Discover

Contents ▶

Canada

Throughout this book, we use these icons to highlight special recommendations:

These icons help you quickly identify reviews in the text and on the map:

 The Best…
Lists for everything from bars to wildlife – to make sure you don't miss out

 Don't Miss
A must-see – don't go home until you've been there

 **Local Knowledge** Local experts reveal their top picks and secret highlights

 Detour
Special places a little off the beaten track

 If you like…
Lesser-known alternatives to world-famous attractions

Sights

Eating

Drinking

Sleeping

Information

This edition written and researched by
Karla Zimmerman, John Lee
Catherine Bodry, Celeste Brash, Emily Matchar,
Brandon Presser, Sarah Richards, Brendan Sainsbury,
Ryan Ver Berkmoes

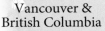

Vancouver &
British Columbia
p51
p115
Banff & the
Canadian Rockies

Nova Scotia &
Maritime
Canada
Montréal &
Québec
p213
p263
Toronto, Niagara
Falls & Ontario
p153

Contents

Contents

On the Road

In Focus

Survival Guide

This Is Canada

Canada is too polite to say so, but it's got the goods: a trio of cultured cities in Montréal, Toronto and Vancouver; an epic amount of terrain to play on outside the urban areas; and a welcoming, progressive vibe throughout.

The globe's second-biggest country has an endless variety of landscapes.
Spiky mountains, glinting glaciers, spectral forests – they're all here, spread across six times zones. Wave-bashed beaches, too. With the Pacific, Arctic and Atlantic oceans on three sides, Canada has a coastline that would reach halfway to the moon, if stretched out. It's the backdrop for plenty of 'ah'-inspiring moments – and for a big provincial menagerie. That's 'big' as in polar bears, grizzly bears, whales and everyone's favorite, shrub-nibblin' moose.

Canada is a land of action.
Whether it's snowboarding Whistler's mountains, surfing Nova Scotia's swell or walking on Banff's glaciers, outfitters will help you gear up for it. Gentler adventures abound, too, such as strolling along Vancouver's Stanley Park seawall, swimming off Prince Edward Island's pink-sand beaches, or ice skating Ottawa's Rideau Canal. Before you know it, you'll be zipping up the fleece and heading outdoors.

Canada is a local food smorgasbord.
If you grazed from east to west across the country, you'd fill your plate like this: lobster with a dab of melted butter in the Maritime provinces, poutine (golden fries soaked in gravy and cheese curds) in Québec and wild salmon and velvety scallops in British Columbia. Tastemakers may not tout Canadian food the way they do with, say, Italian or French fare. So let's just call the distinctive seafood, piquant cheeses and off-the-vine fruits and veggies our little secret. Ditto for the bold reds and crisp whites the country's vine-striped valleys grow.

Canada parties all year long.
Okanagan's icewine festival in January, Québec City's winter carnival in February, Whistler's ski and snowboard fest in April, Montréal's jazz fest in June, Toronto's film fest in September and Niagara's winter festival in December all rock the calendar.

> It's the backdrop for plenty of 'ah'-inspiring moments

The turquoise waters of Moraine Lake (p138), Banff National Park
DAVID TOMLINSON

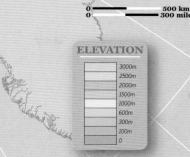

GREENLAND
DENMARK

ICELAND

ELEVATION

3000m
2500m
2000m
1500m
1000m
600m
300m
100m
0

500 km
300 miles

Davis Strait

Nettiling Lake

Amadjuak Lake

◉ Iqaluit

Hudson Strait

Belcher Islands

James Bay

Moosonee ◦

Feuilles R

Mélèzes R

Caniapiscau R

George River

Lac Bienville

Lac Caniapiscau

Réservoir Robert-Bourassa

Réservoir Manicouagan

Lac Mistassini

ATLANTIC OCEAN

Labrador Sea

Labrador

Smallwood Reservoir

Churchill R

NEWFOUNDLAND & LABRADOR

Northern Peninsula

Corner Brook ◦

St John's ◉

❶

Newfoundland

Port aux Basques ◦

Anticosti Island

Îles de la Madeleine

Cape Breton Highlands National Park

QUÉBEC

138

132

Tadoussac ◦

㉑

❷⓪

Îles de la Madeleine

⑯

PEI

❺

NEW BRUNSWICK

Cavendish ◦

Baie St Paul ◦

㉒

Moncton ◦

Québec City ◉

❷

Fredericton ◦

⑲

Halifax

NOVA SCOTIA

North Bay ◦

⑱

❶❶

ME

⑫

109

OTTAWA

★ ㉕

60

Montréal

VT

11

101

Sudbury ◦

North Bay

❼

❾

NH

Kingston ◦

Lake Ontario

NY

MA

CT RI

❽

Lake Huron

Toronto

❹

◦ Niagara Falls

Lake Erie

Detroit ▪

PA

NJ

◉ **Boston**

◉ **New York**

ATLANTIC OCEAN

OH

WV

MD DE

KY

VA

★ **WASHINGTON DC**

20°W

30°W

40°W

40°N

50°N

60°W

70°W

30°N

25
Top Experiences

25 Canada's Top Experiences

Banff National Park

Holy Mother Nature! Banff (p128) is the beautiful, buxom rock star of Canada's national parks. It's impossible to describe without resorting to shameless clichés, so let's get them out of the way: placid, turquoise-tinted lakes; dagger-shaped peaks; bright, jumbled wildflower meadows; and glistening glaciers. While paddling and skiing earn raves, hiking is Banff's tour de force, especially around Lake Louise. Alpine-style teahouses pop up along the trails, so exertion is rewarded with sweet treats (and ethereal, in-the-cloud views).

PHILIP & KAREN SMITH

2

Old Town, Québec

Québec's capital is over 400 years old, and its stone walls, glinting cathedral spires and jazz-playing corner cafes suffuse it with romance, melancholy and intrigue on par with any European city. Soak it up by walking the Old Town's labyrinth of lanes (p244) and get lost amid the street performers and cozy inns, stopping every so often for a café au lait, flaky pastry or plate of poutine (fries smothered in cheese curds and gravy). Le Château Frontenac

Vancouver

Vancouver (p64) always lands atop the 'best places to live' lists, and who's to argue? Sea-to-sky beauty surrounds the laid-back, cocktail-lovin' metropolis. With skiable mountains on the outskirts, beaches fringing the core and Stanley Park's forest just blocks from downtown's glass skyscrapers, it's a harmonic convergence of city and nature. It also mixes Hollywood chic (many movies are filmed here) with buzzing Chinese neighborhoods and a freewheeling counterculture (including a popular nude beach and Marijuana Party headquarters).

The Best...
Tables for Foodies

MONTRÉAL
North America's finest French-influenced cuisine feeds a city with a Bacchanalian love for eating out. p235

VANCOUVER
Fork into salmon, oysters and other West Coast specialties, washed down with local wines and microbrews. p75

TORONTO
Canada's megacity is a wild melting pot of Asian, Greek, Italian and British flavors. p178

CHARLEVOIX
Rustic on-the-farm restaurants pepper Québec's organic growing region. p254

The Best...
Jaw-Dropping Parks

BANFF NATIONAL PARK
Picture-perfect jewel with white-tipped mountains, turquoise lakes and crumbling glaciers. p128

GWAII HAANAS NATIONAL PARK RESERVE
Ancient rainforests reveal lost Haida villages, burial caves and hot springs. p111

CAPE BRETON HIGHLANDS NATIONAL PARK
Misty coastal wilderness of cliffs, whales and eagles. p283

YOHO NATIONAL PARK
Dramatic peaks and pounding waterfalls embody the name: a Cree expression for awe and wonder. p137

STEPHEN SAKS

Niagara Falls

④

Crowded? Cheesy? Well, yes. Niagara (p185) is short, too – it barely cracks the world's highest 500 falls. But when those great muscular bands of water arch over the precipice like liquid glass, roaring into the void below, and when you sail toward it in a misty little boat, Niagara Falls impresses. In terms of sheer volume nowhere in North America beats its thundering cascade, with more than one million bathtubs of water plummeting over the edge every second. Horshoe Falls

HENRY GEORGI/PHOTOLIBRARY

Cape Breton Highlands

⑤

Cape Breton Island crowns Nova Scotia, and Cape Breton Highlands National Park (p283) is the jewel in that crown. It's a heavenly, forested realm of bald eagles, migrating whales, palpable history and foot-tapping music in the wee communities that dot the perimeter. The Cabot Trail, with its scenic views, is the main vein through. The park is best explored on foot, reaching vistas overlooking an endless, icy ocean. Cabot Trail

Whistler

Whistler (p81) is one of the world's most popular ski resorts. Comprising 38 lifts, 34 sq km of skiable terrain and 200 runs, this home to the 2010 Winter Olympics kicks up some serious snowy action. But summer is also a popular time to visit, with adventure hounds lured to the lakes and crags by mountain biking, rafting and scream-triggering zipline runs. Jolly pubs and bistros help you soothe aching muscles.

Victoria & Around

Picture-postcard Victoria (p87) is Vancouver Island's heart, beating with bohemian shops, wood-floored coffee bars and hip, seasonal eateries. After exploring the excellent museums and resident castle, go orca watching, kayaking or cycling – Victoria has more bike routes than any other city in Canada. Nearby, the Cowichan Valley beckons, studded with welcoming little farms and boutique wineries, prime for wandering foodies. Just 20km from Victoria, Butchart Gardens wafts fragrant blooms and serves up afternoon tea and evening concerts.Butchart Gardens

Toronto

A truly global city, Toronto (p166) delivers the multicultural goods. About half its residents were born in another country and the city bubbles with ethnic enclaves, such as Little Italy, Chinatown, Little Korea and Little India. Nowhere is the cultural mash-up more thrilling than in Toronto's restaurants, which fill plates with everything from Korean walnut cakes to Thai curries, jerk chicken and good ol' Canuck pancakes with maple syrup. Markets, bohemian quarters and arts aplenty solidify Toronto's world-class reputation.

The Best...
Adrenaline Towns

WHISTLER
To ski or snowboard Canada's best, Whistler reigns supreme. Ziplining and mountain biking take over in summer. p81

TOFINO
Little Tofino offers big adventure with its surfing, kayaking and storm watching. p100

BANFF
In the heart of the Rockies, this place has it all: skiing, snowboarding, hiking, rafting, horseback riding and mountain biking. p129

THE LAURENTIANS
Sweet mountain villages speckling the landscape outside Montréal let you ski, climb and hike. p240

Thousand Islands

No false advertising here: the 'Thousand Islands' (p193) live up to the number, and then some. The lush archipelago's 1800 isles dot the St Lawrence River between Toronto and Ottawa (and beyond). They offer tufts of fog, showers of trillium petals, quaking tide pools, and 19th-century mansions, whose turrets pierce low-slung clouds. Whether you motor through on the scenic parkway or glide past on a boat, the mist-kissed atmosphere transports visitors to a slower, gentler era. Stately towns and inns let you tuck in overnight.

The Best...
Views

CN TOWER
Rocket up the Western Hemisphere's highest structure and see Toronto in all its glory. p173

GROUSE MOUNTAIN
Hike (or take the gondola) up Vancouver's neighboring crag for excellent mountain-meets-sea vistas. p74

BANFF GONDOLA
Glide to the top of Sulphur Mountain and ogle the Rockies as they sparkle out around you. p129

PEYTO LAKE
Idyllic platform view across the bluest of water. p139

10 Icefields Parkway

Hwy 93 parallels the Continental Divide for 230km between Lake Louise and Jasper Town. Did we just hear a snore? What if we tell you the road is also known as the 'Icefields Parkway' (p139) and fraught with fanning glaciers, foaming waterfalls, aquamarine lakes and hulking mountains? Then what if we say you can get up close and personal with the cold stuff at places such as Athabasca Glacier, where giant-wheeled tour buses rumble onto its craggy surface, as do guided hikes? We thought that'd seal the deal. Jasper National Park

Montréal

Nowhere blends French-inspired *joie de vivre* and cosmopolitan culture like Montréal (p226), Canada's second-largest city and its cultural heart. A flourishing arts scene, an indie rock explosion, a medley of world-renowned boutique hotels, the Plateau's swank cache of eateries and a cool Parisian vibe that pervades every *terrasse* (patio) in the Quartier Latin drive the playful scene. Monster festivals add a high note – the Montréal Jazz Festival and Just for Laughs Festival foremost among them – letting the good times roll 24/7.

GUYLAIN DOYLE

CANADA'S TOP 25 EXPERIENCES ● ● ● 19

12

Grand Manan Island

Cue the Maritime fiddle music. As the ferry from the mainland rounds Grand Manan Island (p288), Swallowtail Lighthouse looms into view, poised atop a rocky, moss-covered cliff. Brightly painted fishing boats bob in the harbor. Clapboard houses surrounded by flower gardens unfurl along the shore. There is plenty of fresh sea air and that rare commodity: silence, broken only by the rhythmic ocean surf. Picnic while seals swim nearby, wave to the seaweed vendor, or go on a whale-watch in this quintessential setting. Seal Cove

13 ## Haida Gwaii

This archipelago (p109) off British Columbia's coast makes a magical trip. Colossal spruce and cedars cloak the wild, rainy landscape. Bald eagles and bears roam the ancient forest, while sea lions and orcas patrol the waters. But the islands' real soul is the resurgent Haida people, best known for their war canoe and totem poles. See the lot at Gwaii Haanas National Park Reserve, which combines lost Haida villages, burial caves and hot springs with some of the continent's best kayaking.

Okanagan Valley

Vines spread across terraced hills in this 180km-long valley (p104), Canada's premier grape-growing region, which suns itself between Vancouver and Banff. More than 100 wineries pour in the lake-spattered area, filling sip-trippers' glasses with fruity whites to the north and complex reds to the south. Even non-oenophiles will enjoy the vineyards' view-worthy terraces and bistros plating regional fare. And everyone will love picking strawberries, cherries, apricots and peaches at the local orchards – or just pulling over at a roadside stand to buy.

14

The Best...
Markets

KENSINGTON MARKET, TORONTO
Have a blast rummaging through the boutiques of bohemian Toronto. p172

MARCHÉ JEAN TALON, MONTRÉAL
Farmers bring fruits, veggies, cheeses and sausages to Montréal's lively marketplace. p241

SALT SPRING ISLAND SATURDAY MARKET
Sail over from Vancouver to peruse island-made arts and crafts. p106

HALIFAX HISTORIC FARMERS' MARKET
North America's oldest market is the prime place to people-watch and buy organic produce, wine, jewelry and clothing. p278

The Best...
Wine Regions

OKANAGAN VALLEY
In the lake-dotted hills, dozens of wineries pour pinot noir, pinot gris, merlot and chardonnay. p108

NIAGARA PENINSULA
Ontario's inn-filled grape-growing area has chardonnay, riesling, pinot noir and cabernet-franc flowing in abundance. p192

COWICHAN VALLEY
Vancouver Island's verdant farming region uncorks blackberry port, apple cider, brandy and pinot noir. p97

PRINCE EDWARD COUNTY
Off the beaten path in pastoral eastern Ontario, the county fills goblets with cooler-climate wines. p206

15

Jasper National Park

Jasper (p140) shares the same majestic mountain-and-wilderness scenery as its sibling park, Banff, though there are a few key differences. Cut the annual visitor number in half, increase the land area by 40%, and multiply the number of bear, elk, moose and caribou threefold, and *then* you've got Jasper. It offers superb hiking, and its rugged backcountry wins plaudits for vertiginous river canyons (loved by white-water paddlers) and adrenalin-charged mountain-bike trails. But it's the park's big hairy wildlife that steals the show.

LEFT: PHILIP & KAREN SMITH; RIGHT: LAWRENCE WORCESTER

Îles de la Madeleine

The six largest islands of this breezy archipelago (p258) are connected by a 200km-long road that curves between white-washed lighthouses, green hills and red sandstone cliffs, all edged by the omnipresent blue sea. If you're not poking in rock pools, windsurfing or keeping your bike upright on a blustery sand spit, artists' studios and seafood huts beckon. At night, listen for wistful Acadian songs being strummed in cafes.

16

Lake Superior

17

Whether the lake got its name from its size (it's the world's largest freshwater lake) or from its beauty, its provincial park (p209) is a stellar place to see the lake's wave-tossed awesomeness. You can travel through misty fjordlike passages braced by thick evergreens. One minute the water is ferocious enough to sink a ship, the next it's blue-green enough to be in the Caribbean (though the moose hovering nearby reminds you otherwise).

ANDREW MCLACHLAN/PHOTOLIBRARY

CANADA'S TOP 25 EXPERIENCES

The Laurentians

Just an hour's drive from Montréal you'll find yourself amid gentle rolling mountains, crystal blue lakes and meandering rivers. Welcome to the Laurentians (p240). Mont-Tremblant rises to the forefront – a killer Canadian ski hill rivaled only by Whistler. Speckling the region are many more lower-profile resort villages, whose pint-sized town centers deliver an air of the Alps with their breezy patios and exclusive, independent-designer clothing shops. Hikers, paddlers and art-gallery hoppers flock in during the summer. Mont-Tremblant

18

The Best...
Scenic Drives

ICEFIELDS PARKWAY
Motor past fanning glaciers, weeping waterfalls, true-blue lakes and elk and bighorn sheep between Lake Louise and Jasper. p139

CABOT TRAIL
Snake by Cape Breton's mountain vistas, sparkling seas and dramatic cliffs. p282

ROUTE 199
Roll along sand dunes and fishing villages on the Îles de la Madeleine. p258

HWY 101
Slowpoke through the convivial Sunshine Coast communities. p84

Halifax

19

The hub of the Maritimes, with the second-largest natural harbor in the world, Halifax (p274) draws its strength from the sea. Pirates once hung out in the waterfront buildings where artisans and buskers now ply their trade. The Maritime Museum of the Atlantic showcases the *Titanic*, whose victims were brought to the city for burial. Alexander Keith's brewery sits by the harbor, slaking visitors' thirst now as it has done for two centuries. Tall-masted schooners, music-filled pubs, seafood and slow-food restaurants bob up in this nautical city, too.

ENAULT PHILIPPE/PHOTOLIBRARY

The Best...
Wildlife-Watching

JASPER NATIONAL PARK
Jasper boasts the Rockies' royal menagerie – grizzlies, elk, moose and caribou. p140

CHURCHILL
Polar bears rule the tundra at Hudson Bay's edge, while beluga whales chatter in the river. p301

DIGBY NECK
Rare North Atlantic right whales, blue whales, humpbacks and seals swim offshore from this spit of land in Nova Scotia. p280

VICTORIA
Resident pods of killer whales ride the local waves. p89

MICHAEL GEBICKI

20 Cavendish

How did the tiny town of Cavendish (p295) become one of Prince Edward Island's biggest moneymakers? It's a long story – a book actually, about a red-pigtailed orphan named Anne. Lucy Maud Montgomery wrote *Anne of Green Gables* in 1908, drawing inspiration from her cousins' bucolic farmhouse. She never would have dreamed of the groupies who descend each year to lay eyes on the gentle, creek-crossed woods and other settings. Bonus for visitors: the surrounding area bursts with fresh-plucked oysters, mussels and lobsters to crack into.

Tadoussac

Location. The captivating town of Tadoussac (p256) has it in spades. Parked at the foot of the Saguenay River fjord – a dramatic waterway bookended by massive cliffs – Tadoussac is perfect for hiking, paddling, vistas and whale-watching, too. Here, the warm, fresh waters of the Saguenay jet out atop the frigid, salt waters of the St Lawrence River, churning up massive volumes of krill. This in turn attracts the whales that put on a splashy show for visitors.

Baie St Paul

Stuffed with superb restaurants and cheerful *gîtes* (B&Bs), Baie St Paul (p255) is almost impossibly relaxing. The *ateliers* (artists' studios), galleries and boutiques lining the town's streets hark back to the artists who, in the late 19th century, gravitated to this region to paint landscapes. Today, food has become an equally important art. The surrounding farm-lands harvest a bounty of organic produce that chefs transform into sublime, rustic cuisine

Tofino

Tofino (p100) is like the Whistler of Vancouver Island. Located on the far west coast, where a wind-bashed ocean meets a Paul Bunyan wilderness, adventurers come here to surf, hike through old-growth forest to hot springs, boat out to see migrating gray whales, and storm watch as winter tempests blow in, rattling windows and spewing waves. It's also a popular destination for kayakers, who glide through the sheltered waters of Clayoquot Sound. Tofino's food trucks, bistros and guesthouses reveal its hippie spirit.

The Best...
Historic Sites

FORTIFICATIONS OF QUÉBEC
History wafts throughout the walled city where the French put down stakes in 1608. p244

LOUISBOURG
Munch soldiers' rations and bribe guards at Nova Scotia's re-created 1744 fortress. p285

KLONDIKE NATIONAL HISTORIC SITES
Preserved structures in the Yukon tell the gold rush tale. p299

CRAIGDARROCH CASTLE
Climb the tower's 87 steps in this turreted coal baron's mansion. p89

23

The Best...
Museums

Churchill

The first polar bear you see up close takes your breath away. Immediately forgotten are the two bum-numbing days on the train that took you beyond the tree zone onto the tundra, to the very edge of Hudson Bay. Churchill (p301) is the lone outpost here, and it happens to be smack in the bears' migration path. From late September to early November, tundra buggies head out in search of the razor-clawed beasts, sometimes getting you close enough to lock eyes.

25

Ottawa

There's no time to waste in Ottawa (p194), Canada's culture-rich capital. From the uber-mod, curvy-walled Canadian Museum of Civilization to the gothic-arched Canadian Museum of Nature and the glass-spired National Gallery of Canada, each attraction is an inspired architectural gesture with an intriguing exhibition space. In winter the Rideau Canal becomes the world's longest skating rink, where people swoosh by, pausing to purchase steaming hot chocolate and scrumptious slabs of fried dough. Rideau Canal

Canada's
Top Itineraries

Fredericton to Québec City
French Canadian Sampler

7 DAYS

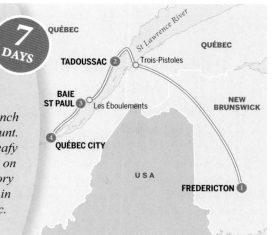

Get a taste of Canada's French side on this 700km jaunt. Ease in with a night in leafy Fredericton, before moving on to whale-watching, art, history and saucy gastronomy in Québec.

① Fredericton (p286)

New Brunswick's capital is quaint – red-brick storefronts, rowboats on the river and concerts on the green. On Saturday, peruse the stalls at **WW Boyce Farmers' Market**. Nip into **Beaverbrook Art Gallery** to see old masters and contemporary Canadian works. Sleep in a Victorian house-turned-inn on an elm-shaded street.

FREDERICTON ➡ TADOUSSAC

🚗🚢 **Six and a half hours** Trans-Canada Hwy (Hwy 2) into Québec, ferry from Trois-Pistoles.

② Tadoussac (p256)

It's a long day of driving, and you'll need to sync with the ferry schedule to get across the St Lawrence River. Your reward is welcoming Tadoussac. It's all about **whale-watching** in this bo-ho little town. Zodiacs go out to see the humpbacks, minkes, belugas and king-of-the-sea blue whales. **Hiking** and **paddling** around the dramatic Saguenay River fjord are also big draws.

TADOUSSAC ➡ BAIE ST PAUL

🚗 **Two hours** Hwy 138 to Hwy 362.

③ Baie St Paul (p255)

Passing through Québec's countryside, you'll see small farms offering everything from foie gras to lamb to cheeses. Pull over for a taste or three before arriving in arty Baie St Paul. Artists' studios, galleries and boutiques line the streets, and the **Musée d'Art Contemporain** shows contemporary works. After your arts fix, commence eating. All those farms you passed earlier supply the sublime restaurants, while local alehouses pour the drink.

BAIE ST PAUL ➡ QUÉBEC CITY

🚗 **One and a half hours** Along Hwy 138.

④ Québec City (p243)

Romantic and history-drenched, Québec's 400-year-old walled capital enchants you into thinking you're an ocean away from North America. Walk over the old **fortifications**, photograph the turreted **Le Château Frontenac**, and sip a café au lait in the soulful **Place Royale**. Search for the ultimate *table d'hôte* in the Old Lower Town before having a nightcap at a jazzy corner cafe. It's easy to linger in the atmospheric city.

Outdoor restaurant in Québec City's Old Town (p244)
WAYNE WALTON

33

Halifax to Îles de la Madeleine
Island Hopper

You're never far from the sea on this 600km journey that jumps two islands (one by bridge, the other by ferry). Nova Scotia, Prince Edward Island (PEI) and Québec's Magdalen Islands are the stars.

ÎLES DE LA MADELEINE

PRINCE EDWARD ISLAND

CAVENDISH

NEW BRUNSWICK

CHARLOTTETOWN

NOVA SCOTIA

HALIFAX

ATLANTIC OCEAN

1 Halifax (p274)

Wander the historic waterfront, making sure to tour **Alexander Keith's Nova Scotia Brewery** and enhance your *Titanic* knowledge at the **Maritime Museum of the Atlantic** (Halifax played a prominent role in the ship's story, as many of the dead were brought here). In the evening, fork into downtown's seafood and slow food restaurants, then see who's playing in the live-music pubs. Make a day trip to **Peggy's Cove** for the prettiest dang lighthouse you ever did see.

HALIFAX ➡ CAVENDISH

🚗 **Four hours** Hwy 102 to Hwy 104 to Hwy 16/ Confederation Bridge.

2 Cavendish (p295)

After a dip into New Brunswick to access the 12.9km Confederation Bridge – voila – you're on Prince Edward Island (PEI). The pastoral land mass was made famous by the 1908 novel *Anne of Green Gables,* and Cavendish is the town that pays homage to the fictional red-headed orphan. Join the groupies goggling at the gentle, creek-crossed woods and other settings, then explore the nearby **pink-sand beaches** and **Prince Edward Island National Park** bluffs. A **lobster supper** is a must; seek out one of the local community halls that sponsor them to get cracking.

CAVENDISH ➡ CHARLOTTETOWN

🚗 **One hour** Along Hwy 13 and Hwy 2.

3 Charlottetown (p291)

PEI's compact, colonial capital Charlottetown is known as the 'birthplace of Canada.' See where it all came together at **Province House National Historic Site**. Enjoy the town's inns, wharfside seafood cafes and lively pubs. The latter often host **ceilidhs** (programs of traditional Celtic music and dance).

CHARLOTTETOWN ➡ ÎLES DE LA MADELEINE

🚗 🚢 **Six hours** Hwy 2 to Souris for ferry to islands.

4 Îles de la Madeleine (p258)

White-washed lighthouses, green hills and red sandstone cliffs dominate Québec's breezy Magdalen Islands. The ferry arrives at **Île du Cap aux Meules**, the archipelago's hub and a fine place to catch a sunset at **Cap du Phare lighthouse**. Wee Rte 199 rolls along the omnipresent blue sea and links several of the islands. **Île Du Havre Aubert** is the Magdalen's largest, popular with kite surfers and sand-castle builders. Days are spent poking in rock pools, waving to folks in fishing villages and trying to keep your bike upright on the blustery sand spits. At night, listen for wistful Acadian songs strummed in cafes.

Lobster boats moored near Cavendish (p295), Prince Edward Island
EMILY RIDDELL

10 DAYS

Niagara Falls to Québec City
Central Corridor

This 1100km route from Niagara Falls to Québec City swoops up Canada's largest cities, mightiest waterfalls and prettiest islands.

QUÉBEC

QUÉBEC CITY ⑥

ONTARIO

④ OTTAWA

⑤ MONTRÉAL

TORONTO ②

③ GANANOQUE

Lake Ontario

Prince Edward County

① NIAGARA FALLS

USA

1 Niagara Falls (p185)

Kitschy but still impressive, Niagara Falls roars, pounds and spews North America's most voluminous cascade. Don a raincoat and board the **Maid of the Mist** for a soggy full frontal, then take advantage of the region's **wineries**. More than 60 vineyards stripe the landscape; drive or cycle the scenic roads between them.

NIAGARA FALLS ➡ TORONTO

🚗 **One and a half hours** Along Queen Elizabeth Way. 🚆 **Two hours**.

2 Toronto (p166)

Spend a few days in multicultural Toronto and wallow in the wealth of architecture, art museums, restaurants and nightclubs. Rocket up the 553m **CN Tower**, dawdle in **St Lawrence Market**, wield chopsticks in **Chinatown**, splash some cash in the shops of **Bloor-Yorkville** and get a tattoo in **Queen West**.

TORONTO ➡ GANANOQUE

🚗 **Three and a half hours** Hwy 401 via Prince Edward County (p206). 🚆 **Three hours**.

3 Gananoque (p194)

The misty Thousand Islands – a constellation of some 1800 rugged isles – dot the St Lawrence River. Victorian Gananoque makes a good break in their midst, where you can take **boat rides** into the archipelago and see castle turrets poke through the fog. Or drive the **Thousand Islands Parkway** as it unfurls dreamy vistas.

GANANOQUE ➡ OTTAWA

🚗 **Two hours** Hwy 401 to Hwy 416. 🚆 **One hour and 45 minutes**.

Maman sculpture by Louise Bourgeois outside the National Gallery of Canada (p197), Ottawa
GLENN VAN DER KNIJFF

4 Ottawa (p194)

Canada's vibrant capital draws applause for its museum cache. From the ubermodern, curvy-walled **Canadian Museum of Civilization** to the gothic-arched **Canadian Museum of Nature** to the glass-spired **National Gallery of Canada**, each attraction is a superb architectural feat with impressive exhibits to boot. The bounteous **ByWard Market** and myriad global eateries provide sustenance.

OTTAWA ➡ MONTRÉAL

🚗 **Two hours and 15 minutes** Along Hwy 417 and Hwy 40. 🚆 **Two hours** To Montréal's Central Station.

5 Montréal (p226)

Ah, Montréal. Canada's second-largest city is an irresistible blend of French-inspired *joie de vivre* and cosmopolitan culture. Hike up **Mont Royal**, explore the cobblestoned alleys of **Old Montréal**, and grab a seat at a boisterous **Plateau** or **Quartier Latin** cafe. Montréalers have a bacchanalian love for good food and drink, so loosen the belt.

MONTRÉAL ➡ QUÉBEC CITY

🚗 **Three hours** Along Hwy 20. 🚆 **Three hours and 15 minutes** Montréal's Central Station to Québec City's Gare du Palais.

6 Québec City (p243)

Québec City packs unparalleled culture, history and romance into its stone walls and soulful plazas. Explore the **fortifications**, the turreted **Le Château Frontenac** and the Old Town's muddling maze of lanes.

Vancouver to Jasper National Park
Rocky Mountain High

Feast on a smorgasbord of scenic delights on this 1200km trek, which rises from valleys to mountains in British Columbia and Alberta.

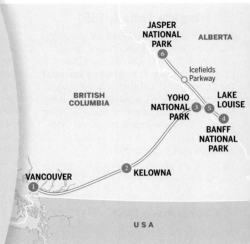

1 Vancouver (p64)

There's loads to do in mountain-meets-sea Vancouver. Hike or bike along the seawall in forested **Stanley Park**, discovering the beaches, totem poles and **Lost Lagoon**. Visit clamorous **Chinatown** for pork buns . And take your pick of freewheeling, foodie-approved restaurants and microbreweries in **Yaletown**, **Gastown** and the **West End**.

VANCOUVER ➡ KELOWNA

🚗 **Five hours** Hwy 1 to Hwy 5 to Hwy 97.

2 Kelowna (p107)

Make Kelowna the base for a tipple trip through the **Okanagan Valley**, famed for its 100 wineries and lake-speckled scenery. Check out **Summerhill Pyramid Winery**, **Quails' Gate Winery** and Aboriginal-owned **Nk'Mip Cellars**. Roadside fruit stands and pick-your-own cherry and peach farms line Hwy 97 in the valley's southern end.

KELOWNA ➡ YOHO NATIONAL PARK

🚗 **Five and a half hours** Hwy 97 to Hwy 1.

3 Yoho National Park (p137)

It may be the smallest of the Rocky Mountain national parks, but Yoho packs a big wallop of looming peaks and crashing waterfalls. **Wapta Falls** and **Lake O'Hara** are worth the hike.

YOHO NATIONAL PARK ➡ BANFF NATIONAL PARK

🚗 **One hour and 15 minutes** Along Hwy 1.

4 Banff National Park (p128)

Cross the border into Alberta and pull over in Banff, Canada's most-visited national park. You won't be able to stop the superlatives from flying forth: grand! majestic! awe-inspiring! Allot plenty of time for hiking, paddling, hot-springs soaking and grizzly-bear spotting (best done from a distance).

BANFF NATIONAL PARK ➡ LAKE LOUISE

🚗 **One hour** Along Bow Valley Pkwy (Hwy 1A). 🚌 **One hour**.

5 Lake Louise (p133)

Bluer-than-blue Lake Louise is a must, surrounded by alpine-style teahouses that fuel day hikes with scones and hot chocolate. There are actually multiple lakes to hike to, including deep-teal **Moraine Lake** and **Mirror Lake**. Feeling lazy? The **Sightseeing Gondola** will do the hard work, and you'll still get those lake-and-glacier snapshots.

LAKE LOUISE ➡ JASPER NATIONAL PARK

🚗 **Three hours** Along Hwy 93, aka Icefields Parkway (p139). 🚌 **Four hours**.

6 Jasper National Park (p140)

Peer into extreme-blue **Peyto Lake**, gape at the gothic, glacier-strewn **Columbia Icefield** and walk over **Athabasca Glacier** – those are just the things to do on the way to Jasper. The park itself is bigger and less crowded than Banff, and offers superb hiking and bear, elk and moose watching, as well as horseback riding, mountain biking and rafting.

The impressive scenery at Moraine Lake (p138), Banff National Park
SEAN CAFFREY

Québec City to Vancouver
Trans-Canada Highway

The Trans-Canada is the world's longest highway, a whopping belt of asphalt cinched around Canada's girth. Scenic stretches alternate with mundane ones. Pack patience and good tunes.

1 Québec City (p243)

Why not start where French Canada started, in Québec's 400-year-old walled capital? Check out the **fortifications**, **citadel** and turreted **Le Château Frontenac**. Walk the **Old Town**'s labyrinth of lanes and get lost amid the street performers and cozy inns, stopping every so often for a café au lait, flaky pastry or heaping plate of poutine (fries covered in cheese curds and gravy).

QUÉBEC CITY ➤ MONTRÉAL

🚗 **Three hours** Along Hwy 20. 🚆 **Three hours and 15 minutes** Québec City's Gare du Palais to Montréal's Central Station.

2 Montréal (p226)

Canada's second-largest city and its cultural heart, Montréal buzzes with a mix of sophistication, playfulness and history-soaked preserved quarters. Hike up **Mont Royal**, explore **Old Montréal's** basilicas and plazas, and indulge at a happening **Plateau** or **Quartier Latin** cafe. Arrive in summer and groove to the Montréal Jazz Festival, Just for Laughs Festival or another city-enveloping event.

MONTRÉAL ➤ OTTAWA

🚗 **Two hours and 15 minutes** Along Hwy 40 and Hwy 417. 🚆 **Two hours** From Montréal's Central Station.

3 Ottawa (p194)

Go museum-crazy in Canada's striking capital, taking in the superb architectual feats of the **Canadian Museum of Civilization**, the **Canadian Museum of Nature** and the **National Gallery of Canada**, each with impressive exhibits. For eats, fill up in the **ByWard Market** and array of international restaurants.

OTTAWA ➤ LAKE SUPERIOR PROVINCIAL PARK

🚗 **13 hours** Along Hwy 17.

4 Lake Superior Provincial Park (p209)

The scenery turns transcendent as the road skirts Lake Superior and coasts through the eponymous provincial park. Wispy beard-like fog and shivering arctic trees give it a distinctly primeval flavor. Day hikes reward with isolated **beaches**, spewing **waterfalls** and mysterious, red-ochre **pictographs**.

the intriguing western art, history and pop culture exhibits in **Glenbow Museum**.

CALGARY ➲ BANFF NATIONAL PARK

🚗 **One and a half hours** Along Hwy 1. 🚆 **Two hours**.

➐ Banff National Park (p128)

Banff is Canada's most-visited national park, and it's easy to see why. Head for the turquoise lakes and white-dipped mountains and prepare to be overwhelmed by breath-catching panoramas. Hiking, paddling, hot-springs soaking and grizzly-bear spotting are the to-do's.

LAKE SUPERIOR PROVINCIAL PARK ➲ WINNIPEG

🚗 **15 hours** Along Hwy 17 in Ontario, Hwy 1 in Manitoba.

BANFF NATIONAL PARK ➲ VANCOUVER

🚗 **10 and a half hours** Along Hwy 1. 🚆 **13 hours** Along Hwy 1. 🚆 **Two days** Calgary to Vancouver on Rocky Mountaineer.

➎ Winnipeg (p300)

Not long after the highway enters the prairie flatlands of Manitoba, Winnipeg rockets up and provides an enlivening patch of cafes and culture. Linger over the mighty Inuit collection at **Winnipeg Art Gallery**, the riverside trails and museums of the **Forks National Historic Site**, and the impressive **fringe theater** scene.

➑ Vancouver (p64)

Sea-to-sky beauty surrounds this laid-back, cocktail-lovin' metropolis. Skiable mountains rise on the outskirts, while beaches fringe the core. The seawalled rainforest at **Stanley Park** is perfect for hiking and biking past totem poles and the occasional seal. **Chinatown** offers tasty Asian food and one-of-a-kind shopping. **Yaletown**, **Gastown** and the **West End** are there with seafood-enriched cuisine and microbrews.

WINNIPEG ➲ CALGARY

🚗 **15 and a half hours** Along Hwy 1. ✈ **Two and a half hours**.

➏ Calgary (p148)

Put on your cowboy boots before arriving in Calgary, a ranching center overtaken by the big new biz in town: oil. Brash and shiny, it's a good place to refuel on a thick-cut steak and peruse

Canada Month by Month

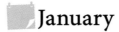 **January**

Ski season is in full swing as snowfall peaks. Cities begin their winter carnivals later in the month.

🍷 Icy Tipples
BC's Okanagan Valley and Ontario's Niagara Peninsula (see www.thewinefestivals.com for both) celebrate their icewines with good-time festivals. The distinctive, sweet libations go down the hatch amid chestnut roasts and cocktail competitions.

❄ Chinese New Year
Dragons dance, firecrackers burst and great food sizzles in Chinatowns throughout the nation on the Chinese lunar New Year. Vancouver (www.vancouver-chinatown.com) hosts the biggest celebration, but Toronto, Calgary, Ottawa and Montréal also have festivities. It's on January 23 in 2012 and February 10 in 2013.

February

Yes, it's cold, but February is a party month, filled with all kinds of wintry events.

❄ Québec City's Winter Carnival
Revelers watch ice-sculpture competitions, hurtle down snow slides, go ice fishing and cheer on their favorite paddlers in an insane canoe race on the half-frozen, ice-floe-ridden St Lawrence River. It's the world's biggest winter fest (www.carnaval.qc.ca).

❄ Winterlude in Ottawa
This snowy bash is along the Rideau Canal, where skaters glide by on the groomed ice. When they're not sipping hot chocolate and eating beavertails (fried, sugared dough), the townfolk build a massive village entirely of ice (www.canadascapital.gc.ca/winterlude).

Top Events

- ⭐ **Montréal Jazz Festival**, June
- ❄ **Québec Winter Carnival**, February
- ⭐ **Stratford Festival**, April–November
- ⭐ **Calgary Stampede**, July
- ❄ **World Ski & Snowboard Festival**, April

May Tulip Festival, Ottawa
BRUCE BI

# March

Snow lessens and temperatures moderate. Ski resorts still do brisk business, especially during the week-long school break.

Vancouver Vinos
Vancouver uncorks 1700 wines from 200 vintners at the Playhouse International Wine Festival (www.playhousewinefest.com), a rite of spring for oenophiles. You're drinking for art's sake, since the event raises funds for the city's contemporary theater company.

April

Apart from the far north, spring sprouts (the weather can waver, so be prepared). Ski season is winding down yet the summer influx hasn't yet begun.

The Bard in Ontario
Canada's Stratford, a few hours outside Toronto, nearly outdoes England's Stratford-upon-Avon. The Stratford Festival (www.stratfordfestival.ca) plays a monster season from April to November. Four theaters stage contemporary drama, music, operas and, of course, works by Shakespeare. Productions are first-rate and feature well-known actors.

World Ski & Snowboard Festival
Ski bums converge on Whistler for 10 days of adrenaline events, outdoor rock and hip hop concerts, film screenings, dog parades and a whole lotta carousing. Heed the motto: 'Party in April. Sleep in May' (www.wssf.com).

May

May is a time for shoulder-season bargains and wildflower jumbles. The weather is warm by day, though nippy at night.

Tiptoe through the Tulips
After a long winter, Ottawa bursts with color – more than three million tulips of 200 types blanket the city for the Canadian Tulip Festival (www.tulipfestival.ca). Festivities include parades, regattas, car rallies, dances, concerts and fireworks.

June

There are warm days to soak up the great outdoors. Attractions don't get mega-busy til later in the month, when school lets out.

Montréal International Jazz Festival
Two million music lovers descend on Montréal in late June, when the heart of downtown explodes in jazz and blues for 11 straight days. Most concerts are outdoors and free, and the party goes on round the clock (www.montrealjazzfest.com).

Pride Toronto
Toronto's most flamboyant event celebrates all kinds of sexuality, climaxing with an out-of-the-closet Dyke March and the outrageous Pride Parade. Pride's G-spot is in the Church-Wellesley Village; most events are free. Held in late June (www.pridetoronto.com).

Elvis Festival
If you're in Penticton, BC, in late June and you keep seeing Elvis, rest assured it's not because you've swilled too much of the local Okanagan Valley wine. The town hosts Elvis Fest (www.pentictonelvisfestival.com), with dozens of impersonators.

July

A prime time for visiting, the weather is at its sunniest, a bounty of fresh produce and seafood fill plates and festivals rock the nights away. Crowds are thick.

 # August

The sunny days and shindigs continue. Visitors throng most provinces, and prices reflect it. It can get hot and humid inland.

 Newfoundland's Big Row
The streets are empty and everyone migrates to the shores of Quidi Vidi Lake for the Royal St John's Regatta (www.stjohns regatta.org). It's the continent's oldest continuously held sporting event.

 Canadian National Exhibition
Akin to a state fair in the USA, 'The Ex' (www.theex.com) features more than 700 exhibitors, agricultural shows, lumberjack competitions, outdoor concerts and carnivalia at Toronto's Exhibition Place. The 18-day event runs through Labour Day and ends with a bang-up fireworks display.

 # September

Labour Day heralds the end of summer, after which crowds (and prices) diminish. But the weather is still decent in most places. Moose mating season begins!

 PEI International Shellfish Festival
This massive kitchen party, set on the Charlottetown waterfront, merges toe-tapping traditional music with incredible seafood. Don't miss the oyster-shucking championships or the chowder challenge (www.peishellfish.com).

 Toronto International Film Festival
Toronto's prestigious 10-day celebration is a major cinematic event. Films of all lengths and styles are screened in late September, as celebs shimmy between gala events and the

 Montréal Chuckles
Everyone gets giddy for two weeks at the Just for Laughs Festival (http://mont real.hahaha.com/en), which features hundreds of comedy shows, including free ones in the Quartier Latin. The biggest names in the biz yuck it up for this one.

 Calgary Stampede
Raging bulls, chuck-wagon racing and bad-ass, boot-wearing cowboys unite for 'The Greatest Outdoor Show on Earth.' A midway of rides and games makes it a family affair well beyond the usual rodeo event, attracting 1.1 million yee-hawin' fans (www.calgarystampede.com).

Wacky Winnipeg
North America's second-largest fringe fest (www.winnipegfringe.com) stages wildly creative, raw and oddball works from a global line-up of performers. Comedy, drama, music, cabaret, even musical memoirs are on tap over 12 days.

gorgeous Bell Lightbox building (www
.torontointernationalfilmfestival.ca).

 Foraging on Vancouver Island

Vancouver Island's Cowichan Wine & Culinary Festival (www.wines.cowichan.net)
lets the valley's small cheese-makers, cider
producers and organic vintners showcase
their wares by tours and tastings.

October

The fall foliage flames bright, the weather
dawns cool but comfortable, and hockey
season gets underway.

 Celtic Colours

With foot-stompin' music, this roving festival in Cape Breton attracts top musicians
from Scotland, Spain and other countries
with Celtic connections. Community sup-
pers, step dancing classes and tin-whistle
lessons round out the cultural celebration
(www.celtic-colours.com).

December

Winter begins in earnest as snow falls,
temperatures drop, and ski resorts ramp
up and soon get busy. 'Tis the holiday
season, too.

 Mountain Time

Powder hounds hit the slopes from east
to west. Whistler in BC, Mont-Tremblant in
Québec and the Canadian Rockies around
Banff, Alberta, pull the biggest crowds, but
there's downhill action going on in every
province (snowboarding and cross-
country skiing, too).

 Niagara Lit Up

The family-friendly Winter Festival of
Lights (www.wfol.com) gets everyone
in the holiday spirit with three million
twinkling bulbs and 125 animated displays
brightening Niagara Falls town and the
waterfall itself. You can ice skate on the
'rink at the brink' of the cascade.

Far Left: July Calgary Stampede; **Left:
December** Ski transport, Whistler

PHOTOGRAPHERS: (FAR LEFT) RICK RUDNICKI;
(LEFT) BILL BACHMANN

What's New

For this new edition of Discover Canada, our authors have hunted down the fresh, the revamped, the hot and the happening. These are some of our favorites. For up-to-the-minute recommendations, see lonelyplanet.com/canada.

1 BIXI, MONTREAL
The city's ingenious solar-powered bike-sharing system makes it easy for both locals and visitors to explore the city with 3000 bikes at 300 depots scattered across downtown's core. (p231)

2 PEAK 2 PEAK GONDOLA, WHISTLER
Powder fans can now ski Whistler and Blackcomb in the same day by hopping on the new gondola. The 4.4km ride between the two mountains takes 11 minutes. (p81)

3 ART GALLERY OF ALBERTA, EDMONTON
Opened in 2010, the silvery, postmodern building vaults the province's western Canadian and international abstract art collection into the big leagues. (p144)

4 HAIDA GWAII, BRITISH COLUMBIA
The Queen Charlotte Islands officially were renamed Haida Gwaii, or 'islands of the people', shaking off their colonial past. A huge new maritime preserve protects the islands' rich sea life. (p109)

5 BLŪMEN GARDEN BISTRO, PRINCE EDWARD COUNTY, ONTARIO
This arty restaurant (☎ 613-476-6841; www .blūmengardenbistro.com; 647 Hwy 49, Picton; lunch $12-16, dinner $19-23; ☉lunch & dinner) takes advantage of the surrounding countryside's vineyards and farms by using local ingredients for its 'honest food'.

6 DISTILLERIES, PRINCE EDWARD ISLAND
Prince Edward Distillery in Hermanville cooks up potato vodka, putting the province's abundant tuber to good use, while Myriad View Distillery in Rollo Bay produces legal, knee-buckling moonshine. (p292)

7 EVANDALE RESORT, NEW BRUNSWICK
By the ferry landing on the Saint John River, this once-abandoned Victorian inn has been restored to its former opulence amid white farmhouses and wildflower fields. (p289)

8 CANADIAN MUSEUM OF NATURE, OTTAWA
The natural history museum emerged massively bulked up after multi-year renovations, with plenty of new space for the dinosaurs and blue whale skeleton. (p198)

9 NORTH COAST TRAIL, VANCOUVER ISLAND, BRITISH COLUMBIA
Giving hikers an alternative to the popular West Coast Trail, this 43km northern-tip trail begins near Port Hardy and winds through dense forest and alongside remote sandy coves.

10 JOGGINS FOSSIL CENTER, NOVA SCOTIA
Soon after the Joggins Fossil Cliffs became a World Heritage site, the town opened a state-of-the-art museum dedicated to the scene, with excellent cliff tours offered.

Get Inspired

Books

- **Beautiful Losers** (1966) Leonard Cohen's experimental oddity involving love, sex and Aboriginals.

- **In the Skin of a Lion** (1987) Michael Ondaatje's story of the immigrants who built Toronto circa 1920.

- **King Leary** (1987) Paul Quarrington's aging hockey player revisits his past.

- **Anne of Green Gables** (1908) Lucy Maud Montgomery's tale of a spunky, pigtailed orphan has made Prince Edward Island a pilgrimage site.

🎵 Music

- **Mass Romantic** (2000) The debut of Vancouver's power pop 'indie supergroup' The New Pornographers.

- **Live at Massey Hall** (2007) Canadian legend Neil Young's 1971 acoustic concert in Toronto, featuring a set list of wistful classics.

- **Moving Pictures** (1981) Rush's defining prog-rock album vaulted them into the 'Limelight.'

- **Fully Completely** (1992) The third and arguably best album by beloved Ontario rockers The Tragically Hip.

🎞 Films

- **The Sweet Hereafter** (1997) A small town in British Columbia copes with a deadly bus crash.

- **Away from Her** (2006) Heart-wrenching film in which Alzheimer's breaks apart a rural Ontario couple.

- **Videodrome** (1983) Early flick by horror master David Cronenberg, set at a Toronto TV station broadcasting S&M and Debbie Harry.

🖱 Websites

- **Environment Canada Weatheroffice** (www .weatheroffice.gc.ca) Forecasts for any town.

- **Lonely Planet** (www .lonelyplanet.com/ canada) Great website for preplanning.

- **Government of Canada** (www.gc.ca) Massive resource, with national (immigration rules) and regional (provincial tourism offices) information.

- **Parks Canada** (www .pc.gc.ca) Lowdown on all national parks.

- **Canadian Broadcasting Corporation** (CBC; www. cbc.ca) The main purveyor of news and cultural programming via TV and radio.

Short on time?

This list will give you an instant insight into the country.

Read *The Apprenticeship of Duddy Kravitz* (1959) is Mordechai Richler's novel about a Jewish boy questing for success in Montréal.

Watch *Bon Cop, Bad Cop* (2006), about an Anglophone and Francophone cracking a case together, is Canada's top-grossing movie ever.

Listen *Neon Bible* (2007) mixes punk and mandolin in Montréal band Arcade Fire's breakout album.

Log on *Canadian Tourism Commission* (www.cana da.travel) is the country's official travel site.

Scene from Montréal's International Jazz Festival (p216)
GUYLAIN DOYLE

Need to Know

Currency
Canadian dollars ($)

Language
English
French

ATMs
ATMs are widely available.

Credit Cards
Credit cards accepted in most hotels and restaurants.

Visas
Generally not required for stays of up to 180 days; some nationalities require a temporary resident visa.

Cell Phones
Local SIM cards can be used in European and Australian phones. Other phones must be set to roaming.

Wi-Fi
Widely available and mostly free.

Internet Access
Main tourist areas have internet cafes. Libraries have free high-speed terminals.

Driving
Drive on the right side of the road; the steering wheel is on the left side of the car.

Tipping
Tipping is standard practice; about 15% to 20% of the bill.

When to Go

Dry climate
Warm to hot summers, mild winters
Mild to hot summers, cold winters
Polar climate

Churchill
GO Sep-Nov

Banff
GO Jul-Sep

Vancouver
GO Jun-Aug

Montréal
GO Jun-Aug

Halifax
GO Jul-Sep

High Season
(Jun–Aug)
o Sunshine and warm weather prevail; far northern regions briefly thaw

o Accommodations prices peak (30% up on average)

o December through March is equally busy and expensive in ski resort towns

Shoulder
(May & Sep–Oct)
o Crowds and prices drop off

o Temperatures are cool but comfortable

o Attractions keep shorter hours

Low Season
(Nov–Apr)
o Places outside the big cities and ski resorts close

o Darkness and cold take over

o April and November are particularly good for bargains

Advance Planning

o **Three months before** Book accommodation and tickets for Montréal Jazz Festival; train tickets to Churchill during polar bear season; and Rocky Mountain train tickets during summer.

o **One month before** Secure lodging and a rental car, especially in summer.

o **Two weeks before** Book tours and activities in busy destinations such as Banff and Whistler; theater tickets in Toronto and Montréal.

o **One week before** Make reservations at coveted restaurants.

Set Your Daily Budget

Budget less than $90
○ Dorm bed: $25-35
○ Campsite: $20-30
○ Plenty of markets and supermarkets for self-catering, plus fast food options

Midrange $90–250
○ B&B or room in a midrange hotel: $80-180
○ Meal in a good local restaurant: from $20 plus drinks
○ Rental car: $35-65 per day
○ Attraction admissions: $5-15

Top End over $250
○ Four-star hotel room: from $180
○ Three-course meal in a top restaurant: from $45 plus drinks
○ Skiing day-pass: $50-80

Exchange Rates

Australia	A$1	$0.94
Euro Zone	€1	$1.34
Japan	¥100	$1.25
New Zealand	NZ$1	$0.74
UK	UK£	$1.64
USA	US$1	$1.05

For current exchange rates see www.xe.com.

What to Bring

○ **Warm clothing** Canada is one of the coldest places on the planet. Even in summer it can get chilly, especially on the coasts and in the Rockies, so bring a jacket.

○ **Rain gear** Coastal British Columbia (BC) and the Maritimes tend toward rain; an umbrella and waterproof clothing are good ideas.

○ **Binoculars** You want to see those moose, bears and whales up close, right?

○ **Insect repellent** Important if you're visiting northern or woodsy regions during summer, when black flies and mosquitoes can be a major annoyance.

Arriving in Canada

○ **Toronto Pearson Airport**

Buses Every 20 to 30 minutes 5am-1am

Taxis $50; 45 minutes to downtown

○ **Montréal Trudeau Airport**

Buses Every 10 to 12 minutes 8:30am-8pm; every 30 to 60 minutes 8pm-8:30am

Taxis $38; 30 to 60 minutes to downtown

○ **Vancouver International Airport**

Trains Every 8 to 20 minutes

Taxis $30-40; 30 minutes to downtown

○ **Land Border Crossings**

Canadian Border Services Agency (www.cbsa-asfc.gc.ca/general/times/menu-e.html) posts wait times.

Getting Around

○ **Car** Extensive highway system links most towns. All major hire car companies are readily available.

○ **Train** Outside the Toronto–Montréal corridor, train travel is mostly for scenic journeys.

○ **Ferry** Public ferry systems operate extensively in BC, Québec and the Maritime provinces.

Accommodations

○ **B&Bs** Common throughout Canada. Standards vary, though most have private bathrooms and a two-night minimum-stay requirement. Called *gîtes* in French.

○ **Hotels** Most are part of international chains, catering to high-end and business travelers. Rooms have cable TV and wi-fi, with access to fitness and business centers.

○ **Inns** Like B&Bs, but with more rooms available.

○ **Motels** More common outside the big cities. Good-value rooms; typically less stylish and amenity-laden than hotels.

Be Forewarned

○ **Summertime** Transportation (rental car, ferry) and sleeping reservations are important in July and August.

○ **Distances** Canada's immense scale means that distances to travel can be long and travel times slow due to single-lane highways and ferries.

○ **Insects** Black flies and mosquitoes can be a major annoyance in the summer in northern and woodsy regions; bring repellent.

Vancouver & British Columbia

Visitors to BC are never short of superlatives when writing home. It's hard not to be moved by towering mountain ranges, wildlife-packed forests and uncountable kilometers of pristine coastline that slow your heartbeat like a sigh-triggering spa treatment. But Canada's westernmost province is much more than a nature-hugging diorama.

Cosmopolitan Vancouver is an animated fusion of cuisines and cultures from Asia and beyond, while vibrant smaller communities such as historic Victoria, surf-loving Tofino and the wine-sipping Okanagan Valley lure ever-curious travelers. And for sheer character, it's hard to beat rustic Haida Gwaii or the winter wonderland of Whistler, one of the world's great ski resorts.

Wherever you head in the region, the great outdoors will always be calling. Don't just point you camera at it. BC is unbeatable for the kind of life-enhancing kayaking, hiking and biking experiences you'll remember fondly for the rest of your life.

Queen Elizabeth Park (p68), Vancouver
DONALD C. & PRISCILLA ALEXANDER EASTMAN

Victoria's imposing Parliament Buildings (p88)

Vancouver & British Columbia

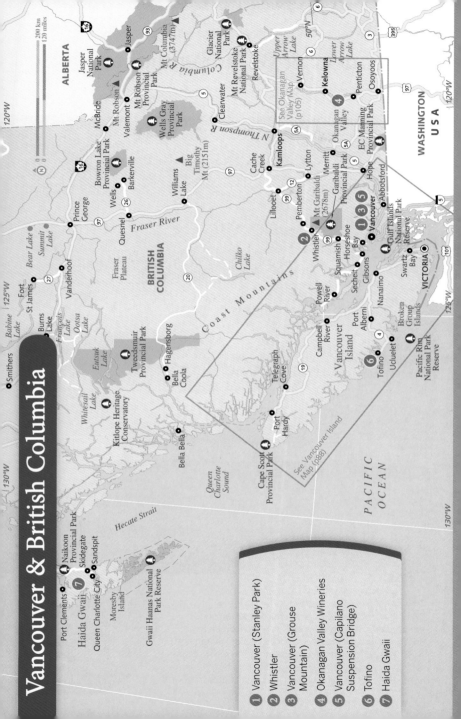

1 Vancouver (Stanley Park)
2 Whistler
3 Vancouver (Grouse Mountain)
4 Okanagan Valley Wineries
5 Vancouver (Capilano Suspension Bridge)
6 Tofino
7 Haida Gwaii

200 km
120 miles

ALBERTA

Jasper National Park
Jasper
Mt Robson (3747m)
Mt Robson Provincial Park
McBride
Valemont
Columbia R
Wells Gray Provincial Park
Clearwater
Glacier National Park
Mt Revelstoke National Park
Revelstoke
Upper Arrow Lake
Lower Arrow Lake
Vernon
Kelowna
Penticton
Osoyoos
WASHINGTON USA

N Thompson R
Kamloops
Cache Creek
Lytton
Merritt
See Okanagan Valley Map (p105)
Okanagan Valley

BRITISH COLUMBIA

Bear Lake
Summit Lake
Fort St James
Vanderhoof
Burns Lake
Ootsa Lake
Francois Lake
Prince George
Quesnel
Fraser River
Wells
Barkerville
Bowron Lake Provincial Park
Big Timothy Mt (2151m)
Williams Lake
Lillooet
Pemberton
Mt Garibaldi (2678m)
Garibaldi Provincial Park
Whistler
Hope
EC Manning Provincial Park
Abbotsford
Vancouver

Smithers
Babine Lake
Whitesail Lake
Eutsuk Lake
Tweedsmuir Provincial Park
Kitlope Heritage Conservatory
Bella Coola
Hagensborg
Bella Bella

Fraser Plateau
Chilko Lake
Chilcotin
Coast Mountains

Telegraph Cove
Powell River
Sechelt
Gibsons
Horseshoe Bay
Squamish
Gulf Islands National Park Reserve
Swartz Bay
VICTORIA

Campbell River
Port Alberni
Vancouver Island
Nanaimo
Broken Group Islands
Ucluelet
Tofino
Pacific Rim National Park Reserve

Port Hardy
Cape Scott Provincial Park
See Vancouver Island Map (p88)

PACIFIC OCEAN

Queen Charlotte Sound

Hecate Strait

Port Clements
Haida Gwaii
Queen Charlotte City
Skidegate
Sandspit
Moresby Island
Naikoon Provincial Park
Gwaii Haanas National Park Reserve

Vancouver & BC's Highlights

1
Stanley Park

One of North America's largest urban green spaces, Vancouver's Stanley Park enjoys a breathtaking setting, surrounded on three sides by rippling ocean and watched over by looming mountains. The park's popular 8.8km seawall skirts a temperate rain forest that's home to beaches, blue herons and excellent attractions.

Need to Know
LOCATION Northwest of downtown. **BEST PHOTO** Prospect Point. **BEST TIME TO VISIT** Early morning or late afternoon. **BEST SUNSET-WATCHING** Third Beach. For further coverage, see p65.

Stanley Park Don't Miss List

BY ROBYN WORCESTER, STANLEY PARK ECOLOGY SOCIETY

1 LOST LAGOON NATURE HOUSE

The Nature House (p65) is a good place to start if you want to learn about the park's ecology and wildlife. We have displays and artifacts and people can borrow our bird books. We also have weekly walks – usually bird spotting – on most Sundays.

2 BIRD-WATCHING

I'm a huge bird nerd and the park has an amazing diversity, from blue herons to bald eagles. The birds are so used to humans that you can often get some great photos, especially around Lost Lagoon (p65) and at the much quieter Beaver Lake, an amazing wetland. Even on the seawall, you'll see great wintering birds. There are also raccoons and beavers in the park: we're always encouraging people not to feed them.

3 WILDLIFE AT THE VANCOUVER AQUARIUM

I know families love the aquarium (p65) for the dolphins and belugas, but its Pacific Northwest Gallery is also excellent. It shows how diverse the region's sea life is – not something we usually see because visibility isn't always great in our coastal waters. The aquarium also has exhibits on local land animals – the frog displays are great!

4 PERUSING THE TOTEM POLES

They're at Brockton Point and they're a good introduction to the First Nations of the Lower Mainland – they show visitors that there have been people living in this region for thousands of years. I like the information signs here and also the one at Siwash Rock, which tells you the First Nations story behind the formation.

5 TRAILING INTO THE PARK'S HEART

There are eight or nine million visitors to the park every year but most stay on the seawall and only a few seem to enter the trails. Circling Lost Lagoon is a good nature walk but heading through the forest just off the lagoon on Cathedral Trail takes you into the heart of the park and up to a 500-year-old Douglas fir tree.

Whistler

Canada's favorite ski resort combines a gabled, Christmas-card village with some jaw-dropping dual-mountain terrain that thrills everyone from beginners to grizzled veterans. But the alpine venue for the 2010 Winter Olympic Games also has plenty of allure for summer visitors – especially cycling fans.

Need to Know

LOCATION 122km north of Vancouver. **TOP TIP** Get Fresh Tracks early morning lift tickets. **BEST ATTRACTION** Squamish Lil'wat Cultural Centre. **For further coverage, see p81.**

2

Whistler Don't Miss List

BY PETER SMART, GUIDE AND SKI INSTRUCTOR WITH EXTREMELY CANADIAN

1 HITTING THE SLOPES

I love the amazing access to challenging terrain here (p81) and also the great backcountry areas that are available. The caliber of the skiers on the hill has really improved in recent years but it's not all about being an advanced skier: there are some great intermediate runs such as Emerald and Symphony.

2 SKI TWO MOUNTAINS ON ONE DAY

The Peak 2 Peak Gondola (p81) is the longest lift of its kind in the world and it's an amazing engineering feat. It's a huge advantage because you can switch mountains and get two totally different experiences: hitting the spring sun on Whistler then the crispy terrain on Blackcomb on the same day. It's also the smoothest lift I've ever been on.

3 SNOWBOARDING PARADISE

Snowboarding (p81) has become bigger every year up here – it's right up there with skiing now and the Terrain Park is definitely one of the best in North America. If you're here for the Ski & Snowboard Festival in April, the skiers and snowboarders take over the village and there's everything from photo contests to live music and great parties.

4 APRES SKI WIND-DOWN

It's an amazing feeling to walk around the Village Stroll area in the evening with like-minded people after a hard day on the slopes. It's comfortable and laid-back and there's a great vibe with a good mix of people shopping, hitting the bars or dining in great restaurants...and maybe comparing stories and bruises from the tumbles they might have had.

5 SUMMER SHENANIGANS

I think winter will always be the best time to come up here, but summer has really risen in popularity in recent years and it's been driven by biking. Mountain biking (p83) is great throughout this region in summer but Whistler is the leader. You have two lifts and access to an excellent park.

57

Grouse Mountain Skiing

Vancouver's favorite winter wonderland, Grouse Mountain (p74) truly is only 20 minutes from the bustle of downtown – so you can ski in the morning and wander the city's beaches in the afternoon. Restaurants and attractions – including a skating rink – offer cold-season respites from the slopes while summer is about alpine hiking, screamy zip-lining and smashing views of the city sparkling below.

Swaying at Capilano Suspension Bridge

The Lower Mainland's most popular attraction, Capilano's massive, gently swaying cabled bridge (p69) spans the waters of a spectacular tree-lined canyon. Hold on tight – or be cool like the hands-free teenagers – then explore the park's woodland trails, tree-canopy walkways and bright-painted totem poles. First Nations carvers often showcase their craft in summer.

LEE FOSTER

Okanagan Valley Wineries

Once a locals-only secret, the blossoming Okanagan fruit and wine region has grown to more than 100 wineries (p108), many of them nationally and internationally celebrated. While the region's rolling lakeside hills are idyllic whether or not you fancy a tipple, most visitors save time by weaving around the tasting rooms or just hitting the fruit stands and farmers markets: you'll likely never have a tastier peach.

Tofino Beach Bumming

A magnet for surf-loving dudes for decades, Tofino (p100) is dramatically licked by the frothing Pacific Ocean throughout the year: hit Long Beach whether or not you have a board and you'll be sucked into one of Canada's most sigh-triggering waterfront vistas. The town itself is a hippy-chic hamlet of cool eateries and galleries and is dripping with soft-eco activities.

Haida Gwaii

It's easy to feel awed by BC's natural beauty, but the northern islands of Haida Gwaii (p109) add a deep First Nations layer that defines the word 'mystical'. Touch base with the locals in the small communities and check out the amazing cultural centre (p110) but don't miss Gwaii Haanas National Park Reserve (p111) where hundreds of Haida settlements have been recorded in this stunning Unesco World Heritage site.

Gwaii Hanaas National Park Reserve

Vancouver & BC's Best...

Dining

- **C Restaurant** (p75) Delectable (and sustainable) seafood fine dining.

- **Raincity Grill** (p75) West coast regional cuisine and a great wine list.

- **Tojo's** (p77) Legendary sushi in a swank top-end room.

- **Araxi Restaurant & Lounge** (p85) Superb service; perfect Pacific Northwest dining.

- **Camille's** (p93) Intimate, romantic and dedicated to seasonal local ingredients.

- **TacoFino** (p101) The best taco truck in the West.

Wineries

- **Quail's Gate Estate Winery** (p108) Charming mid-sized winery with excellent Pinot Noir.

- **Summerhill Pyramid Winery** (p108) With its own 'aging pyramid'; sparkling whites recommended.

- **Nk'Mip Cellars** (p108) Fascinating First Nations winery with award-winning tipples.

- **Cherry Point Vineyards** (p97) Star Vancouver Island vineyard with wines – and a great patio.

- **Salt Spring Vineyards** (p106) Idyllic island winery; perfect for picnicking.

Waterfronts

- **Tofino** (p100) Dramatic wave-licked surf beaches.

- **Stanley Park Seawall** (p65) Forest-fringed seafront path.

- **English Bay Beach** (p67) Vancouver's favorite summertime hangout.

- **Parksville & Qualicum** (p99) Family-friendly beach-studded stretch.

- **Inner Harbour, Victoria** (p87) Bustling, boat-bobbling promenade popular with buskers.

- **Sunshine Coast** (p84) Idyll of little communities; popular with kayakers.

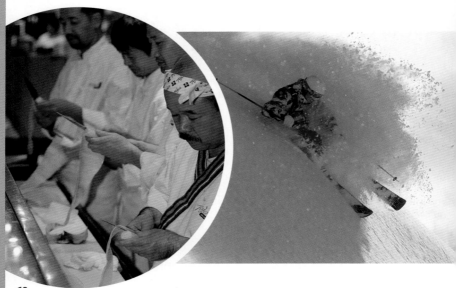

Skiing

○ **Whistler** (p81) Canada's top ski resort, with an amazing array of accessible terrain and a great village vibe.

○ **Big White Ski Resort** (p109) Attractively secluded 118-run resort loved by skiers and snowboarders alike.

○ **Grouse Mountain** (p74) Twenty minutes from downtown Vancouver, it's the city's favorite winter playground.

○ **Apex Mountain Resort** (p106) Best small ski resort in the region, with 68 runs.

Need to Know

ADVANCE PLANNING

○ **One month before** If it's summer, book accommodation as soon as possible.

○ **Two weeks before** Book activities in busy destinations such as Vancouver and Whistler.

○ **One week before** Make restaurant reservations at high-end eateries.

RESOURCES

○ **BC Parks** (www.bcparks .ca) Information, resources and activities on the province's 830 parks.

○ **Tourism British Columbia** (www.hellobc.com) Community information, activities, guides and accommodation booking.

○ **Tourism Vancouver** (www.tourismvancouver .com) Blogs, listings and accommodation bookings in BC's biggest city.

○ **BC Ferries** (www.bc ferries.com) Routes and booking engine for BC's extensive ferry system.

○ **BC Wine Institute** (www.bcwine.com) Information on wineries and festivals across BC.

○ **Cycling BC** (www .cyclingbc.net) Resources for cyclists.

○ **Surfing Vancouver Island** (www.surfing vancouverisland.com) Videos and tips on the region's surfing culture.

○ **Georgia Straight** (www.straight.com) Comprehensive Vancouver listings resource.

GETTING AROUND

○ **Fly** Vancouver International Airport is a hub for travel across the region: services go to Victoria, Kelowna, Haida Gwaii and beyond. Also, floatplane services run from downtown Vancouver across the region.

○ **Car** Extensive highway system links most towns, with all major hire-car companies available.

○ **Ferry** World's largest public ferry system links the mainland with communities on Vancouver Island and throughout BC.

○ **Train** VIA Rail (www.viarail .ca) services from across Canada to Vancouver via Jasper and from Victoria to Courtenay on Vancouver Island. Seasonal services from Vancouver to Whistler and Vancouver to the Rockies via Banff on Rocky Mountaineer (www .rockymountaineer.com).

Vancouver & BC Itineraries

For a taste of BC, take a three-day mainland-and-island loop covering the two main cities and many small towns. Then, visit the spectacular Okanagan wine region, sampling Canada's best tipples and finest fruit.

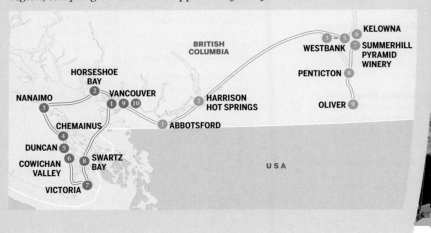

VANCOUVER TO VANCOUVER

3 DAYS Mini BC Circle Tour

Don't leave Vancouver before taking a bracing morning stroll along the seawall in **(1) Stanley Park**. Then drive through the park and across the Lions Gate Bridge to West Vancouver's **(2) Horseshoe Bay**. Trundle on to the Nanaimo-bound ferry and you'll soon be sliding across the glassy waters to Vancouver Island. Get off at **(3) Nanaimo** and take Hwy 1 down the island. Check out colorful small communities such as **(4) Chemainus** and **(5) Duncan** and drop into the **(6) Cowichan Valley** area to pick up a bottle of wine and stay in a local B&B.

Next day, continue south to BC's capital **(7) Victoria** for your next sleepover – two nights is recommended if you want to explore all the attractions and activities and enjoy the city's great restaurants. Conclude your circle tour with a drive to the **(8) Swartz Bay** ferry terminal, where you'll have another idyllic sea crossing back to the mainland. From the dock, follow the signs and you'll be back in **(9) Vancouver** within the hour. Toast your journey, and check out all your digital photos, over a regional microbrewed beer in **(10) Gastown**, the city's old town area.

VANCOUVER TO KELOWNA

Wine Weave Through the Okanagan

5 DAYS

Follow the three-day itinerary, then depart eastwards from Vancouver on Hwy 1 – then Hwys 5 and 97 – through BC's farmland interior. If the Cowichan Valley gave you a taste for local wine, you're about to hit the motherlode: just make sure one of you is a designated driver. It's around 380km to the Okanagan, so consider stopping off in Fraser Valley communities such as **(1) Abbotsford** or **(2) Harrison Hot Springs** before you reach the lakefront community of **(3) Westbank**, home of **(4) Mission Hill Estate Winery**.

After a leisurely tasting, check out nearby **(5) Quail's Gate Estate Winery**.

Continue along Hwy 97 over the bridge into **(6) Kelowna** where you should base yourself for the duration of your trip. From here, spend your time puttering around the verdant region. Include side trips south of Kelowna to **(7) Summerhill Pyramid Winery** and on to **(8) Penticton** and **(9) Oliver** where you'll find Canada's best fresh fruit growing – look out for peaches, apples or cherries. By this stage, you'll be considering moving here: have another glass of wine and hit the Citizenship and Immigration Canada website.

Golden vineyard in Cowichan Valley (p97)

Discover Vancouver & British Columbia

At a Glance

○ **Vancouver** (opposite) BC's main metropolis with city parks and waterfront trails.

○ **Whistler** (p81) Spectacular skiing and snowboarding country.

○ **Vancouver Island** (p86) Victoria, Tofino and many colorful communities in between.

○ **Okanagan Valley** (p104) Verdant fruit, winery and lakefront country.

○ **Haida Gwaii** (p109) Mystical northern islands with rich First Nations culture.

View from the beach at Kitsilano (p67), Vancouver
GLENN VAN DER KNIJFF

VANCOUVER
POP 578,000

Flying into Vancouver International Airport on a cloud-free summer's day, it's not hard to appreciate the nature-bound description of a utopia that sticks to this 'Lotus Land' like a wetsuit. Gently rippling ocean crisscrossed with ferry trails, the crenulated shorelines of dozens of forest-green islands and the ever-present sentinels of snow-dusted crags glinting on the horizon give this city arguably the most spectacular setting of any metropolis on the planet.

But while the city's twinkling outdoor backdrop means you're never far from great skiing, kayaking or hiking, there's much more to Vancouver than appearances. When hitting the streets on foot, you'll come across a kaleidoscope of distinctive neighborhoods, each one almost like a village in itself. This diversity is Vancouver's main strength and a major reason why visitors keep coming back.

If you're a first timer, soak in the breathtaking vistas and hit the verdant forests whenever you can, but also save time to join the locals and do a little exploring off the beaten track; it's in these places that you'll discover what really makes this beautiful metropolis special.

 Sights

Downtown

VANCOUVER ART GALLERY   Art Gallery
(Map p70; www.vanartgallery.bc.ca; 750 Hornby St; adult/child $22.50/7.50, by donation 5-9pm

CHRISTOPHER HERWIG

Don't Miss **Vancouver Aquarium**

Home to 9000 water-loving critters – including wolf eels, beluga whales and mesmerizing jellyfish – the **aquarium** (www.vanaqua.org; adult/child $27/17, reduced in winter; ⏰9:30am-7pm Jul & Aug, 9:30am-5pm Sep-Jun) also has a walk-through rain forest of birds, turtles and a statue-still sloth. Check for feeding times and consider an **Animal Encounter trainer tour** (from $24). The newest draw here is the 4D Experience: a 3D movie theater with added wind, mist and aromas. The aquarium is in Stanley Park.

Tue; ⏰10am-5pm Wed-Mon, to 9pm Tue) The VAG has dramatically transformed since 2000, becoming a vital part of the city's cultural scene. Contemporary exhibitions – often showcasing Vancouver's renowned photoconceptualists – are now combined with blockbuster international traveling shows.

CANADA PLACE   Notable Building
(Map p70; www.canadaplace.ca; 999 Canada Place Way) Shaped like a series of sails jutting into the sky over the harbor, this cruise-ship terminal and convention center is also a pier where you can stroll the waterfront for some camera-triggering North Shore mountain views. Check out the grass-roofed expansion next door and the tripod-like **Olympic**

Cauldron, a permanent reminder of the 2010 Winter Games.

Stanley Park
This magnificent 404-hectare park combines excellent attractions with a mystical natural aura. See also p54.

FREE **LOST LAGOON**   Nature Reserve
Originally an extension of Coal Harbour, this tranquil, watery oasis is now colonized by indigenous plants and beady-eyed birdlife accessed via a shoreline trail. Drop into the **Nature House** (Map p70; www.stanleyparkecology.ca; admission free; ⏰10am-7pm Tue-Sun May-Sep) for an introduction to the park's ecology and ask about the area **walks** (adult/child $10/5).

Vancouver City Overview

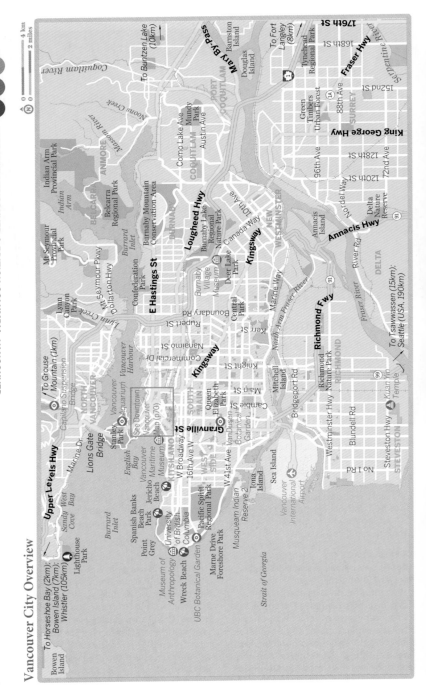

West End

ROEDDE HOUSE MUSEUM
Museum

(Map p70; www.roeddehouse.org; 1415 Barclay St; admission $5; ⏱10am-5pm Tue-Sat, 2-4pm Sun) For a glimpse of pioneer-town Vancouver, drop by this handsome 1893 timber-framed mansion. Packed with antiques, it's a superb re-creation of how well-heeled locals used to live. Sunday entry includes tea and cookies for $1 extra.

ENGLISH BAY BEACH
Beach

(Map p70; cnr Denman & Davie Sts) Whether it's a languid August evening with buskers, sunbathers and volleyballers, or a blustery November day with the dog walkers, this sandy curve is an unmissable highlight. Snap photos of the beach's towering **inukshuk sculpture** or continue along the bustling seawall into neighboring Stanley Park.

Gastown & Chinatown

VANCOUVER POLICE MUSEUM
Museum

(Map p70; www.vancouverpolicemuseum.ca; 240 E Cordova St; adult/student $7/5; ⏱9am-5pm) Charting the city's murky criminal past — complete with confiscated weapons, counterfeit currencies and a mortuary exhibit lined with wall-mounted tissue samples — this excellent little museum also runs recommended **Sins of the City walking tours** (adult/child $15/12).

SCIENCE WORLD AT TELUS WORLD OF SCIENCE
Museum

(Map p70; www.scienceworld.ca; 1455 Quebec St; adult/child $21/14.25; ⏱10am-5pm Mon-Fri, 10am-6pm Sat & Sun) The two levels of hands-on science and natural-history exhibits here bring out the kid in everyone. An ideal place to entertain the family, there's also an **Omnimax Theatre** screening large-format documentaries. Explore without the kids at the regular adults-only **After Dark** ($19.75) events.

Granville Island

GRANVILLE ISLAND PUBLIC MARKET
Market

(Map p70; Johnston St; ⏱9am-7pm) Granville Island's highlight is the covered Public Market, a multisensory smorgasbord of fish, cheese, fruit and bakery treats. Pick up some fixings for a picnic at nearby Vanier Park or hit the international food court (dine off-peak and you're more likely to snag a table). **Edible BC** (www.edible-britishcolumbia.com; tours $49) offers excellent market tours for the foodie-inclined.

GRANVILLE ISLAND BREWING
Brewery

(Map p70; www.gib.ca; 1441 Cartwright St; tours $9.75; ⏱noon, 2pm & 4pm) A short tour of Canada's oldest microbrewery ends with four sample beers in the Taproom — often including summer-favorite Hefeweizen, mildly hopped Brockton IPA or the recommended Kitsilano Maple Cream Ale. You can buy takeout in the adjoining store — look for special-batch tipples like the popular Ginger Ale.

Kitsilano & West Side

HR MACMILLAN SPACE CENTRE
Museum

(www.hrmacmillanspacecentre.com; 1100 Chestnut St; adult/child $15/10.75; ⏱10am-5pm Jul & Aug, 10am-3pm Mon-Fri & 10am-5pm Sat & Sun Sep-Jun) Popular with kids, who hit the hands-on exhibits with maximum force, this high-tech space center offers the chance to battle aliens, design spacecraft and take a Mars-bound simulator ride. There's an additional **observatory** (admission free; ⏱weekends, weather permitting) and a **planetarium**.

MUSEUM OF VANCOUVER
Museum

(Map p70; www.museumofvancouver.ca; 1100 Chestnut St; adult/child $12/8; ⏱10am-5pm Tue-Sun, to 8pm Thu) The recently rebranded MOV has upped its game with cool temporary exhibitions and late-opening parties aimed at an adult crowd. There are still colorful displays on local 1950s pop culture and 1960s hippie counterculture, plus plenty of hands-on kids stuff, including weekend scavenger hunts.

VANDUSEN BOTANICAL GARDEN
Garden

(Map p66; www.vandusengarden.org; 5251 Oak St; adult/child $9.75/5.25; ⏱10am-4pm Nov-Feb, 10am-5pm Mar & Oct, 10am-6pm Apr, 10am-8pm May, 10am-9pm Jun-Aug, 10am-7pm Sep) Four blocks west of the multipurpose

52-hectare **Queen Elizabeth Park**, this garden offers a highly ornamental confection of sculptures, Canadian heritage flowers, rare plants from around the world and a popular hedge maze. The garden is one of Vancouver's top Christmas destinations, complete with thousands of twinkling fairy lights.

University of British Columbia (UBC)

MUSEUM OF ANTHROPOLOGY Museum
(Map p66; www.moa.ubc.ca; 6393 NW Marine Dr; adult/child $14/12; ☺10am-5pm Wed-Mon & 10am-9pm Tue mid-Jan—mid-Oct, closed Mon mid-Oct—mid-Jan) Recently renovated and expanded, Vancouver's best museum houses northwest coast aboriginal artifacts, including Haida houses and totem poles, plus non–First Nations exhibits such as European ceramics and Cantonese opera costumes. The free guided tours are highly recommended, as is the excellent artsy gift shop. Give yourself a couple of hours at this museum.

BOTANICAL GARDEN Garden
(Map p66; www.ubcbotanicalgarden.org; 6804 SW Marine Dr; adult/child $8/4; ☺9am-4:30pm Mon-Fri, 9:30am-4:30pm Sat & Sun, reduced off-season) A giant collection of rhododendrons, a fascinating apothecary plot and a winter green space of off-season bloomers are highlights of this 28-hectare complex of themed gardens. The additional **Greenheart Canopy Walkway** (www.greenheartcanopywalkway.com; adult/child $20/6; ☺9am-5pm) lifts visitors 17m above the forest floor on a 308m guided eco tour. You can buy a combination ticket that includes the Nitobe Memorial Garden.

NITOBE MEMORIAL GARDEN Garden
(www.nitobe.org; 1895 Lower Mall; adult/child $8/4; ☺10am-4pm, reduced off-season) Designed by a top Japanese landscape architect, this lovely green space is a perfect example of the Asian nation's symbolic horticultural art form. Aside from some traffic noise and summer

Left: Punnets at Granville Island Public Market (p67); **Below:** Sightseeing geese, Queen Elizabeth Park (p68)

PHOTOGRAPHER: (LEFT) CHRISTOPHER HERWIG; (BELOW) LAWRENCE WORCESTER

bus tours, it's a tranquil retreat, ideal for meditation.

North Vancouver
For info on Grouse Mountain, see p74.

CAPILANO SUSPENSION BRIDGE Park
(Map p66; www.capbridge.com; 3735 Capilano Rd; adult/child $29.95/10; ☺8:30am-8pm Jun-Aug, 9am-7pm May & Sep, reduced off-season)
Walking gingerly across the world's longest (140m) and highest (70m) suspension bridge, swaying gently over the roiling waters of Capilano Canyon, remember that the steel cables you are gripping are embedded in huge concrete blocks on either side. That should steady your feet – unless the teenagers are stamping their way across. This is the region's most popular attraction – hence the summertime crowds – and the grounds here include rain forest walks, totem poles and some smaller bridges strung between the trees. In summer, First Nations people often showcase their crafts here.

 **Activities**

Running & Cycling
Joggers share the busy Stanley Park seawall with cyclists (and in-line skaters), necessitating a one-way traffic system to prevent pileups. The sea-to-sky vistas are breathtaking, but the exposed route can be hit with crashing waves and icy winds in winter. Since slow-moving, camera-wielding tourists crowd the route in summer, it's best to come early in the morning or late in the afternoon.

There's a plethora of bike and blade rental stores near Stanley Park's W Georgia St entrance, especially around the intersection with Denman St.

Kayaking
Headquartered on Granville Island, the friendly folk at **Ecomarine Ocean Kayak Centre** (Map p70; www.ecomarine.com;

DISCOVER VANCOUVER & BRITISH COLUMBIA

A · **B** · **C** · **D**

Lost Lagoon

Stanley Park

4

Coal Harbour

Devonian Harbour Park

11

Royal Vancouver Yacht Club

Lagoon Dr

Bayshore Dr

Coal Harbour Seawalk

Harbour Green Park

To Second Beach Swimming Pool (800m)

Chilco St

Beach Ave

Gilford St

Denman St

Bidwell St

W Georgia St

Alberni St

W Pender St

Coal Harbour Park

Robson St

14

16

28

Haro St

Cardero St

Barclay St

Nelson St

Barclay Heritage Square

6

13

Melville St

2

Nicola St

Broughton St

Comox St

Jervis St

WEST END

Inukshuk

English Bay

Cardero St

Bute St

Pendrell St

Dave St

Nelson Park

Burnaby St

Thurlow St

Sunset Beach Park

Harwood St

Burrard St

Robson Sq

Provincial Law Courts

34

False Creek Ferry

Pacific St

Hornby St

Helmcken St

29

38

Beach Ave

Howe St

Granville St

Seymour St

Richards St

5

Vanier Park

Whyte Ave

Burrard Bridge

Dave St

Hamilton St

Drake St

15

To Fifth Avenue Cinemas (300m)

Broker's Bay

Pacific Blvd

Yaletown-Roundhouse

22

David Lam Park

Burrard St

To Mickey's Kits Beach Chalet (600m)

Granville Island Public Market

10

Granville Island

Granville Bridge

Granville St

25

Johnston St

3

False Creek Ferry

Fir St

W 1st Ave

W 2nd Ave

Old Bridge St

Cartwright St

Sutcliffe Park

12

The Mound

Aquabus Ferry

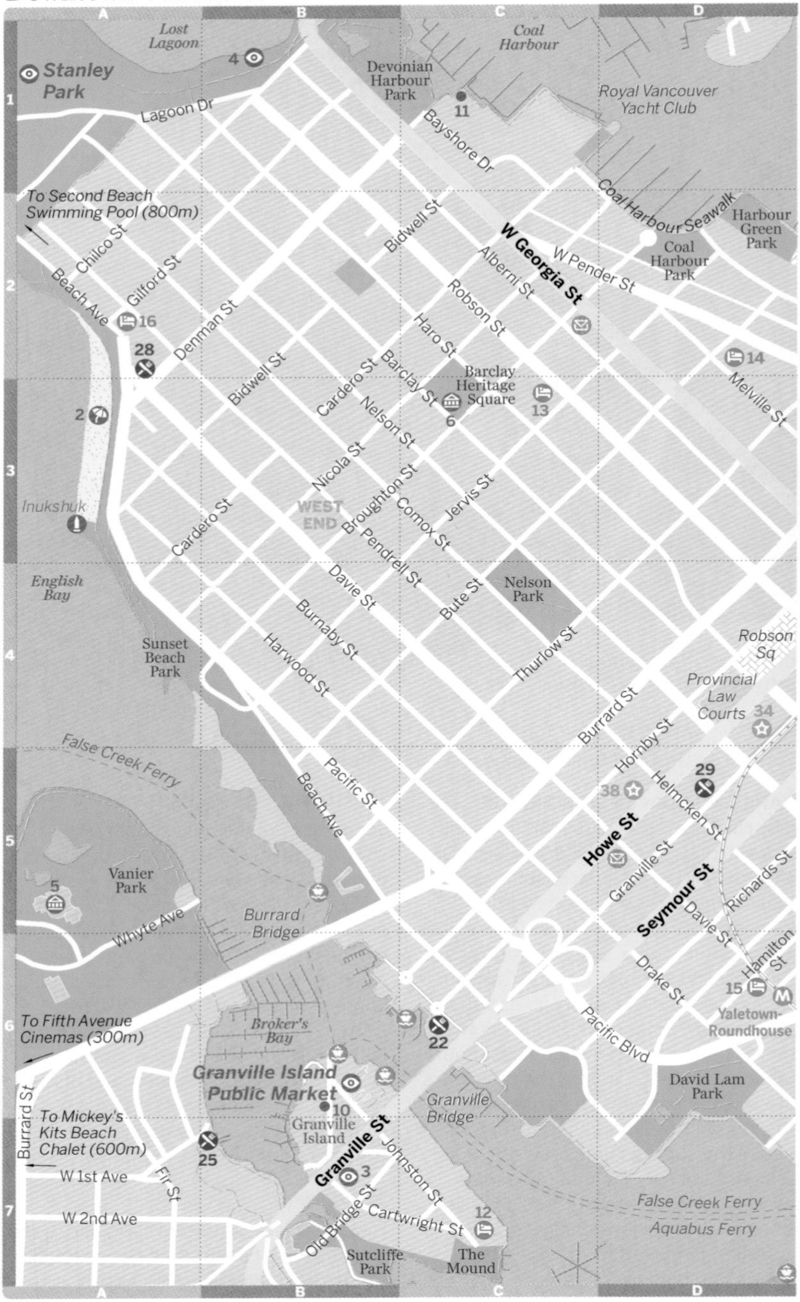

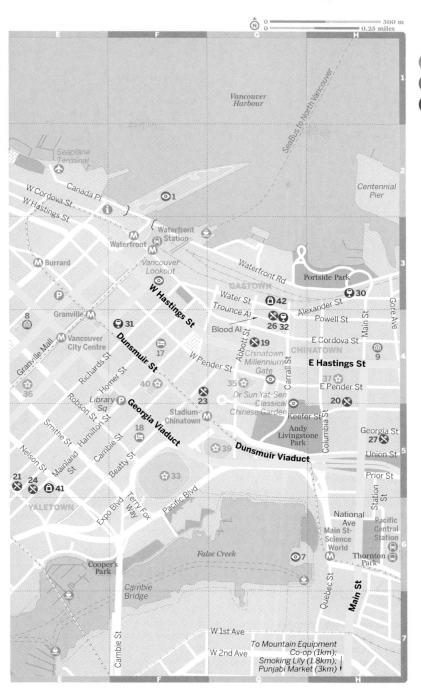

0   500 m
0   0.25 miles

Vancouver Harbour

Seaplane Terminal

W Cordova St
W Hastings St
Canada Pl

Centennial Pier

SeaBus to North Vancouver

Waterfront Station
Waterfront
Vancouver Lookout

Burrard

Waterfront Rd

Portside Park
30

GASTOWN

Water St
Trounce Al
42

Alexander St
Powell St

Main St

Gore Ave

W Hastings St

Granville

26 32

Dunsmuir St

8
Granville
Vancouver City Centre

17

Blood Al
Abbott St
19

E Cordova St

9

CHINATOWN

Richards St

W Pender St

Chinatown Millennium Gate

E Hastings St

Carrall St

36

Homer St

40

Library Sq
Georgia Viaduct

35
23

37
E Pender St

20

Robson St
Smithe St
Hamilton St

18

Stadium-Chinatown

Dr Sun Yat-Sen Classical Chinese Garden

Keefer St

Andy Livingstone Park

Georgia St
27

Cambie St
Beatty St

Dunsmuir Viaduct

Union St

39

Columbia St

Nelson St
Mainland St

21 24
41

33

Prior St

Station St

YALETOWN

Terry Fox Way
Expo Blvd
Pacific Blvd

National Ave
Main St-Science World

Pacific Central Station

Thornton Park

Cooper's Park

False Creek

7

Quebec St

Main St

Cambie Bridge

Cambie St

W 1st Ave
W 2nd Ave

To Mountain Equipment Co-op (1km); Smoking Lily (1.8km); Punjabi Market (3km)

1668 Duranleau St; rentals 2hr/day $36/69;
⏱9am-6pm Sun-Thu & 9am-9pm Fri & Sat Jun-
Aug, 10am-6pm Sep-May) offer equipment
rentals and guided tours. Its **Jericho
Beach branch** (Jericho Sailing Centre, 1300
Discovery St; ⏱9am-dusk May-Aug, 9am-dusk
Sat & Sun Sep) organizes events and semi-
nars where you can rub shoulders with
local paddle nuts.

 Tours

Vancouver Trolley Company   Bus
(☎604-801-5515, 888-451-5581;
www.vancouvertrolley.com; adult/child $38/20)
Red replica trolley buses offering hop-on-hop-off
transportation around popular city stops.

Harbour Cruises   Boat
(Map p70; ☎604-688-7246, 800-663-1500;
www.boatcruises.com; north end of Denman St;
adult/child $30/10; ⏱May-Oct) View the city –
and some unexpected wildlife – from the water
on a 75-minute harbor boat tour. Dinner cruises
are also available.

 Sleeping

While rates peak in the summer months,
there are some great deals available
in fall and early spring. The **Tourism
Vancouver** (www.tourismvancouver.com)
website lists options and packages. Note
that hotels often charge $10 to $20 for
overnight parking.

Downtown & Yaletown

LODEN VANCOUVER
Boutique Hotel $$$

(Map p70; ☎ 604-669-5060, 877-225-6336; www.theloden.com; 1177 Melville St; r from $249; ❄ 🛜) The definition of class, the stylish Loden is the real designer deal. Its 70 rooms combine a knowing contemporary élan with luxe accoutrements like marble-lined bathrooms and those oh-so-civilized heated floors. The attentive service is top-notch, while the glam Voya is one of the city's best hotel bars.

VICTORIAN HOTEL
Hotel $$

(Map p70; ☎ 604-681-6369, 877-681-6369; www.victorianhotel.ca; 514 Homer St; r with/without bathroom from $149/129) Housed in a pair of renovated older properties, the high-ceilinged rooms at this Euro-style pension combine glossy hardwood floors, a sprinkling of antiques, an occasional bay window and plenty of heritage charm. Most are en suite, with TVs and summer fans provided, but the best rooms are in the newer extension.

OPUS HOTEL VANCOUVER
Boutique Hotel $$$

(Map p70; ☎ 604-642-6787, 866-642-6787; www.opushotel.com; 322 Davie St; d & ste from $280; ❄ 🛜) Celebs looking for a place to be seen should look no further. The city's original designer boutique sleepover has been welcoming the likes of Justin Timberlake and that bald bloke from REM for years. The paparazzi magnets come for the chic suites, including feng-shui bed placements and luxe bathrooms with clear windows overlooking the streets (visiting exhibitionists take note).

YWCA HOTEL
Hotel $$

(Map p70; ☎ 604-895-5830, 800-663-1424; www.ywcahotel.com; 733 Beatty St; s/d/tr $69/86/111; ❄ 🛜 👪) One of Canada's best Ys, this popular tower near Yaletown is a useful option for those on a budget. Accommodating men, women, couples and families, it's a bustling place with a communal kitchen on every other floor and rooms ranging from compact singles to group-friendly larger quarters.

Vancouver for Children

Pick up the free *Kids' Guide Vancouver* flyer from racks around town and visit www.kidsvancouver.com for tips and family-focused events. Children under five travel free on all transit services. Child-care equipment – strollers, booster seats, cribs, baby monitors, toys etc – can be rented from **Wee Travel** (☎ 604-222-4722; www.weetravel.ca). Your hotel can usually recommend a licensed and bonded babysitting service.

Stanley Park (p65) can keep most families occupied for a day. If it's hot, make sure you hit the water park at Lumberman's Arch or try the swimming pool at Second Beach; also consider the **miniature railway**. The park is a great place for a picnic, and its beaches – especially Third Beach – are highly kid-friendly. Save time for the **Vancouver Aquarium** (p65) and, if your kids have been good, consider a behind-the-scenes animal trainer tour.

The city's other family-friendly attractions include **Science World at Telus World of Science** (p67) and the **HR MacMillan Space Centre** (p67).

The city has an array of family-friendly festivals, including the **Pacific National Exhibition** (August: www.pne.bc.ca), the **Vancouver International Children's Festival** (May: www.childrensfestival.ca) and the fireworks fiesta known as the **Celebration of Light** (July: www.hsbccelebrationoflight.com).

CHRISTOPHER HERWIG

Don't Miss **Grouse Mountain**

This **mountaintop perch** (www.grousemountain.com; 6400 Nancy Greene Way; adult/child $39/13.95; ☺9am-10pm) is one of the region's most popular outdoor hangouts. In summer, Skyride gondola tickets to the top include access to lumberjack shows, alpine hiking trails and a grizzly-bear refuge. Pay extra for the zipline course ($105) or the new Eye of the Wind tour ($25), which takes you to the top of a 20-story wind turbine tower for spectacular views. In winter, Grouse is also a magnet for skiers and snowboarders.

All are a little institutionalized – think student study bedroom – but each has a sink and refrigerator.

West End

SYLVIA HOTEL Hotel **$$**
(Map p70; ☎ 604-681-9321; www.sylvia hotel.com; 1154 Gilford St; s/d/ste from $110/165/195) Generations of guests keep coming back to this ivy-covered gem for a dollop of old-world charm followed by a side order of first-name service. The lobby decor resembles a Bavarian pension – stained-glass windows and dark-wood paneling – and there's a wide array of comfortable room configurations to suit every need. The best are the 12 apartment suites, which include full kitchens and English Bay panoramas.

LISTEL VANCOUVER Boutique Hotel **$$**
(Map p70; ☎ 604-684-8461, 800-663-5491; www.thelistelhotel.com; 1300 Robson St; d from $169; ❄) Vancouver's self-described 'art hotel' is a graceful cut above the other properties at this end of Robson St. Attracting a grown-up gaggle of sophisticates with its gallery-style art installations (check the little hidden art space just off the lobby), the mood-lit rooms are suffused with a relaxing west-coast ambience.

Granville Island & Kitsilano

GRANVILLE ISLAND HOTEL
Boutique Hotel **$$**
(Map p70; ☎ 604-683-7373, 800-663-1840; www.granvilleislandhotel.com; 1253 Johnston St; d from $159; ❄ @ 🐾) Hugging the quiet

eastern tip of Granville Island, you'll be a five-minute walk from the public market here, with plenty of additional dining, shopping and theater options right on your doorstep. Characterized by contemporary west-coast decor, the rooms feature exposed wood and soothing earth tones. There's also a cool rooftop Jacuzzi, while the on-site brewpub makes its own distinctive beer.

MICKEY'S KITS BEACH CHALET
B&B $$

(☎ 604-739-3342, 888-739-3342; www .mickeysbandb.com; 2142 W 1st Ave; d $135-175; ☎⚑) Eschewing the heritage-home approach of most Kitsilano B&Bs, this modern, Whistler-style chalet has three rooms and a tranquil, hedged-in garden terrace. Rooms – including the gabled, top-floor York Room – are decorated in a comfortable contemporary style, but only the York has an ensuite bathroom. Includes continental breakfast.

 # Eating

With an international diversity that even rival foodie cities such as Toronto and Montréal can't match, Vancouver visitors can fill up on great ethnic dishes and the region's flourishing west-coast cuisine. Tap into the latest reviews at www .urbandiner.ca or pick up a free copy of either *Eat Magazine* or *City Food*.

Downtown & Yaletown

CHAMBAR
European $$

(Map p70; ☎ 604-879-7119; www.chambar.com; 562 Beatty St; mains $14-29) This romantic, brick-lined cave – atmospherically lit by candles at night – is a great place for a lively chat among Vancouver's urban professionals. The sophisticated Euro menu includes perfectly prepared highlights like pan-seared scallops and velvet-soft lamb shank but delectable *moules et frites* are the way to go. An impressive wine and cocktail list (try a Blue Fig Martini) is coupled with a great Belgian beer menu.

TEMPLETON
Breakfast, Burgers $$

(Map p70; www.thetempleton.blogspot.com; 1087 Granville St; mains $8-12) A funky chrome-and-vinyl '50s diner with a twist, Templeton chefs up plus-sized organic burgers, addictive fries, vegetarian quesadillas and perhaps the best hangover cure in town – the 'Big Ass Breakfast.' Sadly, the mini jukeboxes on the tables don't work, but you can console yourself with a waistline-busting chocolate-ice-cream float. The beer here is of the local microbrew variety.

C RESTAURANT
Seafood $$$

(Map p70; ☎ 604-681-1164; www.crestaurant .com; 1600 Howe St; mains $28-40) This pioneering west-coast seafood restaurant overlooking False Creek isn't cheap but its revelatory approach to fish and shellfish makes it possibly the city's best seafood dine-out. You'll be hard pressed to find smoked salmon with cucumber jelly served anywhere else, but there's also a reverence for simple preparation that reveals the delicate flavors in dishes such as local side-stripe prawns and northern BC scallops.

GLOWBAL GRILL STEAKS & SATAY
Fusion $$

(Map p70; www.glowbalgrill.com; 1079 Mainland St; mains $17-40) Casting a wide net that catches the power-lunch, after-work and late-night fashionista crowds, this hip but unpretentious joint has a comfortable, lounge-like feel. Its menu of classy dishes fuses west-coast ingredients with Asian and Mediterranean flourishes – the prawn linguine is ace and the finger-licking satay sticks are a recommended starter.

West End

RAINCITY GRILL
West Coast $$$

(Map p70; ☎ 604-685-7337; www.raincitygrill .com; 1193 Denman St; mains $17-30) This excellent English Bay restaurant was sourcing and serving unique BC ingredients long before the fashion for Fanny Bay oysters and Salt Spring Island lamb took hold. It's a great showcase for fine west-coast cuisine: the $30 three-course tasting menu (served between

5pm and 6pm) is a bargain and the weekend brunch is a local legend. Excellent wine list.

Gastown & Chinatown

JUDAS GOAT
Fusion $

(Map p70; www.judasgoat.ca; 27 Blood Alley; small plates $6-10) This smashing 28-seat, mosaic-and-marble nook became a local foodie favorite soon after its 2010 opening. Named after the goats used to lead sheep off slaughterhouse trucks, it's nailed the art of small, simply prepared but invitingly gourmet tapas treats like beef brisket meatballs, lamb cheek wrapped in savoy cabbage and scallop tartare with pork rinds. Arrive off-peak to avoid lineups.

BAO BEI
Asian Fusion $$

(Map p70; www.bao-bei.ca; 163 Keefer St; mains $10-18) This chic-but-welcoming Chinese brasserie quickly hooked the hipsters when it opened in 2010. From its prawn and chive dumplings to its addictive short-rib-filled buns, it's brought a unique contemporary flair to eating out in the area, combined with an innovative approach to ingredients: top-of-the-

range organic meat and sustainable seafood is used throughout. It's easy to find yourself seduced by the relaxed, candlelit ambience, especially if you hit the excellent cocktail menu.

ACME CAFÉ
Cafe $

(Map p70; www.acmecafe.ca; 51 W Hastings St; mains $8-10) The black-and-white deco-style interior here is enough to warm up anyone on a rainy day – or maybe it's the retro-cool U-shaped counter. The hipsters flock here for good-value hearty breakfasts and heaping comfort-food lunches flavored with a gourmet flourish: meatloaf, chicken club and shrimp guacamole sandwiches are grand but why not drop by for an afternoon coffee and some house-baked fruit pie?

PHNOM PENH
Vietnamese $$

(Map p70; 244 E Georgia St; mains $8-18) Arrive early or late to avoid the queues at this locals' favorite eatery. The dishes here are split between Cambodian and Vietnamese soul-food classics, such as crispy frog legs, spicy garlic crab and prawn- and sprout-filled pancakes. Don't leave without sampling a steamed rice

Tojo's restaurant (p77), Vancouver

LAWRENCE WORCESTER

Gay & Lesbian Vancouver

Vancouver's gay and lesbian scene is part of the city's culture rather than a subsection of it. The legalization of same-sex marriages in BC has resulted in a huge number of couples using Vancouver as a kind of gay Vegas for their destination nuptials. For more information on tying the knot, visit www.vs.gov.bc.ca/marriage/howto.html.

Vancouver's West End district – complete with its pink-painted bus shelters, fluttering rainbow flags and hand-holding locals – houses western Canada's largest 'gayborhood,' while the city's lesbian contingent is centered more on Commercial Dr.

Pick up a free copy of *Xtra!* for a crash course on the local scene, and check www.gayvancouver.net, www.gayvan.com and www.superdyke.com for pertinent listings and resources.

cake, stuffed with pork, shrimp, coconut and scallions, and washed down with an ice-cold bottle of Tsingtao.

Kitsilano & West Side

BISHOP'S West Coast **$$$**
(☎ 604-738-2025; www.bishopsonline.com; 2183 W 4th Ave; mains $28-38) A pioneer of superb west-coast cuisine long before the 'locavore' fashion took hold, modest but legendary chef-owner John Bishop is still at the top of his game in this charming, art-lined little restaurant. Served in an elegant, white-tablecloth room, the weekly changing menu can include stuffed rabbit loin, steamed smoked sablefish and the kind of crisp, seasonal veggies that taste like they've just been plucked from the ground.

TOJO'S Japanese **$$$**
(☎ 604-872-8050; www.tojos.com; 1133 W Broadway; mains $19-26) Hidekazu Tojo's legendary skill with the sushi knife has created one of North America's most revered sushi restaurants. Among his exquisite dishes are favorites such as lightly steamed monkfish, sautéed halibut cheeks and fried red tuna wrapped with seaweed and served with plum sauce. The maplewood sushi bar seats are more sought after than a couple of front-row Stanley Cup tickets.

 Drinking

Distinctive new lounges and pubs are springing up in Vancouver like persistent drunks at an open bar. Granville St, from Robson to Davie Sts, is a party district of mainstream haunts, but Gastown is your best bet for brick-lined character bars.

ALIBI ROOM Pub
(Map p70; www.alibi.ca; 157 Alexander St) Vancouver's favorite craft-brew bar, this hopping brick-walled contemporary tavern stocks an ever-changing roster of around 25 mostly BC beers from celebrated breweries like Phillips, Driftwood, Old Yale, Crannog, Central City and beyond. Adventurous taste-trippers – Main St hipsters and old-lag Camra (Campaign for Real Ale) drinkers alike – enjoy the $9 'frat bat' of four sample tipples: choose your own or ask to be surprised. Food-wise, go for skinny fries with chili garlic vinegar or a bulging, Pemberton-sourced burger.

SIX ACRES Bar
(Map p70; www.sixacres.ca; 203 Carrall St) Perfect for a shared plate of finger food, though it's just as easy to cover all the necessary food groups with the extensive beer selection. There's a small, animated patio out front but inside is great for hid-

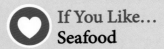

If You Like...
Seafood

If you like the seafood at C Restaurant (p75), BC has a full menu of great aquatic eateries.

1 BLUE WATER CAFÉ
(Map p70; www.bluewatercafe.net; 1095 Hamilton St; mains $22-44) House music gently percolates through the brick-lined interior of this swank Vancouver joint, while seafood towers, arctic char and BC sablefish grace the tables. Hit the semicircular raw bar and watch the whirling blades prepare delectable sushi and sashimi.

2 GO FISH
(Map p70; 1505 W 1st Ave; mains $8-13) A two-minute walk west along the Vancouver seawall from Granville Island, this wildly popular shack is one of the city's best fish-and-chip spots, offering a choice of halibut, salmon or cod encased in crispy golden batter. The fish tacos are highly recommended, while daily specials often include praise-worthy scallop burgers or ahi tuna sandwiches.

3 RED FISH BLUE FISH
(Map p92; www.redfish-bluefish.com; 1006 Wharf St; mains $6-10) On Victoria's waterfront boardwalk, at the foot of Broughton St, this takeout serves a loyal clientele. Highlights such as scallop tacones, wild salmon sandwiches, tempura-battered fish and chips and the signature chunky Pacific Rim Chowder all hit the spot: find a waterfront perch to enjoy your nosh but watch for hovering seagull mobsters.

4 SCHOONER ON SECOND
(www.schoonerrestaurant.ca; 331 Campbell St; mains $12-28) Family-owned for 50 years, this Tofino legend has uncovered many new ways to prepare the region's seafood: halibut stuffed with shrimp, brie and pine nuts is recommended (as are the giant breakfasts). Or try the giant Captain's Plate blowout of salmon, scallops et al.

ing in a candlelit corner and working your way through some exotic bottled brews, often including London Porter and the rather marvelous Draft Dodger from Phillips Brewing. Vancouver's coziest tavern,

you can pull a board game from the shelf for an extended stay.

RAILWAY CLUB Pub
(Map p70; www.therailwayclub.com; 579 Dunsmuir St) Accessed via an unobtrusive wooden door next to a 7-11, this is one of the city's friendliest drinkeries and you'll fit right in as soon as you roll up to the bar – unusually for Vancouver, you have to order at the counter. Expect regional microbrews from the likes of Tree Brewing and Central City (go for its ESB) and hit the hole-in-the-wall kitchen for late-night nosh, including burgers and quesadillas. There's an eclectic roster of live music every night.

 Entertainment

Pick up the free *Georgia Straight* – or check www.straight.com – to tap local happenings.

FORTUNE SOUND CLUB Nightclub
(Map p70; www.fortunesoundclub.com; 147 E Pender St) The city's best club has transformed a grungy old Eastside location – formerly the legendary Ming's Chinese Restaurant – into a slick space with the kind of genuine staff and younger, hipster-cool crowd rarely seen in Vancouver nightspots. Slide inside and you'll find a giant dance floor bristling with party-loving locals out to have a great time. Expect a long wait to get in on weekends: it's worth it, though, for Happy Ending Fridays when you'll possibly dance your ass off.

CAPRICE Nightclub
(Map p70; www.capricenightclub.com; 967 Granville St) Originally a movie theater – hence the giant screen evoking its Tinseltown past – upscale Caprice is one of the Granville strip's best mainstream haunts. The cavernous two-level venue is a thumping magnet for all the local preppies and their miniskirted girlfriends, while the adjoining resto-lounge is great if you need to rest your

eardrums and grab a restorative cocktail and bite to eat. Expect to line up here on weekends when the under-25s visiting from the suburbs dominate.

COMMODORE
Live Music

(Map p70; www.livenation.com; 868 Granville St) Up-and-coming local bands know they've finally made it when they play the city's best midsized music venue, a lovingly restored art deco ballroom that still has the bounciest dance floor in town – courtesy of stacks of tires placed under its floorboards. If you need a break from your moshing shenanigans, collapse at one of the tables lining the perimeter, and catch your breath with a bottled Stella from the back bar.

Cinemark Tinseltown
Cinema

(Map p70; www.cinemark.com; 88 W Pender St) Popular multiplex combining blockbusters and art-house films.

Pacific Cinémathéque
Cinema

(Map p70; www.cinematheque.bc.ca; 1131 Howe St) Art-house cinema screening foreign and underground movies.

Vancouver Playhouse
Theater

(Map p70; www.vancouverplayhouse.com; cnr Hamilton & Dunsmuir Sts) Presenting a six-play season at its large civic venue.

Vancouver Canucks
Sports

(www.canucks.com) The city's NHL team is Vancouver's leading sports franchise. Book ahead for games at downtown's Rogers Arena, also known as GM Place (Map p70).

Vancouver Whitecaps
Sports

(www.whitecapsfc.com) The city's soccer team hits the MLS big league in 2011.

BC Lions
Sports

(www.bclions.com) Playing at Empire Field until BC Place is ready, Vancouver's Canadian Football League (CFL) side is ever-hungry for Grey Cup triumph.

Shopping

JOHN FLUEVOG SHOES
Clothing

(Map p70; www.fluevog.com; 65 Water St) The cavernous Gastown flagship of Vancouver's fave shoe designer (the smaller original store still operates on Granville), Fluevog's funky shoes, sandals and thigh-hugging boots have been a fashion legend since 1970. Some of the footwear looks like Doc Martens on acid, while others could poke your eye out from 20 paces.

MOUNTAIN EQUIPMENT CO-OP
Outdoor Gear

(www.mec.ca; 130 W Broadway, South Main) The massive granddaddy of Vancouver outdoor stores, with an amazing selection of mostly own-brand clothing, kayaks, sleeping bags and clever camping gadgets: MEC has been turning campers into fully fledged outdoor enthusiasts for years. You'll have to be a member to purchase ($5). Equipment – canoes,

Belugas at Vancouver Aquarium (p65).
RICHARD CUMMINS

Grouse Mountain (p74) is also a great playground for bears

CHRISTOPHER HERWIG

kayaks, camping gear etc – can also be rented here.

SMOKING LILY   Clothing

(www.smokinglily.com; 3634 Main St, South Main)
Quirky art-school cool is the approach at this SoMa store, where skirts, belts and halter tops are whimsically accented with prints of ants, skulls or the periodic table. Men's clothing is slowly creeping into the mix, with some fish, skull and tractor T-shirts and ties. A fun spot to browse (the staff are friendly and chatty).

COASTAL PEOPLES FINE ARTS GALLERY
Souvenirs

(Map p70; www.coastalpeoples.com; 1024 Mainland St) This sumptuous Yaletown gallery showcases a fine selection of Inuit and Northwest Coast aboriginal jewelry, carvings and prints. Focusing on the high-art side of aboriginal crafts, you'll find some exquisite items here that will likely have your credit card sweating.

Information

Tourism Vancouver visitor centre (www
.tourismvancouver.com; 200 Burrard St;
⊘8:30am-6pm Jun-Aug, 8:30am-5pm Mon-Sat

Sep-May) Free maps, city and wider BC visitor guides and a half-price theater ticket booth.

ⓘ Getting There & Away

Air

Vancouver International Airport (www.yvr.ca) is the main west-coast hub for airlines from Canada, the US and international locales. It's in Richmond, a 13km (30-minute) drive from downtown. Domestic airlines include Westjet (www.westjet .com) and Air Canada (www.aircanada.com).

Several handy floatplane services can also deliver you directly to the Vancouver waterfront's Seaplane Terminal. These include frequent Harbour Air Seaplanes (www.harbour-air.com) and West Coast Air (www.westcoastair.com) services from Victoria's centrally located Inner Harbour.

Bus & Train

Most out-of-town buses and trains (including those from the USA) bring you to Vancouver's Pacific Central Station (1150 Station St) in Chinatown. Trains go to Seattle and VIA Rail (www.viarail.ca) goes to Jasper (and further east).

The station for the Rocky Mountaineer (www .rockymountaineer.com), which runs train tours to Banff/Calgary, is southeast of Pacific Central.

DISCOVER VANCOUVER & BRITISH COLUMBIA   VANCOUVER

Getting Around

To/From the Airport

SkyTrain's 16-station Canada Line (adult one-way fare to downtown $7.50 to $8.75) operates a rapid-transit train service from the airport to downtown's Waterfront Station.

Public Transportation

The website for TransLink (www.translink .bc.ca) bus, SkyTrain and SeaBus services has a useful trip-planning tool, or you can buy the handy *Getting Around* route map ($1.95) from convenience stores.

A ticket bought on any of the three services is valid for 1½ hours of travel on the entire network, depending on the zone you intend to travel in. One-zone tickets are adult/child $2.50/1.75, two-zone tickets $3.75/2.50 and three-zone tickets $5/3.50. An all-day, all-zone pass costs $9/7. If you're traveling after 6:30pm or on weekends or holidays, all trips are classed as one-zone fares. Children under five travel free.

WHISTLER

POP 9200

Named for the furry marmots that populate the area and whistle like deflating balloons, this gabled alpine village is one of the world's most popular ski resorts. It was home to many of the outdoor events at the 2010 Winter Olympic and Paralympic Games, so feel free to slip on your skis and aim (if only in your imagination) for a gold medal of your own.

Nestled in the shade of the formidable Whistler and Blackcomb Mountains, the wintertime village has a frosted, Christmas-card look. But summer is also an increasingly popular time to visit, with Vancouverites and international travelers lured to the lakes and crags by a wide array of activities, from mountain biking to scream-triggering zipline runs. For an insider's view of Whister, see p57.

 Sights

The dramatic wood-beamed **Squamish Lil'wat Cultural Centre** (www.slcc.ca; 4854 Blackcomb Way; adult/child/youth $18/8/11; ⏱9:30am-5pm) showcases two quite different First Nations groups – one coastal and one interior based – with museum exhibits and artisan presentations. Entry starts with a 15-minute movie and includes a self-guided tour illuminating the heritage and modern-day indigenous communities of the region. There's a wealth of art and crafts on display (check out the amazing two-headed sea serpent carving near the entrance) and the energetic young staff encourage plenty of questions about their twin cultures.

Perched just above the village on Blackcomb, **Whistler Sliding Centre** (www.whistleslidingcentre.com; 4910 Glacier Lane; adult/child $7/free; ⏱10am-5pm) hosted Olympic bobsled, luge and skeleton events and is now open to the public. You can wander exhibits and check out video footage from the track or take a general tour (adult/child $15/free) or behind-the-scenes tour (adult/child $69/59).

The recently revamped **Whistler Museum** (www.whistlermuseum.org; 4333 Main St; adult/child $7/4; ⏱11am-5pm) traces the area's dramatic development, with some colorful exhibits plus evocative photos of old skiing gear and the region's pre-resort days. There's also plenty of information on the 2010 Olympics if you missed it (as well as recollections of the previous Games bid).

 Activities

Skiing & Snowboarding

Comprising 38 lifts and almost 34 sq km of skiable terrain, crisscrossed with over 200 runs (more than half aimed at intermediate-level skiers), the sister mountains of **Whistler-Blackcomb** (www .whistlerblackcomb.com; 1-day lift ticket adult/child/youth $93/46/78) were physically linked for the first time in 2009. The resort's mammoth 4.4km **Peak 2 Peak Gondola** includes the world's longest unsupported span and takes 11 minutes to shuttle wide-eyed powder hogs between

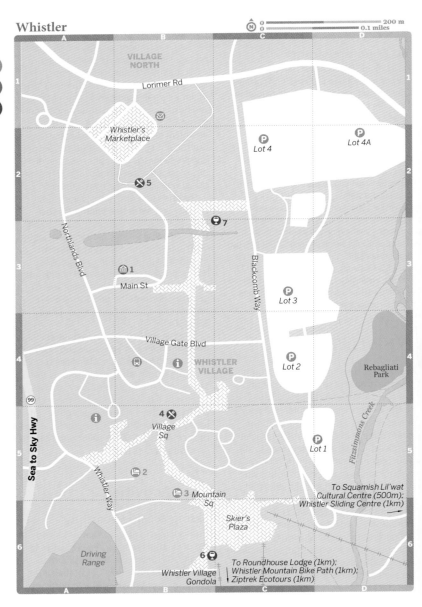

the two high alpine areas, so they can hit the slopes on both mountains on the same day.

The winter season kicks off here in late November and runs to April on Whistler and to June on Blackcomb –

December to February is the peak period. If you want to emulate your favorite Olympic ski heroes, Whistler Creekside was the setting for all the 2010 downhill skiing events.

Whistler

You can beat the crowds with an early morning **Fresh Tracks ticket** (adult/child $17.25/12.60), which must be bought in advance at Whistler Village Gondola Guest Relations. The price includes a buffet breakfast at the Roundhouse Lodge up top. Night owls might prefer the evening **Night Moves** (adult/ child $18/12) program operated via Blackcomb's Magic Chair lift after 5pm.

Cross-country Skiing & Snowshoeing

A pleasant stroll or free shuttle bus away from the village, **Lost Lake** (www.cross countryconnection.bc.ca; day pass adult/child/ youth $17/8.50/10; ☺8am-9pm) is the hub for 22km of wooded cross-country ski trails, suitable for novices and experts alike. Around 4km of the trail is lit for nighttime skiing until 10pm and there's a handy 'warming hut' providing lessons and equipment rentals. Snowshoers are also well served in this area: you can stomp off on your own on 10km of trails or rent equipment and guides.

The **Whistler Olympic Park** (www .whistlerolympicpark.com; 5 Callaghan Valley Rd, Callaghan Valley) is 16km southwest of the village via Hwy 99. It hosted the 2010 Olympic biathlon, Nordic combined, cross-country skiing and ski jumping events. While the site was still being prepared on our visit after the Games, it's expected to become a prime area for public cross-country skiing and snowshoeing. Check the venue's website for information.

Mountain Biking

Taking over the melted ski slopes in summer and accessed via the lift at the village's south end, **Whistler Mountain Bike Park** (www.whistlerbike.com; 1-day pass adult/child/youth $53/29/47; ☺10am-8pm mid-Jun–Aug, 10am-5pm May–mid-Jun & Sep–mid-Oct) offers barreling downhill runs and an orgy of jumps, beams and bridges twisting through 200km of well-maintained forested trails. You don't have to be a bike courier to stand the knee-buckling pace: easier routes are marked in green, while blue intermediate trails and black

Wired For Fun

Stepping out into thin air 70m above the forest floor might seem like a normal activity for a cartoon character but ziplining turns out to be one of the best ways to encounter the Whistler wilderness. Attached via a body harness to the cable you're about to slide down, you soon overcome your fear of flying solo. By the end of your time in the trees, you'll be turning midair somersaults and whooping like a banshee. The two cool courses operated by **Ziptrek Ecotours** (www.ziptrek.com; adult/child from $99/79) are strung between Whistler and Blackcomb mountains and operate in both winter and summer seasons. Its newer **TreeTrek guided canopy walk** (adult/child $39/29) is a gentle web of walkways and suspension bridges for those who prefer to keep their feet on something a little more solid than air. It's ideal for families.

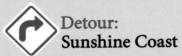

Detour:
Sunshine Coast

Stretching 139km along the water from Langdale to Lund, the Sunshine Coast – separated from the Lower Mainland by the Coast Mountains and the Strait of Georgia – has an independent, island-like mentality that belies the fact it's only a 40-minute ferry ride from Horseshoe Bay. With Hwy 101 linking key communities such as Gibsons, Sechelt and Powell River, it's an easy and convivial region to explore and there are plenty of activities to keep things lively: think kayaking and scuba diving with a side order of artists' studios. Check **Sunshine Coast Tourism** (www.sunshinecoastcanada.com) for information.

Your first port of call after docking in Langdale, the pretty waterfront strip of Gibsons (population 4100) is a rainbow of painted wooden buildings perched over the marina. While the best spot in town for comfort food is **Molly's Reach** (www.mollysreach.ca; 647 School Rd; mains $7-12), gourmet seafood fans shouldn't miss **Smitty's Oyster House** (www.smittysoysterhouse.com; 643 School Rd; mains $12-26). Regionally sourced and perfectly prepared treats here include Fanny Bay oysters and golden halibut fritters.

A useful base for active travelers, with plenty of hiking, biking, kayaking and diving opportunities, **Sechelt** also has plenty of pit-stop amenities if you're just passing through. If you feel like splurging on a sleepover, it's worth continuing your drive along Hwy 101 to **Rockwater Secret Cove Resort** (604-885-7038, 877-296-4593; www.rockwatersecretcoveresort.com; 5356 Ole's Cove Rd; r/cabin/ste/tent $209/209/249/419;), where the highlight accommodations are luxury tent suites perched like nests on a steep cliff.

---

diamond advanced paths are offered if you want to **Crank It Up** – the name of one of the park's most popular routes.

Sleeping

ADARA HOTEL
Hotel $$

(604-905-4665, 866-502-3272; www.adarahotel.com; 4122 Village Green; r from $160;) Unlike all those smaller lodges now claiming to be boutique hotels, the sophisticated and centrally located Adara was built from scratch as the real deal. Lined with sparse but knowing designer details – including fake antler horns in the lobby – the accommodations have spa-like bathrooms, flat-screen TVs and iPod docking stations (the front desk will loan you an iPod if you've left yours at home). Despite the ultracool aesthetics, service is warm and relaxed.

CRYSTAL LODGE
Hotel $$

(604-932-2221, 800-667-3363; www.crystal-lodge.com; 4154 Village Stroll; d/ste from $130/175;) Not all rooms are created equal at the Crystal, a central sleepover forged from the fusion of two quite different hotel towers. Cheaper rooms in the South Tower are standard motel-style – baths and fridges are the highlight – but those in the Lodge Wing match the splendid rock-and-beam lobby, and come complete with small balconies. Both share excellent proximity to village restaurants and are less than 100m from the main ski lift.

CHALET LUISE
B&B $$

(604-932-4187, 800-665-1998; www.chaletluise.com; 7461 Ambassador Cres; r from $125;) A five-minute trail walk from the Lorimer Rd in the village, this recently renovated, Bavarian-look pension has eight bright and sunny rooms – think pine furnishings and crisp white duvets –

and a flower garden that's ideal for a spot of evening wine quaffing. Or you can just hop in the hot tub and dream about the large buffet breakfast coming your way in the morning. The Luise has free parking.

EDGEWATER LODGE
Hotel **$$**

(☎ 604-932-0688, 888-870-9065; www .edgewater-lodge.com; 8020 Alpine Way; r from $150; 🛜) A few minutes' drive north of Whistler on Hwy 99, this 12-room lakeside lodge is a nature lover's idyll and has a celebrated on-site restaurant. Each room overlooks the glassy water through a large picture window – sit in your padded window alcove and watch the ospreys or hit the surface with a kayak rental.

Eating

ARAXI RESTAURANT & LOUNGE
West Coast **$$$**

(☎ 604-932-4540; www.toptable.ca; 4222 Village Sq; mains $30-45) Whistler's best splurge restaurant, Araxi chefs up an inventive and exquisite Pacific Northwest menu plus charming and courteous service. Try the delicious BC halibut and drain the 15,000-bottle wine selection but save room for a dessert: a regional cheese plate or the amazing Okanagan apple cheesecake... or both.

CHRISTINE'S MOUNTAIN TOP DINING
Canadian **$$**

(☎ 604-938-7437; Rendezvous Lodge, Blackcomb Mountain; mains $12-22) The best of the handful of places to eat while you're enjoying a summertime summit stroll or winter ski day on the slopes at Blackcomb Mountain. Loacted at the Rendezvous Lodge,

try for a view-tastic patio table and tuck into a seasonal seafood grill or a lovely applewood smoked cheddar grilled cheese sandwich. Reservations are recommended.

BEET ROOT CAFÉ
Cafe **$**

(129-4340 Lorimer Rd; light mains $6-11) The best home-style hangout in town, pull up a cushion by the window, make yourself at home and tuck into fresh-made soup, bulging sandwiches or the excellent breakfast burritos. Stick around until you smell the cookies emerging from the oven, then scoff yourself into a happy stupor.

Drinking & Entertainment

GARIBALDI LIFT COMPANY
Pub

(Whistler Village Gondola) The closest bar to the slopes – watch the powder geeks or bike nuts on Whistler Mountain skid to a halt from the patio – the GLC is a

Up on the Whistler ski fields (p81)
RANDY LINCKS/PHOTOLIBRARY

rock-lined cave of a place. It's the ideal spot to absorb a Kootenay Mountain Ale and a bulging GLC burger while you rub your muscles and exchange exaggerated stories about your epic battles with the mountain.

WHISTLER BREWHOUSE   Brewery
(www.markjamesgroup.com; 4355 Blackcomb Way) This lodge-like drinkery crafts its own beer on the premises and, like any artwork, the natural surroundings inspire the masterpieces, with names such as Lifty Lager and Twin Peaks Pale Ale. It's an ideal pub if you want to hear yourself think, or if you just want to watch the game on one of the TVs. The food, including pasta, pizza and fish and chips, is superior to the standard pub grub.

ⓘ Information

Whistler visitor center (www.whistler.com; 4230 Gateway Dr; ☉8am-8pm) Flyer-lined visitor center with friendly staff.

ⓘ Getting There & Around

While most visitors arrive by road from Vancouver via Hwy 99, you can also fly in on a **Whistler Air** (www.whistlerair.ca) floatplane to Green Lake (from $149, 30 minutes, two daily May to September).

Train spotters can trundle into town with **Rocky Mountaineer Vacations** (www.rockymountaineer.com), which winds along a picturesque coastal route from North Vancouver (from $129, three hours, one daily May to mid-October).

Whistler's **WAVE** (www.busonline.ca) public buses (adult/child/one-day pass $2/1.50/5) are equipped with ski and bike racks.

VANCOUVER ISLAND

The largest populated landmass off the North American coast – it's around 500km long and 100km wide – Vancouver Island is laced with colorful, often quirky communities. If you want to make a good impression, don't refer to the place as 'Victoria Island,' a frequent mistake that usually provokes involuntary

Left: Hiking on the Sunshine Coast (p84); **Below:** Canada takes on Russia at the Vancouver 2010 Winter Olympics

PHOTOGRAPHER: (LEFT) KELLY FUNK/PHOTOLIBRARY; (BELOW) TODD LAWSON

eye rolls and an almost imperceptible downgrading of your welcome.

While Victoria itself – the history-wrapped BC capital that's stuffed with attractions – is the first port of call for many, it should not be the only place you visit here. Food and wine fans will enjoy weaving through the verdant Cowichan Valley farm region; those craving a laid-back, family-friendly enclave should hit the twin seaside towns of Parksville and Qualicum; and outdoor-activity enthusiasts shouldn't miss the surf-loving west coast area.

For an introduction to the island, contact **Tourism Vancouver Island** (☎ 250-754-3500; www.vancouverisland.travel).

Victoria

POP 78,000

With a population approaching 350,000 when you add in the suburbs, this picture-postcard provincial capital was long touted as North America's most English city. This was a surprise to anyone who actually came from Britain, since Victoria promulgated a dreamy version of England that never really was: every garden (complete with the occasional palm tree) was immaculate; every flagpole was adorned with a Union Jack; and every afternoon was spent quaffing tea from bone-china cups.

Thankfully this tired theme-park version of Ye Olde England has gradually faded in recent years. Fuelled by an increasingly younger demographic, a quiet revolution has seen lame tourist pubs, eateries and stores transformed into the kind of bright-painted bohemian shops, wood-floored coffee bars and surprisingly innovative restaurants that would make any city proud. It's worth seeking out these enclaves on foot but activity fans should also hop on their bikes: Victoria has more cycle routes than any other Canadian city.

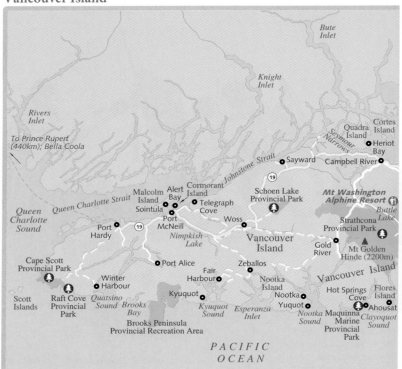

Sights

ROYAL BC MUSEUM
Museum

(Map p92; www.royalbcmuseum.bc.ca; 675 Belleville St; adult/child $14.30/9.10; ⊙10am-5pm) At the province's best museum, start at the 2nd-floor natural-history showcase fronted by a beady-eyed woolly mammoth and lined with realistic dioramas – the forest of elk and grizzlies peeking from behind trees is highly evocative. Then peruse the First Peoples exhibit and its deep exploration of indigenous culture, including a fascinating mask gallery (look for the ferret-faced white man). Possibly the best area, though, is the walk-through re-created street that re-animates the early colonial city, complete with a chatty Chinatown, highly detailed stores and even a little movie house.

FREE PARLIAMENT BUILDINGS
Historical Building

(Map p92; www.leg.bc.ca; 501 Belleville St; admission free; ⊙8:30am-5pm May-Sep, 8:30am-5pm Mon-Fri Oct-Apr) Across from the BC museum, this handsome confection of turrets, domes and stained glass is the province's working legislature but it's also open to history-loving visitors. Peek behind the facade on a colorful 30-minute **tour** led by costumed Victorians, then stop for lunch at the 'secret' politicians' restaurant (see p94). Try to come back in the evening when the building's handsome exterior is lit up like a Christmas tree.

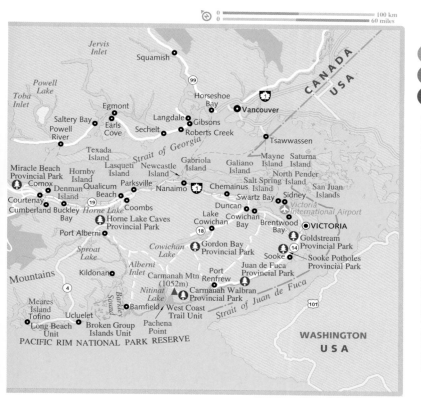

ART GALLERY OF GREATER VICTORIA

Art Gallery

(Map p90; www.aggv.bc.ca; 1040 Moss St; adult/child $13/2.50; ⏱10am-5pm Mon-Wed, Fri & Sat, 10am-9pm Thu, noon-5pm Sun) Head east of downtown on Fort St and follow the gallery signs to find one of Canada's best Emily Carr collections. Aside from Carr's swirling nature canvases, you'll find an ever-changing array of temporary exhibitions. Check online for events, including lectures, presentations and even singles' nights for lonely arts fans. To see more of Emily Carr's art, go to **Emily Carr House** (Map p90; www.emilycarr .com; 207 Government St; admission by donation; ⏱11am-4pm Tue-Sat May-Sep).

CRAIGDARROCH CASTLE

Museum

(Map p90; www.thecastle.ca; 1050 Joan Cres; adult/child $13.75/5; ⏱9am-7pm mid-Jun–Aug,

10am-4:30pm Sep–mid-Jun) If you're in this part of town checking out the gallery, don't miss this elegant turreted mansion a few minutes' walk away. A handsome, 39-room landmark built by a 19th-century coal baron with money to burn, it's dripping with period architecture and antique-packed rooms. Climb the tower's 87 steps (check out the stained-glass windows en route) for views of the snowcapped Olympic Mountains.

 **Activities**

Whale-Watching

Prince of Whales

(Map p92; ☎250-383-4884, 888-383-4884; www.princeofwhales.com; 812 Wharf St; adult/child $100/80) Long-established local operator.

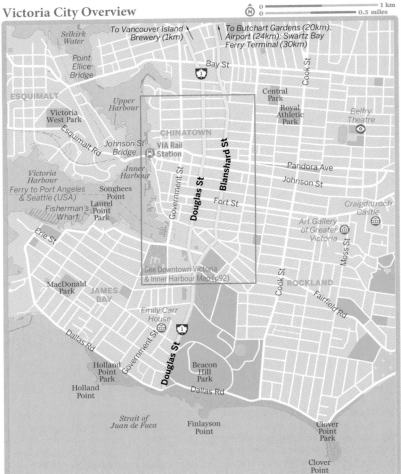

Springtide Charters
(Map p92; ☎250-384-4444, 800-470-3474; www.springtidecharters.com; 1111 Wharf St; adult/child $99/69) Popular local operator.

Kayaking

Ocean River Sports
(Map p92; ☎250-381-4233; www.oceanriver .com; 1824 Store St; rental 2hr/24hr $30/48; ⏰9:30am-6pm Mon-Wed & Sat, 9:30am-8pm Thu & Fri, 10am-5pm Sun) Popular 2½-hour harbor tours ($65).

Sports Rent
(Map p92; ☎250-385-7368; www.sportsrentbc .com; 1950 Government St; ⏰9am-5:30pm Mon-Thu, to 6pm Fri, to 5pm Sat, 10am-5pm Sun) Rents canoes (5hr/24hr $39/49), bikes, tents etc.

Tours

Architectural Institute of BC   Walk
(Map p92; ☎604-683-8588 ext 333, 800-667-0753; www.aibc.ca; 1001 Douglas St; tours $5;

1pm Tue-Sat Jul & Aug) Five great-value, building-themed walking tours covering angles from art deco to ecclesiastical.

Big Bus Victoria Bus
(Map p92; 250-389-2229, 888-434-2229; www.bigbusvictoria.ca; 811 Government St; adult/child $35/17) Offers 90-minute hop-on, hop-off tours around 22 local points of interest.

Sleeping

FAIRMONT EMPRESS HOTEL
Hotel $$$
(Map p92; 250-384-8111, 866-540-4429; www.fairmont.com/empress; 721 Government St; r from $189; ❀@❀) Rooms at this ivy-covered, century-old Inner Harbour landmark are elegant but conservative and some are quite small, but the overall effect is grand and classy – from the Raj-style curry restaurant to the high tea sipped while overlooking the waterfront. Even if you don't stay, stroll through and soak up the ambience.

HOTEL RIALTO
Hotel $$
(Map p92; 250-382-4157, 800-332-9981; www.hotelrialto.ca; 653 Pandora Ave; r $139-249; ☎) Completely refurbished from the faded former budget hotel it used to be, the new Rialto is a well-located downtown option in an attractive century-old heritage building. Each of the 38 mod-decorated rooms has a fridge, microwave and flat-screen TV and some have tubs as well as showers. The lobby's tapas lounge is justifiably popular, whether or not you're staying here.

OSWEGO HOTEL
Hotel $$
(250-294-7500, 877-767-9346; www.oswegovictoria.com; 500 Oswego St; d/ste from $159/229) Victoria's swankiest newer hotel is a designer lounge sleepover in a quiet residential location. Rooms come with granite floors, cedar beams, deep baths and (in most units) small balconies. All have kitchens (think stainless steel) and deep baths, making them more like apartments than hotel suites.

If You Like...
Local Museums

If you like Whistler Museum (p81) you'll likely enjoy these other small BC museums.

1 EMILY CARR HOUSE, VICTORIA
(Map p90; www.emilycarr.com; 207 Government St, Victoria; admission by donation; 11am-4pm Tue-Sat May-Sep) The birthplace of BC's best-known painter, this bright-yellow, gingerbread-style house has plenty of period rooms and displays on the artist's life and work.

2 NANAIMO MUSEUM
(www.nanaimomuseum.ca; 100 Museum Way; adult/child/youth $2/0.75/1.75; 10am-5pm mid-May-Aug, 10am-5pm Tue-Sat Sep-mid-May) Just off Nanaimo's Commercial St drag, this shiny new museum showcases the region's heritage, from First Nations to colonial, maritime, sporting and beyond. Highlights include a walk-through evocation of a coal mine – it's popular with kids.

3 PENTICTON MUSEUM
(250-490-2451; 785 Main St; admission by donation; 10am-5pm Tue-Sat) Inside the town's library, this museum has delightfully eclectic displays, including the de rigueur natural-history exhibit with stuffed animals and birds plus everything you'd want to know about the Peach Festival.

4 OKANAGAN HERITAGE MUSEUM, KELOWNA
(250-763-2417; 470 Queensway Ave; admission by donation; 10am-5pm Mon-Sat) Exploring centuries of social history in an engaging manner, this popular Kelowna spot includes a First Nations pit house, a Chinese grocery and a Pandosy-era trading post.

5 VANCOUVER MARITIME MUSEUM
(www.vancouvermaritimemuseum.com; 1905 Ogden Ave; adult/child $11/8.50; 10am-5pm May-Aug, 10am-5pm Tue-Sat, noon-5pm Sun Sep-Apr) Combining dozens of intricate model ships with detailed re-created boat sections and a few historic vessels, the highlight here is the *St Roch*, an arctic patrol vessel that was the first to navigate the Northwest Passage in both directions.

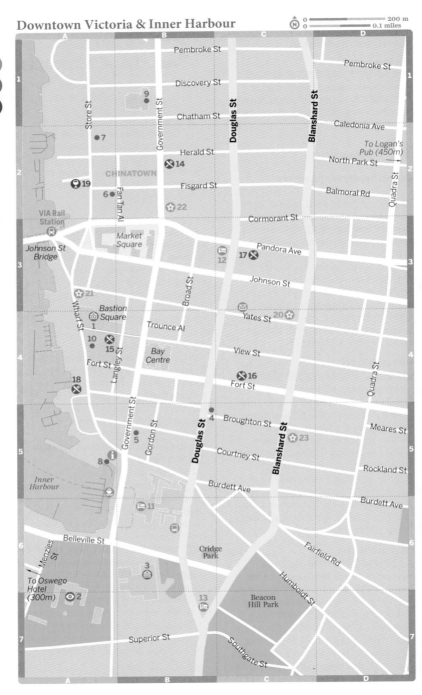

0 | 200 m
0 | 0.1 miles

Pembroke St

Discovery St

Chatham St

Store St

Government St

Douglas St

Blanshard St

Pembroke St

Caledonia Ave

To Logan's
Pub (450m)

North Park St

Quadra St

9

7

Herald St

14

19

CHINATOWN

Fan Tan Al

Fisgard St

Balmoral Rd

6

22

VIA Rail
Station

Market
Square

Cormorant St

Pandora Ave

Johnson St
Bridge

Johnson St

12 17

Broad St

Wharf St

21

Bastion
Square

1

Trounce Al

Yates St 20

10

15

Langley St

Bay
Centre

View St

Fort St

16

18

Fort St

Government St

Gordon St

Douglas St

4

Broughton St

Blanshard St

Quadra St

Meares St

23

5

Courtney St

Rockland St

8

Burdett Ave

Burdett Ave

Inner
Harbour

11

Belleville St

Fairfield Rd

Menzies St

To Oswego
Hotel
(300m)

2

Cridge
Park

3

13

Beacon
Hill Park

Humboldt St

Superior St

Southgate St

Cleverly, the smaller studio rooms have space-saving high-end Murphy beds.

Abbeymoore Manor — B&B $$
(☎ 250-370-1470, 888-801-1811; www.abbey moore.com; 1470 Rockland Ave; r from $165; 🛜) A romantic 1912 arts and crafts mansion, Abbeymoore's handsome colonial exterior hides seven antique-lined rooms furnished with Victorian knickknacks. Some rooms have kitchens and jetted tubs.

Queen Victoria — Hotel $$
(Map p92; ☎ 250-386-1312, 800-663-7007; www.qvhotel.com; 655 Douglas St; d/ste from $133/152; ❄ 🐾) A well-maintained tower-block property near the Inner Harbour with rooms that have a business-hotel feel. All have balconies and handy fridges; some also have kitchenettes.

 Eating

FORT CAFÉ — Canadian $
(Map p92; 742 Fort St; mains $6-10; 🛜) This warm and inviting subterranean hipster haunt offers the perfect combination of great comfort food and cool digs. Among the heaping fresh-made nosh, the turkey avocado wraps and hot pepper beef sandwiches are stand outs, while there's also a rare offering of all the Salt Spring Brewing beers on draft. Check out the Atari game system around the corner at the back, or drop in for Friday's massively popular quiz night (doors open 7:30pm). If you miss it, there's a shelf of board games to keep you busy.

CAMILLE'S — West Coast $$
(Map p92; ☎ 250-381-3433; www.camilles restaurant.com; 45 Bastion Sq; mains $18-26) A charming subterranean dining room with a lively, ever-changing menu reflecting whatever the chef can source locally and seasonally, perhaps ranging from pan-seared BC duck and sweet spot prawns to breathtaking desserts packed with local fruits and berries. With a great wine menu, this spot invites adventurous foodies to linger. Recommended for a romantic night out.

JOHN'S PLACE — Breakfast, Canadian $$
(Map p92; www.johnsplace.ca; 723 Pandora Ave; mains $7-17) Victoria's best weekend brunch spot, this wood-floored, high-ceilinged heritage room is lined with funky memorabilia and the menu is a cut above standard diner fare. It'll start you off with a basket of addictive house-made bread, but save room for heaping pasta dishes or a Belgian waffle breakfast. And don't leave without trying a thick slab of pie from the case at the front.

Downtown Victoria & Inner Harbour

BRASSERIE L'ECOLE
French $$

(Map p92; 📞 250-475-6260; www.lecole.ca; 1715 Government St; mains $20-24) This country-style French bistro has a warm, casual atmosphere and a delectable menu. Locally sourced produce is de rigueur, so the dishes constantly change to reflect seasonal highlights such as figs, salmonberries and heirloom tomatoes. We recommend the lamb shank, served with mustard-creamed root vegetables and braised chard. Beer fans will also love the bottled French, Belgian and Québec brews.

LEGISLATIVE DINING ROOM
Canadian $$

(Map p92; room 606, Parliament Buildings; mains $6-16) One of Victoria's best-kept dining secrets, the Parliament Buildings has its own subsidized restaurant where MLAs (and the public) can drop by for a silver-service menu of regional dishes, ranging from smoked tofu salads to velvety steaks and shrimp quesadillas. It's cash only and entry is via the security desk just inside the building's main entrance.

Drinking

SPINNAKERS GASTRO BREWPUB
Pub

(www.spinnakers.com; 308 Catherine St) A pioneering craft brewer, this wood-floored smasher is a short hop from the Inner Harbour (in Esquimalt) but it's worth it for tongue ticklers like copper-colored Nut Brown Ale and hoppy Blue Bridge Double IPA – named after the sky-blue span that delivers most quaffers to the door. Save room to eat: the seasonal dishes – many designed for beer pairing – often include sharable platters piled high with everything from wild salmon to Cortez Island clams.

CANOE BREWPUB
Pub

(Map p92; www.canoebrewpub.com; 450 Swift St) The cavernous brick-lined interior here is popular on rainy days but the patio is the best in the city with its (usually) sunny views across to the Johnson St Bridge. Indulge in on-site-brewed treats such as the hoppy Red Canoe Lager and the summer-friendly Siren's Song Pale Ale. Grub is also high on the menu here with stomach-stuffing lamb potpie and wild salmon tacos recommended.

Entertainment

Check the freebie *Monday Magazine* weekly for listings or head online to www.livevictoria .com.

Live Music & Nightclubs

LUCKY BAR
Nightclub, Live Music

(Map p92; www.luckybar .ca; 517 Yates St) A Victoria institution, downtown's eclectic Lucky Bar offers live music from ska and indie to electroclash. There are bands here at

Victoria's Parliament Buildings (p88)
JOHN ELK III

Strollable 'Hoods

Sometimes you just need to abandon the guidebook and go for a wander. Luckily, compact and highly walkable downtown Victoria is ideal for that. Start your amble in **Chinatown**, at the handsome gate near the corner of Government and Fisgard Sts. One of Canada's oldest Asian neighborhoods, this tiny strip of businesses is studded with neon signs and traditional grocery stores, while **Fan Tan Alley** – a narrow passageway between Fisgard St and Pandora Ave – is a miniwarren of traditional and trendy stores hawking cheap and cheerful trinkets, cool used records and funky artworks. Consider a guided amble with **Hidden Dragon Tours** (www.oldchinatown.com; adult/child $29/14.50). Its three-hour evening lantern tour will tell you all about the area's historic opium dens and the hardships of 19th-century immigration.

Next up, head over to **Bastion Sq**, located between Government and Wharf Sts. Occupying the site of the old Fort Victoria, this pedestrianized plaza of scrubbed colonial strongholds is also home to the **Maritime Museum of British Columbia** (Map p92; www.mmbc.bc.ca; 28 Bastion Sq; adult/child/youth $12/6/7; ⊙9:30am-5pm mid-Jun–mid-Sep, 9:30am-4:30pm mid-Sep–mid-Jun), where 400 model ships evoke the region's rich and salty nautical heritage.

least twice a week, while the remaining evenings are occupied by dance-floor club nights, including Wednesday's mod fest and Saturday's mix night.

LOGAN'S PUB   Live Music
(www.loganspub.com; 1821 Cook St) A 10-minute walk from downtown and a couple of blocks west of the Belfry Theatre, in Cook St Village, this sports pub looks like nothing special from the outside, but its roster of shows is a fixture of the local indie scene. Fridays and Saturdays are your best bet for performances but other nights are frequently also booked – check the online calendar to see what's coming up.

Theater & Cinemas

Victoria's main stages, **McPherson Playhouse** (Map p92; www.rmts.bc.ca; 3 Centennial Sq) and the rococo-interiored **Royal Theatre** (Map p92; www.rmts.bc.ca; 805 Broughton St), each offer mainstream visiting shows and performances. The latter is also the home of the **Victoria Symphony** (www.victoriasymphony.bc.ca) and **Pacific Opera Victoria** (www.pov.bc.ca). A 20-minute stroll from downtown, the celebrated **Belfry Theatre** (Map p90; www.belfry.bc.ca; 1291 Gladstone Ave) showcases contemporary plays in its lovely former-church-building venue.

The city's main first-run cinema is **Cineplex Odeon** (Map p92; www.cineplex.com; 780 Yates St), while the Royal BC Museum's **IMAX Theatre** (Map p92; www.imaxvictoria.com) shows larger-than-life documentaries and Hollywood blockbusters.

🛈 Information

Visitor centre (Map p92; www.tourismvictoria.com; 812 Wharf St; ⊙8:30am-8:30pm Jun-Aug, 9am-5pm Sep-May) Busy, flyer-lined visitor center overlooking the Inner Harbour.

🛈 Getting There & Away

Air

Victoria International Airport (www.victoriaairport.com) is 26km north of the city via Hwy 17. Air Canada (www.aircanada.com) services arrive here from Vancouver (from $73, 25 minutes, up to 21 daily) while Westjet (www.westjet.com) flights arrive from Calgary (from

$129, 1½ hours, six daily). Both airlines offer competing connections across Canada.

Harbour Air Seaplanes (www.harbour-air .com) arrive in the Inner Harbour from downtown Vancouver ($145, 35 minutes) throughout the day. Alternatively, **Helijet** (www.helijet.com) has helicopter services that arrive from Vancouver (from $149).

Boat

BC Ferries (www.bcferries.com) arrive from mainland Tsawwassen (adult/child/vehicle $14/7/46.75, 1½ hours) at Swartz Bay, 27km north of Victoria via Hwy 17. Services arrive hourly throughout the day in summer but are reduced off-season.

Victoria Clipper (www.clippervacations.com) services arrive in the Inner Harbour from Seattle (adult/child US$93/46, three hours). **Black Ball Transport** (www.ferrytovictoria.com) boats also arrive from Port Angeles (adult/child/vehicle US$15.50/7.75/55, 1½ hours, up to four daily) as do passenger-only **Victoria Express** (www .victoriaexpress.com) services (US$10, one hour, up to three daily).

ⓘ Getting Around

AKAL Airporter (www.victoriaairporter.com) minibuses run between the airport and area hotels

($19, 30 minutes). The service meets all incoming and outgoing flights. A taxi to downtown costs around $50, while transit bus 70 takes around 35 minutes, and costs $2.50.

Nanaimo

POP 79,000

Maligned for years as Vancouver Island's grubby second city, Nanaimo will never have the allure of tourist-magnet Victoria. But the 'Harbour City' has undergone its own quiet renaissance since the 1990s, with the downtown emergence of some good shops and eateries and a slick new museum. With its own ferry service from the mainland, the city is also a handy hub for exploring up-island.

⊚ Sights & Activities

NANAIMO MUSEUM   Museum
(www.nanaimomuseum.ca; 100 Museum Way; adult/child/youth $2/0.75/1.75; ⊙10am-5pm mid-May–Aug, 10am-5pm Tue-Sat Sep–mid-May) Just off the Commercial St main drag, this shiny new museum showcases the region's heritage, from First Nations to colonial, maritime, sporting and beyond. Highlights include a strong Coast Salish

Detail of a totem pole, Royal BC Museum (p88), Victoria

Detour:
Cowichan Wine (& Cider) Country

Eyebrows were raised when the Cowichan Valley region began proclaiming itself as Vancouver Island's version of Provence a few years back, but the wine snobs have been choking on their words ever since.

Favorite stops include **Cherry Point Vineyards** (www.cherrypointvineyards.com; 840 Cherry Point Rd, Cobble Hill; ⊘10am-5pm), with its lip-smacking blackberry port; **Averill Creek** (www.averillcreek.ca; 6552 North Rd, Duncan; ⊘11am-5pm May-Oct), with its view-tastic patio and lovely pinot noirs; and the ever-popular **Merridale Estate Cidery** (www.merridalecider.com; 1230 Merridale Rd, Cobble Hill; ⊘10:30am-4:30pm), an inviting apple-cider producer offering six varieties as well as a new brandy-distilling operation.

If you can, time your visit for the three-day **Cowichan Wine & Culinary Festival** (www.wines.cowichan.net) in September, when regional producers showcase their wares in a series of tasty events.

For more information on the wineries of this area and throughout Vancouver Island, check www.wineislands.ca.

focus and a walk-through evocation of a coal mine that's popular with kids. Ask at the front desk about summertime pub and cemetery tours.

NEWCASTLE ISLAND MARINE PROVINCIAL PARK
Park

(www.newcastleisland.ca) Nanaimo's rustic outdoor gem offers tranquil hiking and cycling, as well as beaches and wildlife-spotting opportunities. Settled by the Coast Salish – and still part of their traditional territory – it was the site of shipyards and coal mines before becoming a popular short-hop summer excursion in the 1930s, when a teahouse was added. Accessed by a 10-minute ferry from the harbor (adult/child $4/3), there's a seasonal eatery and regular First Nations dancing displays.

WILD PLAY ELEMENT PARKS
Amusement Park

(www.wildplay.com; 35 Nanaimo River Rd; adult/child from $40/20; ⊘10am-6pm mid-Jun–Aug, reduced off-season) This former bungee-jumping site has reinvented itself with the creation of five obstacle courses strung between the trees. Once you're harnessed, you can hit ziplines, rope

bridges, tunnels and Tarzan swings, each aimed at different levels of ability.

 Sleeping

KENNEDY HOUSE B&B
B&B $$

(☎250-754-3389, 877-750-3389; www.kennedyhouse.ca; 305 Kennedy St; r $85-125) Uphill from the waterfront, this is one of the few Nanaimo B&Bs nearish to the city center – in fact, it's close to the VIA Rail stop and the Old City Quarter. A restored and outwardly imposing 1913 heritage mansion, it has two lovely rooms, combining antique knickknacks and contemporary flourishes. Elegant, quiet and adult-oriented, there's a smashing cooked breakfast to rouse you from your pleasant morning slumber.

COAST BASTION INN
Hotel $$

(☎250-753-6601, 800-663-1144; www.coasthotels.com; 11 Bastion St; r from $139; ☎) Downtown's leading hotel has an unbeatable location overlooking the harbor, with most rooms having good views. The rooms have been refurbished with a lounge-modern élan in recent years, adding flat-screen TVs

Nanaimo

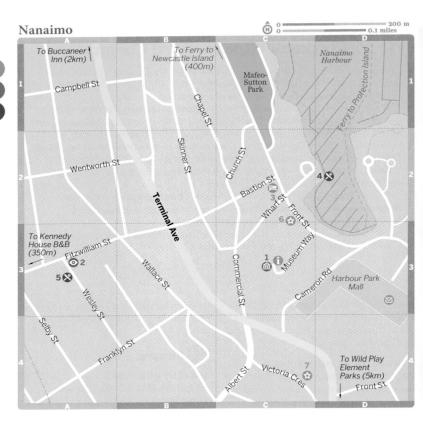

Nanaimo

⊙ Sights

1 Nanaimo Museum C3
2 Old City Quarter A3

⊟ Sleeping
3 Coast Bastion Inn C2

⊗ Eating
4 Penny's Palapa D2
5 Wesley Street Restaurant A3

⊛ Entertainment
6 Port Theatre C2
7 Queen's Hotel C4

and (in most rooms) small fridges. The resto bar in the hotel lobby is a popular hangout but there's also an on-site spa.

⊗ Eating

PENNY'S PALAPA
Mexican $$

(10 Wharf St H Dock; mains $8-12; ☺Apr-Oct)
This tiny, flower-and-flag-decked floating hut and patio in the harbor is a lovely spot for an alfresco meal among the jostling boats. An inventive, well-priced menu of Mexican delights includes seasonal seafood specials – the signature halibut tacos are recommended – plus some good vegetarian options. Arrive early: the dining area fills rapidly on balmy evenings.

WESLEY STREET RESTAURANT
West Coast $$

(www.wesleycafe.com; 321 Wesley St; mains $15-29; ☺11:30am-2:30pm & 5:30-10pm Tue-Sat)
Like a transplant from Victoria, Nanaimo's best splurge-worthy dine-out

---

showcases BC-sourced ingredients prepared with contemporary flair. The oft-changing menu is seasonal, but look out for Haida Gwaii salmon, Qualicum Bay scallops and Cowichan Valley duck. Take your time and savor. And if you're looking for a dinner deal, there's a three-course $30 special from Tuesday to Thursday.

Drinking & Entertainment

DINGHY DOCK PUB Pub
(www.dinghydockpub.com; 8 Pirates Lane) Accessed via a 10-minute mini-ferry hop (return $9) from the harbor, this lively pub and restaurant combo floating offshore from Protection Island is an ideal place to rub shoulders with salty locals and knock back a few malty brews on the deck. The menu doesn't stretch far beyond classic pub fare but there's live music on weekends to keep your toes tapping.

Queen's Hotel Live Music
(www.thequeens.ca; 34 Victoria Cres) The city's best live music and dance spot, hosting an eclectic roster of performances and club nights, ranging from indie to jazz and country.

Port Theatre Theater
(www.porttheatre.com; 125 Front St) Presenting local and touring live-theater shows.

 Information

Tourism Nanaimo (☎ 250-754-8141; www.tourismnanaimo.com; 2290 Bowen Rd; ☺9am-6pm May-Aug, reduced off-season) Edge-of-town site, with downtown satellite operation in the museum building.

Getting There & Away

Nanaimo Airport (www.nanaimoairport.com) is 18km south of town via Hwy 1. Air Canada (www.aircanada.com) flights arrive here from Vancouver (from $98, 25 minutes) throughout the day.

BC Ferries (www.bcferries.com) services from West Vancouver's Horseshoe Bay (passenger/vehicle $14/46.75, one hour 35 minutes) arrive at Departure Bay, 3km north of the city center via Hwy 1.

The daily VIA Rail (www.viarail.com) *Malahat* train trundles in from Victoria ($27, 2½ hours) and Courtenay ($27, two hours).

Parksville & Qualicum

Previously called Oceanside, this mid-island region has reverted to using its twin main towns as its moniker, mainly because no one could tell where Oceanside was just by hearing its name. Find out more about the region – which also includes rustic Coombs – by checking in with the local **tourism board** (☎ 250-248-6300, 888-799-3222; www.visitparksvillequalicumbeach.com).

Sights & Activities

COOMBS OLD COUNTRY MARKET Market
(www.oldcountrymarket.com; 2326 Alberni Hwy, Coombs; ☺9am-7pm Jul & Aug, reduced off-season) The mother of all pit stops,

Say Cheese…

Nibble on the region's 'locavore' credentials at **Morningstar Farm** (www.morningstarfarm.ca; 403 Lowry's Rd, Parksville; admission free; ☺9am-5pm Mon-Sat), a small working farmstead that's also a family-friendly visitor attraction. Let your kids run wild checking out the cowsheds and cheese makers – most will quickly fall in love with the roaming pigs, goats and chickens so you can expect some unusual Christmas pressie requests when you get back home. But it's not just for youngsters here: head to the **Little Qualicum Cheeseworks** shop, where samples of the farm's curdy treats (as well as its own-cured bacon) are provided – this is a great place to pick up picnic supplies.

this ever-expanding menagerie of food and crafts is centered on a large store stuffed with bakery and produce delectables. It attracts huge numbers of visitors on balmy summer days, when cameras are pointed at the grassy roof where a herd of goats spends the season. Nip inside for giant ice-cream cones, heaping pizzas and the deli makings of a great picnic, then spend an hour wandering the attendant stores clustered around the site.

WORLD PARROT REFUGE
Nature Reserve

(www.worldparrotrefuge.org; 2116 Alberni Hwy, Coombs; adult/child $12/8; ☺10am-4pm) Rescuing exotic birds from captivity and nursing them back to health, this excellent educational facility preaches the mantra that parrots are not pets. Pick up your earplugs at reception and stroll among the enclosures, each alive with recovering (and very noisy) birds. Don't be surprised when some screech a chirpy 'hello' as you stroll by.

Tofino
POP 1650

Transforming rapidly in recent years from a sleepy hippy hangout into a soft-eco resort town (it's like the Whistler of Vancouver Island), Tofino is the region's most popular outdoor hangout. It's not surprising that surf fans and other visitors keep coming: packed with activities and blessed with stunning beaches, Tofino sits on Clayoquot (clay-kwot) Sound, where forested mounds rise from roiling waves that batter the coastline in a dramatic, ongoing spectacle.

A short drive south of town, the **visitor center** (☎ 250-725-3414; www.tourismtofino.com; 1426 Pacific Rim Hwy; ☺10am-6pm May-Sep, reduced off-season) has detailed information on area accommodations, hiking trails and hot surf spots. There's also a branch in town at 455 Campbell St.

◎ Sights & Activities

Check out what coastal temperate rain forests are all about by exploring the flora and fauna at the **Tofino Botanical Gardens** (www.tbgf.org; 1084 Pacific Rim Hwy; 3-day admission adult/child/youth $10/free/6; ☺9am-dusk).

SURFING

Live to Surf
(www.livetosurf.com; 1180 Pacific Rim Hwy; 6hr board rental $25) Tofino's original surf shop also supplies skates and skimboards.

Pacific Surf School
(www.pacificsurfschool.com; 430 Campbell St; board rental 6hr/24hr $15/20) Offering rentals, camps and lessons for beginners.

KAYAKING

Rainforest Kayak Adventures
(www.rainforestkayak.com; 316 Main St; multiday courses & tours from $685)

Sunset on the Cowichan Valley (p97)
DAVE BLACKEY/PHOTOLIBRARY

Butchart Gardens

A 30-minute drive from Victoria via West Saanich Rd, the rolling farmlands of waterfront Brentwood Bay are chiefly known for **Butchart Gardens** (www .butchartgardens.com; 800 Benvenuto Ave; adult/child/youth $28.10/2.90/14.05; ☺9am-10pm mid-Jun–Aug, reduced off-season), Vancouver Island's top visitor attraction. The immaculate grounds are divided into separate gardens where there's always something in bloom. Summer is crowded, with tour buses rolling in relentlessly, but evening music performances and Saturday night fireworks (July and August) make it all worthwhile.

Tea fans take note: the **Dining Room Restaurant** serves a smashing afternoon tea, complete with roast-vegetable quiches and Grand Marnier truffles...Leave your diet at the door.

Specializes in four-to-six-day guided tours and courses.

Remote Passages
(www.remotepassages.com; Wharf St; tours from $64) Gives short guided kayaking tours around Clayoquot Sound and the islands.

BOAT TOURS

Jamie's Whaling Station
(www.jamies.com; 606 Campbell St; adult/child $99/65) Whale, bear and sea-lion spotting tours.

Tla-ook Cultural Adventures
(www.tlaook.com; tours from $44) Learn about aboriginal culture by paddling an authentic dugout canoe.

Sleeping

WICKANINNISH INN Hotel $$$
(☎ 250-725-3100, 800-333-4604; www.wickinn .com; Chesterman Beach; r from $399) Cornering the market in luxury winter storm-watching packages, 'the Wick' is worth a stay any time of year. Embodying nature with its recycled wood furnishings, natural stone tiles and the ambience of a place grown rather than constructed, the Wicks' sumptuous guest rooms have push-button gas fireplaces, two-person hot tubs and floor-to-ceiling windows. It's easy to work out that this place is the region's most romantic sleepover.

PACIFIC SANDS BEACH RESORT
Hotel $$$
(☎ 250-725-3322, 800-565-23224; www .pacificsands.com; 1421 Pacific Rim Hwy; r/villa from $220/450) The chic but nevertheless laid-back Pacific Sands has great lodge rooms but its stunning waterfront villas are even better. Great for groups, these huge timber-framed houses open directly onto the beach and include kitchens, stone fireplaces, slate and wood floors and ocean-view bedrooms with private decks.

INN AT TOUGH CITY Hotel $$
(☎ 250-725-2021; www.toughcity.com; 350 Main St; d $169-229; 🛜) Near the heart of the action and monikered after the town's old nickname, this quirky brick-built waterfront inn offers eight wood-floored ensuite rooms, most with balconies and some with those all-important Jacuzzi tubs. Room five has the best views – remember to look out for the bright-red First Nations longhouse across the water.

Eating

TACOFINO Mexican $
(www.tacofino.com; 1180 Pacific Rim Hwy; mains $4-10) Arrive off-peak at this very popular, orange-painted taco truck or you'll be waiting a while for your made-from-scratch nosh. It's worth it, though: these guys have nailed the art

of great Mexican comfort food. Pull up an overturned yellow bucket – that's the seating – and tuck into sustainable fish tacos or bulging burritos stuffed with chicken. Even better are the tasty pulled pork *gringas* and the ever-popular taco soup.

SOBO   Seafood **$$**
(www.sobo.ca; 311 Neill St; mains $6-14) Before TacoFino ruled the vending-cart world, Sobo – it means 'sophisticated bohemian' – was the king with its legendary purple truck. It was so successful it's now upgraded to its own wildly popular bistro-style restaurant. Fish tacos and crispy shrimp cakes remain, but new treats at the table include Vancouver Island seafood stew and roasted duck confit pizza.

SHELTER   West Coast **$$$**
(www.shelterrestaurant.com; 601 Campbell St; mains $25-39) An exquisite west-coast eatery with international accents. Our menu favorite here is the shrimp and crab dumplings. There's a strong commitment to local, sustainable ingredients – the salmon is wild and the sablefish is trap-caught – and there are plenty of nonfishy options for traveling carnivores, including a delectable char-grilled pork chop dish.

ℹ Getting There & Around

Orca Airways (www.flyorcaair.com) flights arrive at Tofino Airport from Vancouver International Airport's South Terminal ($206, 55 minutes, one to four daily).

Tofino Bus (www.tofinobus.com) 'Beach Bus' services roll in along Hwy 4 from Ucluelet ($15, 40 minutes, up to three daily).

Strathcona Provincial Park

Driving inland from Campbell River on Hwy 28, you'll soon come to BC's oldest protected area and also Vancouver Island's largest **park** (www.bcparks.ca). Centered on Mt Golden Hinde, the island's highest point (2200m), Strathcona is a magnificent pristine

Left: Taking in the Strathcona Provincial Park; **Below:** Glorious Butchart Gardens (p101), near Victoria

PHOTOGRAPHER: (LEFT) CHRIS CHEADLE/PHOTOLIBRARY, (BELOW) FRANK CARTER

wilderness crisscrossed with trail systems that deliver you to waterfalls, alpine meadows, glacial lakes and looming mountain crags.

On arrival at the main entrance, get your bearings at **Strathcona Park Lodge & Outdoor Education Centre** (www .strathcona.bc.ca). A one-stop shop for park activities, including kayaking, guided treks, yoga camps, ziplining and rock climbing (all-in adventure packages are available, some aimed specifically at families), this is a great place to rub shoulders with other outdoorsy types – head to the **Whale Dining Room** or **Canoe Club Café** eateries for a fuel up.

The lodge also offers good **accommodations** (r/cabins from $136/175), which, in keeping with its low-impact approach to nature and commitment to eco-education, is sans telephones and TVs. Rooms range from basic college-style bedrooms to secluded timber-framed cottages.

Notable park hiking trails include **Paradise Meadows Loop** (2.2km), an easy amble in a delicate wildflower and evergreen ecosystem; and **Mt Becher** (5km), with its great views over the Comox Valley and mountain-lined Strait of Georgia. The 9km **Comox Glacier Trail** is quite an adventure but is only recommended for advanced hikers. Around Buttle Lake, easier walks include **Lady Falls** (900m) and the trail along **Karst Creek** (2km), which winds past sinkholes, percolating streams and tumbling waterfalls.

FRASER VALLEY

Vancouverites looking for an inland escape shoot east on Hwy 1 through the fertile plains to places such as **Abbotsford**. Most just whiz past this farmland, though self-drive tours are

103

an option (see p327). Further along and a little north of the highway is the town of **Harrison Hot Springs**. At Hope, Hwy 1 continues spectacularly north, literally through the vertical walls of the beautiful **Fraser Canyon**.

OKANAGAN VALLEY

It is hard to know which harvest is growing faster in this fertile and beautiful valley: tourists or fruit. Certainly, bounty abounds in this ever-more-popular and lovely swath midway between Vancouver and Alberta. The moniker 'Canada's Napa Valley' is oft repeated and somewhat apt. The 180km-long Okanagan Valley is home to more than 100 excellent wineries, whose vines spread across the terraced hills, soaking up some of Canada's sunniest weather.

Near the center, Kelowna is one of the fastest growing cities in Canada. It offers a heady mix of culture, lakeside beauty and fun. In July and August, however, the entire valley can seem as overburdened as a grapevine right before the harvest. For many, the best time to visit is late spring and early fall, when the crowds are manageable.

Penticton

POP 32,900

Not as frenetic as Kelowna, Penticton combines the idle pleasures of a beach resort with its own edgy vibe. Long a final stop in life for Canadian retirees (which added a certain spin to its Salish-derived name Pen-Tak-Tin, meaning 'place to stay forever'), the town today is growing fast, along with the rest of the valley.

In late June dozens of Elvis impersonators arrive for the **Elvis festival** (www.pentictonelvisfestival.com).

Sights

Okanagan Beach boasts about 1300m of sand, with average summer water temperatures of about 22°C. If the place is jammed, there are often quieter shores at 1.5km-long **Skaha Beach**, south of the center.

SS SICAMOUS   Historical Site
(☑ 250-492-0405; 1099 Lakeshore Dr W; adult/child $5/1; ⊙9am-9pm May-Oct, 10am-4pm Mon-Fri Nov-Apr) Right on the sand, the SS *Sicamous* hauled passengers and freight on Okanagan Lake from 1914 to 1936. Now restored and beached, it has been joined by the equally old tugboat, SS *Naramata*.

Activities

WATERSPORTS

The paved **Okanagan River Channel Biking & Jogging Path** follows the rather arid channel that links Okanagan Lake to Skaha Lake. But why pound the pavement when you can float? **Coyote Cruises** (☑ 250-492-2115; 215 Riverside Dr; rental & shuttle $11; ⊙10am-4:30pm Jun-Aug) rents out inner tubes that you can float to a midway point on the channel. Coyote Cruises buses you back to the start near Okanagan Lake (if you have your own floatable, it's $5 for the bus ride).

There are several watersports rental places on Okanagan Lake. If it floats you can rent it, including kayaks for $20 an hour and ski boats for $280 for four hours.

Castaways (☑ 250-490-2033; Penticton Lakeside Resort, 21 Lakeshore Dr)
Pier Water Sports (☑ 250-493-8864; Rotary Park, Lakeshore Dr W)

MOUNTAIN BIKING & CYCLING

Long dry days and rolling hills add up to great conditions for mountain biking. Get to popular riding spots by heading east out of town, toward Naramata. Follow signs to the city dump and Campbell's Mountain, where you'll find a single-track and dual-slalom course, both of which aren't too technical. Once you get there, the riding is mostly on the right side, but once you pass the cattle guard, it opens up and you can ride anywhere.

Rent bikes and pick up a wealth of information at **Freedom – The Bike Shop** (☑ 250-493-0686; www.freedombikeshop .com; 533 Main St; bikes per day $40). **Fun City**

Okanagan Valley

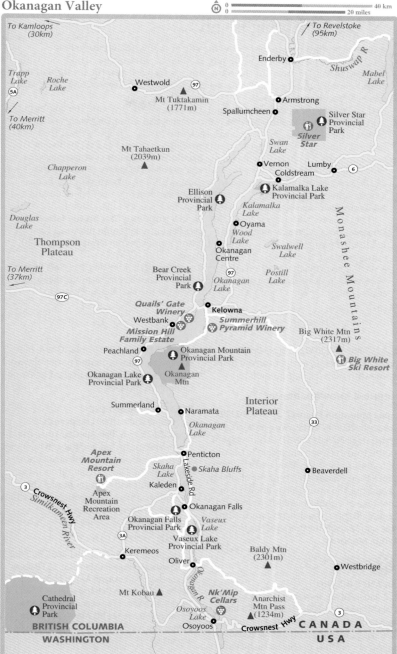

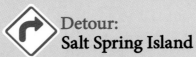

Detour:
Salt Spring Island

A former hippie enclave that's now the site of many rich vacation homes, pretty Salt Spring (population 10,500) justifiably receives the majority of Gulf Island visitors. The heart of the community is Ganges, also the location of the **visitor center** (📞250-537-5252; www.saltspringtourism.com; 121 Lower Ganges Rd; ⏰9am-5pm Jul & Aug, reduced off-season).

If you arrive on a summer weekend, the best way to dive into the community is at the thriving **Saturday Market** (www.saltspringmarket.com; Centennial Park, Ganges; ⏰8am-4pm Sat Apr-Oct), where you can tuck into luscious island-grown fruit and piquant cheeses while perusing locally produced arts and crafts. Visit some of these artisans via a free downloadable **Studio Tour Map** (www.saltspringstudiotour .com). One of the best is the rustic **Blue Horse Folk Art Gallery** (www.bluehorse. ca; 175 North View Dr; ⏰10am-5pm Sun-Fri Mar-Dec), with its funky carvings of horses, among other cool creations. The friendly owners recently opened an on-site **B&B** (www.bloomorganicbandb.com; d $150) if you feel like sticking around.

If you haven't eaten your fill at the market, drop into **Salt Spring Island Cheese** (www.saltspringcheese.com; 285 Reynolds Rd) for a self-guided tour of the facilities. Be sure to check out the miniature ponies before sampling up to 10 curdy treats in the winery-style tasting room.

Pick a favorite cheese, then add to your picnic with a bottle from **Salt Spring Vineyards** (www.saltspringvineyards.com; 151 Lee Rd; ⏰11am-5pm mid-Jun–Aug, reduced off-season), where you can sample a few tipples – try the rich blackberry port.

(📞250-462-1151; 1070 Lakeshore Dr; bikes per day $40) lives up to the promise of its name with maps of self-guiding tours.

SKIING & SNOWBOARDING

Apex Mountain Resort (📞877-777-2739, conditions 250-487-4848; www.apexresort.com; lift tickets adult/child $60/37), 37km west of Penticton off Green Mountain Rd, is one of Canada's best small ski resorts. It has more than 68 downhill runs for all ability levels, but the mountain is known for its plethora of double-black-diamond and technical runs (the drop is over 600m). It is usually quieter than nearby Big White Mountain.

 Eating

AMANTE BISTRO　　　　　Fusion **$$**
(📞250-493-1961; www.amantebistro.com; 483 Main St; mains $10-30; ⏰11am-2pm & 5-10pm Mon-Sat) There's intimate dining for those who want to enjoy a changing seasonal menu of carefully prepared dishes such

as small pizzas with Poplar Grove blue cheese or a slow-roasted pork belly with scallops; local produce stars. Excellent Okanagan wine list.

SALTY'S BEACHOUSE　　Seafood **$$**
(📞250-493-5001; 1000 Lakeshore Dr W; mains $12-25; ⏰5-10pm Apr-Oct) You expect deep-fried but what you get is a nuanced menu of seafood with global accents. Typical is the Cayman Island chowder, which is rich and multifaceted. Dine under the stars on the patio or enjoy the lake views from the upper level.

ℹ️ Information

The **visitor center** (📞250-493-4055, 800-663-5052; www.tourismpenticton.com; 553 Railway St, cnr Hwy 97 & Eckhardt Ave W; ⏰8am-8pm May-Sep, 10am-6pm Oct-Apr) is one of BC's best. There's free internet on offer and, even better, a room devoted to the **BC Wine Information Centre** with regional wine information, tasting and sales.

ℹ️ Getting There & Away

Penticton Regional Airport (YYF; ☎ 250-492-6042; www.cyyf.org) There are daily flights by Air Canada Jazz to Vancouver (one hour).

Kelowna

POP 120,300

A kayaker paddles past scores of new tract houses up on a hillside: it's an iconic image for fast-growing Kelowna, the unofficial 'capital' of the Okanagan Valley and the sprawling center of all that's good and not-so-good with the region.

Entering from the north, the ever-lengthening urban sprawl of tree-lined Hwy 97 seems to go on forever. Once past the waves of chains and strip malls, the downtown is a welcome reward. Museums, culture, nightlife and the park-lined lakefront feature. About 2km south is charming, lakeside Pandosy Village.

👁️ Sights

CITY PARK & PROMENADE   Park
The focal point of the city's shoreline, this immaculate downtown park is home to manicured gardens, water features and **Hot Sands Beach**, where the water is a respite from the summer air. Among the many statues (the visitor center has a good guide) look for the one of the **Ogopogo**, the lake's mythical – and hokey – monster. Restaurants and pubs take advantage of the uninterrupted views of the lake and forested shore opposite. North of the marina, **Waterfront Park** has a variegated shoreline and a popular open-air stage.

CULTURAL DISTRICT
                         Historic Site
Pick up the Cultural District walking-tour

and public-art brochures at the visitor center and visit www.kelowna museums.ca.

Located in the old Laurel Packing House, the **BC Orchard Industry Museum** (☎ 250-763-0433; 1304 Ellis St; admission by donation; 🕙10am-5pm Mon-Sat) recounts the history of the Okanagan Valley from its ranchland past, grazed by cows, to its present, grazed by tourists. The old fruit packing-crate labels are works of art. It was due to reopen in 2011 after a major restoration.

In the same building, the knowledgeable staff at the **Wine Museum** (☎ 250-868-0441; admission free; 🕙10am-6pm Mon-Sat, 11am-5pm Sun) can recommend tours, steer you to the best wineries for tastings and help you fill your trunk with the many local wines on sale.

🛏️ Sleeping

HOTEL ELDORADO   Hotel $$$
(☎ 250-763-7500, 866-608-7500; www.hotelel doradokelowna.com; 500 Cook Rd; r $180-400;

Apple harvest at Okangan Valley
(p104)
T KITCHIN & V HURST/PHOTOLIBRARY

107

DAVE BLACKEY/PHOTOLIBRARY

Don't Miss **Visiting the Okanagan Valley Wineries**

Among the dozens of options, the following (listed north to south) are recommended. Summerhill Pyramid and Cedar Creek Estate are south of Kelowna along the lake's east shore. The rest of the wineries can be reached via Hwy 97. Two good sources of information on Okanagan Valley wines are the BC Wine Information Centre in Penticton's visitor center and the Wine Museum in Kelowna.

Summerhill Pyramid Winery (☎250-764-8000; www.summerhill.bc.ca; 4870 Chute Lake Rd, Kelowna) On Kelowna's eastern shore, the wines are aged in a huge pyramid.

Quails' Gate Winery (☎250-769-4451; www.quailsgate.com; 3303 Boucherie Rd, Kelowna; ◯10am-5pm) A small winery with a huge reputation, it's known for its pinot noir and sauvignon blanc. The **Old Vines Restaurant** (mains $10-20; ◯11am-9pm) is among the best.

Mission Hill Family Estate (☎250-768-7611; www.missionhillwinery.com; 1730 Mission Hill Rd, Westbank; ◯10am-5pm) Go for a taste of one of the blended reds (try the Bordeaux) or the thirst-quenching pinot gris. Luncheons at the **Terrace** (mains $24-27; ◯11am-3pm mid-May–mid-Sep) are a seasonal treat.

Nk'Mip Cellars (☎250-495-2985; www.nkmipcellars.com; 1400 Rancher Creek Rd, Osoyoos) Excellent winery owned by an entrepreneurial First Nations band. Simple meals with aboriginal touches such as corn bread are served at the **Patio** (mains $16-18; ◯11:30am-8pm May-Sep).

❄@🛜🏊) This historic lakeshore retreat, south of Pandosy Village, has 19 heritage rooms where you can bask in antique-filled luxury. A modern low-key wing has 30 more rooms and six opulent waterfront suites. It's classy, artful and funky all at once. This place is definitely the choice spot in town for a luxurious getaway.

ROYAL ANNE HOTEL Hotel $$

(☏ 250-763-2277, 888-811-3400; www.royal annehotel.com; 348 Bernard Ave; r $100-200; ✳@☎) Location, location, location are the three amenities that count at this otherwise unexciting, older five-story motel in the heart of town. Rooms have standard modern decor, fridges and huge, openable windows.

PRESTIGE HOTEL Motel $$

(☏ 250-860-7900, 877-737-8443; www .prestigeinn.com; 1675 Abbott St; r $120-250; ✳@☎⚓) This 66-room place has a great location across from City Park and once you're inside, you can't see the rather hideous exterior. The rooms are just fine, in an upscale-motel sort of way (nice soap, LCD TVs, piles of decorative pillows etc).

 Eating & Drinking

RAUDZ Fusion $$

(☏ 250-868-8805; www.raudz.com; 1560 Water St; mains $12-25; ☺5-10pm) Noted chef Rod Butters returns with this casual bistro that is a temple to Okanagan produce and wine. The dining room is as airy and open as the kitchen and the seasonal menu takes global inspiration for Med-infused dishes good for sharing, as well as steaks and seafood. Suppliers include locally renowned Carmelis goat cheese.

ROTTEN GRAPE Tapas $$

(☏ 250-717-8466; 231 Bernard Ave; mains $8-15; ☺5pm-midnight Wed-Sun) Enjoy flights of local wines without the fru-fru in the heart of town. If you utter 'tannin, the hobgoblin of pinot' at any point, be quiet and eat some of the tasty tapas (from $10).

DOC WILLOUGHBY'S Pub

(☏ 250-868-8288; 353 Bernard Ave; ☺11:30am-2am) Right downtown, this pub boasts a vaulted interior lined with wood and tables on the street; it's perfect for a drink or a meal. The beer selection is excellent, including brews from Tree Brewing and Penticton's Cannery Brewing.

 Information

Visitor center (☏ 250-861-1515, 800-663-4345; www.tourismkelowna.com; 544 Harvey Ave; ☺8am-7pm daily summer, 8am-5pm Mon-Fri & 10am-3pm Sat & Sun winter) Near the corner of Ellis St; excellent touring maps.

 Getting There & Away

From Kelowna airport (YLW; ☏ 250-765-5125; www.kelownaairport.com), Westjet (www.westjet .com) serves Vancouver, Victoria, Edmonton, Calgary and Toronto. Air Canada Jazz (www .aircanada.com) serves Vancouver and Calgary. Horizon Air (www.alaskaair.com) serves Seattle. The airport is a long 20km north of the center on Hwy 97.

ⓘ Getting Around

To/From the Airport

Kelowna Airport Shuttle (☏ 250-888-434-8687; www.kelownashuttle.com) costs $12 to $15 per person. Cabs cost about $30.

Big White Ski Resort

Perfect powder is the big deal at **Big White Ski Resort** (☏ 250-765-8888, 800-663-2772, snow report 250-765-7669; www .bigwhite.com; 1-day lift passes adult/child $71/35), located 55km east of Kelowna off Hwy 33. With a vertical drop of 777m, it features 16 lifts and 118 runs that offer excellent downhill and backcountry skiing, while deep gullies make for killer snowboarding. Because of Big White's isolation, most people stay up here. The resort includes numerous restaurants, bars, hotels, condos, rental homes and a hostel. The resort has lodging info and details of the ski-season Kelowna shuttle.

HAIDA GWAII

Haida Gwaii, which means 'Islands of the People', offers a magical trip for those who make the effort. Attention has long focused on its many unique species of flora and fauna to the extent that 'Canada's Galapagos' is a popular moniker. But each year it becomes more apparent that the real soul of the islands is the Haida culture itself. Long one of the most advanced and powerful First Nations, the Haida suffered terribly after Westerners arrived.

Now, however, their culture is resurgent and can be found across the islands in myriad ways beyond their iconic totem poles. Haida reverence for the environment is protecting the last stands of superb old-growth rain forests, where the spruce and cedars are some of the world's largest. Amid this sparsely populated, wild and rainy place are bald eagles, bears and much more wildlife. Offshore, sea lions, whales and orcas abound.

In 2010 two events further confirmed the islands' and their people's resurgence. The name used by Europeans since the 18th century, Queen Charlotte Islands, was officially ditched; and the federal government moved forward with its plans to make the waters off Haida Gwaii a marine preserve.

 ## Sights & Activities

The Haida Gwaii portion of the **Yellowhead Hwy** (Hwy 16) heads 110km north from Queen Charlotte City (QCC) past Skidegate, Tlell and Port Clements. The latter was where the famous golden spruce tree on the banks of the Yakoun River was cut down by a demented forester in 1997. The incident is detailed in the best-selling *The Golden Spruce* by John Vaillant, one of the best books on the islands and the Haida culture in print.

All along the road to **Masset**, look for little seaside pullouts, oddball boutiques and funky cafes that are typical of the islands' character.

HAIDA HERITAGE CENTRE AT QAY'LLNAGAAY   Cultural Center

One of the top attractions in the north is this marvelous **cultural center** (☎ 250-559-7885; www.haidaheritagecentre.com; Skidegate; adult/child $15/5; ⏱9am-6pm Jun-Aug, 11am-5pm Tue-Sat Sep-May). With exhibits on history, wildlife and culture, it alone is reason to visit the islands. The rich traditions of the Haida are explored in galleries, programs and work areas where contemporary artists create new works such as the totem poles lining the shore.

YAKOUN LAKE   Landmark

Hike about 20 minutes through ancient stands of spruce and cedar to pristine **Yakoun Lake**, a large wilderness lake towards the west side of Graham Island. A small beach near the trail is shaded by gnarly Sitka alders. Dare to take a dip in the bracing waters or just enjoy the sweeping views.

The trailhead to the lake is at the end of a rough track that is off a branch from the main dirt and gravel logging road between QCC and Port Clements. It runs for 70km – watch for signs for the lake. On weekdays, check in by phone (☎250-557-6810) for logging trucks.

 ## Sleeping

Small inns and B&Bs are mostly found on Graham Island. There are numerous choices in QCC and Masset, with many in between and along the spectacular north coast.

It's Time for Fruit

Roadside stands and farms where you can pick your own fruit line Hwy 97 between Osoyoos and Penticton via the town of Oliver. Major Okanagan Valley crops and their harvest times:

Strawberries Mid-June to early July

Raspberries Early to mid-July

Cherries Mid-June to mid-August

Apricots Mid-July to mid-August

Peaches Mid-July to mid-September

Pears Mid-August to late September

Apples Early September to late October

TODD LAWSON

Don't Miss Gwaii Haanas National Park Reserve & Haida Heritage Site

This huge Unesco World Heritage site encompasses Moresby and 137 smaller islands at the southern end of the islands. It combines a time-capsule look at abandoned Haida villages, hot springs, amazing natural beauty and some of the continent's best kayaking.

Access to the park is by boat or plane only. A visit demands a decent amount of advance planning and usually requires several days. From May to September, you must obtain a reservation, unless you're with a tour operator.

Contact **Parks Canada** (☎250-559-8818; www.pc.gc.ca/gwaiihaanas; Haida Heritage Centre at Qay'llnagaay, Skidegate; ⏰8:30am-noon & 1-4:30pm Mon-Fri) with questions. The website has links to the **essential annual trip planner**. Anyone who has not visited the park during the previous three years must attend a free orientation at the park office (all visitors also must register).

The number of daily **reservations** (☎877-559-8818) is limited: plan well in advance. There are user fees (adult/child $20/10 per night). Nightly fees are waived if you have a Parks Canada Season Excursion Pass. A few much-coveted standby spaces are made available daily: call Parks Canada.

The easiest way to get into the park is with a tour company. Parks Canada can provide you with lists of operators; tours last from one day to two weeks. Many can also set you up with **rental kayaks** (average per day/week $60/300) and gear for independent travel.

PREMIER CREEK LODGING　Inn $
(☎ 250-559-8415, 888-322-3388; www.qcislands.net/premier; 3101 3rd Ave, QCC; dm $25, r $35-100; @) Dating from 1910, this friendly lodge has eight beds in a hostel building out back and 12 rooms in the main building, ranging from tiny but great-value singles to spacious rooms with views and porches. There's high-speed internet.

111

If You Like...
Provincial Parks

If you like Strathcona Provincial Park
(p102), check out these parks.

1 **NAIKOON PROVINCIAL PARK**
(☎250-626-5115; www.bcparks.ca) Haida
Gwaii's northeastern side is devoted to this
beautiful 72,640-hectare park, combining sand
dunes and low sphagnum bogs surrounded by
stunted lodgepole pine, and red and yellow cedar.
The beaches on the north coast feature strong
winds, pounding surf and flotsam. They can be
reached via the stunning 26km-long Tow Hill Rd, east
of Masset.

2 **HORNE LAKE CAVES PROVINCIAL PARK**
(www.hornelake.com; tours adult/child from
$20/17; ⊙10am-5pm Jul & Aug, reduced off-season)
A 45-minute drive southwest from Parksville
on Vancouver Island delivers you to BC's best
spelunking spot. Two caves are open to the public for
self-exploring, or you can take a guided tour of the
spectacular Riverbend Cave.

3 **MAQUINNA MARINE PROVINCIAL PARK**
(www.bcparks.ca) One of the most popular day
trips from Tofino, the highlight is Hot Spring Cove.
Tranquility-minded trekkers travel to the park by
Zodiac boat or seaplane, watching for whales and
other sea critters en route. From the boat landing,
2km of boardwalks lead to the natural hot pools.

4 **NEWCASTLE ISLAND MARINE
PROVINCIAL PARK**
(www.newcastleisland.ca) Nanaimo's rustic outdoor
gem offers tranquil hiking and cycling, as well
as beaches and wildlife-spotting opportunities.
Settled by the Coast Salish – and still part of their
traditional territory – it's acessed via a 10-minute
ferry from the harbor (adult/child $4/3), there's
a seasonal eatery and regular First Nations
dancing displays.

COPPER BEECH HOUSE   B&B $$
(☎250-626-5441; www.copperbeechhouse.com;
1590 Delkatla Rd, Masset; r from $100) David
Phillips has created a legendary B&B in
a rambling old house on Masset Harbor.

It has three unique rooms and there's
always something amazing cooking in
the kitchen.

🍴 Eating & Drinking

The best selection of restaurants is
in QCC, although there are also a few
in Skidegate, Tlell and Masset. Ask at
the visitor centers about local Haida
feasts, where you'll enjoy the best
salmon, blueberries and more you've
ever had. Good supermarkets are
found in Skidegate and Masset.

QUEEN B'S   Cafe $
(☎250-559-4463; 3201 Wharf St, QCC;
mains $3-10; ⊙9am-5pm) This funky
place excels at baked goods, which
emerge from the oven all day long.
There are tables with water views
outside and lots of local art inside.

OCEAN VIEW RESTAURANT
                              Seafood $$
(☎250-559-8503; Sea Raven Motel, 3301
3rd Ave, QCC; mains $10-25; ⊙11am-9pm)
Good fresh seafood (try the halibut)
is the specialty at this casual dining
room, where some tables look out to
the harbor.

ℹ Information

QCC visitor center (☎250-559-8316; www
.qcinfo.ca; 3220 Wharf St, QCC; ⊙8:30am-
9pm daily Jul & Aug, 9am-5pm Tue-Sat Oct-Apr,
9am-5pm May, Jun & Sep) is handy, although
there's been a recent encroachment of gift
items. Get a free copy of *Art Route*, a guide to
more than 40 studios and galleries. A desk at
Sandspit Airport opens for incoming flights.

ℹ Getting There & Away

Air
The main airport for Haida Gwaii is at Sandspit
(YZP; ☎250-559-0052) on Moresby Island. Note
that reaching the airport from Graham Island
is time-consuming: if your flight is at 3:30pm,
you need to line up at the car ferry at Skidegate
Landing at 12:30pm (earlier in summer). There's

One Tall Tale

Though most Aboriginal groups on the northwest coast lack formal written history as we know it, centuries of traditions manage to live on through artistic creations such as totem poles.

Carved from a single cedar trunk, totems identify a household's lineage in the same way a family crest might identify a group or clan in Britain, although the totem pole is more of a historical pictograph depicting the entire ancestry.

Unless you're an expert, it's not easy to decipher a totem. But you can start by looking for the creatures that are key to the narrative. Try to pick out the following.

Eagle Signifies intelligence and power.

Killer whale Symbolizes dignity and strength (often depicted as a reincarnated spirit of a great chief).

Raven Signifies mischievousness and cunning.

Shark Exemplifies an ominous and fierce solitude.

Thunderbird Represents the wisdom of proud ancestors.

also a small airport at Masset (YMT; ☎250-626-3995).

Air Canada Jazz (☎888-247-2262; www.aircanada.com) flies daily between Sandspit and Vancouver.

Ferry

BC Ferries (☎250-386-3431; www.bcferries.com) Prince Rupert to/from Skidegate Landing (adult $33-39, child fare 50%, car $115-140, seven hours) runs six times a week in summer, and three per week in winter on the *Northern Adventure*. Cabins are useful for overnight schedules (from $85). Prince Rupert can be reached from Jasper by trains run by VIA Rail.

❶ Getting Around

Off Hwy 16, most roads are gravel or worse.

BC Ferries (adult/child $9/4.50, cars from $20, 20 minutes, almost hourly 7am to 10pm) operates a small car ferry linking the two main islands at Skidegate Landing and Alliford Bay.

Eagle Transit (☎877-747-4461; www.haidagwaii.net/eagle) meets flights and ferries. The fare from the airport to QCC is $27.

Banff & the Canadian Rockies

When dreamers from around the world imagine trips to Canada, they almost always think of the Rockies. Their mammoth snow-frosted peaks looming over glassy turquoise lakes encircled by wildlife – elk, wolves, grizzlies and much more – are usually spotted only on TV wildlife programs. But unlike most dreams of the perfect vacation destination, this serene, jaw-dropping mountain region really delivers. The trick, though, is not to rush through too quickly.

Be sure to linger in Banff for its dramatic scenery but don't miss Jasper for its camera-twitching wildlife-viewing. Both areas offer excellent hiking for all energy levels, with easy wanders around amazing Lake Louise or Moraine Lake shorelines being especially popular. And it's not all about nature here either: city slickers should also check out the scenes in Calgary and Edmonton, the main Alberta access points for the Rockies region.

Sun-fired mountains above Moraine Lake (p138)
SEAN CAFFREY

Taking in the wild side of the Canadian Rockies
RADIUS IMAGES/PHOTOLIBRARY

Banff & the Canadian Rockies

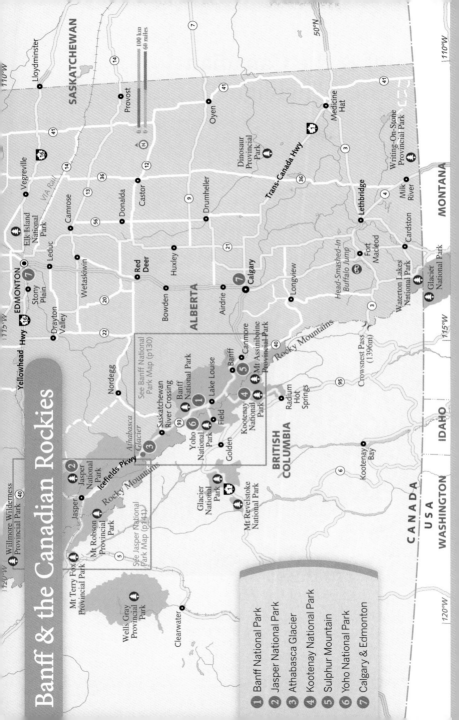

100 km
60 miles

1 Banff National Park
2 Jasper National Park
3 Athabasca Glacier
4 Kootenay National Park
5 Sulphur Mountain
6 Yoho National Park
7 Calgary & Edmonton

Banff & the Canadian Rockies' Highlights

① Banff National Park

Banff township is jam-packed during peak season, but rather than queuing in the souvenir shops, make a bee-line for the real reason people started coming here: head for the lakes and mountains and prepare to be overwhelmed by Canada's most dramatic panoramas. It's what hiking was invented for.

Need to Know

LOCATION 128km east of Calgary. **PEAK TIME TO VISIT** July and August. **TOP PHOTOS** Moraine Lake and Lake Louise. **BEST SKIING** Sunshine Village. **For further coverage, see p128.**

Banff National Park Don't Miss List

BY TAMARA DYKSHOORN,
LOCAL HIKING GUIDE

1 LAKE LOUISE

Once at the lake (p133), walk along the shoreline: the trail offers 2km of flat walking. From here you have many options: hiking a full day to two high teahouses or perhaps hitting the top of Fairview Mountain. All the while, the summit of Victoria and its surrounding glacier-covered peaks are in your view.

2 SUNSHINE MEADOWS

The stunning meadows area (p129) is dotted with wildflowers and alpine lakes, and offers an opportunity to see wildlife. Take a 10-minute shuttle bus to the treeline and begin your hike – perhaps sign-up for a guided walk and you'll see even more! Trails in this special area are well maintained and have something for every hiker's ability.

3 MORAINE LAKE

Also known as the Valley of Ten Peaks, Moraine Lake (p138) is a short drive from Lake Louise. There's a short trail up the Moraine that gives great vistas of the area and there's a level walking trail along the shoreline. Because of the high elevation, the autumn colors of the Larch trees here are a big draw.

4 BANFF TOWN

There's much more to Banff (p128) than wandering the main strip. Hikers can hit Tunnel Mountain in the evening or spend a few hours hiking up Sulphur and taking the gondola down. Consider a self-guided trip through the historic cemetery: the beginnings of Banff and its stories lie here. Ask at the Whyte Museum about guided tours.

5 JOHNSTON CANYON

On Highway 1A west of Banff, this is a pretty, any-weather hiking path. You'll witness water erosion first hand as the creek cuts through the landscape – waterfalls are many. Keep your eyes out for the Dipper and many other birds living along the creek side. If it's raining on your Banff visit, Johnston Canyon's partially sheltered trails are a good way to avoid the elements.

Jasper National Park

Smaller and cozier than its Banff big brother, Jasper Town is the hub of a magical wilderness that's dripping with natural allure. You'll find crystal-clear lakes and razor-sharp mountains studding this forested region, but it's the wildlife – elk, wolves, bears *et al* – that takes your breath away.

2

Need to Know

LOCATION 292km northwest of Banff. **BEST TIME TO VISIT** July to September. **BEST WILDLIFE-WATCHING** Discovery Trail and Miette Hot Springs. **For further coverage, see p128.**

Jasper National Park Don't Miss List

BY WES BRADFORD, RETIRED PARKS CANADA WARDEN AND JASPER WILDLIFE SPECIALIST

1 JASPER TRAMWAY

The Tramway (p140) takes you up Whistlers Mountain for excellent views of the Athabasca and Miette river valleys. Mountain goats, hoary marmots and golden-mantled ground squirrels are observed on the slopes near the lower trail. Hiking along the upper ridge and onto the backside of the mountain provides opportunities to see grizzly bears, elk and mule deer. Be equipped: sudden weather changes are common.

2 MIETTE HOT SPRINGS

The road to the hot springs (p137) climbs out of the Athabasca Valley and then descends steeply into the Riddle River Valley – watch for golden eagles soaring above the cliffs. At the hot springs, where you can enjoy a soothing soak in these sulphur-rich hot pools, bighorn sheep are often observed on the slopes above. Black bear, red fox and mule deer are common in this area.

3 MALIGNE LAKE

Wildlife-viewing along the road to the lake (p146) in spring and fall is superb, with black bears, bighorn sheep, mule deer, moose, and osprey common. The Maligne River is also an excellent place to test your fly-fishing (with no bait) skills against rainbow trout during August and September.

4 LAKES ANNETTE & EDITH

These lakes (p140) have large day use areas for family outings, plus beaches for those warm summer days. Swimming is popular – enjoy the spectacular views and abundant wildlife. Watch for elk, whitetail deer, coyotes, osprey, bald eagles, loons and river otters here.

5 JASPER TOWN

Take an evening or early morning walk on the Discovery Trail (p140) that transects Jasper town to observe elk, mule deer, coyotes, ground squirrels and abundant birdlife. Watch for black bears in spring on the south-facing slopes to the north where they're often searching for the first green grass and dandelions.

121

Hopping onto the Athabasca Glacier

Just off the highway, the multitudes stop to gaze at the icy toe of this mighty glacier (p144), the most accessible of the vast Columbia Icefield. But you don't just get to look: giant-wheeled tour buses rumble onto its craggy surface all day long or you can walk out yourself on a fascinating guided tour, gear supplied.

3

Riding up Sulphur Mountain

5

Hop on the slick Banff Gondola (p129) and you'll be atop Sulphur Mountain within 10 minutes – which is a lot easier than hiking the 5.6km trail alternative. While the peak's name comes from the hot springs at its base, the ride provides you with great views en route as well as some spectacular craggy panoramas up top: look out for Cascade Mountain and Table Mountain.

Hot springs, Sulphur Mountain

Kootenay National Park

Across the border in BC, Kootenay National Park (p135) is an accessible Rocky Mountain favorite, especially if your idea of wilderness encompasses cacti as well as glaciers: you'll find them both in this comparatively mild region. Plan ahead and hit some of the park's interpretative trails or consider a white-water rafting adventure.

Yoho National Park

The tiniest of BC's four Rocky Mountain national parks, dramatic Yoho (p137) contains more than its fair share of looming peaks, glacial lakes and pretty meadows. And if you're a waterfall fan, you'll find plenty of opportunities to run down your camera battery.

Calgary & Edmonton

Before you start thinking that Alberta is home only to countless mountains and hungry grizzlies, check out the region's two main cities. Oil-town Calgary (p148) still wears its cowboy heart on its sleeve – this is your best opportunity for a giant steak – while northerly Edmonton (p143) has an unexpected artsy feel. Both have museums, galleries and explorable neighborhoods.

Calgary

Banff & the Canadian Rockies' Best...

Vistas

o **Banff Gondola** (p129) Takes you to the top of Sulphur Mountain for great summer or winter summit views.

o **Big Beehive** (p134) Challenging hike to an unexpected gazebo viewpoint.

o **Peyto Lake** (p139) Idyllic platform view across the water.

o **Jasper Tramway** (p140) Breathtaking mountain and glacier views.

o **Meadows in the Sky Parkway** (p140) Mountain-summit views of the Columbia River valley.

Wildlife

o **Icefields Parkway** (p139) Scenic drive with frequent elk, deer and bighorn sheep sightings.

o **Maligne Lake** (p146) Spectacular lake vistas with moose and grizzly locals.

o **Discovery Trail** (p140) Encircling Jasper, expect to catch sight of wandering elk.

o **Miette Hot Springs** (p137) Sit in the pool while bighorn sheep hangout on the surrounding crags.

o **Lakes Annette & Edith** (p140) Prime area for elk, white-tailed deer and soaring bald eagles.

Hiking

o **Lake Minnewanka** (p129) Easy shoreline hike, plus sailing and swimming.

o **Bow River Falls** (p129) Popular waterfall trail, also leading to oddball Hoodoo rock formations.

o **Moraine Lake** (p138) Short or day-long hikes from a magical teal-colored lake.

o **Lake Louise** (p133) Via Mirror Lake to Lake Agnes Teahouse, a great hike.

Need to Know

Glaciers

o **Victoria Glacier** (p134) Great views of the glacier from the Lake Louise Sightseeing Gondola.

o **Columbia Icefield** (p139) Access point to a 30-glacier complex with large visitor center.

o **Athabasca Glacier** (p144) Breathtaking ice walks or bus trips from the glacier base.

o **Path of the Glacier Trail** (p140) Day hike to the foot of Angel Glacier.

o **Glacier National Park** (p140) BC's 430-glacier parkland treasure.

Left: Elk, Jasper National Park (p140);
Above: Jasper National Park (p140)

PHOTOGRAPHERS: (LEFT) LAWRENCE WORCESTER; (ABOVE) ANDREW BAIN

ADVANCE PLANNING

o **One month before** For peak summer accommodation, book well ahead.

o **Two weeks before** Book tours and activities in Banff and Jasper.

o **One week before** Start wearing-in your new hiking boots.

RESOURCES

o **Banff Lake Louise Tourism** (www.banff lakelouise.com) Information, resources and activities on the region.

o **Tourism Jasper** (www .jasper.travel) Local sights and resources for visitors.

o **Parks Canada** (www .parkscanada.gc.ca) Visitor information for national parks throughout the Rockies.

o **Travel Alberta** (www .travelalberta.com) General visitor resources for the province.

o **Friends of Jasper** (www.friendsofjasper.com) Volunteer organization dedicated to stewardship of the park.

o **Tourism Edmonton** (www.edmonton.com) Resources for city visitors.

o **Tourism Calgary** (www .visitcalgary.com) Visitor information for Calgary-bound tourists.

o **Association of Canadian Mountain Guides** (www.acmg.ca) Resources and links for climbing in the region.

o **Banff webcam** (www .explorerockies.com/banff -webcam) View-tastic images from Banff Gondola.

GETTING AROUND

o **Fly** Many visitors arrive via either Calgary or Edmonton International Airports, before heading on to Jasper (closer to Edmonton) or Banff (closer to Calgary).

o **Car** All major car-hire car companies are available, and highways link the region's main sites: Hwy 16 runs from Edmonton to Jasper; Hwy 93 (Icefields Parkway) from Jasper to Banff; and Hwy 1 from Banff to Calgary.

o **Train** VIA Rail (www .viarail.ca) services run from Vancouver to Jasper and Edmonton then across the country. Luxury Rocky Mountaineer services (www.rockymountaineer.com) run from Vancouver to Jasper, Banff and Calgary.

125

Banff & the Canadian Rockies Itineraries

For a whirlwind Rockies tour, take a three-day jaunt from Jasper to Banff, stopping off at the Athabasca Glacier en route. Augment this on the five-day route by starting and finishing in Alberta's two biggest cities.

3 DAYS

JASPER TO BANFF
Rocky Mountains Highlights

Start your north to south jaunt in **(1) Jasper**, where you should focus on snapping as many wildlife photos as possible in the national park: extras points for wolf and grizzly bear sightings in this region. After a sleepover in the charming, mountain-encircled town, plan for an early start the next day and hit the **(2) Icefields Parkway** southwards. There's a good chance that any wildlife you failed to spot in Jasper will be hanging around the sides of the highway here – this area is especially good for catching a longhorn sheep or three. Save some juice in your camera, though: the Columbia Icefields are also en route and

you should plan to pull over at the popular **(3) Athabasca Glacier**. There's an ever-busy cafeteria across the street if it's time for lunch, but make sure you're back on the road in time to make it to **(4) Banff** before sunset. Aim to spend a night or two here – it's bigger than Jasper.

After exploring the many top attractions in **(5) Banff National Park** such as the Banff Gondola and Whyte Museum of the Canadian Rockies, don't miss taking a drive/bus out to picture-perfect **(6) Lake Louise**.

EDMONTON TO CALGARY

The Big 'C' Tour

5 DAYS

Use the three-day itinerary for the middle of this tour, but bookend it with visits to the region's two biggest cities – this C-shaped route is handy for flying into one airport and departing from another. Start your journey in **(1) Edmonton**, where a sleepover in town should be combined with visits to the excellent Royal Alberta Museum and the new Art Gallery of Alberta. On the road early the next morning, head westwards on Hwy 16.

There are places to stop en route for lunch but you should be in **(2) Jasper** within five hours. Switch to the three-day itinerary here and, if time allows, add in

extra visits to **(3) Maligne Lake**, 50km from Jasper; **(4) Peyto Lake** along the Icefields Parkway; and **(5) Moraine Lake** in the Lake Louise area of Banff National Park.

Once you've had your fill of the Rockies – which could take a lot longer than you imagine – hop back in the car and take Hwy 1 eastwards to **(6) Calgary**. Take a break from all that driving by booking a downtown hotel and checking out the excellent Glenbow Museum and Heritage Park Historical Village.

Getting aquainted with Lake Louise (p133) by canoe
PHOTOGRAPHER: EMILY RIDDELL

Discover Banff & the Canadian Rockies

BANFF & JASPER NATIONAL PARKS

While Italy has Venice and Florence, Canada has Banff and Jasper, legendary natural marvels that are as spectacular and vital as anything the ancient Romans ever built. But don't think these protected areas have no history. Of the thousands of national parks scattered around the world today, Banff, created in 1885, is the third oldest while adjacent Jasper was only 22 years behind. Situated on the eastern side of the Canadian Rockies, the two bordering parks were designated Unesco World Heritage sites in 1984, along with British Columbia's (BC's) Yoho and Kootenay, for their exceptional natural beauty coupled with their manifestation of important glacial and alluvial geological processes. In contrast to some of North America's wilder parks, they both support small towns that lure between 2 to 5 million visitors each year. Despite all this, the precious balance between humans and nature continues to be delicately maintained – just. The one-day park entry fee (for entry to both parks) is $9.80/4.90 per adult/child; the passes are good until 4pm the following day.

Banff Town

Like the province in which it resides, Banff is something of an enigma. A resort town with souvenir shops, nightclubs and fancy restaurants is not something any national park purist would want to claim credit for. But looks can be misleading. First, Banff is no ordinary town. It developed historically, not as a residential district, but as a service

A rocky pool at Banff National Park

GREG GAWLOWSKI

center for the park that surrounds it. Second, the commercialism of Banff Ave is delusory. Wander five minutes in either direction and (though you may not initially realize it) you're in wild country, a primeval food chain of bears, elk, wolves and bighorn sheep. Banff civilized? It's just a rumor.

Sights

WHYTE MUSEUM OF THE CANADIAN ROCKIES   Museum

(www.whyte.org; 111 Bear St; adult/child $8/5; ⊙10am-5pm) The century-old Whyte Museum is more than just a rainy-day option. There is a beautiful gallery displaying some great pieces on an ever-changing basis. The permanent collection tells the story of Banff and the hearty men and women who forged a home among the mountains. Attached to the museum is an archive with thousands of photographs spanning the history of the town and park; these are available for reprint. The museum also gives out leaflets for a self-guided **Banff Culture Walk**.

BANFF GONDOLA   Landmark

(Mountain Ave; adult/6-15yr $29/14; ⊙8:30am-9pm summer, reduced hours rest of year) In summer or winter you can summit a peak 4km south of Banff thanks to the Banff Gondola, whose four-person enclosed cars glide you up to the top of Sulphur Mountain in less than 10 minutes. Named for the thermal springs that emanate from its base, this peak is a perfect viewing point and a tick-box Banff attraction. Some people hike all the way up on a zigzagging 5.6km trail. You can travel back down on the gondola for half price and recover in the hot springs.

BANFF PARK MUSEUM   Museum

(93 Banff Ave; adult/child $3.95/1.95; ⊙10am-6pm May-Sep, 1-5pm Oct-Apr) Occupying an old wooden Canadian Pacific Railway building dating from 1903, this museum is a national historic site. Its exhibits – a

taxidermic collection of animals found in the park, including grizzly and black bear, plus a tree carved with graffiti dating from 1841 – have changed little since the museum opened about a century ago.

Activities

Canoeing & Kayaking

Despite a modern penchant for big cars, canoe travel is still very much a quintessential Canadian method of transportation. The best options near Banff Town are **Lake Minnewanka** and nearby **Two Jack Lake**, both to the northeast, or – closer to the town itself – the **Vermilion Lakes**. Unless you have your own canoe, you'll need to rent one; try **Blue Canoe** (403-760-5007; cnr Wolf St & Bow Ave; rental 1st hr/additional hours $34/20).

Hiking

Hiking is Banff's tour de force and the main focus of many travelers' visit to the area. The trails are easy to find, well signposted and maintained enough to be comfortable to walk on, yet rugged enough to still provide a wilderness experience.

In general, the closer to Banff Town you are, the more people you can expect to see and the more developed the trail will be. But regardless of where in the park you decide to go walking, you are assured to be rewarded for your efforts.

Before you head out, check at the Banff Information Centre (p133) for trail conditions and possible closures. Keep in mind that trails are often snow-covered much later into the summer season than you might realize, and bear trail closures are a possibility, especially in berry season (from June to September).

One of the best hikes from the town center is the **Bow River Falls and the Hoodoos Trail** that starts by the Bow River Bridge and tracks past the falls to the Hoodoos, weird rock spires caused by wind and water erosion. The trail plies its way around the back of Tunnel Mountain through forest and some river meadows and is 10.2km return.

Some of the best multiday hikes start at the Sunshine parking lot where skiers grab the gondola in winter. From here you can get a bus up to Sunshine Village where you can cross the border into BC and head out across **Sunshine Meadows** and also **Mount Assiniboine Provincial Park**.

Skiing & Snowboarding

Sunshine Village (www.skibanff.com; day ski passes $75) straddles the Alberta–BC border. Though slightly smaller than Lake Louise in terms of skiable terrain it gets much bigger dumpings of snow, or 'Champagne powder' as Albertans like to call it (up to 9m annually). Aficionados laud Sunshine's advanced runs and lengthy ski season, which lingers until Victoria Day weekend in late May. A high-speed gondola whisks skiers up in 17 minutes to the village which sports Banff's only ski-in hotel, the Sunshine Mountain Lodge.

 Tours

DISCOVER BANFF TOURS
Wildlife, Sightseeing
(403-760-5007; www.banfftours.com; Sundance Mall, 215 Banff Ave; tours $39-145) Discover Banff has a great selection of tours to choose from: there are three-hour Banff Town tours, sunrise and evening wildlife tours, Columbia Icefield day trips and even a 10-hour grizzly bear tour, where if you don't see a bear you get your money back.

Banff National Park

0 _____ 40 km
0 _____ 20 miles

Athabasca Glacier Icewalks; Brewster; Icefield Centre

Athabasca Glacier

Abraham Lake

Kootenay Plains

Rocky Mountain Forest Reserve

Saskatchewan River Crossing

David Thompson Hwy

Icefields Pkwy

ALBERTA

Peyto Lake

Bow Lake

Banff National Park

To Glacier National Park (20km); Revelstoke (60km)

Yoho National Park

93

Trans-Canada Hwy

Field

Lake Louise

See Lake Louise Area Map (p136)

Golden

Moraine Lake

Mt Norquay (2133m)

Lake Minnewanka

Castle Mountain

Anthracite

Sawback

Banff Town

BRITISH COLUMBIA

95

Kootenay National Park

Sunshine Village

Canmore

Bow River

93

Mt Assiniboine National Park

To Calgary (66km)

Spillimacheen

Kootenay Crossing

Mt Assiniboine (3618m)

40

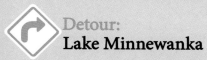

Detour:
Lake Minnewanka

Lake Minnewanka, pronounced mini-wonka, as in Willy Wonka (not mini-wanker, as Australian visitors enjoy saying), sits 13km east of Banff Town, making it a popular escape from downtown. The scenic recreational area features plenty of hiking, swimming, sailing, boating and fishing opportunities. The nonchallenging trail around the lake is a good option for a walk; the path is easy to follow and popular. **Minnewanka Lake Cruises** (www.explorerockies.com/minnewanka; adult/child $44/19; ⏱5-9 departures 10am-6pm mid-May–early Oct) offers a 60-minute interpretive cruise on the lake giving plenty of insight into the region's history and geology.

 # Sleeping

FAIRMONT BANFF SPRINGS
Hotel $$$

(☎ 403-762-2211; www.fairmont.com/banffsprings; 405 Spray Ave; r from $337; P@🌐☒) Imagine crossing a Scottish castle with a French chateau and then plonking it in the middle of one of the world's most spectacular (and accessible) wilderness areas. Rising like a Gaelic Balmoral above the trees at the base of Sulphur Mountain and visible from miles away, the Banff Springs is a wonder of early 1920s revivalist architecture and one of Canada's most iconic buildings. Wandering around its museumlike interior, it's easy to forget that it's also a hotel.

BANFF ROCKY MOUNTAIN RESORT
Hotel $$

(☎ 403-762-5531; www.bestofbanff.com; 1029 Banff Ave; r from $119; P🌐☒) Being 4km out of town at the far, far end of Banff Ave is a small price to pay for the preferential prices and excellent all-round facilities here (including a hot tub, pool, tennis courts and cafe/restaurant). Added to this is the greater sense of detachment, quiet tree-filled grounds (it never feels like a 'resort') and generously sized bedrooms with sofas, desks and extra beds. There's a free shuttle into town (hourly) or you can walk or cycle 4km along the Legacy Trail.

INNS OF BANFF
Hotel $$

(☎ 403-762-4581; www.bestofbanff.com; 600 Banff Ave; r from $129; P@🌐☒) The last hotel on Banff Ave and slightly out of the hustle and bustle, there are some good deals to be found here. Though the architecture is a little passé, there are loads of facilities including both indoor and outdoor pools, ski and bike rentals, and a Japanese restaurant.

 # Eating

COYOTE'S DELI & GRILL
Fusion $$

(www.coyotesbanff.com; 206 Caribou St; lunch mains $8-14, dinner mains $20; ⏱7:30am-10:30pm) Coyote's is best at lunchtime when you can skip hiking and choose a treat from the deli and grill menu inflected with a strong southwestern slant. Perch on a stool and listen to the behind-the-bar banter as you order up flatbreads, seafood cakes, quesadillas or some interesting soups (try the sweet potato and corn chowder).

BISON MOUNTAIN BISTRO
Fusion $$

(www.thebison.ca; 211 Bear St; lunch mains from $11, dinner mains from $18; ⏱11am-late Mon-Fri, 10am-late Sat & Sun) The Bison might look like it's full of trendy, well-off Calgarians dressed in expensive hiking gear, but its prices are actually very reasonable (nothing over $20). And rather than saturating the menu in AAA Alberta

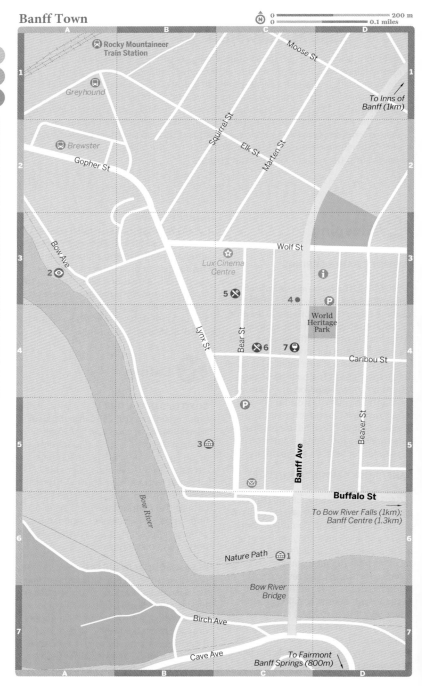

N

0 ──────────── 200 m
0 ──────────── 0.1 miles

Rocky Mountaineer
Train Station

Greyhound

Brewster

Gopher St

Moose St

Squirrel St

Elk St

Marten St

To Inns of
Banff (1km)

Bow Ave

2 ◉

Wolf St

Lux Cinema
Centre

ℹ

5 ✕

4 ●

P

World
Heritage
Park

Lynx St

Bear St

✕ 6   7 🚌

Caribou St

Beaver St

P

3 🏛

Banff Ave

✉

Buffalo St →

To Bow River Falls (1km);
Banff Centre (1.3km)

Bow River

Nature Path   🏛 1

Bow River
Bridge

Birch Ave

Cave Ave

To Fairmont
Banff Springs (800m) ↘

Banff Town

beef, there are big salads here and weird starch-heavy pizzas with butternut squash and rosemary potato toppings. The modern decor is set off by an outdoor patio and ground-floor boutique deli that serves up gourmet cheese and other such delights.

Drinking & Entertainment

WILD BILL'S LEGENDARY SALOON   Bar
(www.wbsaloon.com; 201 Banff Ave) Cowboys – where would Alberta be without them? Check this bar out if you're into line-dancing, calf-roping, karaoke and live music of the twangy Willy Nelson variety. The saloon is named after Wild Bill Peyto, a colorful 'local' character who was actually born and raised in that not-so-famous cowboy county of Kent in England.

BANFF CENTRE   Theater
(www.banffcentre.ca; 107 Tunnel Mountain Dr) A cultural center in a national park? Banff never ceases to surprise. This is the cultural hub of the Bow Valley – concerts, art exhibitions and the popular Banff Mountain Film Festival are all held here.

ℹ Information

Banff Information Centre (www.parkscanada .gc.ca/banff; 224 Banff Ave; ⏲8am-8pm Jun-Sep, 9am-5pm Oct-May) Offices for Parks Canada.

Banff/Lake Louise Tourism Bureau (www .banfflakelouise.com; ⏲8am-8pm May-Sep, 9am-noon & 1-5pm Oct-Apr) In the same building as the Banff Information Centre; gives advice on services and activities in and around Banff Town.

ℹ Getting There & Away

The nearest airport is in Calgary.

All of the major car-rental companies (see p359) have branches in Banff Town. During summer all the cars might be reserved in advance, so call ahead.

Shuttle buses operate daily year-round between Calgary International Airport and Banff. Buses are less frequent in the spring and fall. Companies include Brewster Transportation (www.brewster.ca) and Banff Airporter (www .banffairporter.com). The adult fare for both is around $50 one way and $98 round-trip.

Lake Louise

Famous for its teahouses, grizzly bears, skiing, Victoria Glacier, hiking and lakes (yes, plural), Lake Louise is what makes Banff National Park the phenomenon it is, an awe-inspiring natural feature that is impossible to describe without resorting to shameless clichés. Yes, there is a placid turquoise-tinted lake here; yes, the natural world feels (and is) tantalizingly close; and yes, the water is surrounded by an amphitheater of finely chiseled mountains that Michelangelo couldn't have made more aesthetically pleasing.

The **Lake Louise Visitor Centre** (Samson Mall, Lake Louise village; ⏲9am-8pm May-Sep, to 5pm Oct & Apr, to 4pm Nov-Mar) has some good geological displays, a Parks Canada desk and a small film theater.

The Bow Valley Parkway between Banff Town and Lake Louise is a slightly slower but much more scenic drive than Hwy 1.

◎ Sights

LAKE LOUISE   Natural Site
Named for Queen Victoria's otherwise anonymous fourth daughter (who also lent her name to the province), Lake Louise is a place that requires multiple

viewings. Aside from the standard picture-postcard shot (glorious blue sky, even bluer lake), try visiting at six in the morning, at dusk in August, in the October rain or after a heavy winter storm.

You can rent an unethically priced canoe from the **Lake Louise Boathouse** (per hr $45; ⊙9am-4pm Jun-Oct) and go for a paddle around the lake. Be sure you don't fall overboard – the water is freezing.

LAKE LOUISE SIGHTSEEING GONDOLA
Landmark

(www.lakelouisegondola.com; 1 Whitehorn Rd; round-trip adult/child $25.95/12.95; ⊙9am-5pm) To the east of Hwy 1, this sightseeing gondola will lever you to the top of Mt Whitehorn, where the views of the lake and **Victoria Glacier** are phenomenal. At the top, there's a restaurant and a Wildlife Interpretive Centre that offers 45-minute **guided hikes** (per person $5; ⊙11am, 1pm & 3pm).

Activities

HIKING

In Lake Louise beauty isn't skin-deep. The hikes behind the stunning views are just as impressive. Most of the classic walks start from Lake Louise and Moraine Lake. Some are straightforward, while others will give even the most seasoned alpinist reason to huff and puff.

From Chateau Lake Louise, two popular day walks head out to alpine-style teahouses perched above the lake. The shorter but slightly harder hike is the 3.4km grunt past **Mirror Lake** up to the Lake Agnes Teahouse (see p135) on its eponymous body of water. After tea and scones you can trek 1.6km further and higher to the view-enhanced **Big Beehive** lookout and Canada's most unexpectedly sited gazebo. Continue on this path to the Highline Trail to link up with the **Plain of Six Glaciers** for views of the Victoria Glacier.

Left: Skating on a frozen Lake Louise (p133); Below: The rugged beauty of Banff National Park (p128)
PHOTOGRAPHER: (LEFT) ANDREW BAIN; (BELOW) JOHN E MARRIOTT/PHOTOLIBRARY

Eating

LAKE AGNES TEAHOUSE   Cafe $
(Lake Agnes Trail; snacks from $3; ⊙Jun-Oct)
You thought the view from Lake Louise was good? Wait till you get up to this precariously perched alpine-style teahouse that seems to hang in the clouds beside ethereal Lake Agnes and its adjacent waterfall. The small log cabin runs on gas power and is hike-in only (3.4km uphill from the Chateau). Perhaps it's the thinner air or the seductiveness of the surrounding scenery but the rustic $6 tea and scones here taste just as good as the $39 spread at the Chateau Lake Louise.

LAKE LOUISE STATION RESTAURANT
                             Canadian $$
(mains from $14; ⊙11:30am-9:30pm) Restaurants with a theme have to be handled so carefully – thankfully this railway-inspired eatery, at the end of Sentinel Rd, does it just right. You can either dine in the station among the discarded luggage or in one of the dining cars, which are nothing short of elegant. The food is simple yet effective. A must-stop for trainspotters.

ⓘ Getting There & Around

The bus terminal is basically a marked stop at Samson Mall. The easiest way to get here from Banff is by car or Greyhound bus.

Kootenay National Park

Shaped like a lightning bolt, **Kootenay National Park** (☎ 250-347-9505; www.pc.gc.ca/kootenay; adult/child $10/5) is centered on a long, wide tree-covered valley shadowed by cold, grey peaks. Encompassing 1406 sq km, Kootenay has a more moderate climate than the other Rocky Mountains parks and, in the southern regions especially, summers can be hot and dry (which is a factor in the frequent fires). It's the only national

135

Lake Louise Area

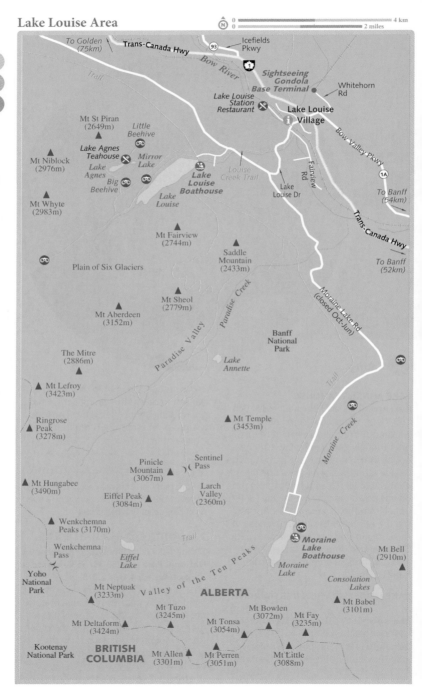

To Golden (75km)

Trans-Canada Hwy

Icefields Pkwy

Bow River

Sightseeing Gondola Base Terminal

Whitehorn Rd

Lake Louise Station Restaurant

Lake Louise Village

Bow Valley Pkwy

Mt St Piran (2649m)

Little Beehive

Lake Agnes Teahouse

Mirror Lake

Louise Creek Trail

Mt Niblock (2976m)

Lake Agnes

Big Beehive

Lake Louise Boathouse

Lake Louise Dr

Fairview Rd

To Banff (54km)

Mt Whyte (2983m)

Lake Louise

Trans-Canada Hwy

Mt Fairview (2744m)

Saddle Mountain (2433m)

To Banff (52km)

Plain of Six Glaciers

Mt Sheol (2779m)

Paradise Creek

Banff National Park

Moraine Lake Rd (closed Oct-Jun)

Mt Aberdeen (3152m)

Paradise Valley

Lake Annette

The Mitre (2886m)

Mt Lefroy (3423m)

Ringrose Peak (3278m)

Mt Temple (3453m)

Moraine Creek

Mt Hungabee (3490m)

Pinicle Mountain (3067m)

Sentinel Pass

Eiffel Peak (3084m)

Larch Valley (2360m)

Wenkchemna Peaks (3170m)

Wenkchemna Pass

Eiffel Lake

Moraine Lake Boathouse

Mt Bell (2910m)

Yoho National Park

Valley of the Ten Peaks

ALBERTA

Moraine Lake

Consolation Lakes

Mt Neptuak (3233m)

Mt Tuzo (3245m)

Mt Bowlen (3072m)

Mt Babel (3101m)

Mt Deltaform (3424m)

Mt Tonsa (3054m)

Mt Fay (3235m)

Kootenay National Park

BRITISH COLUMBIA

Mt Allen (3301m)

Mt Perren (3051m)

Mt Little (3088m)

0 — 4 km
0 — 2 miles

DISCOVER BANFF & THE CANADIAN ROCKIES BANFF & JASPER NATIONAL PARKS

park in Canada to contain both glaciers and cacti.

The short interpretive **Fireweed Trail** loops through the surrounding forest at the north end of Hwy 93. Panels explain how nature is recovering from a 1968 fire here. Some 7km further on, **Marble Canyon** has a pounding creek flowing through a nascent forest. Another 3km south on the main road is the short, easy trail through forest to ochre pools known as the **Paint Pots**. Panels describe both the mining history of this rusty earth and its past importance to Aboriginal people.

Learn how the park's appearance has changed over time at the **Kootenay Valley Viewpoint** where informative panels vie with the view. Just 3km south, **Olive Lake** makes a perfect picnic or rest stop. A lakeside interpretive trail describes some of the visitors who've come before you.

Yoho National Park

Although the smallest (1310 sq km) of the national parks in the Rockies, **Yoho National Park** (☎ 250-343-6783; www.pc.gc.ca/yoho; adult/child $10/5) is a diamond in the (very) rough countryside. This wilderness of looming peaks, ice-blue river, pounding waterfalls and glacial lakes is the real deal; it's some of the continent's least tarnished.

East of Field on Hwy 1 is the **Takakkaw Falls road** (⊙late-Jun–early Oct). At 254m, Takakkaw is one of the highest waterfalls in Canada. From here **Iceline**, a 20km hiking loop, passes many glaciers and spectacular scenery.

This World Heritage site protects the amazing Cambrian-age **fossil beds** on Mt Stephen and Mt Field. These 515-million-year-old fossils preserve the remains of marine creatures that were some of the earliest forms of life on earth. You can only get to the fossil beds by guided hikes, which are led by naturalists from the **Yoho-Burgess Shale**

♥ If You Like...
Hot Springs

If you like the luxury spa at the Fairmont Banff Springs (p131), you'll likely love these natural hot springs.

1 BANFF UPPER HOT SPRINGS
(Mountain Ave; adult/student $7.30/6.30; ⊙9am-11pm May-Sep, 10am-10pm Sun-Thu, 10am-11pm Fri & Sat Oct-Apr) You'll find a soothing hot pool, steam room, spa and excellent mountain views at these hot springs, near the Banff Gondola, 4km south of town. The water emerges from the spring at 47°C; in winter it has to be cooled to 39°C before entering the pool, but in spring the snowmelt does that job. In addition to the pool, you can indulge in a massage or an aromatherapy wrap. Bathing suits, towels and lockers can be rented.

2 MIETTE HOT SPRINGS
(Map p141; www.parkscanada.gc.ca/hotsprings; Miette Rd; adult/child/family $6.05/5.15/18.45; ⊙10:30am-9pm late May-Jun) A good spot for a soak is the remote Miette Hot Springs, 61km northeast of Jasper off Hwy 16, near the park boundary. The soothing waters are kept at a pleasant 39°C and are especially enjoyable when the fall snow is falling on your head and steam envelops the crowd. There are a couple of hot pools and a cold one, too – just to get the heart going – so it's best to stick a toe in before doing your cannonball.

3 RADIUM HOT SPRINGS
(☎ 250-347-9485; adult/child $7/6; ⊙9am-11pm mid-May–early Oct, noon-9pm rest of yr) Just outside the southwest corner of Kootenay National Park, the pools here are quite modern and can get very busy in summer. The water comes from the ground at 44°C, enters the first pool at 39°C and hits the final one at 29°C.

Foundation (☎ 800-343-3006; www.burgess -shale.bc.ca; tours from $55). Reservations are essential.

Near the south gate of the park, you can reach pretty **Wapta Falls** via a 2.4km trail. The easy walk takes about 45 minutes each way.

SEAN CAFFREY

Don't Miss **Moraine Lake**

The scenery will dazzle you long before you reach the spectacular deep-teal colored waters of Moraine Lake. The lake is set in the Valley of the Ten Peaks, and the narrow winding road leading to it offers views of these distant imposing summits. With little hustle or bustle and lots of beauty, many people prefer the more rugged and remote setting of Moraine Lake to Lake Louise. There are some excellent day hikes from the lake, or rent a boat at the **Moraine Lake Boathouse** (per hr $40; ⏰9am-4pm Jun-Oct) and paddle through the glacier-fed waters.

Moraine Lake Rd and its facilities are open from June to early October.

LAKE O'HARA

Perched high in the mountains east of Field, **Lake O'Hara** is worth the significant hassle involved in reaching this place, an encapsulation of the whole Rockies. Compact wooded hillsides, alpine meadows, snow-covered passes, mountain vistas and glaciers are all wrapped around the stunning lake. A basic day trip is worthwhile, but stay overnight in the backcountry and you'll be able to access many more trails, some quite difficult, all quite spectacular. The **Alpine Circuit** (12km) has a bit of everything.

To reach the lake, you can take the **shuttle bus** (adult/child $15/7.50; ⏰mid-

Jun–early Oct) from the Lake O'Hara parking lot, 15km east of Field on Hwy 1. A quota system governs bus access to the lake and limits permits for the 30 backcountry campsites. You can freely walk the 11km from the parking area, but no bikes are allowed. The area around Lake O'Hara usually remains snow-covered or very muddy until mid-July.

Make reservations for the **bus trip** (📞 250-343-6433) or for **camping** (backcountry permit adult $10) up to three months in advance. Given the popularity of Lake O'Hara, reservations are basically mandatory (unless you want to walk). However, if you don't have advance reservations, six day-use seats on the bus and three to five campsites are set aside for 'standby' users. To try to snare these, call ☎250-343-6433 at 8am the day before.

 Information

Yoho National Park Information Centre (☎250-343-6783; off Hwy 1, Field; ⊙9am-4pm Sep-Apr, 9am-5pm May & Jun, 9am-7pm Jul & Aug)

Icefields Parkway

Paralleling the Continental Divide for 230km between Lake Louise and Jasper Town, plain old Hwy 93 has been wisely rebranded as the Icefields Parkway (or the slightly more romantic 'Promenade des Glaciers' in French) as a means of somehow preparing people for the majesty of its surroundings. And what majesty! The highlight is undoubtedly the humungous Columbia Icefield and its numerous fanning glaciers, and this dynamic lesson in erosive geography is complemented by weeping waterfalls, aquamarine lakes, dramatic mountains and the sudden dart of a bear, an elk, or was it a moose?

⊙ **Sights**

PEYTO LAKE   Natural Site

This is the sort of scenery you come to the Canadian Rockies to find. This bluer than blue glacier-fed lake has been photographed more than Brangelina. Don't let the inevitable zoo of people sharing the sight deter you – the view is one of the best anywhere. The lake is best visited between the time the sun first illuminates the water and the the time the first tour bus arrives. From the

bottom of the lake parking lot, follow a paved trail for 15 minutes up a steady gradual incline to the wooden platform overlooking the lake. From here you can continue up the paved trail, keeping right along the edge of the ridge.

COLUMBIA ICEFIELD   Museum

About halfway between Lake Louise Village and Jasper Town you'll encounter the only accessible section of the vast Columbia Icefield, which contains about 30 glaciers and is up to 350m thick. This remnant of the last ice age covers 325 sq km on the plateau between Mt Columbia (3747m) and Mt Athabasca (3491m). It's the largest icefield in the Rockies and feeds the North Saskatchewan, Columbia, Athabasca, Mackenzie and Fraser River systems with its meltwaters.

Be sure to stop here at the FREE **Icefield Centre** (☎780-852-6288; admission free; ⊙9am-6pm May–mid-Oct). The downstairs **Glacial Gallery** explains the science of glaciers and provides a comprehensive snapshot of the area's history. On the

Glacier-fed Peyto Lake
ORIEN HARVEY

If You Like…
BC's Rocky Mountain Parks

If you like Yoho and Kootenay National Parks over in BC, you'll also like these.

1 GLACIER NATIONAL PARK
(www.pc.gc.ca/glacier) To be accurate, this 1350-sq-km park should be called 430 Glaciers National Park. Whether you travel by car, bus, trail or bicycle (more power to you), Rogers will likely rank as one of the most beautiful mountain passes you'll ever traverse. Be sure to pause at the Hemlock Grove Trail, 54km west of Revelstoke, where a 400m boardwalk winds through an ancient hemlock rain forest.

2 MT REVELSTOKE NATIONAL PARK
(www.pc.gc.ca/revelstoke) Grand in beauty if not in size (only 260 sq km), this national park just northeast of its namesake town is a vision of peaks and valleys – many all-but-untrod. From the 2223m summit of Mt Revelstoke, the views of the mountains and the Columbia River valley are excellent. To ascend, take the 26km Meadows in the Sky Parkway, 1.5km east of Revelstoke off Hwy 1. From here walk to the top or take the free shuttle.

main level you can have a chat to the rangers from **Parks Canada** (780-852-6288), who can advise you on camping options and climbing conditions and answer any questions you might have regarding the park.

The Icefields Centre is close to the easily accessible Athabasca Glacier (see the boxed text, p144).

Jasper Town & Around

Take Banff, halve the annual visitor count, increase the total land area by 40%, and multiply the number of bears, elk, moose and caribou by the power of three. The result: Jasper, a larger, less-trammeled more wildlife-rich version of the other Rocky Mountains parks whose rugged backcountry wins admiring plaudits for its vertiginous river canyons,

adrenalin-charged mountain-bike trails, rampartlike mountain ranges and delicate ecosystems.

Most people enter Jasper Town from the south via the magnificently Gothic Icefields Parkway that meanders up from Lake Louise amid foaming waterfalls and glacier-sculpted mountains, including iconic Mt Edith Cavell, easily visible from the town. About 50km southeast of Jasper take a detour to spectacular Maligne Lake (see the boxed text, p146).

 Sights

JASPER TRAMWAY   Landmark
(Map p141; www.jaspertramway.com; Whistlers Mountain Rd; adult/child $29/15; ⏰Apr-Oct) If the average, boring views from Jasper just aren't blowing your hair back, go for a ride up this sightseeing tramway which is open 9am to 8pm from June to August and closes earlier in the shoulder seasons. The vista is sure to take your breath away, with views, on a clear day, of the Columbia Icefield 75km to the south.

LAKES ANNETTE & EDITH
Natural Site
On the opposite side of the highway to the town, Lakes Annette and Edith are popular for water activities in the summer and skating in the winter. If you're brave and it's very hot, Annette is good for a quick summer dip – just remember the water was in a glacier not too long ago! Edith is more frequented by kayakers and boaters. Both are ringed by cycling/hiking trails and picnic areas. The one that circumnavigates Lake Annette is wheelchair accessible.

 **Activities**

Hiking
Even when judged against other Canadian national parks, Jasper's trail network is mighty, and with comparatively fewer

people than its sister park to the south, you've a better chance of seeing more wildlife and less humans.

Initiate yourself on the interpretative **Discovery Trail**, an 8km easy hike that encircles the town highlighting its natural, historical and railway heritage.

Other short, less radical trails include the 3.2km **Mary Schäffer Loop** by Maligne Lake named for one of the earliest European visitors to the area; the **Old Fort Loop** (3.5km) to the site of an old fur-trading post; and the 9km **Mina and Riley Lakes Loop** that leads out directly from the town.

Further away and slightly harder is the famous 9.1km **Path of the Glacier Trail** below the impressive face of Mt Edith Cavell that takes you to the foot of the Angel Glacier through the flower-scattered Cavell meadows.

White-water Rafting

There's nothing like a glacial splash-down to fight the summer heat. The Jasper area has lots of good rafting

Jasper National Park

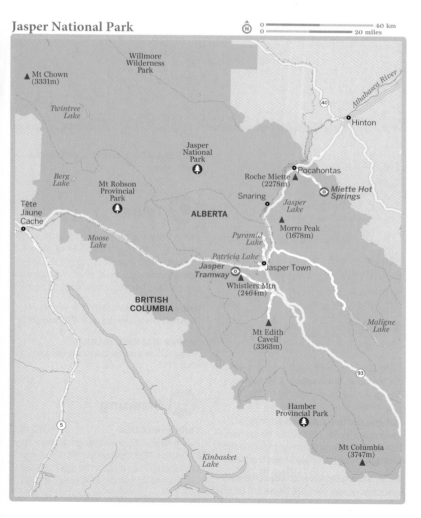

0 ——————— 40 km
0 ——————— 20 miles

Mt Chown (3331m)

Willmore Wilderness Park

Twintree Lake

Jasper National Park

Berg Lake

Mt Robson Provincial Park

Tête Jaune Cache

Moose Lake

BRITISH COLUMBIA

Athabasca River

Hinton

Roche Miette (2278m)

Pocahontas

Miette Hot Springs

Snaring

Jasper Lake

ALBERTA

Morro Peak (1678m)

Pyramid Lake

Patricia Lake

Jasper Tramway

Jasper Town

Whistlers Mtn (2464m)

Maligne Lake

Mt Edith Cavell (3363m)

Hamber Provincial Park

Kinbasket Lake

Mt Columbia (3747m)

Jasper Town

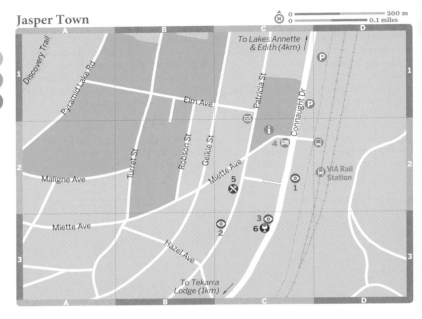

Jasper Town

◎ Sights

1 Brewster Gray Line	C2
Jasper Walks & Talks	(see 3)
2 Maligne Rafting Adventures	C3
Maligne Tours	(see 3)
3 Rocky Mountain River Guides	C3

🛏 Sleeping

4 Whistlers Inn	C2

🍴 Eating

5 Andy's Bistro	C2

🍷 Drinking

6 Jasper Brewing Co	C3

opportunities, from raging to relaxed on the **Maligne**, **Sunwapta** and **Athabasca Rivers**. The season runs from May to September.

Maligne Rafting Adventures (Map p142; www.raftjasper.com; 616 Patricia St; trips from $59) Everything from float trips to class II and III adventures, plus the option of overnight trips.

Rocky Mountain River Guides (Map p142; www.rmriverguides.com; 626 Connaught Dr; trips

from $59) Fun for beginners or experienced river-runners.

👉 Tours

There is a variety of tour companies and booking centers in Jasper. They run a host of tours, including trips to the icefields, train rides, boat rides, wildlife viewing, rafting, horseback riding and more.

BREWSTER GRAY LINE   Sightseeing
(Map p142; www.brewster.ca; 607 Connaught Dr)

JASPER WALKS & TALKS   Hikes
(Map p142; www.walksntalks.com; 626 Connaught Dr)

🛏 Sleeping

TEKARRA LODGE   Hotel $$
(📞 780-852-3058; www.tekarralodge.com; Hwy 93A; d from $169; ⏱ May-Oct; 🅿) The most atmospheric cabins in the park are set next to the Athabasca River amid tall trees and splendid tranquility. Hard-

wood floors, wood-paneled walls plus fireplaces and kitchenettes inspire coziness. It's only 1km from the townsite, but has a distinct backcountry feel.

WHISTLERS INN   Hotel **$$$**
(Map p142; ☎ 780-852-9919; www.whistlersinn .com; cnr Connaught Dr & Miette Ave; r $195; ◙⃝🛇) A central location and above-standard rooms give Whistlers an edge over many of its rivals. The rooftop hot tub alone is worth spending the night for – watch the sun dip behind the hills as the recuperative waters soak away the stress of the day. What more could you ask for?

 Eating & Drinking

ANDY'S BISTRO   Fusion **$$$**
(Map p142; ☎ 780-852-3323; 622 Patricia St; mains from $22; ⏲5-11pm) Following a new trend for fine-dining in outdoor adventure areas (led by Whistler), Andy's is one of two posh Jasper options where you can take off your filthy hiking boots and quaff one of 70 wines. The European-inspired menu (escargot, vol-au-vents, pan-fired veal) has various Indian and Asian inflections.

🍃 JASPER BREWING CO
             Brewery, Pub
(Map p142; www.jasperbrewingco.ca; 624 Connaught Dr) Open since 2005, this brewpub uses glacial water to make its fine ales including the signature Rockhopper IPA or – slightly more adventurous – the Rocket Ridge Raspberry Ale. It's a sit-down affair with TVs and a good food menu.

 **Information**

Jasper Information Centre (www.parkscanada. gc.ca/jasper; 500 Connaught Dr; ⏲8am-7pm Jun-Sep,

9am-4pm Oct-May) Informative office in historic 'parkitecture' building.

🛈 **Getting There & Around**

Car
International car-rental agencies (p359) have offices in Jasper.

Train
VIA Rail (www.viarail.ca) offers tri-weekly train services west to Vancouver ($168, 20 hours) and east to Toronto ($456, 62 hours) via Edmonton. Trains also run tri-weekly to Prince Rupert, BC ($117, 32 hours). Contact the **train station** (607 Connaught Dr) for details.

EDMONTON

POP 730,000

Despite advance publicity regaling everything from dirty oil sands to North America's largest mall, Alberta's often ignored capital is more refined than many outsiders imagine. Count on a

EDMONTON

Having fun at Jasper National Park (p140)
PHILIP & KAREN SMITH

JOSH MCCULLOCH/PHOTOLIBRARY

Don't Miss **Athabasca Glacier**

The best way to experience the Columbia Icefield is to walk on it at the Athabasca Glacier, which almost extends down to the road opposite the Icefields Centre. For that you will need the help of **Athabasca Glacier Icewalks** (📞 780-852-5595, 800-565-7547; www .icewalks.com; Icefield Centre), which supplies all the gear you'll need and a guide to show you the ropes. It offers a three-hour tour (adult/child $60/30, departing 10:40am daily June to September), and a six-hour option ($70/35) on Sundays and Thursdays for those wanting to venture further onto the glacier.

The other far easier (and more popular) way to get on the glacier is via a 'Snocoach' ice tour offered by **Brewster** (📞 877-423-7433; www.brewster.ca; adult/child $49/24; ⏱ tours every 15-30min 9am-5pm May-Oct). For many people this is the defining experience of their Columbia Icefield visit. The large hybrid bus-truck grinds a track onto the ice where it stops to allow you to go for a short walk in a controlled area on the glacier.

large annual calendar of festivals, the redbrick and vaguely bohemian neighborhood of Old Strathcona and a huge swath of riverside parkland that cuts through the downtown district like a pair of green lungs.

 Sights & Activities

ROYAL ALBERTA MUSEUM   Museum
(www.royalalbertamuseum.ca; 12845 102nd Ave; adult/child $10/5; ⏱ 9am-5pm) Edmonton's

leading museum contains numerous exhibits including sections on insects and diamonds, and a lauded display of Alberta's First Nations' culture. The highlight, however, is the 'Wild Alberta' gallery, which splits the province into different geographical zones and displays plants and animals from each.

ART GALLERY OF ALBERTA
Art Gallery
(www.youraga.ca; 2 Sir Winston Churchill Sq; adult/child $12/8; ⏱ 11am-7pm Tue-Fri, 10am-

5pm Sat & Sun, closed Mon) With the opening of this fantastic new art gallery in January 2010, Edmonton at last gained a modern signature building to emulate any great city and doubled the display space of its less-exalted predecessor, the Edmonton Art Gallery. Looking like a giant glass and metal space helmet, the new futuristic structure in Churchill Sq is an exhibit in its own right and houses over 6000 historical and contemporary works of art, many of which have a strong Canadian bias.

Sleeping

MATRIX   Boutique Hotel   **$$**
(☎ 780-429-2861; www.matrixedmonton.com; 10001 107th St; r Mon-Fri $135, Sat & Sun $170; P @ 🛜) One of a triumvirate of Edmonton boutique hotels (along with the Varscona and the Metterra), the Matrix is the new kid on the block (opened in 2007) that claims to serve the 'sophisticated traveler,' with cool minimalist architecture punctuated with woody color accents and plenty of handy modern gadgets. In keeping with its boutique image, there's free wine and cheese every evening at 5:30pm.

VARSCONA   Boutique Hotel   **$$**
(☎ 780-434-6111; www.varscona.com; 8208 106th St, cnr Whyte Ave; r from $145; P @ 🛜) Right in the heart of Old Strathcona, this charming hotel styles itself as 'casually elegant,' suggesting you can roll up either in a tracksuit or a business suit – or some kind of combination of the two. With the coolest neighborhood in town right on the doorstep, your ability to stick your finger on the collective pulse of Edmonton is made all the easier. Breakfast, parking and evening wine and cheese are thrown in to sweeten the deal.

Eating & Drinking

TASTE OF UKRAINE   Ukrainian   **$$**
(www.tasteofukraine.com; 12210 Jasper Ave) There's mum in the kitchen, the eldest son behind the bar, the chatty daughter waiting tables, and dad out back updating the books. Taste of Ukraine is a true family affair and a friendly one at that.

Sweeping aerial view of Edmonton (p143)

MILES ERTMAN/PHOTOLIBRARY

Don't Miss **Maligne Lake**

Almost 50km southeast of Jasper at the end of the road that bears its name, 22km-long Maligne Lake is the recipient of a lot of hype. It is billed as one of the most beautiful lakes within the park and there's no denying its aesthetics: the baby-blue water and a craning circle of rocky, photogenic peaks are feasts for the eyes. Although the north end of the lake is heavy with the summer tour bus brigade, most of the rest of the shoreline is accessible only by foot or boat – hence it's quieter. Numerous campgrounds are available lakeside and are ideal for adventurous kayakers and backcountry hikers. Moose and grizzly bears are also sometimes seen here.

The **Maligne Lake Boathouse** (boat rentals per hr/day $30/90) rents canoes for a paddle around the lake. Not many people paddle all the way to Spirit Island – the lake's most classic view – as it would take all day. If you are really keen to see it, **Maligne Tours** (Map p142; ☎780-852-3370; www.malignelake.com; 627 Patricia St, Jasper; adult/child $55/27.50; ⏰10am-5pm May-Oct) will zip you out there. The company runs a 1½-hour boat tour to the island.

The real test, of course, is the food but you don't need to be a Tolstoy-reading Cossack to realize that the cabbage rolls, sauerkraut, buckwheat, fresh bread and vodka shots are spot on.

DA-DE-O   Cajun **$$**
(www.dadeo.ca; 10548A Whyte Ave; mains $10-16; ⏰11:30am-11pm Mon, Tue & Thu-Sat, noon-10pm Sun, closed Wed) A classic diner-style restaurant serving Cajun food, Da-De-O

competes for the prize of Edmonton's most memorable eating joint. With retro jukeboxes, art-deco lighting and jazz etchings on the wall, the decor is eye-catching and interesting, while the food – oysters, jambalaya and filling po'boys – is the stuff of Louisiana legend. The perennial highlight is the spice-dusted sweet potato fries. Forget the Big Easy. Save yourself the airfare and eat here.

BLACK DOG FREEHOUSE
Pub

(www.blackdog.ca; 10425 Whyte Ave) Insanely popular with all types, the Black Dog is essentially a pub with a couple of hidden extras: a rooftop patio, known as the 'wooftop patio,' with heaters (naturally, this is Alberta), a traditional ground-floor bar (normally packed cheek to jowl on weekday nights), and a basement that features live music and occasional parties. The sum of the three parts has become a rollicking Edmonton institution.

 Entertainment

See and *Vue* are free local alternative weekly papers with extensive arts and entertainment listings. For daily listings, see the *Edmonton Journal* newspaper.

BLUES ON WHYTE
Live Music

(www.bluesonwhyte.ca; 10329 Whyte Ave) This is the sort of place your mother warned you about: dirty, rough, but still somehow cool. It's a great place to check out some live music; blues and rock are the standards here. The small dance floor is a good place to shake a leg.

EDMONTON OILERS
Sports

(www.edmontonoilers.com; tickets from $38.50) The Oilers are the local National Hockey League (NHL) team – the season runs from October to April. Games are played at oft-renamed **Rexall Place** (7424 118th Ave NW), once the stomping ground of 'The Great One,' former ice-hockey pro Wayne Gretzky.

 **Information**

Edmonton Tourism (9990 Jasper Ave; ⊙8am-5pm) Friendly place with tones of flyers and brochures.

Getting There & Away

Air

Edmonton International Airport (YEG; www.edmontonairports.com) is about 30km south of the city along the Calgary Trail, about a 45-minute drive from downtown.

Train

The small **VIA Rail station** (www.viarail.ca; 12360 121st St) is 5km northwest of the city center near Edmonton City Centre Airport. Trains travel east to Toronto and west to Vancouver via Jasper,

Getting Around

To/From the Airport

City buses unfortunately don't make it all the way to the airport, so your best option is to jump on a **Sky Shuttle Airport Service** (www.edmontonskyshuttle.com; adult/child $18/10). It runs three different routes that service hotels in most areas of town, including downtown and the Strathcona area.

West Edmonton Mall

A kitsch lover who is tired of Vegas could still have a field day in **West Edmonton Mall** (www.westedmontonmall.com; 170th St; ⊙10am-9pm Mon-Fri, to 6pm Sat, noon-6pm Sun; 🚻). Not content to simply be a shopping mall, this urban behemoth has the world's largest waterslides, an equipped indoor wave pool, a full-sized amusement park, a skating rink, two (yes, two) minigolf courses, a fake reef with real seals swimming around, a petting zoo, a hotel and 800 stores thrown in as a bonus. Stroll through Chinatown, grab a meal on the delightfully unauthentic Bourbon St, or go for a skate or bungee jump. Then dive into the sea of chain retail shops. The mall is about 8km southwest of the downtown area.

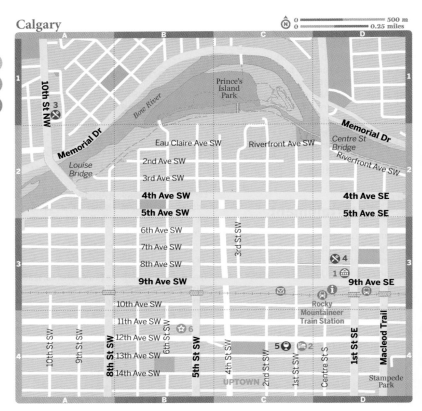

Calgary

⊙ Sights
1 Glenbow Museum D3

🛏 Sleeping
2 Hotel Arts C4

✖ Eating
3 Broken Plate A1
4 Catch D3

🍷 Drinking
5 The Hop in Brew C4

✪ Entertainment
6 Broken City B4

Car & Motorcycle

There is metered parking throughout the city. If you're staying in Old Strathcona, most hotels offer complimentary parking to guests. Edmonton also has public parking lots.

Public Transportation

City buses and a 10-stop tram system – the Light Rail Transit (LRT) – cover most of the city. The fare is $2.75 (day passes $8.25) – check out www.edmonton.ca.

CALGARY

POP 1,065,000

Livable but sometimes characterless, prosperous but economically precarious, super-modern but not always pretty, 21st-century Calgary isn't a place that any unbiased out-of-towner is likely to fall in love with (although the locals can be fanatically loyal). Most visitors either come here on business and deposit their briefcases in one of a plethora of generic business hotels, or arrive in outdoor garb and use it as a springboard for the more alluring attractions of Banff.

Shoehorned among the Stetsons and SUVs of downtown, there's a decent dining scene, an excellent museum, remnants of the 1988 Winter Olympics and – contrary to popular belief – a good public transportation system.

The world-famous **Calgary Stampede** (www.calgarystampede.com; tickets from $24) is held in the second week of July. During this time, civic spirits are on a yearly high with live music, stampede breakfasts and a rowdy party atmosphere.

 ## Sights

HERITAGE PARK HISTORICAL VILLAGE
Historic Park

(www.heritagepark.ab.ca; 1900 Heritage Dr SW at 14th St SW; adult/child $19/14; ⊙9.30am-5pm mid-May–early Sep, 9.30am-5pm Sat & Sun early Sep–mid-Oct) Want to see what Calgary used to look like? Head down to this historical park and step right into the past. With a policy that all buildings within the village are from 1915 or earlier, it really is the opposite of modern Calgary. There are 10 hectares of re-created town to explore, with a fort, grain mill, church, school and lots more.

 ## Sleeping

HOTEL ALMA
Boutique Hotel $$

(☎403-220-3203; www.hotelalma.ca; 169 University Gate NW; r from $129; ☎) Get ready for something different. Operated and run by the University of Calgary and situated on the campus (7km from downtown), the

Alma opened in October 2009 with small Euro-style rooms decked out in boutique fashion and located in an old student residence. Guests get access to all on-campus facilities that include everything from a gym to a florist, plus there's free long-distance phone calls (within North America).

HOTEL ARTS
Boutique Hotel $$$

(☎403-266-4611, 800-661-9378; www.hotelarts.ca; 119 12th Ave SW; ste from $250; P✳@☎⊠) Setting a new standard in Calgary, this boutique hotel plays hard on the fact that it's not part of an international chain. Aimed at the modern discerning traveler with an aesthetic eye, there are hardwood floors, thread counts Egyptians would be envious of, and art on the walls that should be in a gallery.

 ## Eating & Drinking

CATCH
Seafood $$

(☎403-206-0000; www.catchrestaurant.ca; 100 8th Ave SW; mains $17-27) The problem

Action at the Calgary Stampede
RICK RUDNICKI

DAVE PATTINSON/ALAMY

Don't Miss **Glenbow Museum**

For a town with such a short history, Calgary does a fine job in telling it at this commendable **museum** (www.glenbow.org; 130 9th Ave SE; adult/student & youth/senior $14/9/10; ⊙9am-5pm Fri-Wed, to 9pm Thu), which traces the legacy of Calgary and Alberta both pre- and post-oil. Contemporary art exhibitions and stunning artifacts dating back centuries fill its halls and galleries. With an extensive permanent collection and an ever-changing array of traveling exhibitions, there is always something for the history buff, art lover and pop culture fanatic to ponder. The best museum in the province – hands down.

for any saltwater fish restaurant in landlocked Calgary is that, if you're calling it fresh, it can't be local. Overcoming the conundrum, Catch, situated in an old bank building in Stephen St, flies its 'fresh catch' in daily from both coasts. You can work out the carbon-offsets for your lobster, crab and oysters on one of three different floors: an oyster bar, a dining room or an upstairs atrium.

BROKEN PLATE Mediterranean $$
(www.brokenplate.ca; 302 10th St NW; mains from $15) One of three Greek-themed restaurants in the city (all under the same name), this one, in the independently minded neighborhood of Kensington, is the original and best. Excellent pastas,

pizzas and traditional Greek fare are enthusiastically consumed in the open, light-filled dining area. And yes, they break plates to dancing waiters Friday and Saturday nights.

THE HOP IN BREW Pub
(www.hopinbrew.com; 213 12th Ave SW) Imagine if you took an old house, turned it into a dive bar, and then threw a great party every weekend. Tucked down a quiet street just off the main drag, the Hop in Brew has got some style. The converted house has a bar upstairs and down, a pool table up top and winding steps right through the middle. There are good tunes, a grungy atmosphere and plenty on tap.

Entertainment

BROKEN CITY   Music Venue
(www.brokencity.ca; 613 11th Ave SW) If you
fancy a bit of rock and roll and are looking for a club with a 4/4 heartbeat, then
Broken City is your scene. Indie rock, alt
country and punk all do the rounds and
get the crowds going. Gigs are usually on
Thursday and Friday nights.

CALGARY FLAMES   Sports
(☏ 403-777-0000; tickets from $15) Archrival
of the Edmonton Oilers, the Calgary
Flames play ice hockey from October to
April at the **Saddledome (Stampede Park)**.
Make sure you wear red to the game and
head down to 17th Ave afterwards, or the
'Red Mile' as they call it during playoff
time.

ℹ Information

Tourism Calgary (www.tourismcalgary.com; 101
9th Ave SW; ⊙ 8am-5pm) Operates a visitors
center in the base of the Calgary Tower. The
staff will help you find accommodations. It has
booths at the airport.

ℹ Getting There & Away

Calgary International Airport (YYC; www
.calgaryairport.com) is about 15km northeast
of the center off Barlow Trail, a 25-minute drive
away.

Rocky Mountaineer (www.rockymountaineer
.com) runs train tours to Vancouver via Banff.

Winter Road Conditions

For up-to-date road conditions on
the Trans-Canada Hwy and across
the province, consult **DriveBC**
(☏ 800-550-4997; www.drivebc.ca).
This is essential in winter when
storms can close roads for extended
periods.

ℹ Getting Around

To/From the Airport

Sundog Tours (☏ 403-291-9617; tickets adult/
child $15/8) runs every half hour from around
8:30am to 9:45pm between all the major
downtown hotels and the airport.

You can also take bus 57 to the Whitehorn stop
and transfer to the C-Train.

Car & Motorcycle

Parking in downtown Calgary is an absolute
nightmare. Luckily, downtown hotels generally
have garages, and pricey private lots are available
for about $20 per day.

Public Transportation

Calgary Transit (www.calgarytransit.com) is
efficient and clean. You can choose from the
Light Rapid Transit (LRT) rail system, also known
as the C-Train, and ordinary buses.

Toronto, Niagara Falls & Ontario

When it comes to culture, cuisine and sophistication, Ontario is on top of its game. When you're here, you can't help but feel a palpable connection with the rest of the planet. Forget ice fishing, conifers and bears for a minute – this is global Canada, big-city Canada, sexy, progressive, urbane Canada.

Toronto, Canada's largest city, is a blazing metropolis overflowing with multicultural arts, entertainment and eating opportunities. Ottawa, Canada's capital, is no longer a steadfast political filing cabinet: contemporary Ottawa is as hip as you want it to be.

Not far from the madding crowds, low-key agricultural towns and historic settlements define Ontario's country civility. And if you're into wildlife, excellent national parks abound. From north to south you'll find more than enough boreal forests, undulating hills and vineyards to keep you feeling green.

Algonquin Provincial Park (p201) during fall
PHOTOGRAPHER: GARRY BLACK/PHOTOLIBRARY

Pitching at the Rogers Centre (p183), Toronto
KLAUS LANG/PHOTOLIBRARY

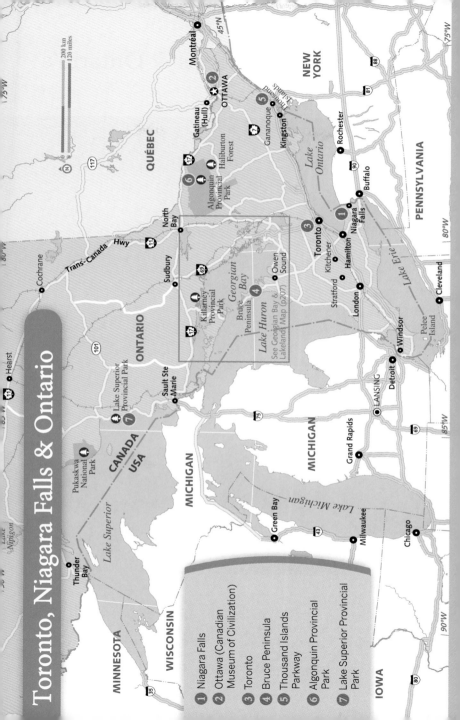

Toronto, Niagara Falls & Ontario

1 Niagara Falls
2 Ottawa (Canadian Museum of Civilization)
3 Toronto
4 Bruce Peninsula
5 Thousand Islands Parkway
6 Algonquin Provincial Park
7 Lake Superior Provincial Park

Toronto, Niagara Falls & Ontario's Highlights

Niagara's Natural Wonders

Of course there's the falls, one of the world's most famous torrents, to ogle. But the Niagara region also struts its pretty stuff with leafy trails and slowpoke backroads to cycle, wooded gorges and nature-reserve paths to hike, and a lush, vineyard-striped landscape to explore.

Need to Know
LEAST CROWDED TIME Around 9am. **SAVINGS TIP** Jump queues and save money with the Great Gorge Adventure Pass. **For further coverage, see p185 and Map p186.**

Niagara Don't Miss List

BY DARLENE ERSKINE, SUPERVISOR
AT TABLE ROCK WELCOME CENTRE
AND LIFELONG NIAGARA AREA RESIDENT

1 QUICK THRILLS

If you're short on time, focus on three things. First, head to Table Rock for a view of the falls right at their brink. At Table Rock you also can experience the 'Fury,' a film and simulation of how the falls were formed, where you feel the ground shake and temperature drop 20°. 'The Journey Behind the Falls' is also here, where you walk right beside the waterfall with just a fence and 6ft to 8ft (2m to 3m) between you and the flow. It's exhilarating.

2 CATCHING A RAINBOW

The most panoramic view of the falls is from Table Rock's upper deck. The best time to see rainbows is in the afternoon, around 3pm.

3 NIAGARA PARKWAY

Winston Churchill called the Niagara Parkway (p189) 'the prettiest Sunday afternoon drive in the world.' Heritage sites pop up all along the 56km road. It's a must-do.

4 FLORAL SHOWHOUSE

Table Rock gets 8 million visitors per year. For a respite from the hustle and bustle, head to the Floral Showhouse (p187) to wander through the exquisite indoor displays of tropical plants. It's free, and an easy 10-minute walk down the road.

5 FREE ACTIVITIES

The park has a **fireworks show** on Wednesday, Friday and Sunday nights at 10pm in summer. The **Botanical Gardens** (p190) at the park's north end are gorgeous and a good place to escape the crowds. And the **Maid of the Mist Plaza** (p190), where the boats dock, is always alive with free music and buskers.

Canadian Museum of Civilization

In one stop: the history of Canada in one museum, plus all-encompassing views of the nation's capital and Parliament. Learn about everything from Aboriginal creation stories to civil rights, Basque whaling ships to Jackrabbit Johannsen, a trailblazing skier. Ottawa has several more museums right out the front door.

Need to Know

LOCATION It's actually in Québec, across the river. **FREE MOBILE APP** Available for iPhone and Blackberry users. **FREE ENTRY** 4pm to 8pm Thursdays. **For further coverage, see p199.**

Canadian Museum of Civilization Don't Miss List

BY VICTOR RABINOVITCH, MUSEUM PRESIDENT AND CEO

1 THE ARCHITECTURE

The building's sinuous design gives the impression of a traditional Haida mask. As you approach you're entering through the mask into the main lobby. The architect, Douglas Cardinal, also was the concept designer behind the Smithsonian's National Museum of the American Indian in Washington DC.

2 THE BALCONY OVERLOOKING THE GRAND HALL

From here you see out huge glass windows toward Parliament and the Rideau Canal. It's breathtakingly beautiful. Look down, and you see the museum's collection of totem poles and Pacific Coast nations' traditional houses. The dual view draws gasps.

3 THE HIDDEN GALLERY

A lot of visitors miss the 'Face to Face' biography hall on the museum's top floor. It's where we depict influential Canadians through artifacts, recordings and multiple points of view. So you might learn about author Mordecai Richler and some of his controversial writings, or Tommy Douglas, the father of Canada's national health system, or Generals Wolfe and Montcalm and their battle on the Plains of Abraham.

4 PICNICKING

We have beautiful lawns and a sculpture display along the river. People picnic out there if the weather is good. For a quiet place to relax inside, head to the end of the Grand Hall — you'll find a semicircular gallery with comfortable seats and lovely river views.

5 OTHER GREAT MUSEUMS WITHIN WALKING DISTANCE

The **Canadian War Museum** (p199) shows how conflict has touched and shaped us. Discount tickets are available since the museum is our partner organization. **The National Gallery** (p197) holds the country's core collection of fine arts. And the **ByWard Market** (p204), while not a museum, is also an easy walk over the bridge and well worth wandering around.

Toronto's Mega Style

A hyperactive stew of cultures and neighborhoods, Toronto (p166) strikes you with sheer urban awe. Will you have dinner in Chinatown or Greektown? Five-star fusion or a peameal bacon sandwich? Designer shoes from Bloor-Yorkville are accessorized with tattoos in Queen West. Mod art galleries, theater par excellence and hockey mania add to the megalo polis, and it's all viewable atop the CN Tower, the Western Hemisphere's highest structure.

Queen St, Toronto

Thousand Islands Parkway

The Thousand Islands Parkway rolls along a pastoral strip by the St Lawrence River where a fog-cloaked constellation of 1800 islands floats. The road offers picture-perfect vistas and dreamy picnic areas, as well as dainty Victoria towns such as Gananoque (p194). Pull over to spend the night at an inn or tak a boat ride through the isles, many of which hold rambling old mansions and castles.

Bruce Peninsula

Thumbing out into the water, with Lake Huron on one side and dreamy Georgian Bay on the other, the Bruce Peninsula (p206) features dramatic cliffs, lighthouses, clapboard villages and dockside fish-and-chip shanties. The Bruce Trail, Ontario's oldest and longest footpath, tracks all the way to Niagara if you're feeling ambitious. Otherwise, it's perfect for a serene day hike. Kayaking and wreck diving also draw visitors to the area. Cove Island lighthouse

Algonquin Provincial Park

Equally accessible from Toronto or Ottawa, lake-riddled Algonquin Provincial Park (p201) is a must-see gem for canoeists, hikers and wildlife-watchers. Moose sightings are common, especially in spring as the beasts flee the woods to escape blackflies. The park also is known for public wolf howls, when groups of people get together and – literally – answer the call of the wild.

Lake Superior Provincial Park

It might not have sky-high mountains or whale sightings like its counterparts east and west, but Lake Superior Provincial Park (p209) offers a landscape every bit as dramatic. Wispy beardlike fog and shivering arctic trees give it a distinctly primeval flavor. Shore-clasping drives and day hikes reward with isolated beaches, spewing waterfalls and mysterious, red-ochre pictographs.

Toronto, Niagara Falls & Ontario's Best…

Dining

○ **The Swan** (p181) Art deco diner to linger over mussels, sandwiches and egg scrambles

○ **ZenKitchen** (p202) Vegan-chic eats from a couple of TV-star chefs

○ **Queen Mother Café** (p180) Spot-on pan-Asian and Canadian comfort food

○ **Sweetgrass Aboriginal Bistro** (p203) Bannock, corn soup, elk and other dishes from the aboriginal kitchen

Art

○ **National Gallery of Canada** (p197) Ottawa's sprawling trove with Rembrandts, Warhols, Canadian and Inuit art

○ **Art Gallery of Ontario** (p172) From rare Québecois religious statuary to the Henry Moore sculpture pavilion

○ **Owen Sound** (p209) Fifty-plus studios pepper the region around this thriving artists' colony

○ **401 Richmond** (p169) A rambling old lithographer's warehouse bursting with mod galleries

Uncommon Museums

○ **Bata Shoe Museum** (p175) Polar boots, crushing clogs and Elton John's bedazzlers rest among the soles

○ **Hockey Hall of Fame** (p169) Skate against Gretzky and hoist the Stanley Cup (virtually, of course)

○ **Daredevil Gallery** (p188) Cautionary tales of what happens when you go over Niagara Falls in a barrel

○ **Canadian War Museum** (p199) Explores human conflict in an admirably nonheroic way

Need to Know

Scenic Parks

o **Lake Superior Provincial Park** (p209) Shore-clasping drives and hikes to mysterious pictographs

o **Pukaskwa National Park** (p210) Wildlife-rich hinterland with only 4km of road

o **Algonquin Provincial Park** (p201) Moose and wolves, and sapphire lakes prime for paddlers

o **Fathom Five National Marine Park** (p206) Lightstations, shipwrecks and eerie, wave-bashed rock formations

Left: Algonquin Provincial Park (p201);
Above: Lake Superior park area (p209)

ADVANCE PLANNING

o **One month before** If it's summer, book accommodation as soon as possible.

o **Two weeks before** Book theater tickets in Toronto, and cycling and paddling excursions in Niagara and other parks.

o **One week before** Make dinner reservations at trendy restaurants where you covet a plateful.

RESOURCES

o **Ontario Tourism** (www.ontariotravel.net) Wide-ranging resource, including activity and accommodation information.

o **Tourism Toronto** (www.seetorontonow.com) Theater listings and accommodation bookings for Canada's biggest city.

o **Niagara Falls Tourism** (www.niagarafallstourism .com) Everything you ever wanted to know about the waterfall and its carnival attractions.

o **Ontario Parks** (www .ontarioparks.com) The low-down for visiting any of the province's 104 parks.

o **Wine Council of Ontario** (www.winesofontario .ca) Information on wines, vineyards and boozy festivals across the province.

o **Now** (www.nowtoronto.com) Music and entertainment listings from Toronto's alt weekly newspaper.

GETTING AROUND

o **Fly** Many visitors arrive via Toronto's Lester B Pearson International Airport, Canada's busiest. Small Toronto City Centre Airport (TCCA) is home to regional airlines. Flights to and from Ottawa often land at TCCA.

o **Car** Extensive highway system links most towns, with all major hire car companies readily available. Surprisingly, no major highway shoots directly between Toronto and Ottawa. The speediest option is to take Hwy 401 from Toronto to Prescott, and use Hwy 416 to complete the L-shaped journey.

o **Train** From Toronto, VIA Rail trains run three times per week to Vancouver via Edmonton, and several times daily to Montréal. There's Amtrak service to/ from New York City.

Toronto, Niagara Falls & Ontario Itineraries

It sure is handy that Toronto sits a mere 140km from Niagara's vineyards and pounding falls. Helpful, too, that Ottawa is a straight shot northeast via pretty islands prime for pit stops.

3 DAYS

TORONTO TO NIAGARA
ALL THINGS BIG

Prime yourself for high times in the neighborhoods of multicultural **(1) Toronto**. Take a rocket ride up the **(2) CN Tower** – as high as Torontonians get without wings or drugs. Have lunch at **(3) St Lawrence Market** – perhaps a peameal bacon sandwich – then head up to **(4) Bloor-Yorkville** to splash some cash in the shops. Compensate by having a thrifty dumpling dinner in **(5) Chinatown**.

On day two check out the amazing **(6) Royal Ontario Museum**, **(7) Hockey Hall of Fame** or **(8) Art Gallery of Ontario** – then take a long lunch in **(9) Baldwin Village**. Afterward, ride the ferry to the

(10) Toronto Islands; hire a bike and wheel away the afternoon. Back on the mainland, relax with a pint at a downtown pub.

On day three, bow down before the power and grace of **(11) Niagara Falls**. Don a raincoat and board the **(12) Maid of the Mist** for a splashy good time, then trundle up the **(13) Niagara Parkway** to Niagara-on-the-Lake to find out what the definition of 'quaint' really is. By now you've noticed signposts for more than a few wineries. Pick one to stop at, sip from the vines and toast your three-day jaunt.

TORONTO TO OTTAWA
ONTARIO'S MAIN VEIN

5 DAYS

Start in **(1) Toronto**, and wallow in the wealth of architecture, museums, restaurants and nightclubs. Consider a day trip to Niagara (see the three-day itinerary).

Pastoral **(2) Prince Edward County** makes a fine pit stop, especially for foodies. The hilly island, attached by bridges to the mainland, is a budding region for new wineries and rustic gourmet restaurants.

Next up: more islands. The misty, mansion-covered **(3) Thousand Islands** dot the St Lawrence River. Victorian **(4) Gananoque**, where you can take boat rides into the archipelago and see castle

turrets poking through the prevailing fog, also makes a good break.

Then it's on to **(5) Ottawa**, Canada's capital. Start at **(6) Parliament Hill** for Kodak moments with the Peace Tower, swap copper towers for shimmering glass spires at the **(7) National Gallery of Canada**, then pause for lunch at the **(8) ByWard Market** where vendors hawk fresh farm produce. Don't forget to see the gorgeous **(9) Canadian Museum of Civilization**. Take in the awesome architecture and the skyline.

Parliament Hill (p195), Ottawa
PHOTOGRAPHER: GLENN VAN DER KNIJFF

Discover Toronto, Niagara Falls & Ontario

Skaters enjoy winter festival event in Toronto
PHOTOGRAPHER: COREY WISE

TORONTO

POP 5.5 MILLION

Polite yet edgy, urban yet green: Toronto is one of those places where you can get it all. A cultural leader, Toronto has a thriving art community and food scene. And while you could spend weeks pin-balling between Toronto's urban virtues, it's a green city too. Parks and natural spaces fill in city gaps, and public transport is top notch.

Toronto is a city driven by the seasons. Dramatic shifts in weather elicit almost schizophrenic behavior from the locals. Washed-out by winter, reticent residents scuttle between doorways to stay out of the April wind – spring here is far from frivolous. Come back in July and it's a whole new ball game: patios overflow with laughing crowds, pubs heave and sway, people play in the parks and along the lakeshore till late. Humidity clogs the avenues and the streetlife hum approaches a roar.

In October, Torontonians have a haunted look – reddening maples bring a tight-lipped, melancholy realization that winter isn't far away. Spanked across the face by bitter February, locals head underground into the PATH network of subterranean walkways. Snowy streets are no place to be – instead it's galleries, coffee shops and cozy pubs. And of course, winter is hockey season!

Toronto's many immigrants play along with this performance, their relocated cultures transforming the city into a hyperactive human stew of ethnic, subcultural and historic districts. Far from ghettos, this patchwork of neighborhoods shapes the city's social agenda and fuels its progress. Overlaid by typically laconic Canadian attitude, Toronto is as unpretentious and tolerant as it is complex.

Sights

Downtown Toronto is an easy-to-navigate grid, bounded by a hodge-podge of bohemian, ethnic and historic neighborhoods. A plethora of Toronto sights – breweries, water parks, sports stadiums, gardens, historic sites – huddle around the Harbourfront and Financial District at the southern end of downtown. Toronto's oldest and best-preserved buildings sit just east of here in the Old York neighborhood. The Toronto Islands are where locals retreat to for a bit of peace and quiet.

North from the lake, modernity and history collide at Dundas Sq: shopping centers, office blocks, museums and majestic theaters all stake their claim. The mixed-bag continues along Yonge St into Bloor-Yorkville and The Annex, where you'll find gracious old mansions, museums, eccentric markets and even a faux castle.

Kensington Market, Little Italy, Queen West and West Queen West are attractions in their own right – multicultural enclaves bubbling with human activity.

Car parking in Toronto is expensive and traffic congestion is an issue; public transportation is usually the best option.

Harbourfront

HARBOURFRONT CENTRE Landmark
(Map p174; ☎ 416-973-4000; www.harbourfrontcentre.com; York Quay, 235 Queens Quay W; ☉box office 1-6pm Tue-Sat, to 8pm show nights; ☐509, 510; Ⓟ) The 4-hectare Harbourfront Centre puts on a kaleido-scopic variety of performing arts events at the **York Quay Centre**; many are kid-focused, some are free. Performances sometimes take place on the covered outdoor concert stage by the lake. Also

outside are a lakeside ice-skating rink where you can slice up the winter ice, and the ramshackle **Artists' Gardens** – seasonally rotating raised planter beds constructed by local artists in the spirit of 'guerilla gardening.' Parking costs $12 to $15.

Don't miss the free galleries, including the **Photo Passage** and the functioning **Craft Studio**.

Power Plant (☎ 416-973-4949; www.thepowerplant.org; adult/child/concession $6/free/3, admission free 5-8pm Wed; ☉noon-6pm Tue-Sun, to 8pm Wed) is a big-reputation gallery celebrating contemporary Canadian art.

TORONTO MUSIC GARDEN Garden
(Map p174; www.harbourfrontcentre.com; 475 Queens Quay W; admission free; ☉dawn-dusk; ☐509, 510) Delicately strung along the western harbourfront, the Toronto Music Garden was designed in collaboration with cellist Yo-Yo Ma. It expresses Bach's *Suite No 1 for Unaccompanied Cello* through landscape, with an arc-shaped grove of conifers, a swirling path through a wildflower meadow and a grass-stepped amphitheater where free concerts are held. Contact the Harbourfront Centre box office for performance schedules and guided tour details.

STEAM WHISTLE BREWING
Historical Building
(Map p174; www.steamwhistle.ca; 255 Bremner Blvd; 45min tour $10; ☉noon-6pm Mon-Thu, from 11am Fri & Sat, to 5pm Sun; Ⓢ Union, ☐509, 510; Ⓟ) 'Do one thing and do it well' is the motto of Steam Whistle Brewing, a microbrewery that makes only a crisp European-style pilsner. Bubbling away in a 1929 train depot, Steam Whistle continually works on being environmentally friendly, in part by using renewable energy, steam heating, all-natural (and often local) ingredients, and super-cool ginger ale bottles that can be reused up to 40 times. During snappy tours of the premises, guides explain the brewing process in great detail. Tours depart half-hourly from 1pm to 5pm and include tastings.

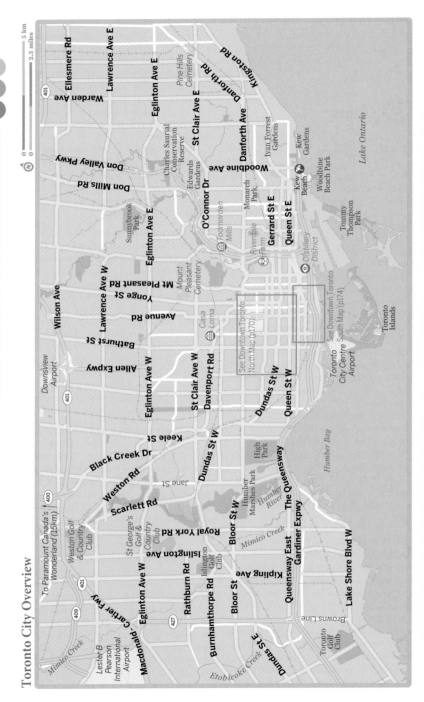

Financial & Entertainment Districts

HOCKEY HALL OF FAME   Museum

(Map p174; ☎ 416-360-7765; www.hhof.com; BCE Pl, 30 Yonge St; adult/child/concession $15/10/12; ☼10am-5pm Mon-Fri, 9:30am-6pm Sat, 10:30am-5pm Sun, 9:30am-6pm Jun-Aug; ⑤Union) Inside an ornate rococo gray stone Bank of Montréal building (c 1885) on the Yonge St lower concourse, the Hockey Hall of Fame gives hockey fans everything they could possibly want. Check out the collection of *Texas Chainsaw Massacre*–esque goalkeeping masks, attempt to stop Wayne Gretzky's virtual shot or have your photo taken with hockey's biggest prize – the hefty Stanley Cup (no trifling shield or pint-sized urn for these boys, oh no). Even visitors unfamiliar with this super-fast, ultraviolent sport will be impressed with the interactive multimedia exhibits and hockey nostalgia.

CLOUD FOREST CONSERVATORY   Garden

(Map p170; ☎ 416-392-7288; admission free; ☼10am-2:30pm Mon-Fri; ⑤Queen) An unexpected sanctuary, the steamy Cloud Forest Conservatory is crowded with enormous jungle leaves, vines and palms. Information plaques answer the question 'What Are Rain Forests?' for temperate Torontonians, distracting accountants from their spreadsheets for a few minutes. It's a great place to warm up during winter, but avoid the area after dark – the adjacent park attracts some pretty lewd types. It's between Richmond and Temperance Sts, west of Yonge St.

FREE TORONTO DOMINION GALLERY OF INUIT ART   Museum

(Map p174; ☎ 416-982-8473; ground fl & mezzanine, Maritime Life Tower, 79 Wellington St W; ☼8am-6pm Mon-Fri, 10am-4pm Sat & Sun; ⑤St Andrew) An unexpectedly calm sanctuary in the bustle of the Financial District, the Toronto Dominion Gallery of Inuit Art provides an exceptional insight into Inuit culture. Inside the Toronto-Dominion Centre, a succession of glass cases displays otter, bear, eagles and carved Inuit figures in day-to-day scenes.

401 RICHMOND   Art Gallery

(Map p170; www.401richmond.net; 401 Richmond St W; ☼Tue-Sat; 🚌510) Inside an early-20th-century lithographer's warehouse, restored in 1994, the 18,500-sq-m 401 Richmond bursts forth with 130 diverse contemporary art and design galleries displaying the heartfelt works of painters, architects, photographers, printmakers, sculptors and publishers. The original floorboards creak between the glass elevator, ground-floor cafe, leafy courtyard and rooftop garden. A new lounge space livens things up. Check the website for events and tours.

CANADIAN BROADCASTING CENTRE   Museum

(CBC; Map p174; ☎ 416-205-3311; www.cbc.ca; 250 Front St W; ☼museum & theater Mon-Fri; ⑤Union, 🚌504) Toronto's enormous Canadian Broadcasting Centre is the headquarters for English-language radio and TV across Canada. French-language production is in Montréal, which leaves the president (in a truly Canadian spirit of compromise) stranded in Ottawa.

You can peek at the radio newsrooms anytime or attend a concert in the world-class Glenn Gould Studio. Don't miss the miniature-sized **CBC Museum** with its amazing collection of antique microphones (the 1949 RCA 74DX is a doozy!), sound-effects machines, tape recorders and puppets from kids' TV shows. Next door the **Graham Spry Theatre** screens ever-changing CBC programming.

Queen Street & Dundas Square

CITY HALL   Historical Building

(Map p170; ☎ 311, 416-392-2489; www.toronto.ca; 100 Queen St W; admission free; ☼8:30am-4:30pm Mon-Fri; ⑤Queen; Ⓟ) The much-maligned City Hall was Toronto's bold leap of faith into architectural modernity. Its twin clamshell towers, flying-saucer central structure, sexy ramps and funky mosaics were completed in 1965 to Finnish architect Viljo Revell's award-winning design. An irritable Frank

DISCOVER TORONTO, NIAGARA FALLS & ONTARIO TORONTO

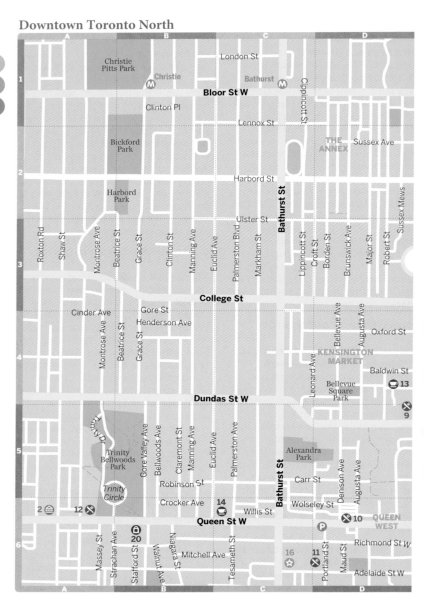

Lloyd Wright called it a 'headmarker for a grave'; in a macabre twist, Revell died before construction of the building was finished.

Collect a self-guided tour pamphlet at the information desk; don't miss the geeky 1:1250 Toronto scale model in the lobby. Parking here costs $13.

Out the front is **Nathan Phillips Square**, a meeting place for skaters, demonstrators and office workers on their lunch breaks. In summer, look

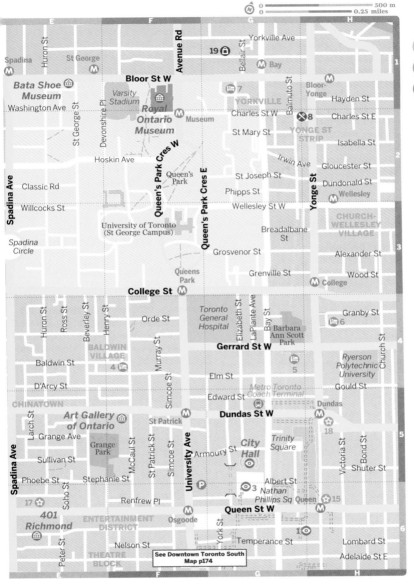

for the **Fresh Wednesdays farmers' market** (⏰10am-2:30pm), free concerts and special events. The fountain pool becomes an ice-skating rink in winter.

North of Dundas Sq, the Yonge St Strip falls between College and Bloor Sts,

peppered with sex shops, cheap eateries and strip clubs. One block east is Church St, Toronto's gay quarter. The rainbow flag–festooned Church-Wellesley Village centers on the intersection of Church and Wellesley Sts.

Chinatown & Baldwin Village

ART GALLERY OF ONTARIO
                                    Art Gallery

(AGO; Map p170; ☎ 416-979-6648, 877-225-4246; www.ago.net; 317 Dundas St W; adult/child/concession/family $19.50/11/16/49, admission free 6-8:30pm Wed; ☺10am-5:30pm Tue, to 8:30 Wed, to 5:30 Thu-Su; ☒505) The AGO houses art collections both excellent and extensive (bring your stamina). Extensive renovations, designed by Frank Gehry, were completed in 2008, and include a new entrance and a massive glass and wood facade. Other highlights include rare Québecois religious statuary, First Nations and Inuit carvings, major Canadian works by the Group of Seven, the Henry Moore sculpture pavilion, and a restored Georgian house called **The Grange**. There's a surcharge for special exhibits.

While you're in the 'hood, note that TIFF Cinematheque screens movies at the AGO's Jackman Hall.

Kensington Market & Little Italy

Tattered around the edges, elegantly wasted Kensington Market is multicultural Toronto at its most authentic. Eating here is an absolute joy, and shopping is a blast. The streets are full of artists, dreadlocked urban hippies, tattooed punks, potheads, junkies, dealers, bikers, goths, musicians and anarchists. Shady characters on bicycles whisper their drug menus as they glide by; hooch and Hendrix tinge the air.

Further along College St, Little Italy is an established trendsetting strip of outdoor cafes, hip bars and stylish restaurants that are almost always changing hands – the affluent clientele is notoriously fickle. The further west you go, the more traditional things become, with aromatic bakeries, sidewalk *gelaterias* and rootsy *ristoranti*.

Queen West & West Queen West

MUSEUM OF CONTEMPORARY CANADIAN ART   Museum

(MOCCA; Map p170; ☎ 416-395-0067; www.mocca.ca; 952 Queen St W; admission by donation; ☺11-6pm Tue-Sun; ☒501; Ⓟ) The MOCCA is the city's only museum mandated to collect works by living Canadian and international visual artists. West Queen

Downtown Toronto North

SEAN CAFFREY

Don't Miss **CN Tower**

Though it's been around for more than 30 years, the funky **CN Tower** (Canadian National Tower, La Tour CN; Map p174; www.cntower.ca; 301 Front St W; adult/child $23/15; ⊙9am-10pm Sun-Thu, to 10:30pm Fri & Sat, to 11pm summer; ⓢUnion) still warrants 'icon' status. Its primary function is as a radio and TV communications tower, but relieving tourists of as much cash as possible seems to be the next order of business. It's expensive, but riding the great glass elevators up the highest freestanding structure in the Western Hemisphere (553m) is one of those things in life you just *have* to do. On a clear day, the views from the Observation Deck are astounding; if it's hazy, you won't see a thing. Beware: two million visitors each year means summer queues for the elevator can be up to two hours long – going up *and* coming back down. For those with reservations and sacks of cash, the award-winning revolving restaurant **360°** (☎416-362-5411; mains $32-65; ⊙dinner, lunch & dinner summer) awaits, with 'the world's highest wine cellar'. Elevator price is free for diners.

West has consolidated as an arts and design precinct – the perfect location for this facility. Permanent holdings only number about 400 works, curated since 1985, but award-winning temporary exhibitions promote emerging artists from Nova Scotia to British Columbia.

Bloor-Yorkville & University of Toronto

ROYAL ONTARIO MUSEUM Museum (ROM; Map p170; ☎416-586-8000; www.rom.on.ca; 100 Queen's Park; adult/child/concession $20/14/17; ⊙10am-6pm Sat-Thu, to 9:30pm Fri; ⓢMuseum) The multidisciplinary ROM was already Canada's biggest natural history museum, even before embarking upon the 'Renaissance ROM' building project, which should be complete by the time you read this. The new work involves a magnificent explosion of architectural crystals on Bloor St, housing an array of new galleries.

ROM's collections bounce between natural science, ancient civilization and art exhibits. The Chinese temple

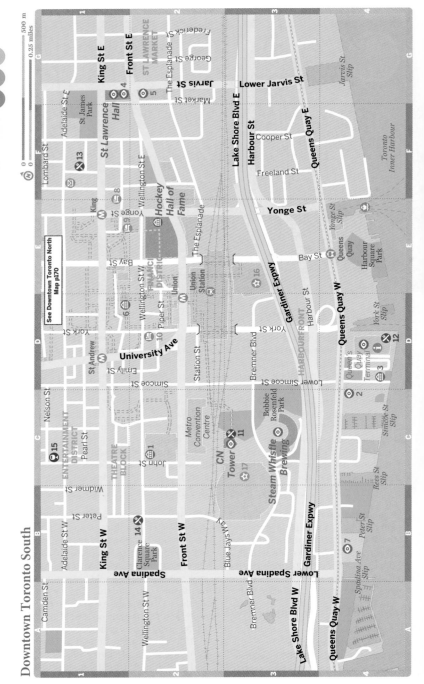

Downtown Toronto South

500 m
0.25 miles

See Downtown Toronto North
Map p170

**ENTERTAINMENT
DISTRICT**

**THEATRE
BLOCK**

**FINANCIAL
DISTRICT**

HARBOURFRONT

Camden St
Adelaide St W
King St W
Wellington St W
Front St W
Spadina Ave
Lower Spadina Ave
Queens Quay W
Lake Shore Blvd W
Gardiner Expwy
Bremner Blvd
Blue Jays Way
Peter St
Widmer St
John St
Nelson St
Pearl St
Clarence
Square
Park
Metro
Convention
Centre
CN
Tower
Steam Whistle
Brewing
Bobbie
Rosenfeld
Park
Spadina Ave
Slip
Peter St
Slip
Rees St
Slip
Simcoe St
Slip
York St
Slip
Yonge St
Slip
Jarvis St
Slip
Queens Quay W
Gardiner Expwy
Lake Shore Blvd W
Bremner Blvd
Lower Simcoe St
Simcoe St
Emily St
University Ave
St Andrew
Bay St
York St
Station St
Union
Station
The Esplanade
Union
Bay St
Yonge St
King
Wellington St W
Piper St
Wellington St E
Wellington St E
Lombard St
Adelaide St E
King St E
Front St E
FREDERICK St
George St
The Esplanade
Jarvis St
Market St
ST LAWRENCE
MARKET
St Lawrence
Hall
St James
Park
St Lawrence
Hockey
Hall of
Fame
The Esplanade
Yonge St
Lake Shore Blvd E
Harbour St
Cooper St
Freeland St
Queens Quay E
Lower Jarvis St
Harbour St
Queens Quay E
Bay St
Queens
Quay
Harbour
Square
Park
Queen's
Quay
Terminal
Gardiner Expwy
York St
Toronto
Inner Harbour

15
1
17
11
14
6
10
8
9
13
5
4
16
7
2
3
12

sculptures, **Gallery of Korean Art** and costumery and textile collections are some of the best in the world. Kids file out of yellow school buses chugging by the sidewalk and rush to the dinosaur rooms, Egyptian mummies and Jamaican bat-cave replica. Don't miss the cedar **crest poles** carved by First Nations tribes in British Columbia. The on-site **Institute of Contemporary Culture** explores current issues through art, architecture, lectures and moving image. There are free museum tours daily; call or check the website for times. There's a surcharge for special exhibits.

BATA SHOE MUSEUM   Museum
(Map p170; ☎ 416-979-7799; www.batashoemu seum.ca; 327 Bloor St W; adult/child/concession/family $12/4/10/30, admission free 5-8pm Thu; ☺10am-5pm Tue, Wed, Fri & Sat, to 8pm Thu, noon-5pm Sun; ⑤ St George) It's important in life to be well shod, a stance the Bata Shoe Museum takes seriously. Designed by architect Raymond Moriyama to re-semble a stylized shoebox, the museum displays over 10,000 'pedi-artifacts' from around the globe. Peruse some 19th-century French chestnut-crushing clogs, aboriginal Canadian polar boots

or famous modern pairs worn by Elton John, Indira Gandhi and Pablo Picasso. Permanent and rotating exhibits cover the evolution of shoemaking, with a focus on how shoes have signified social status throughout human history.

CASA LOMA   Historical Building
(Map p168; ☎ 416-923-1171; www.casaloma .org; 1 Austin Tce; adult/child/concession $19/10.50/13.60; ☺9:30am-5pm, last entry 4pm; ⑤ Dupont; ℗) The mock medieval Casa Loma lords over The Annex on a cliff that was once the shoreline of the glacial Lake Iroquois, from which Lake Ontario derived. Climb the 27m **Baldwin Steps** up the slope from Spadina Ave, north of Davenport Rd.

The eccentric 98-room mansion – a crass architectural orgasm of castellations, chimneys, flagpoles, turrets and Rapunzel balconies – was built between 1911 and 1914 for Sir Henry Pellat, a wealthy financier who made bags of cash from his exclusive contract to provide Toronto with electricity. He later lost everything in land speculation, the resultant foreclosure forcing Hank and his wife to move out. The castle briefly reopened as a luxury hotel, but

Downtown Toronto South

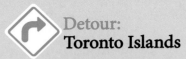

Detour:
Toronto Islands

Once upon a time there were no Toronto Islands, just an immense sandbar stretching 9km into the lake. On April 13, 1858, a hurricane blasted through the sandbar and created the gap now known as the Eastern Channel. Toronto's jewel-like islands were born – nearly two-dozen isles covering 240 hectares. When you visit the close-knit, 800-strong artistic communities on gorgeous **Algonquin Island** and **Ward's Island**, expect to feel pangs of jealousy.

The islands are only accessible by a 15-minute ferry ride. From April to September, **Toronto Islands Ferries** (✆ 416-392-8193; www.city.toronto.on.ca/parks/island/ferry.htm; adult/child/concession $6/2.50/3.50) run every 15 to 30 minutes from 8am to 11pm. Queues can be long on weekends and holidays – show up early. From October to March, ferry services are slashed (roughly hourly), only servicing Ward's Island, plus a couple per day to Hanlan's Point. The Toronto Islands Ferry Terminal is at the foot of Bay St, off Queens Quay (see Map p174).

its big-band nightclub attracted more patrons than the hotel did, and it too failed. Parking here costs $3/9 per hour/day.

Tours

Walking & Cycling

The easiest way to experience Toronto is on foot, though cycling tours allow you to cover a bit more territory.

FREE **ROMWalks**   Walking Tours
(✆ 416-586-8097; www.rom.on.ca; ☾ Wed & Sun evenings May-Sep) Volunteers from the Royal Ontario Museum lead one- to two-hour historical and architectural walking tours, rain or shine.

A Taste of the World   Walking Tours
(✆ 416-923-6813; www.torontowalksbikes.com; 2-3½hr tours $25-45) Quirky, well-qualified guides lead offbeat walking and cycling tours of Toronto's nooks and crannies, usually with a foodie focus. Reservations recommended.

FREE **Heritage Toronto**   Walking Tours
(✆ 416-338-3886; www.heritagetoronto.org; ☾ weekends May-Sep) Excellent historical, cultural and nature walks led by museum experts and neighborhood historical society members last from one to three hours.

Reservations not required. You can also download an audio tour from the website.

 Sleeping

Hold onto your wallets, this is gonna get ugly... Finding good-value accommodations in Toronto will be the most difficult and expensive part of your trip. Reservations outside of winter are mandatory – decent options are full every night from Victoria Day (around mid-May) through to the last vestiges of summer. Booking ahead also limits the sting of many places charging double or triple the off-peak rates during summer and major festivals. Some hostels, guesthouses and B&Bs don't charge tax, but hotels always do.

Downtown Toronto offers historic hotels, boutique digs and lakefront properties. It can be pricey here, but you don't have to spend all your dough to be close to the action. Guesthouses and B&Bs are prolific in eastern Toronto and the Church-Wellesley Village. Budget beds are harder to find, but there are some top-quality youth hostels around town.

Toronto's thriving B&B industry caters to most budgets. Reliable agencies:

Bed & Breakfast Homes of Toronto B&B
(☎416-363-6362; www.bbcanada.com/associations/toronto2) Anything from modest family homes to deluxe suites.

Downtown Toronto Association of Bed and Breakfast Guest Houses B&B
(☎416-483-8032; www.bnbinfo.com) Rooms in various neighborhoods, mostly in renovated Victorian houses.

Toronto Bed & Breakfast Reservation Service B&B
(☎705-738-9449, 877-922-6522; www.torontobandb.com) The oldest agency in town with a dozen central listings.

Financial & Entertainment Districts

HOTEL VICTORIA   Boutique Hotel $$
(Map p174; ☎ 416-363-1666, 800-363-8228; www.hotelvictoria-toronto.com; 56 Yonge St; d $134-164; S King; ⊖✳🤝) The early-20th-century Victoria is one of Toronto's best small downtown hotels. Refurbished, it maintains a few old-fashioned features, including a fine lobby and a warm welcome at the 24-hour reception desk. Rates include health club privileges.

COSMOPOLITAN
                    Boutique Hotel $$$
(Map p174; ☎ 416-945-5455, 866-852-1777; www.cosmotoronto.com; 8 Colborne St; ste from $228; S King; P⊖✳🤝) Sleek and quiet, with only five rooms per floor, this Asian-inspired hotel oozes calm. Suites have lake views, bedroom-sized showers and CD

players tinkling meditation music. Both the spa and downstairs wine bar, Eight, will further ease your sink into relaxation. Parking is $33.

STRATHCONA HOTEL   Hotel $$
(Map p174; ☎ 416-363-3321, 800-268-8304; www.thestrathconahotel.com; 60 York St; d from $125; S St Andrew; ⊖✳🤝) With many refurbished rooms (and more on the way), this 65-year-old hotel is unpretentious and reasonably priced for its downtown location. Downstairs, a pub and cafe offer good deals on grub.

SOHO METROPOLITAN HOTEL
                  Boutique Hotel $$$
(Map p174; ☎ 416-599-8800; www.soho.metropolitan.com; 318 Wellington St W; d from $475; 🚌510; P✳🤝🏊) Have a seat in the lap of luxury. With heated floors in the bathrooms, private dressing rooms, floor-to-ceiling windows and top-end linens, you'll have all the pampering you can handle. The excellent Sen5es restaurant is right downstairs. Parking here costs $30.

Queen Street & Dundas Square

LES AMIS BED & BREAKFAST B&B $$
(Map p170; ☎ 416-928-0635; www.bbtoronto.com; 31 Granby St; s/d with shared bathroom incl breakfast from $90/125; S College; P⊖✳🤝) Run by a multilingual Parisian couple, this cheery B&B offers full, gourmet vegetarian (or vegan) breakfasts. Colorful rooms are adorned with the owners' art, and a leafy back deck is a great spot to chill out. It's a short walk from the Eaton Centre. Parking costs $10.

Toronto's Top Vegetarian

Meat-free restaurants in Toronto run the gamut from gourmet to gourmet greasy spoon. Here's a couple for you to start out with.

Fressen (Map p170; ☎416-504-5127; 478 Queen St W; mains $10-14; ⏰dinner Mon-Fri, brunch Sat & Sun; 🍴; 🚌501)

Sadie's Diner (Map p170; 504 Adelaide St W; mains $7-10; ⏰breakfast & lunch daily, dinner Wed-Sat; 🍴; 🚌504, 511)

DELTA CHELSEA TORONTO DOWNTOWN
Hotel **$$**

(Map p170; 416-595-1975, 800-268-1133; www
.deltahotels.com; 33 Gerrard St W; d/ste from
$100/250; College;) With
nearly 1600 rooms, Toronto's largest and
arguably best-value hotel caters to all
people. If you're with kids, you'll like the
apartment-style family suites and indoor
waterslide. Prices vary with season and
day of the week. Parking costs from $27.

Chinatown & Baldwin Village
BALDWIN VILLAGE INN
B&B **$$**

(Map p170; 416-591-5359; www.baldwininn
.com; 9 Baldwin St; d with shared bathroom
$85-105; 505, 506;) This yellow-
painted B&B plugs a gap in the local
Baldwin Village market. Facing a leafy
street filled with dim sum cafes and art
galleries, the front courtyard is perfect
for lounging about.

Bloor-Yorkville
WINDSOR ARMS
Boutique Hotel **$$$**

(Map p170; 416-971-9666; www.windsor
armshotel.com; 18 St Thomas St; ste from $300;
Bay;) The Windsor Arms is
an exquisite piece of Toronto history –
stay the night or drop in for afternoon
tea. It's a 1927 neo-Gothic mansion
boasting a grand entryway, stained-
glass windows, polished service and its
own coat of arms. When we visited, the
swish establishment was ready to open
a Russian tearoom, where ornate service
costs $85. Parking is $35.

 Eating

Executive diners file into classy restau-
rants in the Financial District and Old
York, while eclectic, affordable eateries

Gay & Lesbian Toronto

To say Toronto is G&L-friendly is understating things just a tad. 'Gay is the new
straight' is closer to the mark! During Pride Toronto, about a million visitors
descend on the city. The focus of the action is the Church-Wellesley Village, or
simply the 'Gay Village.' Spread along Church St north and south of Wellesley
St E is a busy commercial strip that draws mustachioed crowds, promenading
and people-watching. Other gay-focused neighborhoods include The Annex,
Kensington Market, Queen West and Cabbagetown.

Gay nightlife venues are abundant and although men's bars and clubs vastly
outnumber lesbian venues, Toronto is also home to drag kings, women-only
bathhouse nights and lesbian reading series.

In 2003 Toronto became the first city in North America to legalize same-sex
marriage; apply at **City Hall** (Map p170; 416-392-7036; www.toronto.ca/registry
-services; 100 Queen St W; license $110; 8:30am-4:15pm Mon-Fri; Queen). In September
2004 an Ontario Court also recognized the first legal same-sex divorce.

See p345 for Canada-wide G&L resources. Helpful Toronto resources:

519 Community Centre (416-392-6874; www.the519.org; 519 Church St; 9am-10pm
Mon-Fri, to 5pm Sat, 10am-5pm Sun; Wellesley)

Canadian Lesbian & Gay Archives (416-777-2755; www.clga.ca; 34 Isabella St; 7:30-
10pm Tue-Thu; Wellesley)

Queer West (www.queerwest.org) Info on west Toronto's gay scene.

Xtra! Free G&L alternative weekly.

BARRETT & MACKAY/PHOTOLIBRARY

fill Baldwin Village, Kensington Market, Queen West and the Yonge St Strip. More ethnically consistent are Little Italy, Greektown (The Danforth), Little India and Chinatown.

Harbourfront

IL FORNELLO   Italian $$
(Map p174; ☎ 416-861-1028; 207 Queen's Quay W; mains $12-24; ⊙11:30am-1am Mon-Fri, from 5pm Sat & Sun; ⌕509, 510) One of five Il Fornellos in Toronto, this insider's favorite is popular not only for its seafood-favoring menu but also its 200-seat patio overlooking Lake Ontario. If you're not fancying fish, there are plenty of other options, including gourmet pizza. We like the fig pizza: mascarpone, figs, honey and prosciutto are a few of the delicious ingredients. Delightful.

Financial & Entertainment Districts

MERCATTO   Italian $$
(Map p174; ☎ 416-306-0467; 330 Bay St; meals $8-14; ⊙Mon-Fri; ⑤King) One of an effervescent string of Italian deli-cafes, Mercatto serves up creative panini, pasta, risotto, frittata and pizza dishes

at a central dining bench beneath entirely out-of-place chandeliers. Espresso in the morning or wine at night; dine in or take out: you've got options.

BYMARK   Fusion $$$
(Map p174; ☎ 416-777-1144; Toronto-Dominion Centre, 66 Wellington St W; mains $34-50; ⊙lunch & dinner Mon-Fri, dinner Sat; ⑤St Andrew) Celebrity chef Mark McEwan of North 44° brings his sophisticated menu of continentally hewn cuisine to this hip, bi-level downtowner. His creative kitchen crew whips seasonal regional ingredients (wild truffles, quail, soft-shell crab) into sensational combinations, each with suggested wine or beer pairings. It's on street level.

SEN5ES   Fusion $$$
(Map p174; ☎ 416-935-0400; 318 Wellington St W; breakfast & lunch $5-17, dinner $32-45; ⊙7am-2pm daily, 6-11pm Tue-Sat, lounge 5pm-1am daily; ⌕510) Sen5es' sun-drenched, airy cafe serves breakfast (try an impeccable cappuccino and chocolate croissant), while the sleek modern dining room harbors a chef's table and nocturnal offerings like goat cheese and beef ravioli or seared scallops with citrus salad and curry

179

CHRIS CHEADLE/PHOTOLIBRARY

Don't Miss **St Lawrence Market**

Old York's sensational **St Lawrence Market** (Map p174; 📞 416-392-7129; www.stlawrencemarket .com; 95 Front St E; ⏱8am-6pm Tue-Thu, to 7pm Fri, 5am-5pm Sat; 🚌503, 504; **P**) has been a neighborhood meeting place for over two centuries. The restored, high-trussed 1845 **South Market** houses more than 50 specialty food stalls: cheese vendors, fishmongers, butchers, bakers and pasta makers. Inside the old council chambers upstairs, the **St Lawrence Market Gallery** (📞 416-392-7604; admission free; ⏱10am-4pm Wed-Fri, 9am-4pm Sat) has rotating displays of paintings, photographs, documents and historical relics.

On the opposite side of Front St, the dull-looking **North Market** is redeemed by a Saturday farmers' market and a Sunday antique market (get there at dawn – literally – for the good stuff). Neglected for decades, it was rebuilt around the time of Canada's centenary in 1967. A few steps further north, the glorious **St Lawrence Hall** (1849) is topped by a mansard roof and a copper-clad clock tower that can be seen for blocks.

Parking at the market costs $2 to 6.

---

yoghurt. Alternatively, dine in the lounge to sample from the same amazing menu for under $25 per plate.

Queen Street & Chinatown
QUEEN MOTHER CAFÉ
Fusion $$

(📞 416-598-4719; 208 Queen St W; mains $9-18; ⏱11:30am-1am Mon-Sat, to 11pm Sun; **S**Osgoode) A Queen St institution, the Queen Mother is beloved for its cozy, dark wooden booths and excellent pan-

Asian menu. Canadian comfort food is also on offer – try the Queen Mum burger. Check out the display of old stuff the owners found in the walls the last time they renovated. The patio is hidden and one of the best you'll find in the city.

DUMPLING HOUSE RESTAURANT
Chinese $

(Map p170; 328 Spadina Ave; 12 dumplings $4-6; ⏱lunch & dinner; 🚌510) Watch dumplings being rolled in the window, then walk right in, sit right down and order a steaming mass of them. Impale steamed or pan-fried pork, chicken, beef, seafood or vegetarian dumplings on your chopsticks, dunk them in soy sauce and dispense with them forthwith.

Yonge Street Strip

7 WEST CAFÉ   Cafe $$
(Map p170; ☎ 416-928-9041; 7 Charles St W; mains $9-15; ⏱24hr; **S**Bloor-Yonge) Three floors of moody lighting, textured jade paint, framed nudes, wooden church pews and jaunty ceiling angels set the scene for a dazzling selection of pizzas, pastas and sandwiches, and 24-hour breakfasts. Make like a vampire sipping blood-red wine as the moon dapples shadows across the street.

Queen West & West Queen West

THE SWAN   Cafe $$
(Map p170; 892 Queen St W; mains $18-13; ⏱noon-10pm Mon-Fri, from 10am Sat & Sun; 🚋501) This art-deco diner features a small and deceptively simple menu, with items like smoked oyster with pancetta and egg scrambles, club sandwiches, and mussels that sit iced in a vintage Coca-Cola cooler. The coffee is divine, and it's a great place to sit at the counter and read the paper on a rainy Sunday.

 **Drinking**

The following pubs open at 11am and stay open until 2am. Bars keep serving until 2am too, but don't generally open their doors until around 4pm.

C'EST WHAT   Pub
(67 Front St E; 🚋503, 504) Over 30 whiskeys and six dozen Canadian microbrews (mostly from Ontario) are on hand

at this underground pub. An in-house brewmaster tightly edits the all-natural, preservative-free beers on tap. There's live music most nights at the Music Showbar next door. There's good grub as well – the menu encompasses all-local meats, including peameal bacon from St Lawrence Market next door as well as free-range bison (mains about $10 to $15).

SMOKELESS JOE   Bar
(Map p174; ☎ 416-728-4503; 125 John St; 🚋501) Buried below street level in Clubland, this narrow where-everybody-knows-your-name bar sells over 250 different types of beer (the menu is a book). Some of the rarest brews aren't sold in stores, so stop by for a pint or three. It was one of the first places in TO to ban smoking. Thanks, Joe.

 Entertainment

To stay attuned to club, alt-culture and live-music options, scan the city's free street press: *Now*, *Xtra!* and *Eye Weekly*.

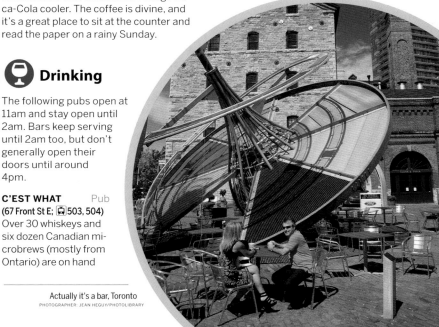

Actually it's a bar, Toronto
PHOTOGRAPHER: JEAN HEGUY/PHOTOLIBRARY

Toronto for Children

Special events for children take place throughout the year in Toronto; the Harbourfront Centre produces ongoing events through HarbourKIDS.

Climb a rock wall, journey to the center of a human heart, catch a criminal with DNA fingerprinting and race an Olympic bobsled at the excellent, interactive **Ontario Science Centre** (www.ontariosciencecentre.ca; 770 Don Mills Rd; Science Centre adult/child/concession $18/11/13.50, Omnimax $12/8/9, combined ticket $25/15/19; ⏰10am-7pm; P). Over 800 high-tech exhibits and live demonstrations wow the kids (and the adults pretending not to be interested). Also here is the giant domed Omnimax Cinema. To get here, take the subway to Eglinton then bus 34, or Pape then bus 25.

The interactive exhibits at the **Royal Ontario Museum** (p173) are also fabulous.

During summer keep 'em occupied at **Paramount Canada's Wonderland** (www.canadas-wonderland.com; 9580 Jane St, Vaughan; day pass adult/child/concession $55/32/32; ⏰10am-10pm Jun-Aug, Sat & Sun only late Apr-late May & early Sep-early Oct; P), a state-of-the-art amusement park with over 60 rides. Highlights include some lunch-losing roller coasters, an exploding volcano, a 20-hectare Splash Works water park, and the Fantastic World of Hanna-Barbera for the young 'uns. Queues can be lengthy; most rides operate rain or shine. Wonderland is a 45-minute drive northwest of downtown Toronto on Hwy 400. Exit at Rutherford Rd, 10 minutes north of Hwy 401.

A handy online resource for parents is www.helpwevegotkids.com, which lists everything child-related in Toronto, including babysitters and day-care options.

The daily newspapers also provide weekly entertainment listings.

Ticketmaster (☎416-870-8000; www.ticketmaster.ca) sells tickets for major concerts, sports games, theater and performing arts events. **TO Tix** (Map p170; ☎416-536-6468, ext 40; www.totix.ca; Dundas Sq, 1 Dundas St E; ⏰noon-6:30pm Tue-Sat; S Dundas) sells half-price and discount same-day 'rush' tickets. **TicketKing** (☎416-872-1212, 800-461-3333; www.mirvish.com) represents several venues in town, including various theaters.

RIVOLI Live Music
(Map p170; www.rivoli.ca; 334 Queen St W; 🚋501) Songbird Feist got her start here, and the talent keeps rolling in. Nightly live music (rock, indie and solo singer-songwriters), weekly stand-up comedy and monthly hip-hop nights are all part of the line-up. CD launches, art shows and Saturday-night DJs complete the renaissance picture. There's also a pool hall, and the food is fabulous!

GLENN GOULD STUDIO Live Music
(Map p174; ☎416-205-5555; www.cbc.ca/glenngould; Canadian Broadcasting Centre, 250 Front St W; tickets $15-40; ⏰box office 2-6:30pm Mon-Fri, to 8pm Sat; S Union, 🚋504) Glenn Gould Studio's acoustics do the name-sake famous pianist honors. Purchase advance tickets for evening concerts of classical and contemporary music by soloists, chamber groups, choirs and sinfonia between September and June. Young international artists are often featured.

FACTORY THEATRE Theater
(Map p170; ☎416-504-9971; www.factorytheatre.ca; 125 Bathurst St; ⏰box office 1-7pm

Tue-Sat; 511) This innovative theater company – 'Home of the Canadian Playwright' – has been busy for more than 35 years. The independent **Summer-Works Theatre Festival** (416-504-7529; www.summerworks.ca) stages plays at the Factory Theatre too, as do performers from the Toronto Fringe Festival. Sunday matinees are on a 'Pay What You Can' basis.

TORONTO BLUE JAYS   Sports
(416-341-1234; www.toronto.bluejays.mlb.com; regular season Apr-Sep) Toronto's Major League Baseball team plays at the **Rogers Centre** (Map p174; 416-341-2770; www.rogerscentre.com; 1 Blue Jays Way; Union). Buy tickets through Ticketmaster or at the Rogers Centre box office near Gate 9. Try for the dearer seats along the lower level baselines where you have a better chance of catching (or wearing) a fly-ball. Incidentally, the Rogers Centre has a fully retractable roof.

TORONTO MAPLE LEAFS   Sports
(416-815-5982; www.mapleleafs.com; regular season Oct-Apr) The 13-time Stanley Cup–winning Toronto Maple Leafs slap the puck around the **Air Canada Centre** (ACC; Map p174; 416-815-5500; www.theaircanadacentre.com; 40 Bay St; Union) in the National Hockey League (NHL). Every game sells out, but a limited number of same-day tickets go on sale through Ticketmaster at 10am and at the Air Canada Centre ticket window from 5pm. You can also buy tickets via the website from season ticket-holders who aren't attending – expect to pay around $80 and up.

Shopping

GUILD SHOP   Souvenirs
(Map p170; www.theguildshop.ca; 118 Cumberland St; 10am-6pm Mon-Wed, to 7pm Thu & Fri, to 6pm Sat, noon-5pm Sun; Bay) The **Ontario Crafts Council** (www.craft.on.ca) has been promoting local artisans for more than 70 years. Ceramics, jewelry, glassworks, prints and carvings make up most of the displays, but you could also catch a special exhibition of Pangnirtung weaving or Cape Dorset graphics.

The Toronto Maple Leafs put on a show at the Air Canada Centre

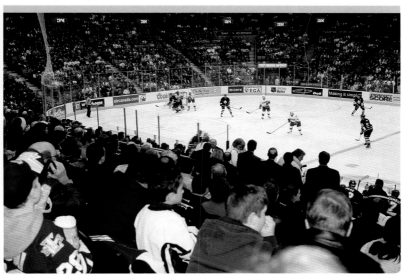

COREY WISE

Top Coffee Shops

Too early for beer? Sidestep the awful coffee chains for some *real* caffeine:

Moonbean Coffee Company (Map p170; 30 St Andrews St; ⏰7am-9pm; 🚌510) Kensington Market.

B Espresso Bar (111 Queen St E; ⏰7:30am-5pm Mon-Fri, 10am-3pm Sat; 🚌501) East Toronto.

Quaff (Map p170; 668 Queen St W; ⏰8am-7pm; 🚌501) West Queen West.

PRELOVED Clothing
(Map p170; www.preloved.ca; 881 Queen St W; ⏰11am-7pm Mon-Wed, to 8pm Thu & Fri, to 7pm Sat, noon-6pm Sun; 🚌501) Preloved is all about reusing and recycling, but this is no thrift store: you can find Preloved designs on the runway. Reclaimed vintage fabrics are reassembled to create all-new, one-of-a-kind clothing.

Information

Money

ATMs are on every street corner. American Express (www.americanexpress.com/canada) branches function as travel agencies and don't handle financial transactions. Instead, tackle the banks or try Money Mart (www.moneymart.ca; 617 Yonge St; ⏰24hr; Ⓢ Wellesley).

Tourist Information

Tourism Toronto (Map p174; ☏ 416-203-2500, 800-499-2514; www.seetorontonow.com; 207 Queens Quay W; ⏰8:30am-6pm Mon-Fri; Ⓢ Union).

Getting There & Away

Air

Most Canadian airlines and international carriers arrive at Canada's busiest airport, Lester B Pearson International Airport (YYZ; ☏866-207-1690, Terminals 1 & 2 416-247-7678, Terminal 3 416-776-5100; www.gtaa.com), 27km northwest of downtown Toronto. Terminal assignments are subject to change; call ahead or check airport entrance signs.

On the Toronto Islands, small Toronto City Centre Airport (TCCA; Map p168; ☏416-203-6942; www.torontoport.com/airport.asp) is home to regional airlines, helicopter companies and private flyers. Air Canada Jazz flights from Ottawa land at TCCA rather than Pearson.

Bus

Long-distance buses operate from the Metro Toronto Coach Terminal (www.torontocoachterminal.com; 610 Bay St; Ⓢ Dundas). Union Station downtown serves as the bus and train depot for GO Transit (www.gotransit.com) that services nearby towns.

Car & Motorcycle

Toronto is served by expressways from all directions; expect congestion. Along the lake, the Gardiner Expresway runs west into Queen Elizabeth Way (QEW) to Niagara Falls. At the city's western border is Hwy 427, running north to the airport. The tolled (and often bumper-to-bumper) Hwy 401 runs east–west above the downtown area: east to Montréal, west to Windsor. On the eastern side of the city, the Don Valley Parkway connects Hwy 401 to the Gardiner Expressway. Hwy 400 and Hwy 404 run north from Toronto.

Train

Grand Union Station (Map p174; ☏416-869-300; www.viarail.com; 140 Bay St) is Toronto's main rail hub. Trains from Toronto go west to Edmonton and Vancouver, south to Niagara Falls, and northeast to Ottawa, Montréal and Québec City. Amtrak trains run to New York City via Buffalo.

ℹ️ Getting Around

To/From the Airport

Airport Express (📞905-564-3232, 800-387-6787; www.torontoairportexpress.com) operates an express bus connecting Pearson International with the **Metro Toronto Coach Terminal** (Map p170; 📞416-393-7911; www.greyhound.ca; 610 Bay St; 🕐5:30am-midnight; **S** Dundas) and major downtown hotels. Allow 1½ hours to get to/from the airport (one way/return $17/30). Students and seniors receive $2 off one-way fares; kids under 11 travel free.

A taxi from Pearson into the city takes around 45 minutes, depending on traffic ($46 to downtown Toronto). A metered taxi from central Toronto to Pearson costs around $50.

Public Transportation

The **Toronto Transit Commission** (**TTC**; 📞416-393-4636; www.toronto.ca/ttc) operates Toronto's efficient subway, streetcar and bus system. The regular fare is adult/child/concession $3/0.70/1.85 (cash), or 10 tickets (or tokens) for $21. Day passes ($8.50) and weekly Metropasses ($30) are also available. Tickets or tokens are available in the subway and at some convenience stores. You can transfer to any other TTC bus, subway or streetcar for free using your paper streetcar/bus ticket or transfer ticket from automated dispensers near subway exits. Exact change is required for streetcars and buses; subway attendants are more forgiving.

Subway lines operate from approximately 6am (9am on Sunday) until 1:30am daily, with trains every five minutes. The main lines are the crosstown Bloor–Danforth line, and the U-shaped Yonge–University–Spadina line, which bends through Union Station.

Streetcars are slower than the subway, but they stop every block or two. Streetcars operate from 5am until 1:30am on weekdays with reduced weekend services. The main east–west routes are along St Clair Ave (512), College St (506), Dundas St (505), Queen St (501 and 502) and King St (503 and 504). North–south streetcars grind along Bathurst St (511) and Spadina Ave (510).

NIAGARA FALLS

POP 79,000

Niagara Falls: great muscular bands of water arch over the precipice like liquid glass, roaring into the void below; a vast plume of spray boils up from the cauldron, feathering into the air hundreds of meters above. There are dozens of taller

Checking out clothes in the Kensington Market area (p172), Toronto

NIAGARA FALLS

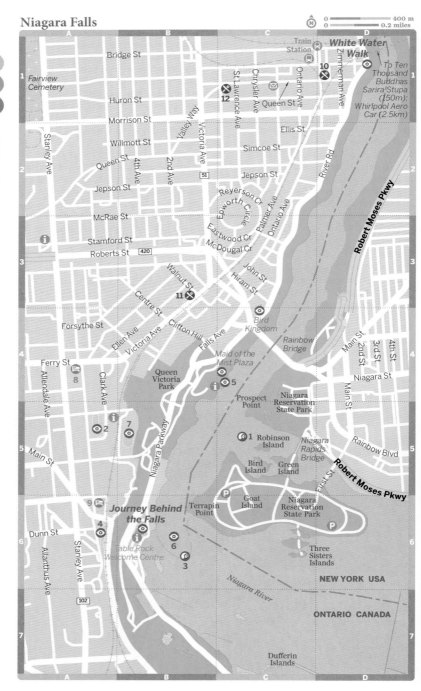

waterfalls in the world (Niagara ranks a lowly 50th), but in terms of sheer volume these falls are almost unbeatable: more than a million bathtubs of water plummet over the edge every second.

By day or night, regardless of the season, the falls never fail to awe (14 million visitors annually can't be wrong!). Even in winter, when the flow is partially hidden and the edges freeze solid, the watery extravaganza is undiminished. Very occasionally the falls stop altogether. This first happened on Easter Sunday morning in 1848, when ice completely jammed the flow. Pious locals feared the end of the world was nigh...

Piety, however, isn't something Niagara Falls strives for these days. It's been a saucy honeymoon destination ever since Napoléon's brother brought his bride here – tags such as 'For newlyweds and nearly deads' and 'Viagra Falls' are apt. More recently, a crass morass of casinos, fast-food joints, sleazy motels, cheesy tourist attractions and sex shops has bloomed parasitically around the falls in the Clifton Hill area – a Little Las Vegas!

Love it or loathe it, there's nowhere quite like Niagara Falls.

Sights & Activities

For sights and activities around the falls and Clifton Hill, park elsewhere (see p192).

The Falls & Around

Niagara Falls forms a natural rift between Ontario and New York State. On the US side, **Bridal Veil Falls** (aka the American Falls) crash onto mammoth fallen rocks. On the Canadian side, the grander, more powerful **Horseshoe Falls** plunge into the cloudy **Maid of the Mist Pool**. The prime falls-watching spot is **Table Rock**, poised just meters from the drop – arrive early to beat the crowds.

Around 1km south of Horseshoe Falls, the **Floral Showhouse** (☑ 905-353-5407; www.niagaraparks.com; 7145 Niagara Parkway; admission free; ☉9:30am-8pm) offers year-round floral displays and some warm respite on a chilly day. Opposite, lodged on rocks in the rapids, the **Old Scow** is a rusty steel barge that's been waiting to be washed over the falls since 1918 – a teetering symbol of Western imperialism, perhaps?

Tickets for the following three main falls attractions (and the Maid of the Mist, see boxed text, p190) can be bought separately, or purchase the **Niagara Falls Great Gorge Adventure Pass** (www.niagaraparks.com; adult/child $40/28), a discount pass for admission to all four attractions, plus Niagara Parkway and Queenston sites, and all-day transportation on the Niagara Parks People Mover. Passes are available from the Niagara Parks Commission at Table Rock Welcome Centre and various attractions.

JOURNEY BEHIND THE FALLS
Walking Tour
(www.niagaraparks.com; 6650 Niagara Parkway; adult/child $13/8; ☉9am-5:30pm Mon-Fri, to 7:30pm Sat & Sun) From Table Rock Welcome Centre you can don a very un-sexy

plastic poncho and traverse rock-cut tunnels halfway down the cliff – as close as you can get to the falls without getting in a barrel. It's open year-round, but be prepared to queue.

WHITE WATER WALK   Walking Tour
(www.niagaraparks.com; 4330 Niagara Parkway; adult/child $9/6; ⏱9am-7:45pm Jun-Aug, 9am-4:45pm Mon-Fri, to 5:45pm Sat & Sun Apr-May & Sep-Oct) At the northern end of town, next to Whirlpool Bridge, the White Water Walk is another way to get up close and personal, this time via an elevator down to a 325m boardwalk suspended above the rampaging torrents, just downstream from the falls.

WHIRLPOOL AERO CAR   Gondola
(3850 Niagara Parkway; adult/child $12/7; ⏱9am-8pm Jun-Aug, 9am-5pm Mon-Fri, to 6pm Sat & Sun Apr-May & Sep-Oct) Dangling above the Niagara River, 4.5km north of Horseshoe Falls, the Whirlpool Aero Car was designed by Spanish engineer Leonardo Torres Quevedo and has been operating since 1916 (but don't worry – it's still in good shape). The gondola travels 550m between two outcrops above a deadly whirlpool created by the falls – count the logs and tires spinning in the eddies below. No wheelchair access.

Clifton Hill & Around
Clifton Hill is a street name, but refers to a broader area near the falls occupied by a sensory bombardment of artificial enticements. You name it – House of Frankenstein, Madame Tussaud's Wax Museum, Castle Dracula – they're all here. In most cases, paying the admission will leave you feeling like a sucker.

DAREDEVIL GALLERY   Museum
(www.imaxniagara.com; 6170 Fallsview Blvd; adult/child $8/6.50; ⏱9am-9pm) The most engaging thing around the area is the Daredevil Gallery attached to IMAX Niagara. Scratch your head in amazement at the battered collection of barrels and padded bubbles in which people have

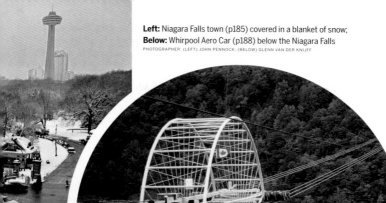

Left: Niagara Falls town (p185) covered in a blanket of snow;
Below: Whirlpool Aero Car (p188) below the Niagara Falls
PHOTOGRAPHER: (LEFT) JOHN PENNOCK; (BELOW) GLENN VAN DER KNIJFF

ridden over the falls (not all of them successfully). There's also a history of falls 'fun-ambulism' (tightrope walking) here.

FREE **TEN THOUSAND BUDDHAS SARIRA STUPA** Temple
(4303 River Rd; 9am-5pm, main temple Sat & Sun only) If the tourist bustle is messing with your yang, find tranquility at the totally out-of-context Buddhist temple Ten Thousand Buddhas Sarira Stupa. Visitors are welcome to wander the serene complex and view the various sculptures, bells and artworks.

KONICA MINOLTA TOWER
Observation Deck
(www.niagaratower.com; 6732 Fallsview Blvd; adult/child $5.50/3.50; 7am-11pm) Leering over the falls, the Minolta Tower is a bodacious vantage point, with indoor and outdoor observation galleries. On a clear day the view extends from Toronto to Buffalo, New York. There's a restaurant and hotel here, too.

SKYLON TOWER Observation Deck
(www.skylon.com; 5200 Robinson St; adult/child $13/7.50; 8am-midnight Apr-Oct, 11am-9pm Nov-Mar) The Skylon Tower is a 158m spire with yellow elevators crawling like bugs up the exterior. The views up high are real eye-poppers, and the revolving restaurant is worth a spin or two.

Niagara Parkway

NIAGARA PARKWAY Scenic Drive
The slow-roaming, leafy Niagara Parkway runs for 56km along the Niagara River, from Niagara-on-the-Lake past the falls to Fort Erie. Along the way are parks, picnic areas and viewpoints. The 3m-wide **Niagara River Recreation Trail** (www.niagaraparks.com/nature/rectrailarea .php) for cycling, jogging or walking runs parallel to the parkway – an idyllic short or long cycling excursion.

FREE **NIAGARA GLEN NATURE RESERVE**
Nature Reserve

(www.niagaraparks.com; Niagara Parkway; ☺dawn-dusk; **P**) About 8km north of the falls is this exceptional reserve, where you can get a sense of what the area was like pre-Europeans. There are 4km of walking trails winding down into a gorge, past huge boulders, cold caves, wildflowers and woods. The Niagara Parks Commission offers **guided nature walks** daily during the summer season for a nominal fee. Don't drink water from the river.

FREE **BOTANICAL GARDENS** Garden
(www.niagaraparks.com; 2565 Niagara Parkway; ☺dawn-dusk; **P**) Almost opposite Niagara Glen are the neatly pruned botanical gardens with 40 hectares of herbs, vegetables and trees – a spot to chill out.

BUTTERFLY CONSERVATORY Garden
(www.niagaraparks.com; 2565 Niagara Parkway; adult/child $11.75/8; ☺10am-7pm Jun-Aug, 10am-4pm Mon-Fri, to 5pm Sat & Sun Nov-May, 10am-7pm Jun-Sep; **P**) Inside the botanical gardens, the conservatory has more than 50 species of butterflies (some as big as birds) flitting around 130 species of flowers and plants. This is also a breeding facility where you can see young butterflies released.

 **Sleeping**

There are more beds than heads in Niagara Falls, but the town is sometimes completely booked up. Prices spike sharply in summer, on weekends and during holidays (Canadian and US). Check B&B availability at www.bbnia garafalls.com. Lundy's Lane is motel central.

OAKES HOTEL Hotel **$$$**
(☎905-356-4514, 877-843-6253; www.oakes hotel.com; 6546 Fallsview Blvd; d $119-269; **P**😑❄️🛜✈️) A jaunty silver spire next to the Fallsview Casino, the Oakes has front-row-center views of the great cascades. For a lofty establishment, staff are remarkably down to earth. Not all rooms have falls views, but ask and ye shall receive. The pricier rooms have Jacuzzis, floor-to-ceiling windows, fireplaces, terraces and the best views. Wi-fi is an additional $13; parking is $15.

CRYSTAL INN Motel **$$**
(☎905-354-1436; www.crystalinn.ca; 4249 River Rd; r $50-90; **P**😑❄️🛜) Run by the same family since it was built in 1955, this basic motel has plain but remodeled rooms. It has a great location across from the river and about a 20-minute walk to the falls. Some rooms have heart-shaped Jacuzzi tubs.

CADILLAC MOTEL Motel **$$**
(☎905-356-0830, 800-650-0049; www .cadillacmotelniagara.com; 2 Ferry St; r $59-149; **P**❄️) What killer architecture! Straight out of a 1950s design dreambook, the old Cadillac has resisted the urge to scrap its neon sign, funky pink-and-

Maid of the Mist

This brave little **boat** (www.maidofthemist.com; 5920 River Rd; adult/child $15.60/9.60; ☺8:45am-7:45pm Jun-Aug, 8:45am-4:45pm Mon-Fri, to 5:45pm Sat & Sun Apr, May, Sep & Oct) has been plowing headlong into the falls' misty veil since 1846. It's loud and wet and lots of fun. Everyone heads for the boat's upper deck, but views from either end of the lower deck are just as good. Departures are every 15 minutes, weather permitting. Back on land, **Maid of the Mist Plaza**, where the boats dock, is the stage for local musicians and buskers.

peach brickwork, retro plastic chairs, lewd tiling and geometric carpets. The walls are a little thin (an eavesdropper's delight), but the location is brilliant.

Eating

The old downtown section is seeing a lot of new restaurants crop up and is worth exploring. In general, though, finding food in Niagara is no problem, but be prepared for quantity rather than quality. For cuisine a cut above, you're better off heading to the Wine Country. Aside from the following there are sky-high restaurants at both the Skylon Tower and Minolta Tower.

TAPS ON QUEEN BREWHOUSE & GRILL Brewery $$
(www.tapsbeer.com; 4680 Queen St; mains $9-14; ⊙noon-10pm Mon, Tue & Sun, to midnight Wed-Sat) Taps does a mix of stuff, from shepherd's pie to ancient grains curry (quinoa, couscous, adzuki beans, mung beans and veggies). All dishes are, naturally, best when paired with one of the brewery's tasty beers.

EDWIN'S Fusion $$
(4616 Erie Ave; mains $8-10) Born in Jamaica, trained in England, the illustrious Edwin blends Caribbean and Mediterranean cuisine at this little spot near the train station. Jerk chicken, fried plantains, curried goat and salmon salad are all on offer, as is a weekend breakfast buffet ($6.99).

GURU Indian $$
(☑ 905-354-3444; 5705 Victoria Ave; mains $11-16; ⊙noon-11pm Mon-Thu, to midnight Fri-Sun) Take alternate sips of cold mango lassi with forks of red-hot curry at the Guru, an unexpected gem located in Clifton Hill. Dark-wood wicker chairs and Ganesh-skin tablecloths set the scene for smooth vegetable curries, tangy chicken masalas and a surprisingly global wine list.

If You Like...
Theater

If the Factory Theatre (p182) draws your applause, check out what's playing on these other stages around Toronto:

1 ELGIN & WINTER GARDEN THEATRE
(Map p170; ☑416-314-2901; www.heritagefdn.on.ca; 189 Yonge St, Dundas Sq; ⊙box office 11am-5pm Tue-Sat; Ⓢ Queen) The restored Elgin & Winter Garden Theatre stages high-profile productions in an amazing, double-decker setting.

2 STRATFORD FESTIVAL
(☑519-273-1600, 800-567-1600; www.stratfordfestival.ca; Festival Theatre, Queen's Park, 55 Queen St; ⊙box office 9am-5pm Mon-Sat Dec-Mar, 9am-8pm Mon-Fri, to 5pm Sat, to 2pm Sun Apr-Nov) You'll have to road trip for this one. Canada's Stratford is a lot like the Bard's birthplace in England, primped to country-garden, swan-rivered perfection. And every April to November, theater buffs flock in to see internationally acclaimed productions of Shakespeare's works. Stratford is 150km west of Toronto.

3 SHAW FESTIVAL
(☑905-468-2172, 800-511-7429; www.shawfest.com; ⊙box office 10am-8pm Apr-Oct) In pretty, touristy Niagara-on-the-Lake, 135km south of Toronto, the much-esteemed Shaw Fest lures global audiences. Aside from an opening Shaw showstopper, the season offers Victorian drama, European and US plays, musicals, mystery and suspense, and classics from Wilde, Woolf and Coward.

ℹ Information

Niagara Falls Tourism (☑ 905-356-6061, 800-563-2557; www.niagarafallstourism.com; 5400 Robinson St; ⊙8am-5pm Mon-Fri, 10am-4pm Sat & Sun) Everything you need to know about Niagara, served with a smile.

Niagara Parks Commission (www.niagaraparks.com; ⊙9am-11pm Jun-Aug, to 4pm Sep-May) The falls' governing body, with information desks at Maid of the Mist Plaza and Table Rock Welcome Centre.

Detour:
Niagara Peninsula Wine Country

The Niagara Peninsula adheres to the 43rd parallel – a similar latitude to northern California and further south than Bordeaux, France. A primo vino location, mineral-rich soils and a moderate microclimate: the perfect recipe for viticulture success!

There are two main areas to focus on: west of St Catharines around Vineland, and north of the Queen Elizabeth Way (QEW) around Niagara-on-the-Lake. For more info check out www.winesofontario.ca.

Some of our favorites (in order, coming from Toronto):

Vineland Estates Winery (www.vineland.com; 3620 Moyer Rd, Vineland; tastings $3, tours $6; ⊙10am-6pm May-Oct, 11am-5pm Nov-Apr) It's the elder statesman of Niagara viticulture. Almost all the wines here are excellent – riesling and cabernet franc are the flavors of the moment. The restaurant and accommodations are fabulous too.

Wayne Gretzky Estate (www.gretzky.com; 3751 King St, Vineland, ⊙10am-6pm Mon-Sat, from 11am Sun summer, 10am-5pm Mon-Sat, from 11am Sun winter) Canada's beloved hockey star has dipped into the wine business, producing a veritable rainbow of wines, from cab-merlot blends to ice-wine to rieslings.

Stratus (www.stratuswines.com; 2059 Niagara Stone Rd, Niagara-on-the-Lake; tastings $10; ⊙11am-5pm May-Dec, noon-5pm Wed-Sat Jan-Apr) The building's design addresses complex recycling, organic, energy-efficient and indigenous concerns. Your wine choice is less complex: Stratus White or Stratus Red.

Inniskillin (www.inniskillin.com; 1499 Line 3, cnr Niagara Parkway, Niagara-on-the-Lake; tastings $1-20, tours $5; ⊙9am-6pm, tours hourly 10:30am-4:30pm daily May-Oct, reduced schedule Nov-Apr) It's a master of the icewine craft.

While in Niagara-on-the-Lake, don't forget to see who's treading the boards at the Shaw Festival (p191).

ⓘ Getting There & Away

Car

From Toronto, the Gardiner Expressway runs west into Queen Elizabeth Way (QEW) to Niagara Falls.

Train

From Niagara Falls Train Station (☏888-842-7245; www.viarail.ca; 4267 Bridge St), opposite the bus station, VIA trains run to Toronto ($37, two hours, two daily) and New York City ($85, 10 hours, once daily).

ⓘ Getting Around

Car, Motorcycle & Parking

Driving and parking around the center is an expensive headache. Park way out and walk, or follow the parking district signs and stash the car for the day (around $6 per 30 minutes, or $15 per day). The huge Rapidsview parking lot (also the Niagara Parks People Mover depot) is 3km south of the falls off River Rd.

Public Transportation

Cranking up and down the steep 50m slope between the falls and Fallsview Blvd is a quaint Incline Railway (www.niagaraparks.com; 6635 Niagara Parkway; one way $2.50; ⊙9am-11pm Jul-Aug, to 8pm Sep-Nov & Apr-Jun).

The Niagara Parks People Mover (www.niagaraparks.com; day pass adult/child $7.60/4.60; ⊙every 20min 9am-9pm Mar-Oct) is an economical and efficient bus system, departing the huge Rapidsview parking lot south of the falls. Day passes can be purchased at most stops. Shuttles follow a 15km path from the parking lot north past the Horseshoe Falls,

Rainbow and Whirlpool bridges and Whirlpool Aero Car, continuing along Niagara Parkway to Queenston in peak season. Tickets include a ride on the Incline Railway.

....

Walking

Put on your sneakers and get t'steppin' – walking is the way to go! You'll only need wheels to visit outlying sights along the Niagara Parkway.

THOUSAND ISLANDS & AROUND

Thousand Islands

The 'Thousand Islands' is a constella-tion of over 1800 rugged islands dotting the St Lawrence River from Kingston to Brockville. The lush archipelago offers loose tufts of fog, showers of trillium petals, quaking tide-pools and opulent 19th-century summer mansions, whose turrets pierce the prevailing mist.

The narrow, slow-paced **Thousand Islands Parkway** dips south of Hwy 401 between Gananoque and Elizabethtown, running along the river for 35km before rejoining the highway. The scenic journey winds along the pastoral strip of shoreline offering picture-perfect vistas and dreamy picnic areas. The **Bikeway** bicycle path extends the full length of the parkway.

In **Ivylea**, a series of soaring bridges link Ontario to New York State over several islands. Halfway across, you'll find the **Skydeck** (✆ 613-659-2335; www.1000islandsskydeck .com; Hill Island; adult/ child $9.75/5.75; ⊙9am-dusk mid-Apr–Oct), a 125m observation tower offering some fantastic views of the archipelago from three different balconies.

Rockport, the largest village along the Thousand Islands Parkway, lies just beyond a cluster of stone churches.

There are two large cruise lines that operate out of Rockport, both offering optional stopovers at the gorgeous, rambling **Boldt Castle**, an unfinished Gothic palace of dark spires and stone facades. The castle is technically in the USA, so make sure all your papers are in order if you are planning to visit. **Rockport Boat Line** (✆ 613-659-3402, 800-563-8687; www.rockportcruises.com; 23 Front St; ⊙May-Oct) offers a variety of cruising options including a popular two-hour cruise ($28), which departs three times per day and offers a look-see past the castle. Cruises with a stopover at the castle (adult/child/concession $30/12/26, plus admission fee adult/child US$7/4.50) allow you to explore the grounds. Lunch and dinner cruise options are also available ($39 and $59 respectively).

In nearby Mallorytown, the **St Lawrence Islands National Park** (✆ 613-923-5261) preserves a gentle green archipelago of 20 islands.

Niagara Peninsula vineyard (opposite)

If You Like…
Cycling

If you like cycling along the Niagara River Recreation Trail (p189), the area offers other breezy (and boozy) opportunities to pedal:

1 NIAGARA WINE & CULINARY TOURS (905-468-1300, 800-680-7006; www .niagaraworldwinetours.com; 92 Picton St; tours $65-165; ☉tour times & months vary) Cycle backroads from winery to winery on these guided trips, tailored to all fitness levels. Based in Niagara-on-the-Lake.

2 ZOOM LEISURE BICYCLE RENTALS (905-468-2366, 866-811-6993; www .zoomleisure.com; 2017 Niagara Stone Rd; rental per half-day/day/two days $20/30/50, delivery free; ☉9am-5pm) Also based in Niagara-on-the-Lake, but Zoom will deliver a bike to you anywhere in the Niagara region. Longer rentals and two-wheeled wine tours available, too.

Gananoque

Pleasant Gananoque (gan-an-*awk*-way) is the perfect place to rest your eyes after a long day of squinting at the furry green islands on the misty St Lawrence.

The **Chamber of Commerce** (613-382-3250, 800-561-1595; www.1000islands gananoque.com; 10 King St E; ☉8:30am-8pm Jun-Aug, 9am-5pm Sep-May) offers basic services such as lodging recommendations. Check out www .gananoque.com for additional info.

Like most other towns in the Thousand Islands region, Gananoque is home to several river cruise operators. Shop around before choosing a company – some trips stop at several islands, others don't; some offer dinner cruises, while others specialize in quicker trips on faster boats. The **Gananoque Boat Line** (613-382-2144, 888-717-4837; www.ganboatline.com; 6 Water St; 1hr tours adult/child $20/11, 2½hr tours $30/11, castle cruise $36/11; ☉May–mid-Oct) is a

popular choice, with several trip options including a stopover at Boldt Castle.

Gananoque sports an abundance of memorable accommodations, including several upmarket and architecturally eye-catching inns.

Victoria Rose Inn (613-382-3386, 888-246-2893; www.victoriaroseinn.com; 279 King St W; d incl breakfast $155-255; ✱☺☎), once the mayor's house and a monument to Victorian splendor, has been refurbished to its original elegance. A glassed-in veranda overlooks garden terraces, and the rooms are comfortable and spacious. A friendly family runs the Victoria Rose and is an excellent source of local information.

The large **Gananoque Inn** (888-565-3101; www.gananoqueinn.com; 550 Stone St S; r $179-395), with its signature green shutters, regally sits at the junction of the Gananoque River and the St Lawrence Seaway. The old carriage-works inn opened its doors in 1896, and has retained much of its charm while surreptitiously adding modern amenities like a luxurious day spa. Bike and boat rentals are offered. Half-priced rooms are available in the off-season.

OTTAWA
POP 900,000

Descriptions of Ottawa read like an appealing personal ad: young, vibrant, clean, bilingual, likes kids, long walks on the river. And the attractive capital continues to impress in person.

The postcard-perfect Parliament regally anchors the downtown core at the confluence of three gushing rivers. An inspiring jumble of pulsing districts – each with their own flavor – lies beyond the sleek government offices. In the distance, the rolling Gatineau hills tenderly hug the cloudless valley.

The city's main attraction is the vast assortment of state-of-the-art museums. From the smooth undulating walls of the ubermodern Museum of Civilization (just across the river in Gatineau) to the haunting Gothic arches of the Museum of Nature, each attraction is an inspired architectural gesture with an intriguing exhibition space.

Sights

Ottawa's best feature is its collection of stunning, state-of-the-art museums. Most of these attractions are within walking distance of one another. Many museums are closed on Mondays in the winter, and several attractions will let you in for free if you arrive less than an hour before closing.

PARLIAMENT HILL
Historical Building

(www.parliamenthill.gc.ca) Vast yawning archways dominate this stunning complex of copper-topped towers. The city's most picture-perfect attraction by far, Parliament is Canada's nexus of political activity. The primary building, **Centre Block**, supports the iconic **Peace Tower**, the highest structure in the city. Venture inside to peruse the hand-carved limestone and make a stop at the gorgeous library with its wood and wrought iron. Visitors are allowed to see the Commons and Senate while they're in session. Question Period in the House of Commons is particularly popular, occurring every afternoon and at 11am on Fridays. Admission is on a first-come first-served basis.

Free 45-minute **tours** (📞 613-996-0896) run frequently; be prepared for tight security. In summer you can book tours at the conspicuous white tent; in winter there's a reservation desk inside the building. The grounds can be explored on one's own as well. Pick up a free copy of the *Walking Tour of Parliament Hill* at the information center across the street. The pamphlet details little-known facts about the buildings – learn about the gargoyles and grotesques that haunt the sculpted sandstone.

The tour schedule is quite convoluted and confusing – the best bet is to check out the parliament's website.

At 10am daily in summer, see the colorful **changing of the guard** on the front lawns. At night during summer, there's a free bilingual sound-and-light show called *Mosaika* on Parliament Hill.

Snowslide in Jacques Cartier Park during Ottawa's Winterlude festival (p42)

BRUCE BI

Ottawa

DISCOVER TORONTO, NIAGARA FALLS & ONTARIO OTTAWA

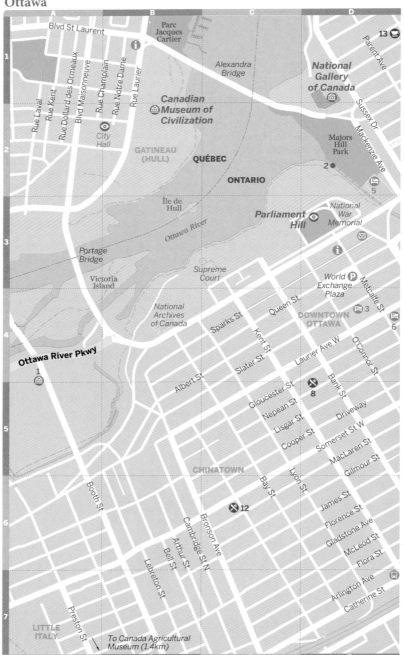

Blvd St Laurent

Parc Jacques Cartier

Alexandra Bridge

National Gallery of Canada

13

Rue Laval
Rue Kent
Rue Dollard des Ormeaux
Blvd Maisonneuve
Rue Champlain
Rue Notre Dame
Rue Laurier

Parent Ave

Canadian Museum of Civilization

City Hall

GATINEAU (HULL)

QUÉBEC

ONTARIO

Majors Hill Park

Sussex Dr
Mackenzie Ave

2

5

Île de Hull

Ottawa River

Parliament Hill

National War Memorial

Portage Bridge

Victoria Island

Supreme Court

World Exchange Plaza

Metcalfe St

DOWNTOWN OTTAWA

3

6

National Archives of Canada

Sparks St

Queen St

Ottawa River Pkwy

1

Kent St
Slater St

Laurier Ave W

O'Connor St

Albert St

Gloucester St

Bank St

8

Nepean St
Lisgar St
Cooper St

Driveway

Somerset St W

MacLaren St

Gilmour St

CHINATOWN

Bay St
Lyon St

Booth St

12

Bronson Ave
Cambridge St N
Arthur St
Bell St
Lebreton St

James St
Florence St
Gladstone Ave
McLeod St
Flora St
Arlington Ave
Catherine St

LITTLE ITALY

Preston St

To Canada Agricultural Museum (1.4km)

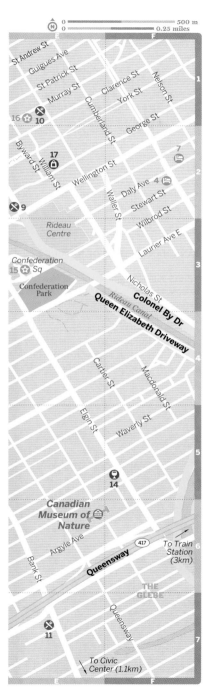

After exploring the architectural allegories to nationalist ideals, there's a bizarre, little-known quirk that should not be missed. The **stray-cat sanctuary**, with its dollhouse shelters, sits on Parliament Hill between the West Block and Centre Block, toward the river. Some say, loftily, that it represents the Canadian ideal of welcoming and caring for the world's needy, but then again, maybe it's just nutty.

NATIONAL GALLERY OF CANADA
Art Gallery

(613-990-1985; www.gallery.ca; 380 Sussex Dr; adult/child under 12yr/child 12-19yr/concession/family $9/free/4/7/18, audioguide $6; 10am-5pm, to 8pm Thu May-Sep, closed Mon

OTTAWA SIGHTS

197

Oct-Apr) Canada's largest art gallery is a must, housing the largest collection of Canadian and Inuit art in the world. The structure is a piece of art in itself – one of Ottawa's modern architectural gems. The striking ensemble of glass and pink granite was concocted by Moshe Safdie, a noted architect who also created Montréal's well-known 'Habitat' (a unique apartment complex). His emphatic glass spires at the museum's rear echo the ornate copper-topped towers of the Parliament nearby. The dialogue between the heavy metallic roof and the floating crystalline steeple is magical, even on the dreariest of days.

In the interior, the vaulted galleries display classic and contemporary pieces with an emphasis on Canadian artists. The thoughtful chronological displays guide visitors through an annotated retelling of the nation's history. The **Inuit Gallery** on the ground level fuses ancestral themes with modern media in the dedicated **photography gallery** next door (room B102 and B103). Beyond the slew of Canadian art, galleries of US and European works will please the eye with several recognizable names and masterpieces.

There are two smooth courtyards deep within the museum's interior – both ooze Zen and tranquility, making them the perfect place to rest your eyes. Also hidden deep within is the unusual **Rideau Street Convent Chapel**. Built in 1888, this stunning wooden chapel was saved from demolition and restored piece-by-piece inside the gallery.

The complex, a 15-minute walk north of Parliament, takes at least two hours to navigate, and that's without checking out the latest rotating exhibitions, video presentations and film archives.

Two levels of underground parking hide beneath the museum ($12 per day).

CANADIAN MUSEUM OF NATURE
Museum

(☎ 613-566-4700; 240 McLeod St; www.nature.ca; adult/child/family $10/8/25, free Sat morning; ☉9am-6pm Sat-Wed, to 8pm Thu-Fri) Sparkling after a massive, seemingly endless renovation, this vast museum pokes its Gothic head up just beyond the skyline, south of downtown. The gaping four-story museum houses an

Locks at the Rideau Canal (p200), Ottawa

GLENN VAN DER KNIJFF

198

RICK GERHARTER

Don't Miss **Canadian Museum of Civilization**

This must-see **museum** (☎819-776-7000; www.civilization.ca; 100 Rue Laurier; adult/child/senior $12/8/10; ⏱9am-6pm Sat-Wed, to 8pm Thu-Fri) documents the history of Canada through a spectacular range of exhibits. Designed by Douglas Cardinal, the stone exterior has been sculpted into smooth ripples – like the undulating wave of a current. Note that you won't find any corners at the museum, as it is believed in Aboriginal lore that the evil spirits live in these angled nooks. Allow at least an entire afternoon to explore the museum and to take in the stunning views of the Parliament across the river.

The **Grand Hall**, with its simulated forest and seashore, illuminates the northwest coastal aboriginal cultures with towering colorful totem poles. Kids get a passport when they enter the **Canadian Children's Museum**, a vast educational and hands-on space offering glimpses into different cultures from around the world. Even adults may find that this is their favorite part of the museum. A slew of temporary exhibits supplement the already-incredible collection, and **Cineplus** adds an additional dimension, showing IMAX and Omnimax films.

impressive collection of fossils, minerals and animals, a full skeleton of a blue whale, and an excellent stock of dinosaurs from Alberta. Everyone's favorite section is the realistic mammal and bird dioramas depicting Canadian wildlife. The taxidermic creatures are so lifelike, you'll be glad that they're behind a sheet of glass.

Buses 5, 6 and 14 transport passengers to McLeod St.

CANADIAN WAR MUSEUM   Museum
(☎ 800-555-5621; www.warmuseum.ca; 1 Vimy Pl; adult/child $12/8; ⏱9am-6pm Fri-Wed, to 9pm Thu May–mid-Oct, 9am-5pm Tue-Sun, to 9pm Thu mid-Oct–Apr) This museum, built in 2005, still has that new-car smell. The metallic building is itself an eye-catching sculptural gesture. Fascinating displays wind through the labyrinthine interior, tracing the country's military history with Canada's most comprehensive

collection of military artifacts. Many of the exhibits were constructed on a human scale, including a haunting life-sized replica of a WWI trench. Don't forget to take a second look at the facade in the evening – flickering lights pulse on and off spelling 'Lest We Forget' and 'CWM' in Morse code (in both English and French, of course).

 ## Activities

For a city with harsh, endless winters, its residents sure love to be outside. Tourists will find a glut of outdoor activities during all seasons.

Ice-Skating

The **Rideau Canal**, Ottawa's most famous outdoor attraction, doubles as the largest skating rink in the world. The 7.8km of groomed ice is roughly the size of 90 Olympic-sized hockey rinks. Rest stops and changing stations are sprinkled throughout, but, more importantly,

take note of the wooden kiosks dispensing scrumptious slabs of fried dough called BeaverTails. The three skate and sled rental stations are located at the steps of the National Arts Centre, Dow's Lake and 5th Ave.

 ## Tours

The Capital Infocentre offers handy brochures for self-guided walking tours.

Around About Ottawa Walking Tours
(☎613-599-1016; www.aroundaboutottawa.com; ⏰Mon–Fri) Two-hour guided walking tours exploring the city's historic landmarks.

Ottawa Walking Tours Walking Tours
(☎613-799-1774; www.ottawawalkingtours.com; adult/family $15/45) Run by a local high school teacher, these informative tours – great for older tourists – depart from in front of the Capital Infocentre.

Paul's Boat Lines Boat Tours
(☎613-255-6781; www.paulsboatcruises.com; Ottawa Locks or Rideau Canal Dock; 1½hr Ottawa River tour adult/child $20/12, 1¼hr Rideau Canal cruise $18/10; ⏰mid-May–Oct) Scenic cruises offer picture-perfect moments.

Sleeping

The city has an impressive array of lodgings in all price ranges. The urban downtown district, stocked with high-rises, offers some unique upmarket lodging options in addition to the usual suspects (franchises and the like). During summer, reservations are recommended. February and May are bustling months as well, due to popular festivals. Ottawa's two major B&B hubs are on the east side of downtown.

A sign best not ignored, Algonquin Provincial Park (opposite)

Detour:
Algonquin Provincial Park

About 300km west of Ottawa, Algonquin is a sight for sore eyes. Established in 1893, Ontario's oldest and largest park offers 7800 sq km of thick pine forests, jagged cliffs, trickling crystal streams, mossy bogs and thousands (thousands!) of lakes. An easily accessible outdoor gem, this rugged expanse is a must-see for canoeists and hikers.

Algonquin is famous for its wildlife-watching and scenic lookouts. During spring, you're almost certain to see moose along Hwy 60, as they escape the pesky black flies to lick the leftover salt from winter de-icing. Other spotable creatures include deer, beaver, otter, mink and many bird species.

The park is primarily a nature preserve, which means that most noncamping accommodations are outside the park's boundaries. Numerous outfitters offer tours in the park. Scores of accommodations are available just beyond the protected lands, including resorts, motels and hostels (check www.algonquinpark.on.ca for a lengthy list).

Algonquin Provincial Park is accessible year-round. Drivers can pass through the park along Hwy 60; you must pay the day-use fee to stop and look around ($15 per vehicle).

The Sandy Hill district – a posh pocket of heritage houses – offers several architectural gems, and the ByWard Market district has some colorful options as well. Both areas offer walkable access to the city's major attractions.

FAIRMONT CHÂTEAU LAURIER
Historic Hotel $$$
(☎ 613-241-1414, 866-540-4410; www.fairmont.com/laurier; 1 Rideau St; r $250-400; ❄ @ ☎ ❧) This opulent castle gives the Parliament a run for its money. The city's best-known hotel is a landmark in its own right. You won't want for creature comforts and the location is unbeatable. If you're cashed-up, there's no better place to stay in town. If you don't have the bucks, recline on the overstuffed chaises as though you were the toast of the town.

HOTEL INDIGO
Boutique Hotel $$
(☎ 613-216-2903; www.ottawadowntownhotel.com; 123 Metcalfe St; r $139-199; ❄ @ ☎) This boutique hotel was designed with one lofty concept in mind: Fibonacci's Sequence – a natural order governing visual aesthetics. It's a tad complicated, but basically it involves mathematical harmony; where the ratio of two quantities equals the ratio between the larger of the two quantities and the two quantities combined (whew!). Additional perks and quirks include a floor-to-ceiling mural in each room, plasma TVs, and customer information written in haiku form. Reserve at least two weeks in advance.

BELLA NOTTE
B&B $$
(☎ 613-565-0497; www.bellanottebb.com; 108 Daly Ave; r incl breakfast $128-148; ☎) This charming little gem was once the home of Alexander Campbell, a prominent politician during Canada's founding. Evenings are filled with beautiful piano-playing from the owners, who happen to be professional musicians. The hosts proudly boast an infinite breakfast – 'you can eat till you die.'

MCGEE'S INN
B&B $$
(☎ 613-262-4337; www.mcgeesinn.com; 185 Daly Ave; r $108-198; @ ☎) This vast Victorian mansion has all the period trappings, from floral prints and embroidered chair

Ottawa for Children

Nope, the **Canada Agricultural Museum** (613-991-3044; www.agriculture.techno muses.ca; 930 Carling Ave at Prince of Wales Dr; adult/child $7/4; 9am-5pm Mar-Oct) isn't about the history of the pitchfork – it's a fascinating experimental farm. The government-owned property, southwest of downtown, includes about 500 hectares of gardens and ranches. Kids will love the livestock as they hoot and snort around the barn. The affable farmhands will even let the tots help out during feeding time. Guided tours lead visitors to an observatory, a tropical greenhouse and an arboretum. The rolling farmland is the perfect place for a scenic summer picnic, and in winter the grounds become a prime tobogganing locale. The farm can be reached on the city's network of cycling routes.

In addition to the experimental farm, virtually all of Ottawa's museums have been designed with families in mind; several options have entire wings devoted to child's play, such as the **Canadian Museum of Nature** and the **Canadian Museum of Civilization**.

caning to plush button-eyed teddy bears and varnished sewing machines. The John McGee room still contains some of the inn's original furnishings, including a cherry-wood desk and sleigh bed. Enjoy breakfast amid chirps from antique cuckoo clocks.

ARC Boutique Hotel **$$$**
(613-238-2888; www.arcthehotel.com; 140 Slater St; r $169-450;) Arc is a savvy boutique hotel with 112 minimal-yet-elegant rooms; call it low-key, muted and restfully hip. This mellow adult atmosphere continues through the quiet bar and trendy restaurant.

Eating

Little Ottawa's smorgasbord of gastronomic choices could give Toronto a run for its money. Bounteous ByWard Market boasts 150 options squished into one condensed epicurean district. During the warm month(s), eateries spill out onto the streets, creating charming cobblestone verandas. Follow Bank St south to the colorful Glebe neighborhood for a surplus of less-touristy pubs, restaurants and cafes between First St and Fifth St.

Take an evening stroll down Preston St, known as 'Corso Italia' – Ottawa's Little Italy – and choose from one of the many delicious options cluttering the street. The city's small but lively Chinatown is also worth a visit. Chinese restaurants spread along Somerset St W near Bronson Ave, and a tasty smattering of Vietnamese joints can be scouted west of Booth St.

Check out www.savourottawa.ca for details about the burgeoning local initiative that strives to match regional restaurants with the area's farmers.

ZENKITCHEN Vegan **$$**
(613-233-6404; www.zenkitchen.ca; 634 Somerset St W; mains $18-21; lunch Thu-Fri, dinner daily;) Let's face it folks, this could mean the end of the meat industry – ZenKitchen will baffle even the biggest of carnivores with its savvy menu of vegan-chic superlatives. The owners, Caroline and Dave, have years of culinary training between the two of 'em – they're also the stars of a hit reality TV show that documented their 'restaurant adventures.' Voted the best new restaurant in the city in 2009, this unique restaurant concept offers up healthy dishes that pay tribute to a colorful clash of continents. Oh, and the

wine! Let's not forget about the wine! Enjoy a lip-smacking selection of expertly chosen bottles – most come from Ontario, and although the region may not have a global reputation in the industry, we guarantee you'll be surprised by the quality.

BECKTA DINING & WINE
Fusion $$$

(☎ 613-238-7063; www.beckta.com; 226 Nepean St; mains $27-37; ☺dinner) This excellent upmarket option puts an original spin on regional cuisine. The inspired five-course tasting menu ($79) is the collective brainchild of the chef and sommelier. Ingredients are unpronounceable, which must mean they're gourmet. A second location – dubbed 'Play Food & Wine' – has recently opened in the Market district, and offers similar fare with a tapas twist.

BRASSERIE MÉTROPOLITAIN
French $$

(www.metropolitainbrasserie.com; 700 Sussex Dr; mains $10-19; ☺lunch & dinner) This trendy hot spot puts a modern spin on the typical brasserie with a swirling zinc countertop, flamboyant fixtures and the subtle oompah-pah from a distant accordion – you'll feel like you're dining on the set of *Moulin Rouge*. 'Hill Hour' (4pm to 7pm weekdays) buzzes with the spirited chatter of hot-blooded politicos as they down discounted drinks and $1 oysters.

WORKS
Burgers $$

(580 Bank St; burgers $9.50-13; ☺lunch & dinner) This western-style chow house takes burgers to a new level. At the Works you can brand your juicy patty with over 60 quirky toppings, be it spinach leaves, fried eggs, brie cheese or even peanut butter. It'll fill you up without emptying your wallet.

SWEETGRASS ABORIGINAL BISTRO
Aboriginal $$

(www.sweetgrassbistro.ca; 108 Murray St; mains $12-28; ☺lunch Mon-Fri, dinner daily) Usually, you would have to travel to a distant reservation to sample bannock, corn soup or elk. This unique aboriginal kitchen will save you that grueling $200 train ride, so why not leave an extra-big tip.

 Drinking

IDEAL COFFEE
Cafe

(www.idealcoffees.com; 176 Dalhousie St) Ideal indeed; handcrafted blends are produced and roasted on-site. The decor is thin – it's all about rich, flavorful cups of joe.

MANX
Bar

(370 Elgin St) A homey velvet sea awaits you at this basement pub-style hangout. Most people come for the great selection of Canadian microbrews (including the beloved Creemore) served on copper-top tables.

 Entertainment

Express is the city's free entertainment weekly. It can be found around town in various cafes, restaurants, bars and bookshops. Try www.upfrontottawa

Culture Passport: 9 Museums, 7 Days

Capital-ize on Ottawa's cache of fantastic museums with the **Culture Passport** (adult/family $30/75), a discount card that grants carriers admission to the city's nine best museums. Additional perks include 20% discounts on performances at the National Arts Centre. The card can be purchased at any of the participating museums and is valid for seven days.

.com and www.ottawaentertainment
.ca for additional information, and check
out Thursday's *Ottawa Citizen* for complete listings of club and entertainment
options.

RAINBOW BISTRO   Live Music
(☎ 613-241-5123; 76 Murray St) This upstairs
joint north of the Byward Market is the
best place in town to catch some live
blues tunes.

NATIONAL ARTS CENTRE   Theater
(NAC; ☎ 613-755-1111; www.nac-cna.ca; 53 Elgin
St) The capital's premier performing
arts complex delivers opera, drama, and
performances from the symphony orchestra. The modish complex stretches
along the canal in Confederation Sq.

NHL SENATORS   Sports
Ottawa is a hard-core hockey town. It's
worth getting tickets to a game even if
you're not into hockey – the ballistic fans
put on a show of their own. The NHL's
Senators play at the **ScotiaBank Place**
(☎ 613-599-0100, tickets 800-444-7367;

www.senators.com; Palladium Dr, Kanata), in the
city's west end.

 **Shopping**

The **ByWard Market** (www.byward-market
.com), at the corner of George St and
ByWard St, is the best place in town for
one-stop shopping. Vendors cluster
around the old maroon-brick market
building, erected in the 1840s. Outdoor merchants operate booths from
6am to 6pm year-round (although the
winter weather drastically reduces the
number of businesses). In summer, over
175 stalls fill the streets, selling fresh
produce from local farms, flowers, seafood, cheese, baked goods and kitschy
souvenirs.

Dalhousie St, a block east of the
market, has been rising in popularity
with a smattering of hipster boutiques
and fashion houses.

The Glebe, a colorful neighborhood
just south of the Queensway, bustles

with quirky antique shops and charismatic cafes. Most of the action happens along Bank St.

ℹ Information

Ottawa Tourism (www.ottawatourism .ca) offers a comprehensive glance at the nation's capital and can assist with planning itineraries and booking accommodations. Several banks and currency exchange outlets cluster along the Sparks St mall.

ℹ Getting There & Away

Air

The state-of-the-art **Ottawa MacDonald-Cartier International Airport** (YOW; ☎ 613-248-2000; www.ottawa airport.ca; 1000 Airport Rd) is 15km south of the city and is, perhaps surprisingly, very small. Main airlines serving the city include Air Canada, Air Canada Jazz, American Airlines, British Airways, Northwest Airlines, KLM, Porter, US Airways and WestJet.

Train

The **VIA Rail Station** (☎ 888-842-7245; 200 Tremblay Rd) is 7km southeast of downtown, near the Riverside Dr exit of Hwy 417. VIA Rail operates five daily trains to Kingston (two hours) with continued service to Toronto (4¼ hours) and Montréal (1¾ hours).

ℹ Getting Around

To/From the Airport

YOW Airporter (☎ 613-247-1779; www. yowshuttle.com; per person $15) makes an hourly round between most major hotels. Check online for exact departure times. Plan on a 35-minute ride, and call ahead to reserve a seat.

Blue Line Taxis (☎ 613-238-1111; www .bluelinetaxi.com) and **Capital Taxi** (☎ 613-744-3333) offer cab service to and from the airport ($20 to $30). If you're having a hard time snagging a cab, there's always a cluster on Metcalfe St between Sparks and Queen Sts.

If You Like…
Island Hopping

If you like the Thousand Islands region (p193), glide over to these destinations to further your explorations:

1 **PRINCE EDWARD COUNTY**
(www.pecchamber.com) An emerging foodie hot spot, Prince Edward County's undulating pastoral hills are extremely photogenic, as are the myriad water views. New wineries and rustic gourmet restaurants pop up every season. The Taste Trail (www.tastetrail.ca) provides a flavorful self-guided way to explore the island, which is 75km east of Kingston. Various bridges connects the island to the mainland.

2 **WOLFE ISLAND**
(www.wolfeisland.com) It's the largest in the Thousand Islands chain, offshore from Kingston and linked via a free, hourly car ferry. The cool, 25-minute trip affords views of the city and various other isles. Wolfe itself is home to 86 wind turbines, cycle-friendly farmland and the General Wolfe Hotel. Kingston's ferry terminal is at the intersection of Ontario and Barrack Sts.

Public Transportation

Ottawa and Hull/Gatineau operate separate bus systems. A transfer is valid from one system to the other, but may require an extra payment.

OC Transpo (☏613-741-4390, 613-741-6440; www.octranspo.com) operates buses and a light-rail system known as the O-train. Generally, the transportation network functions more rapidly and efficiently in the east end of town.

GEORGIAN BAY & LAKELANDS

A vast realm of blues and greens, Georgian Bay is a land of infinite dreaming. Summer breezes amble along curving lakes and sandy shores, while thick pines quiver at winter's frosty kiss. These ethereal landscapes inspired Canada's best-known painters, the

Group of Seven, and today the bay is home to hundreds of artists who use their backyard as inspiration. Evidence of these creative enclaves is conspicuous in Owen Sound and Manitoulin Island.

Bruce Peninsula

The Bruce, as it's known, is an 80km-long limestone outcrop of craggy shorelines and green woodlands at the northern end of the Niagara Escarpment. The fingerlike protrusion separates the cool crystal waters of Georgian Bay from the warm churning water of Lake Huron.

The main base for travelers is Tobermory, a charmingly unpretentious village at the tip of the peninsula. Activity centers on the harbor area known as Little Tub, which bustles during ferry season and is all but deserted in the winter. The 100km stretch of highway from Wiarton to Tobermory is dismal at best. Consider taking a side road or two to get a taste of the rural, often rugged scenery that makes the Bruce so special.

◉ Sights

From Hwy 6 just south of the Bruce Peninsula National Park boundary, take Dyer's Bay Rd to the quaint village of **Dyer's Bay**. The wee village is reminiscent of Cape Cod, with pretty clapboard houses and shoreline scenery. (Do not get out of your car along Dyer's Bay Rd as the street is lined with poison ivy.) **Cabot Head Lighthouse** (admission by donation; ⊙May–mid-Oct), about 7km from Dyer's Bay, contains a small museum and stunning views from the keeper's perch. There are other more accessible lighthouses on the peninsula, but the rugged journey is all part of the fun.

The best-known, most visited feature of **Fathom Five National Marine Park** is Flowerpot Island, named after the 'flowerpots' of the area: top-heavy, precarious-looking rock formations created by wave erosion. Several small glass-bottom cruises depart from the ferry dock offering privileged views of the rusty barnacle-ridden ships below.

Sleeping & Eating

In summer it's absolutely essential to book accommodations in advance. Visit the website www.bbgreybruce.com for information on lodging options in the region.

The following lodging and dining options are situated in the picturesque town of Tobermory, at the tip of the peninsula.

CEDAR VISTA MOTEL   Motel $$
(☎ 519-596-2395; 7370 Hwy 6; r $69-99) This super-tidy motel is on the right-hand side of the highway just before arriving in Tobermory, and attracts a lot of repeat visitors. The free coffee available in the lobby helps get you going.

INNISFREE   B&B $$
(☎ 519-596-8190; www.bbcanada.com/innis free; 46 Bay St; r $84-144; ⊙May-Oct; ℗😊) Whether it's the scent of fresh blueberry muffins, or the stunning harbor views from the sunroom and large deck, guests will adore this charming country home.

MERMAID'S SECRET   Cafe $$
(7433 Hwy 6; mains $8-14) This is a colorful shack with a screened-in back porch that looks out to a mossy forest. The menu has it all: organic fair-trade coffee, gourmet sandwiches, fresh and smoked local fish, and homemade pastries. After you're full, check out the boutique next door.

CRAIGIE'S   Fast Food $$
(fish & chips $10.50; ⊙7am-7pm May-Oct) This white sea shanty has been serving fish and chips in Tobermory since 1932, so by now they've pretty much perfected their recipe. The hearty breakfast menu is a solid second choice if you don't feel like battered fish in the wee hours of the morning.

ℹ Information

Tobermory Chamber of Commerce (☎ 519-596-2452; www.tobermory.org; Hwy 6; ⊙9am-5pm Sep-Jun, to 9pm Jul & Aug)

Georgian Bay & Lakelands

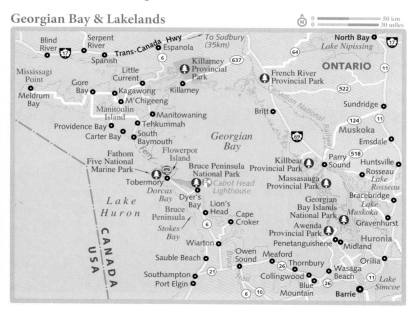

Owen Sound

Owen Sound's sordid past as a shipping center is rife with slow boats and fast women. Known to sailors as 'Little Liverpool,' the skanky port became so overrun with uncouth characters that alcohol was strictly prohibited for over 60 years. By the time the embargo was lifted in 1972, Owen Sound had transformed into a thriving artists' colony.

Sights & Activities

TOM THOMSON ART GALLERY
Museum

(www.tomthomson.org; 840 1st Ave W; adult/child $5/3; ☺10am-5pm Mon-Sat, from noon Sun Jun-Aug, 11am-5pm Tue-Fri, from noon Sat & Sun Sep-Jun) This gallery displays the work of Tom Thomson, a passionate outdoorsman and the granddaddy of modern Canadian landscape painting. His intimate and smoldering portrayal of nature is said to have inspired the formation of Canada's famous Group of Seven painters. Thomson grew up in Leath, and many of his works were composed in nearby thickets of fall leaves. Rotating exhibits in the gallery also include selections from the collection of contemporary Canadian art.

WATERFALLS
Parks

There are eight scenic waterfalls in the area, four of which are almost right in town. Rent a bike at **Jolley's Alternative Wheels** (☎ 519-371-1812; www.alternativewheels.com; 939 2nd Ave E; rental per day $39; ☺11:30am-6:30pm Tue-Fri, 11am-6pm Sat) to explore the nearby falls, or take a ride along Grey County Rd 1, which winds along the scenic shoreline of staggering pines between Owen Sound and Wiarton.

Sleeping & Eating

If you're into B&B-ing, have a peek at www.bbgreybruce.com for a lengthy list of options in the region.

BUTCHART ESTATE
B&B $$

(☎ 519-371-0208, 877-280-2403; www.butchartestate.com; 919 5th Ave E; s/d $109/129; P ☎) When the Butchart family, of Butchart Gardens fame (p101), first emigrated from Scotland, they constructed this rambling estate. The Queen Anne home, with a spiky turret and brick

Evening light at Lake Superior Provincial Park (opposite)

DON JOHNSTON/PHOTOLIBRARY

Travel on the Bruce Trail

For 800km, the Bruce Trail winds along the top of the Niagara Escarpment, from the Niagara Peninsula to the Bruce Peninsula. This wide, well-maintained path is excellent for hiking during summer months, while those armed with cross-country skis and snowshoes make good use of it in winter. Opened in 1967, it's the oldest hiking trail in Canada, and the longest in Ontario.

The trail winds through public and private land, as well as roadways. In Niagara you'll wander past wineries, while up north you'll have clear views of Georgian Bay's blue water from the escarpment's white cliffs. In-between has scenery just as unique and gorgeous.

Multiple entry points make day hikes along 'the Bruce' an appealing way to spend a sunny afternoon, and a multitude of campsites offer budget accommodation for those who are looking for longer trips. In towns where the trail passes through, B&Bs and inns are available to travelers.

Check www.thebruce.org for all sorts of information including trail conditions and accommodations.

gables, is a jumble of architectural styles, which is further exaggerated by the modern addition of a large indoor pool and hot tub. Unfortunately, a housing tract is going up around the lush grounds.

ROCKY RACOON CAFÉ Fusion $$$ (☑ 519-376-2232; 941 2nd Ave E; mains $15-23; ⏱11am-11pm Mon-Sat; 🖉) These organic-produce advocates serve up wild boar and Tibetan dumplings, with vegan and vegetarian options. You'll find plenty of South Asian flavors, especially in the delicious curries.

🄰 Shopping

Pick up *The Art Map*, or check out www.theartmap.com, for a list of over 50 local artists' studios.

OWEN SOUND ARTISTS' CO-OP
Gallery
(www.osartistsco-op.com; 279 10th St E; ⏱9:30am-5:30pm Mon-Sat, noon-4pm Sun) The co-op features an assortment of crafts from regional artists. Spend countless hours browsing the high-quality pottery, photography, basketwork, woodwork, weaving and jewelry while listening to the experimental melodies of new-age music.

NORTHERN ONTARIO

Canada's version of the outback is a stunning, silent expanse where ancient aboriginal canoe routes ignite under the ethereal evening lightshow of aurora borealis. If you're traveling to Ontario and you don't squeeze in a visit, you'll regret it, big-time.

Lake Superior Provincial Park

Most people think Lake Superior got its name from its superior size (it's the largest freshwater lake in the world), but we're pretty sure the lake gets its name from its superior beauty. Shoreline drives are sure to turn car-ride conversations into extended periods of awe-induced silence interspersed with the occasional 'wow.' Whether you're looking to become one with nature, or just want some instant gratification, **Lake Superior Provincial Park** (☑ 705-856-2284, 705-882-2026; www.lakesuperiorpark.ca; Hwy 17; day use per vehicle $13, backcountry sites $9.50, campsites $27.25-32.75) is the perfect introduction to the great Lake. The 1600-sq-km park is one of the most scenic areas along the lake, offering misty fjordlike passages, thick ever-greens, and empty beaches that could have been lifted from an advert for the Caribbean.

All visitors should stop at the park's high-quality interactive museum in the **Agawa Bay Visitor Centre** (☎ 705-882-2026; Hwy 17; ⏱ 9am-8pm Jul-Aug, to 5pm Jun & Sep), roughly 8.7km north of the park's southern boundary. The outdoorsy staff members are an excellent resource for making the most of your visit, however long it may be. In the quieter months visitors can stop at **Red Rock** (☎ 705-856-2284; ⏱ 9am-4pm Mon-Fri), 53km north of the visitor's center, for additional details.

If you're on a tight schedule, pull off Hwy 17 at the **Katherine Cove** picnic area for paradigmatic panoramas of misty sand-strewn shores. Culture junkies should make a pit stop at the **Agawa Rock Pictographs**. These animal and anthropomorphic images, painted in red ochre, are roughly 150 to 400 years old. A short-but-rugged 500m trail connects the visitor parking lot to a rock ledge where, if the lake is calm, the mysterious sketches can be viewed.

For those who have a bit more time, there are 11 excellent hiking trails to explore.

Try the **Nokomis Trail** (5km), which loops around the iconic Old Woman Bay (so named because it is said you can see the face of an old woman in the cliffs). This moderate trek feels like a walk through the past – the wispy beardlike fog and shivering arctic trees give off a distinctly primeval flavor.

The diverse **Orphan Lake Trail** (8km), just north of Katherine Cove, is a veritable pupu platter of the park's ethereal features: isolated cobble beaches, spewing waterfalls, elevated lookouts and dense maple forests.

There are three campgrounds just off Hwy 17: Crescent Lake (no flushing toilets), Awaga Bay and Rabbit Blanket Lake. Bookings must be made through **Ontario Parks** (☎ 888-668-7275; www .ontarioparks.com).

Keep an eye out for scraggly moose along the highway, especially at dusk or dawn.

Pukaskwa National Park

At Pukaskwa (*puck*-a-saw), bear hugs are taken literally. The **park** (☎ 807-229-0801, ext 242; www.parkscanada.gc.ca/pukas kwa; Hwy 627; day use adult/ child $5.80/2.90, backcoun-try sites $9.80, campsites $15-29) features an intact predator-prey ecosys-tem, which continues to thrive since there is only 4km of road in the entire preserve (and just 1km in winter). Pukaskwa offers many of the same

Suspension bridge at Pukaskwa National Park
PHOTOGRAPHER: JA. KRAULIS/PHOTOLIBRARY

topographical features as Lake Superior Provincial Park and includes a small herd of elusive caribou.

There are two ways to explore this majestic hinterland. Those pressed for time can do a trip through the frontcountry, and for those with a flexible itinerary, an adventure through the park's backcountry will be an unforgettable experience.

Pukaskwa's frontcountry is based around **Hattie Cove**, the park's only campground, about 2km from the park's entrance. The **visitor center** (⊙9am-4pm **Jul-Aug**) offers a wealth of information about local wildlife and the boreal forest. On most summer evenings (starting around 7pm) there are guided hikes and activities departing from the center.

Three short trails depart from the campground area, offering glimpses of the pristine setting. The popular spear-shaped **Southern Headland Trail** (2.2km) pokes along a rocky route offering elevated photo ops of the shoreline and the craggy Canadian Shield. The track also acquaints hikers with bonsai-esque trees, severely stunted by harsh winds blowing off the lake. The **Halfway Lake Trail** (2.6km) loops around a small

squiggly lake. Informative signs, dotted along the path, annotate the trek by offering an informed perspective on the inner workings of the ecosystem. A third route, the **Beach Trail** (1.5km), winds along Horseshoe Bay and Lake Superior revealing sweeping vistas of crashing waves and undulating sand dunes. Hattie Cove and Halfway Lake offer tranquil day-long paddling options as well.

It's possible to get a taste for the rugged backcountry even if you're only here for the day. Many fit hikers opt to traverse the first 7.6km of the Coastal Hiking Trail, which culminates at the 30m-long, 25m-high White Water Suspension Bridge. The trek is arduous, even wet, and you must return the way you came (making it a 15km total), but few will complain about the stunning surroundings.

If you don't have the time to plan your own trip, **Naturally Superior Adventures** (☏705-856-2939, 800-203-9092; www.natu rallysuperior.com) in Wawa and **Caribou Expeditions** (☏800-970-6662; www.caribou -expeditions.com; 1021 Goulais Mission Rd, Goulais Bay; tours $135-1495) near Sault Ste Marie offer a variety of guided excursions through Pukaskwa's backcountry.

Montréal & Québec

Once an outpost of Catholic conservatism, an isolated island of *francophonie* languishing in a sea of Anglo culture, Québec province has finally come into its own. It has crafted a rich, spirited culture independent of its European motherland. The Québecois are as vibrant and inviting as the colorful Victorian facades, lush rolling hills and romantic bistros strewn across the province.

And there's plenty to choose from. Montréal and Québec City are bustling metropolises with a perfect mixture of sophistication, playfulness and history-soaked preserved quarters. Produce from bucolic Charlevoix graces the tables of the region's stellar restaurants. The Laurentians abound with ski resorts and peaks, while the cliffs soaring above the Saguenay River at Tadoussac are equally breathtaking (as are the resident beluga whales). The easygoing, red-tinged Îles de la Madeleine freckle the sea to the east.

Québecois enjoy the outdoors in all manner of ways **213**
PHOTOGRAPHER: CHERYL FORBES

View of Montréal's (p226) skyline

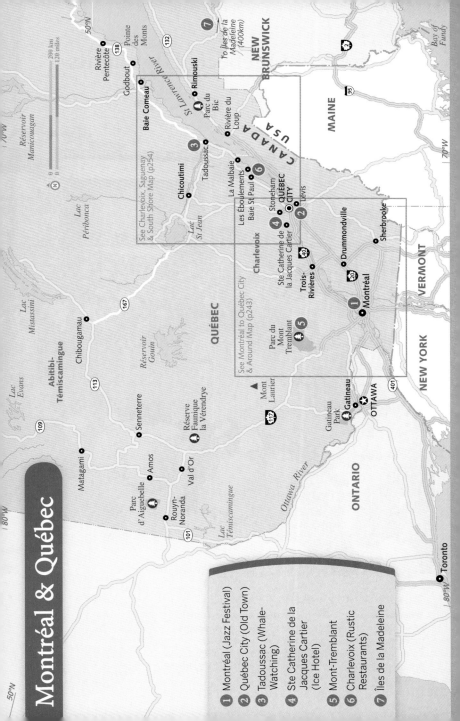

Montréal & Québec

1 Montréal (Jazz Festival)
2 Québec City (Old Town)
3 Tadoussac (Whale-Watching)
4 Ste Catherine de la Jacques Cartier (Ice Hotel)
5 Mont-Tremblant
6 Charlevoix (Rustic Restaurants)
7 Îles de la Madeleine

Montréal & Québec's Highlights

1

Montréal Jazz Festival

Where else can you join more than two million music lovers and watch the best jazz-influenced musicians in the world, choosing from 500 shows of which countless are free? BB King, Prince and Astor Piazzolla are among those who've plugged in at the 10-day bash during late June.

Need to Know

LOCATION Festival venues are within a four-block span downtown. **FREE MOBILE APP** Available for iPhone and Blackberry users, with performance schedules and venue info.

Montréal Jazz Festival Don't Miss List

BY ANDRÉ MÉNARD, FESTIVAL CO-FOUNDER AND ARTISTIC DIRECTOR

1 GESU

My favorite small club to see a show at the festival is **Gesu** (Map p231; ☎514-861-4378; 1200 Bleury Ave). Contemporary jazz is featured there. It's in the stone-walled basement of a church that dates from the mid-19th century. The acoustics are great, and you're close to the stage.

2 METROPOLIS

Metropolis (p238) is a massive rock club that's my favorite big venue. It's an old opera house where we hold reggae and world-music shows. There's a huge dance floor downstage, while the balcony is a different scene with bars, tables and chairs. It has flair combined with excellent sightlines and sound for such a large theater.

3 L'ASTRAL

L'Astral (Map p231; www.sallelastral.com; 305 Ste Catherine St W) is the 'house' and meeting place of the festival, where jam sessions and surprise players from the stages show up between midnight and 3am each night. The festival actually owns the venue, and it's open year-round hosting performances.

4 PLACE DES FESTIVALS

This is the main outdoor space for free shows, where up to 100,000 people attend concerts by the likes of Stevie Wonder (in 2009) and the Brian Seltzer Orchestra (in 2010). We just added the plaza a few years ago, for the festival's 30th anniversary. Here, as elsewhere throughout the event, there is no VIP area. The public is the VIP. It's a very democratic festival!

5 BEYOND JAZZ FEST

Montréal has a huge array of restaurants. Schwartz's (p237) is an Eastern European–style deli that has a famous smoked meat recipe. For live music throughout the year, Upstairs (p239) is the most dignified jazz club in the city.

Québec City Old Town

Inside the walled quarter high on a hill, castle-like towers poke at the sky, glasses clink at sidewalk cafes, and the soft murmurs of a foreign language waft through the air. Stroll through narrow cobblestone lanes and 400-year-old plazas, and it's easy to believe you're an ocean away from North America.

Need to Know

BEST BARS & NIGHTLIFE Grande Allée. **BEST FOR ARTISAN BOUTIQUES** Rue du Petit-Champlain. **BEST DISTRICT FOR HIP BARS & CAFES** St Roch. For further coverage, see p243

Québec City Old Town Don't Miss List

BY RICHARD SÉGUIN, RESIDENT SINCE 1974 AND FORMER TOUR GUIDE

1 PLACE ROYALE

Champlain built Québec's first home here in 1608. It's now a beautiful little plaza surrounded by 17th-century stone buildings. Just to be there and look around is a great way to feel the soul of the city. Then stop in Le Cochon Dingue (p252) for coffee, a *croque monsieur* and nice desserts. In summer you can grab a seat outdoors.

2 WALKING THE FORTIFICATIONS

At the St Louis gate, in the old powder house, there's an interpretive center (p244). Get a guide there for your walk over the fortifications, because they'll take you to places you wouldn't think of going on your own. They know where all the stairways lead.

3 TOURING THE FRONTENAC

The guided tours of Le Château Frontenac (p250) are a well-done way to learn the hotel's history such as how Churchill and Roosevelt planned D-Day there. Afterward, look for Chez Temporel (p251), down a narrow street nearby. It's a cafe with intimate tables, as in Paris, where writers and artists hang out.

4 PLAINS OF ABRAHAM

The Plains of Abraham (p247) is outside the walls, but it's an important part of the city. The battle of 1759 took place there between generals Montcalm and Wolfe. The Discovery Pavilion (p248) is next to it, and you can watch 'Odyssey,' a high-tech show with holograms of the generals and the battle. You can also arrange a tour from the pavilion – the site is huge and best seen by bus.

5 MUSÉE DE LA CIVILISATION

The Museum of Civilization (p247) is especially good for families –a sort of playground with interactive exhibits. There's a real birch-bark canoe, a real teepee and similar displays in the First Nations hall.

219

Wet & Wild Tadoussac

Whale-watching is Tadoussac's (p256) main claim to fame, especially glimpsing the white belugas – the only population outside the Arctic. But it has lots to offer beyond leviathans, such as sea kayaking, 'surfbiking,' hiking in the Saguenay fjord's rugged parks, or simply wandering the local dunes and headlands. Post-adventure, settle into a cafe in the historic, bohemian town, where residents invariably have time for a chat.

Mont-Tremblant

The Laurentians' jagged peaks offer skiing and snowboarding opportunities galore, but it's the region's star, Mont-Tremblant (p241), that draws the international crowds. Throw in a little French panache and it makes for one heck of an après-ski party in the boisterous village surrounding this majestic mountain. In summer, the mountain lords over a lake-jeweled landscape for hikers, bikers, golfers and watersports fans.

CHRIS CHEADLE/PHOTOLIBRARY

YVETTE CARDOZO/ALAMY

Chillin' at the Ice Hotel

Even if you don't sleep in its frosty chambers, Hôtel de Glace (p257) is a sight to behold. Ice beds, ice bar, ice pens to sign the guestbook – you get the theme. Each winter workers scoop up 12,000 tons of snow and 400 tons of ice to build the cool structure, and by April it melts away. The mighty igloo chills a short distance west of Québec City.

GUYLAIN DOYLE

Charlevoix's Rustic Restaurants

A pastoral strip of rolling hills northeast of Quebec City, the Charlevoix region harvests much of the province's food. Gastronomes take a road trip out to get plates heaped with everything from foie gras to lamb to cheeses from the organic farms and rustic eateries that pepper the area. It's farm-to-fork dining in action, especially in towns such as Baie St Paul (p255), Les Éboulements (p258) and La Malbaie (p258).

Sunset in the Magdalen Islands

Sunsets are something on the archipelago, as the sinking orb fires up the ubiquitous red cliffs of the îles. Take your pick on Île du Cap Aux Meules (p259): watch atop the bluff at Cap du Phare lighthouse, or cruise to a beachside microbrewery to see the spectacle. Follow up with a lobster dinner and evening mingling with locals at *boîtes à chansons*, the lively small music venues.

MONTRÉAL & QUÉBEC'S HIGHLIGHTS ● ● ● 221

Montréal & Québec's Best…

Dining

○ **L'Express** (p237) It's so French it could be serving frites under the Eiffel Tower

○ **Le Lapin Sauté** (p252) Country cookin' in cozy environs

○ **Vice Versa** (p258) Creative meats under peppery sauces

○ **Les Saveurs Oubliées** (p258) Lamb in all its glory down on the farm

○ **Le Patriarche** (p251) Nouvelle cuisine and local ingredients amid contemporary art

Gathering Spots

○ **Place du Jacques Cartier** (p227) Buskers, vendors and cafes in Old Montréal's heart

○ **Place Royale** (p245) Québec City's atmospheric soul, where it all began 400 years ago

○ **Georges Étienne Cartier monument** (p229) Hit the bongos with the hippies during Tam Tam Sundays

○ **Grande Allée** (p252) Nightlife and twinkling lights by Québec City's walls

Hotels/B&Bs

○ **Auberge Saint Antoine** (p250) Part archaeological site, part boutique hotel with grand views

○ **Maison Historique James Thompson** (p249) The 18th-century residence of a Plains of Abraham veteran

○ **Hotel Gault** (p233) Minimalist, loft-style rooms for design buffs

○ **Nature et Pinceaux** (p255) Mountain-top B&B with four-course breakfast

Outdoor Adventures

○ **Mont-Tremblant** (p241) Whistler-esque skiing in winter, hiking and paddling in summer

○ **Tadoussac** (p256) Get sprayed by whales on a Zodiac or kayak trip

○ **Îles de la Madeleine** (p258) Windsurfing, kitesurfing, cycling, kayaking and cave visits

○ **Canal de Lachine** (p231) Cycle from Old Montréal to its outskirts along the waterway

Need to Know

ADVANCE PLANNING

○ **One month before** In summer book accommodation as soon as possible, especially in festival-crazy Montréal. Same for winter visits to Québec City or the Laurentians.

○ **Two weeks before** Get Cirque du Soleil and other theater tickets.

○ **One week before** Secure dinner reservations at well-known restaurants in Montréal and Charlevoix.

RESOURCES

○ **Tourism Québec** (www .bonjourquebec.com) Lets you book rooms, show tickets, even car rentals and train tickets.

○ **Tourism Montréal** (www.tourisme-montreal.org) Accommodation bookings, videos and a buzzy blog; the last-minute hotel search engine guarantees a minimum 10% discount.

○ **Tourism Québec City** (www.quebecregion.com) Listings of what to see and do, and where to eat and sleep.

○ **Québec Parks** (www .sepaq.com/pq) The low-down for visiting the province's 23 'national' (aka provincial) parks.

○ **Midnight Poutine** (www .midnightpoutine.ca) Lifestyle blog by hip Montréal urbanites with good 'city and culture' listings.

○ **Montréal Clubs** (www .montreal-clubs.com) Keeps the finger on the pulse of Montréal's latest nightlife hotspots.

GETTING AROUND

○ **Fly** Montréal's Trudeau International Airport is Canada's third-busiest and a regional hub. Québec City's airport is much smaller.

○ **Car** The Trans-Canada Hwy (Hwy 40 within Québec) runs through Montréal and Québec City. Highways throughout the province are good. Rental cars are readily available.

○ **Ferry** Several different ferry services glide across the St Lawrence River, as well as to islands in the Gulf, such as the Îles de la Madeleine.

○ **Train** From Montréal, VIA Rail (www.viarail.ca) has fast and frequent daily service to Toronto and Québec City, and one train daily to Halifax. There's Amtrak service (www.amtrak.com) from New York City to Montréal.

Left: Ski lift at Mont-Tremblant (p241);
Above: Hôtel Tadoussac (257), Tadoussac
(LEFT) GLENN VAN DER KNIJFF; (ABOVE) OLIVIER CIRENDINI

Montréal & Québec Itineraries

Oh la la! Montréal and Québec City wow with romance, history and gastronomic delights. From there the roads hugging the St Lawrence River lead to art towns, on-the farm restaurants and whales.

3 DAYS

MONTRÉAL TO QUÉBEC CITY
Provincial Pillars

Start in **(1) Montréal** in the **(2) Mile End** district, partaking in a local ritual – a long and leisurely brunch. Hike up **(3) Mont Royal**, stopping to catch your breath and snap the cityscape from the **(4) Kondiaronk Lookout** before ending up in the boisterous **(5) Plateau Mont-Royal** for dinner and evening entertainment.

Begin day two by exploring the cobblestoned alleys of Old Montréal. Get a dose of history at **(6) Musée d'Archéologie et d'Histoire Pointe-à-Callière**, or soak up some culture at **(7) Musée des Beaux Arts**. Head to **(8) Little Italy** for a pasta-wine-espresso

dinner, then sample the club scene in **(9) the Village**.

It's tough to leave such a playful place, but history-drenched **(10) Québec City** awaits. Set out on foot through the Old Town's labyrinth of cobbled lanes and squares. Walk over the 400-year-old **(11) fortifications**; point the camera at turreted **(12) Le Château Frontenac**; and sip a cafe au lait in the soulful **(13) Place Royale**, the cradle of Nouvelle France. Search for the ultimate *table d'hôte* (fixed price menu) in the Old Lower Town for dinner before tucking into the covers at a romantic inn come nightfall.

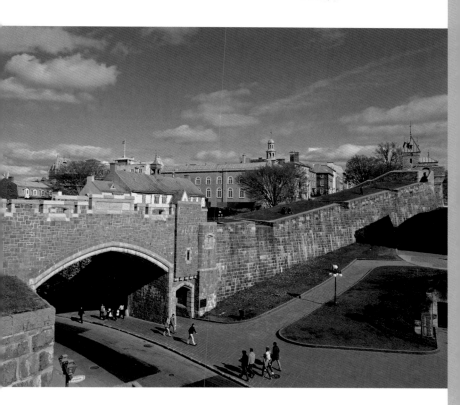

5 DAYS

QUÉBEC CITY TO TADOUSSAC
River Route

Rattle around **(1) Québec City** for two days, absorbing the historic sites, street performers and jazz-playing corner cafes. If it's summer, hop on the ferry to **(2) Lévis** for city views. If it's winter, do a day-trip a half-hour west to see **(3) Hôtel de Glace**, aka the 'Ice Hotel,' a gleaming marvel made entirely of – that's right – ice.

Begin the journey northeast, following the St Lawrence River as it slices through flowery **(4) Charlevoix**. Foodies often make a pilgrimage to this region, known for its organic farms and stellar eateries. Stop in **(5) Baie St Paul**, an arty town stuffed with galleries, cheerful B&Bs, alehouses

and, of course, fine French cuisine. Further on, dine at the lamb farm in **(6) Les Éboulements**. Onward still, **(7) La Malbaie** offers country manors and more rustic restaurants specializing in local fare.

Once you get your fill, continue following the river to **(8) Tadoussac**. The historic, bohemian town is a top place for whale-watching. Humpbacks, minkes and king-of-the-sea blue whales swim by, as do beluga whales, which otherwise are seen only in the Arctic. Hiking and paddling around the dramatic scenery are the other big draws.

Québec City's fortifications (p244)

Discover Montréal & Québec

MONTRÉAL

POP 3.4 MILLION

Historically Montréal, the only de facto bilingual city on the continent, has been torn right in half, the 'Main' (Blvd St-Laurent) being the dividing line between the east-end Francophones and the west-side Anglos. Today French pockets dot both sides of the map, a new wave of English-speaking Canadians have taken residence in some formerly French enclaves and thanks to constant waves of immigration, it's not uncommon for Montréalers to speak not one, or two, but three languages in their daily life. With the new generation concerned more with global issues (namely the environment), language battles have become so passé.

One thing not up for debate is what makes Montréal so irresistible. It's a secret blend of French-inspired joie de vivre and cosmopolitan dynamism that has come together to foster a flourishing arts scene, an indie rock explosion, a medley of world-renowned boutique hotels, the Plateau's extraordinary cache of swank eateries and a cool Parisian vibe that pervades every *terrasse* (patio) in the Quartier Latin. It's easy to imagine you've been transported to a distant locale, where hedonism is the national mandate.

 Sights

Old Montréal

BASILIQUE NOTRE-DAME Church

(Map p230; www.basiliquenddm.org; 110 Rue Notre-Dame Ouest; adult/child $5/4; ⏲8am-

View from Old Montréal
PHOTOGRAPHER: RENAULT PHILIPPE/PHOTOLIBRARY

4:30pm Mon-Sat, noon-4:15pm Sun) Montréal's famous landmark, Notre-Dame Basilica, is a visually pleasing if slightly gaudy symphony of carved wood, paintings, gilded sculptures and stained-glass windows. Built in 1829 on the site of an older and smaller church, it also sports a famous Casavant organ and the Gros Bourdon, said to be the biggest bell in North America. The interior looks especially impressive during an otherwise overly melodramatic **sound and light show** (adult/child $10/5), staged from Tuesday to Saturday night.

PLACE D'ARMES   Historical Site

The twin-towered Notre-Dame Basilica lords over this dignified square, where the early settlers once battled it out with the local Iroquois. A statue of Maisonneuve stands in the middle of the square, which is surrounded by some of Old Montréal's finest historic buildings. In fact, the **Old Seminary** (Map p230), next to the basilica, is the city's oldest, built by Sulpician missionaries in 1685 and still occupied today.

Behind the temple-like curtain of columns in the northwest corner lurks the **Bank of Montreal** (Map p230; 119 Rue St-Jacques Ouest; admission free; ☺10am-4pm Mon-Fri). It harbors the head office of Canada's oldest bank, founded in 1817. The opulent marble interior is worth a gander and there's a small money museum as well.

Looming on the square's east side is the red sandstone **New York Life Building** (1888; Map p230), which was the city's first skyscraper. Today it is dwarfed by the art-deco **Aldred Building** (1937; Map p230), which was intended to emulate the Empire State Building until the Great Crash of 1929 put an end to such lofty ambitions.

PLACE JACQUES CARTIER & AROUND
Historical Site

Gently sloped Place Jacques Cartier in the heart of Old Montréal is a beehive of activity, especially in summer when it's filled with flowers, street musicians, vendors and visitors. The cafes and res-

taurants lining it are neither cheap nor good, but they do offer front-row seats for the action. There is a tourist office (p240) in the northwest corner.

At the square's north end stands the **Colonne Nelson** (Nelson's Column; Map p230), a monument erected by the British to the general who defeated the French and Spanish fleet at Trafalgar. Nelson faces a small statue of Admiral Vauquelin across the street, put there as a riposte by the French.

Looking mightily majestic with its green copper roof and perky turret, the **Hôtel de Ville** (City Hall; Map p230; 275 Rue Notre-Dame Est; admission & tours free; ☺8:30am-4:30pm, tours late Jun–mid-Aug) towers above the square's northeast end. Modeled on the city hall of Tours, France, and completed in 1878, its grandeur reflects the city's 19th-century wealth and confidence.

MARCHÉ BONSECOURS   Market

(Bonsecours Market; Map p230; 350 Rue St-Paul Est; ☺10am-9pm late Jun-early Sep, to 6pm Sep-Mar) The silvery dome standing sentinel over Old Montréal like a glamorous lighthouse belongs to Bonsecours Market. After a stint as city hall, the neoclassical structure served as the city's main market hall until supermarkets drove it out of business in the 1960s. These days, the flower and vegetable stands have been replaced with fancy boutiques selling arts, crafts and clothing produced in Québec. This is not a bad place to pick up some quality souvenirs.

OLD PORT   Landmark

Montréal's Old Port has morphed into a park and fun zone paralleling the mighty St Lawrence River for 2.5km and punctuated by four grand *quais*. Locals and visitors alike come here for strolling, cycling and in-line skating. Cruise boats, ferries, jet boats and speedboats all depart for tours from various docks (see p240). In winter, you can cut a fine figure on an outdoor **ice-skating rink** (p231).

Historical relics include the striking white **Clock Tower** (Map p230; Clock Tower Pier; admission free; ☺10am-9pm mid-May–Sep)

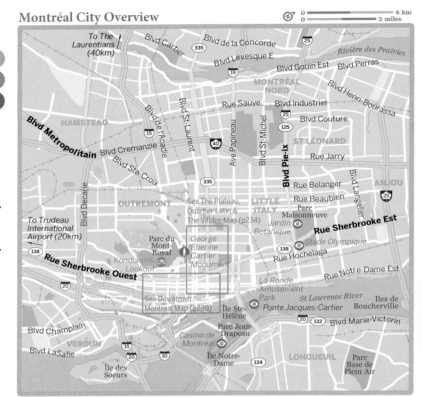

at the northern end of Quai Jacques Cartier. Built in 1922 to honor sailors who died in WWI, it affords commanding views of the river and city.

A perennial family favorite is the **Centre des Sciences de Montréal** (Montréal Science Centre; Map p230; www .montrealsciencecentre.com; King Edward Pier; adult/child $12/9, with IMAX 3-D movie $20/15; ⏰9am-4pm Mon-Fri, to 5pm Sat & Sun). There are plenty of buttons to push, knobs to pull and games to play as you make your way through the high-tech exhibition halls.

MUSÉE D'ARCHÉOLOGIE ET D'HISTOIRE POINTE-À-CALLIÈRE   Museum
(Museum of Archaeology & History; Map p230; www.pacmuseum.qc.ca; 350 Place Royale; adult/ child $14/6; ⏰11am-6pm mid-Jun–mid-Sep, 11am-5pm mid-Sep–mid-Jun) Housed in a

striking, contemporary building, this excellent museum sits near the original landing spot of the early settlers and provides a good overview of the city's beginnings. Make time for the multimedia show before plunging underground into a maze of excavated foundations, an ancient sewerage system and vestiges of the first European cemetery. The lookout tower and restaurant can be visited free of charge.

Downtown

FREE MUSÉE DES BEAUX-ARTS
Museum

(Museum of Fine Arts; Map p230; www.mbam .qc.ca; 1380 Rue Sherbrooke Ouest; permanent collection admission free, special exhibitions adult/child $15/free, half-price Wed after 5pm; ⏰11am-5pm Tue, Sat & Sun, to 9pm Wed-Fri) A must for art lovers, the Museum of

Fine Arts has amassed several millennia worth of paintings, sculpture, decorative arts, furniture, prints, drawings and photographs. European heavyweights include Rembrandt, Picasso and Monet, but the museum really shines when it comes to Canadian art. Highlights include works by Jean-Baptiste Roy-Audy and Paul Kane, landscapes by the Group of Seven and abstractions by Jean-Paul Riopelle.

CHINATOWN   Landmark

Although this neighborhood, perfectly packed into a few easily navigable streets, has no sites per se, it's a nice area for lunch or for shopping for quirky knickknacks. The main thoroughfare, Rue de la Gauchetière, between Blvd St-Laurent and Rue Jeanne Mance, is enlivened with Taiwanese bubble-tea parlors, Hong Kong–style bakeries and Vietnamese soup restaurants. The public square, **Place Sun-Yat-Sen** (Map p230), attracts crowds of elderly Chinese and the occasional gaggle of Falun Gong demonstrators.

MUSÉE D'ART CONTEMPORAIN
Museum

(Map p234; www.macm.org; 185 Rue Ste-Catherine Ouest; adult/child $10/free, admission free 5-9pm Wed; ◷11am-6pm Tue & Thu-Sun, to 9pm Wed) Canada's only major showcase of contemporary art, this museum offers an excellent survey of Canadian, and in particular Québécois, creativity. All the local legends, including Jean-Paul Riopelle, Paul-Émile Borduas and Géneviève Cadieux, are well represented. There are great temporary shows, too. Free English-language tours run at 6:30pm Wednesday and at 1pm and 3pm on weekends.

Parc du Mont Royal Area
GEORGES ÉTIENNE CARTIER
MONUMENT   Statue

On the park's northeastern edge, on Ave du Parc, this statue draws hundreds of revelers every Sunday for tribal playing and spontaneous dancing in what has been dubbed 'Tam Tam Sundays' (tam-tams are bongo-like drums). It's nothing less than an institution. If the noise doesn't lead you all the way there, just follow your nose toward whiffs of 'wacky tabaccy.' This is also a good spot to pick up some unusual handicrafts sold by local artisans.

Mont Royal can be entered via the steps at the top of Rue Peel. Buses 80 and 129 make their way from the Place des Arts métro station to the Georges Étienne Cartier monument. Bus 11 from the Mont Royal métro stop traverses the park.

Quartier Latin & The Village

The Quartier Latin is Montréal's most boisterous neighborhood, a slightly grungy entertainment district made glitzy with an infusion of French panache.

A hotbed of activity, especially during the **International Jazz Festival** (www.montrealjazzfest.com; late June/early July), **FrancoFolies** (www.francofolies.com; late June) and **Just for Laughs** (http://montreal.hahaha.com/en; July), the quarter bubbles 24 hours a day in its densely packed rows of bars, trendy bistros, music clubs and record shops.

Over the past decade or so, Montréal's gay community has breathed new life into The Village, a once poverty-stricken corner of the east end. Today,

Montréal Museum Pass

Custom-made for culture buffs, this handy **pass** ($45) is valid for three consecutive days and gets you admission to 34 museums, plus unlimited use of the bus and métro system. It's available at tourist offices, major hotels and participating museums. Note that most museums are closed on Monday.

Downtown Montréal

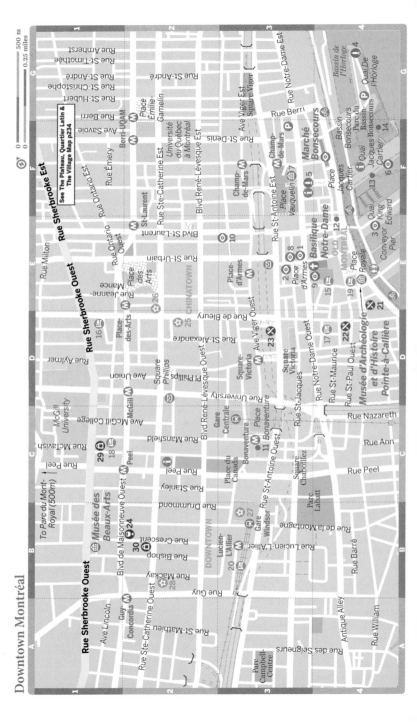

Downtown Montréal

gay-friendly doesn't even begin to describe the neighborhood. People of all persuasions wander Rue Ste-Catherine and savor the joie de vivre in its cafes, bistros and discerning eateries.

Plateau Mont-Royal

East of Parc du Mont Royal, the Plateau (Map p234) is Montréal's youngest, liveliest and artiest neighborhood.

The main drags are Blvd St-Laurent (aka The Main), Rue St-Denis and Ave du Mont-Royal, all lined with sidewalk cafes, restaurants, clubs and boutiques. Rue Prince Arthur, Montréal's quintessential hippie hangout in the 1960s, and Rue Duluth are alive with BYOW eateries.

Little Italy & Mile End

The zest and flavor of the old country find their way into the lively Little Italy district, north of the Plateau, where the espresso seems stiffer, the pasta sauce thicker and the chefs plumper. Soak up the atmosphere on a stroll, and don't

miss the **Marché Jean Talon** (p241), which always hums with activity.

Dubbed the 'new Plateau' by the exodus of students and artists seeking a more affordable, less polished hangout, the Mile End district has all the coolness of its predecessor as well as two phenomenal bagel shops, upscale dining along Ave Laurier and tons of increasingly trendy hangouts at its epicenter: Rue St-Viateur and Blvd St-Laurent.

 Activities

Cycling & In-line Skating

Montréal is a cyclist's haven. One popular route parallels the Canal de Lachine (p239) for 14.5km, starting in Old Montréal and passing a lot of history en route. Picnic tables are scattered along the way, so pick up some tasty victuals at the fabulous Marché Atwater (p237).

Bixi (http://montreal.bixi.com; refundable security deposit $250, basic fees 24hr/30 days/1 year $5/28/78, usage fees up to 30min/60min/90min free/$1.50/3; ⊙24hr Apr-Nov) Three hundred pickup and dropoff stations are located every few blocks and at every main attraction throughout the city.

Ça Roule Montréal (Map p230; www .caroulemontreal.com; 27 Rue de la Commune Est, Old Port; bicycles per hr/24hr $9/35, in-line skates 1st/additional hr $9/4; ⊙9am-8pm Apr-Oct)

Ice Skating

Atrium (Map p230; www.le1000.com; 1000 Rue de la Gauchetière Ouest; adult/child $6.50/4.50, skate rental $6; ⊙11:30am-9pm Tue-Sun, to 6pm Mon Oct-Apr, 11:30am-6pm Tue-Fri, noon-10pm Sat, noon-6pm Sun May-Sep) Take to the ice any time the mood strikes at this gigantic, state-of-the-art glass-domed indoor rink in Montréal's tallest tower.

Patinoire du Bassin Bonsecours (Map p230; Parc du Bassin Bonsecours, Old Port; adult/child $5/3, skate rental $6; ⊙11am-6pm

in winter, weather permitting) This is one of Montréal's most popular outdoor skating rinks.

 Tours

Le Bateau Mouche Boat Tour
(Map p230; ☏514-849-9952; www.bateau -mouche.com; 1hr tours adult/child $23/11; ⊙11am, 2:30pm & 4:30pm mid-May–mid-Oct) Leaving from Quai Jacques Cartier, hour-long cruises aboard climate-controlled, glass-roofed boats explore the Old Port and Parc Jean-Drapeau. A 90-minute version ($27/14) departs at 12:30pm.

Guidatour Walking Tour
(☏514-844-4021; www.guidatour.qc.ca; adult/ child $19.50/10.50; ⊙11am & 1:30pm Sat & Sun mid-May–late Jun, daily late Jun–mid-Oct) Guidatour's bilingual guides spice up historical tours of Old Montréal with colorful tales and anecdotes. Tours depart from the Basilique Notre-Dame (Map p230).

Left: Tranquil Parc du Mont Royal (p236); Below: Toboggan slope near Montréal

PHOTOGRAPHER: (LEFT) GUYLAIN DOYLE; (BELOW) BRIAN CRUICKSHANK

🛏 Sleeping

Hotels fill up fast in the summer when warm weather and festivals galore bring hordes of tourists to Montréal, making reservations essential.

The following agencies can help book accommodations.

BB Select (www.bbselect.com/quebec)

BBCanada (www.bbcanada.com/quebec)

BedandBreakfast.com (www.bedand breakfast.com/montreal-quebec.html)

Centre Infotouriste (see p240)

Old Montréal

HOTEL GAULT   Boutique Hotel $$$
(Map p230; ✆ 514-904-1616, 866-904-1616; www.hotelgault.com; 449 Rue Ste-Hélène; r $220-750; ❄ 🛜) A design aficionado's haven, the Hotel Gault features a sooth-ing minimalist palette with polished concrete floors and steel accents, original 19th-century cast-iron columns and the occasional splash of warm blond wood. Flou beds, iPod docks, flat-screen TVs and heated bathroom floors add warmth and comfort to each of the 30 serenely stark loft-style rooms.

BONAPARTE   Inn $$
(Map p230; ✆ 514-844-1448; www.bonaparte .com; 447 Rue St-François-Xavier; r $145-230, ste $355; ❄ 🛜) This elegant property exudes refined, classic European ambi-ence with wooden floors, Louis-Philippe furniture, French windows – some with views of the Basilique Notre-Dame – and exposed stone walls. After a satis-fying three-course breakfast head up to the rooftop patio for snap-worthy views.

LE PETIT HÔTEL   Boutique Hotel $$
(Map p230; ✆ 514-940-0360, 877-530-0360; www.petithotelmontreal.com; 168 Rue St-Paul Ouest; r $138-268; ❄ @ 🛜) The newest kid on the boutique hotel block, this 'small

233

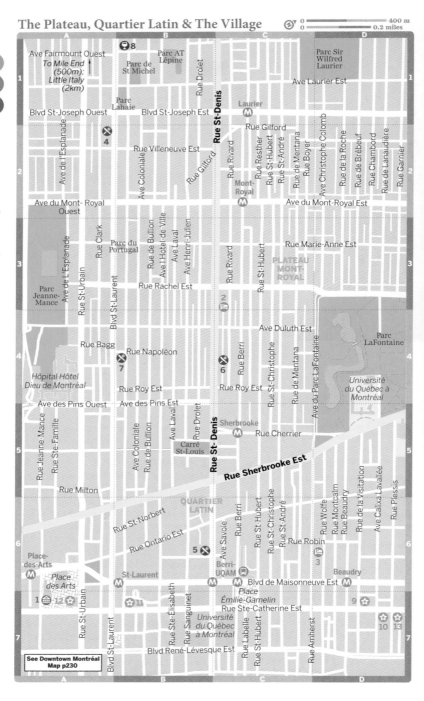

The Plateau, Quartier Latin & The Village

hotel' is indeed tiny with only 24 small, medium, large and extra-large rooms, but *très* chic with hardwood floors, colorful furniture and plenty of modern electronic gadgets.

Downtown

HÔTEL LE GERMAIN　　Hotel　$$$
(Map p230; ☎ 514-849-2050, 877-333-2050; www.germainmontreal.com; 2050 Rue Mansfield; r $170-475; ✳@☎) An air of calm and sophistication greets you from the moment you walk in to this unassuming former office building just a stone's throw from the McGill University campus. The rooms are sexy with crisp white linens, dark, seductive Québec-crafted furniture, and see-through walls into the shower (with blinds, for shy bathers).

LES BONS MATINS　　B&B　$$
(Map p230; ☎ 514-931-9167, 800-588-5280; www.bonsmatins.com; 1401 Ave Argyle; r $129-149, ste $199-239; ✳☎) Charming and seductive with exposed bricks and vibrant colors splashed across bed sheets and wall hangings, this classy establishment fills a series of adjoining turn-of-the-century step-ups. Breakfasts couldn't get better, with gourmet quiche, homemade waffles and Italian-style espresso. Parking is $12 per night.

HILTON GARDEN INN　　Hotel　$$
(Map p230; ☎ 877-840-0010; www.hiltongarden montreal.com; 380 Rue Sherbrooke Ouest; r $179-209; ✳@☎) The brand-new incarnation of this popular hotel chain's budget series has garnered quite a reputation for its spacious rooms, friendly staff

and excellent location. The airy rooftop swimming pool and exercise room are big pluses for families, and the free internet access and in-room fridges and microwaves only sweeten the deal. No rooms are situated near the elevator or ice machines.

Quartier Latin & Around

LA LOGGIA ART & BREAKFAST　B&B　$$
(Map p234; ☎ 514-524-2493, 866-520-2493; www.laloggia.ca; 1637 Rue Amherst; r without bathroom $80-130, with bathroom $105-155; @☎) Although plain-looking from the exterior, the inside of this 19th-century townhouse in the Gay Village is anything but average. The artwork of co-host, Joel, brings the five modern guest rooms alive; a sprawling breakfast buffet prepared by his partner, Rob, is served in a leafy sculpture garden behind the house.

ANNE MA SOEUR ANNE　　Hotel　$$
(Map p234; ☎ 514-281-3187; www.annema soeuranne.com; 4119 Rue St-Denis; s $70-180, d $80-210; ✳☎) Buttery croissants delivered to your door and a fresh pot of coffee brewed in your own small kitchen is the way mornings get started in this hotel. Smallish rooms feature clever beds that fold up to reveal a full dining table, but the real draw here is the central Plateau location.

 Eating

Downtown and especially the Plateau are a foodie's nirvana. More than any

BRIAN CRUICKSHANK

Don't Miss **Parc du Mont Royal**

Montréalers are proud of their **'mountain'** (Map p228; www.lemontroyal.qc.ca), the work of New York Central Park designer Frederick Law Olmsted. It's a sprawling, leafy playground that's perfect for cycling, jogging, horseback riding, picnicking and, in winter, cross-country skiing and tobogganing. In fine weather, enjoy panoramic views from the **Kondiaronk Lookout** near **Chalet du Mont-Royal**, a grand old stone villa that hosts big-band concerts in summer, or further north from the **Observatoire de l'Est**, a favorite rendezvous for lovebirds. It takes about 30 minutes to walk between the two. En route you'll spot the landmark 40m-high **Cross of Montréal** (1924), which is illuminated at night. It's there to commemorate city founder Maisonneuve, who single-handedly carried a wooden cross up the mountain in 1643 to give thanks to God for sparing his fledgling village from flooding.

other street, Blvd St-Laurent epitomizes the city's gastronomic wealth, from boisterous soup parlors in Chinatown to Schwartz's smoked meat emporium to funky Plateau trendsetters. Further north, the Marché Jean Talon (see boxed text, p241) is a great place to sample local produce.

Old Montréal

GIBBY'S Steakhouse **$$$**
(Map p230; 📞 514-282-1837; www.gibbys.com; 298 Place d'Youville; meals $25.50-48.50; ⏰5:30pm-late Mon-Fri, from 5pm Sat & Sun)

The setting alone, in a 200-year-old converted stable, offers eye candy galore, but it's the food, especially expertly cut steaks, that truly shines. A drink in the bar is a perfect overture to an evening of fine dining. Reservations essential.

OLIVE + GOURMANDO Cafe **$**
(Map p230; www.oliveetgourmando.com; 351 Rue St-Paul Ouest; meals $5-10; ⏰8am-6pm Tue-Sat; 🖋) Push and shove (if necessary) through thick lunchtime crowds in this little corner cafe for a little bit of heaven, manifest in hot paninis and sultry soups

using fresh, often organic produce. Leave room for the infamous chocolate brownies, infused with rich illy coffee.

Downtown

TOQUÉ!   French $$$

(Map p230; ☎ 514-499-2084; www.restaurant
-toque.com; 900 Place Jean-Paul-Riopelle; tasting menu $92-171; ⊙5:30-10:30pm Tue-Sat)
This restaurant is consistently touted as Montréal's top restaurant, with a long list of accolades to add credence to this claim. Chef Normand Laprise's seven-course tasting menu brings fresh Québec produce to the table in a symphony of taste ingenuity and flawless presentation. Reservations essential.

MARCHÉ ATWATER   Market $

(138 Ave Atwater; ⊙7am-6pm Mon-Wed, to 8pm
Thu & Fri, to 5pm Sat & Sun; ⏲; Ⓜ Atwater)
This superb market brims with vendors selling mostly local and regional products, from perfectly matured cheeses to crusty breads, exquisite ice wines and tangy tapenades. It's all housed in a 1933 brick hall just west of downtown, at the intersection of Ave Atwater and Rue Ste-Catherine Ouest.

Quartier Latin & The Village

LES 3 BRASSEURS   Pub $$

(Map p234; www.les3brasseurs.ca; 1658 Rue St-
Denis; mains $11-14; ⊙11am-1am) If you'd like
to cap a day of sightseeing with belly-filling fare and a few pints of handcrafted beer, stop by this convivial brewpub with its stylized warehouse looks and rooftop terrace. The house specialty is 'Flamm's,' a French spin on pizza.

Plateau Mont-Royal

L'EXPRESS   French $$

(Map p234; ☎ 514-845-5333; 3927 Rue St-Denis;
mains $14-29; ⊙8am-2am) This place is so fantastically French, you'd half expect to see the Eiffel Tower out the window, especially after guzzling too much of the excellent wines. The food's classic Parisian bistro – think steak *frites*, bouillabaisse, tarragon chicken – and so is the attitude. Reservations are essential.

SCHWARTZ'S   Sandwich Shop $

(Map p234; www.schwartzsdeli.com; 3895 Blvd
St-Laurent; meals $6-17; ⊙9am-12:30am Sun-
Thu, to 1:30am Fri, to 2:30am Sat) Don't be deterred by the line that inevitably forms outside this legendary smoked meat parlor. Join the eclectic clientele – from students to celebrities – at the communal tables, and don't forget to order the pickles, fries and coleslaw.

LA SALA ROSA   Spanish $$

(Map p234; 4848 Blvd St-Laurent; meals $12-15;
⊙5-11pm Tue-Sun; ⏲) Wash down some

Montréal for Children

Children adore Montréal. The Stade Olympique (Olympic Park; Map p228) area is the ultimate kid-friendly zone: the **Biodôme**, home to porcupines, penguins and other local and exotic critters, is a sure winner, and the nearby **Insectarium's** (p239) creepy crawlies provide plenty of gasps and tickles.

Budding scientists will have a field day at the **Centre des Sciences de Montréal** (p228), which has dozens of interactive stations and video games. Many museums have special kid-oriented workshops and guided tours.

On nearby Île Ste-Hélène awaits **La Ronde** (p239) amusement park, where the stomach-churning roller coasters and other diversions are especially thrilling for teens. There's ice skating all year long at the grand **Atrium** (p232), which offers special kids' sessions on Sundays until 11:30am.

Many hotels can provide referrals to reliable, qualified babysitting services.

flavorful tapas and every shade of paella with a pitcher of sangria in this unique restaurant, which shares a floor with the Spanish Social Club. Thursdays sees the venue hosting free flamenco dance performances.

 # Drinking

BU
Wine Bar

(Map p234; www.bu-mtl.com; 5245 Blvd St-Laurent; ⏱5pm-1am) Subtle just about sums up the nonabrasive crowds and cool-as-a-cucumber decor in this pleasant *bar à vins*. Knowledgeable staff can advise on the bible-like wine list, or shop around with a trio of tasters. You must order at least a snack ($4 to $9) to be permitted to drink.

SIR WINSTON CHURCHILL PUB
Pub

(Map p230; www.winniesbar.com; 1455 Rue Crescent; ⏱11:30am-3am) A quintessential Crescent St watering hole, founded in 1967 by Johnny Vale, a one-time comrade of Che Guevara. The late local author Mordecai Richler used to knock back cold ones in the bar upstairs.

The colors of fall, Montréal (p226)

Things get clamorous between 5pm and 8pm when it's two-for-one happy hour.

 # Entertainment

The city positively grooves during the Jazz Festival (see p216).

For details about top clubs and DJs *du jour*, pick up a copy of the glossy *ME* (Montréal Entertainment). **Info-Arts Bell** (☎ 514-790-2787) is an information line for cultural events, plays and concerts. The free alternative weeklies, the *Mirror* and the *Hour*, have useful 'what's on' listings.

CIRQUE DU SOLEIL
Theater

(☎ 514-722-2234; www.cirquedusoleil.com) For the past two decades, this phenomenally successful troupe has redefined what circuses are all about. Headquartered in Montréal, it usually inaugurates new shows in the city every year or two. Call or check with the tourist office.

METROPOLIS
Live Music

(Map p234; ☎ 514-844-3500; www.montreal metropolis.ca; 59 Rue Ste-Catherine Est) Of its

many faces – as a skating rink, a porn movie theater and disco among others – a rock venue suits this 2300-person-capacity concert hall best. The stage was graced by the likes of Radiohead, David Bowie and Coldplay earlier in their careers.

UPSTAIRS   Live Music
(Map p230; ☎ 514-931-6808; www.upstairs jazz.com; 1254 Rue Mackay; ☺noon-1am Tue-Fri, 5pm-1am Sat & Sun) Some mighty fine talent, both home-grown and imported, has tickled the ivories of the baby grand in this intimate jazz joint. Shows start at 10pm. The venue also has an ice terrace and respectable dinner menu.

MONTRÉAL CANADIENS   Sports
(Map p230; ☎ 514-932-2582; www .canadiens.com; Bell Centre, 1200 Rue de la Gauchetière Ouest; tickets $29-261) Bell Centre is home base for this National Hockey League team and 24-time Stanley Cup winners (the last time in 1993). After the first drop of the puck you might be able to snag a half-price ticket from the scalpers lurking by the entrance. Bring binoculars for the rafter seats.

MONTRÉAL ALOUETTES   Sports
(☎ 514-871-2255; www.montrealalouettes .com; Molson Stadium, Ave des Pins Ouest; tickets $20-75; Ⓜ Square Victoria, then free shuttle bus) This once-defunct Canadian Football League team is now the unlikely hottie of the city's sports scene, especially since winning the league's Grey Cup trophy in 2009. They have sold out every game since 1999, so order tickets early. Free shuttle buses to the games start two hours before kickoff.

 Shopping

PARASUCO   Clothing
(Map p230; www.parasuco.com; 1414 Rue Crescent) Made right here in Montréal, Parasuco has become one of Canada's hottest labels for jeans and casual wear.

If You Like…
Urban Oases

If you like Parc du Mont Royal (p236), check out these other natural areas in Montréal:

1 JARDIN BOTANIQUE & INSECTARIUM
(www2.ville.montreal.qc.ca/jardin; 4101 Rue Sherbrooke Est; adult/child May-Oct $16.50/8.25, Nov-Apr $14/7, combination ticket with Biodôme $28/14; ☺9am-6pm mid-May–mid-Sep, to 9pm mid-Sep–Oct, to 5pm Tue-Sun Nov–mid-Jun; Ⓜ Pie-IX) Montréal's Botanical Garden is the world's third largest after those in London and Berlin. Some 22,000 species of plants grow in 30 outdoor gardens. Tickets also include a visit to the Insectarium with its intriguing collection of creepy crawlies, and the Butterfly House, which shouldn't be missed. The facility is east of central downtown near Olympic Park (Stade Olympique). A trolley traverses the park, so you don't have to foot it all the way.

2 PARC JEAN-DRAPEAU
(www.parcjeandrapeau.com) The site of the 1967 World's Fair, Parc Jean-Drapeau consists of two islands surrounded by the St Lawrence: Île Ste-Hélène and Île Notre-Dame. Although nature is the main appeal, the park is also home to a Vegas-sized casino and the scream-inducing **La Ronde** (Map p228; www.laronde.com) amusement park. Ferries ($6) depart from Quai Jacques Cartier to shuttle pedestrians and bicycles to the park.

3 CANAL DE LACHINE
The waterway stretches for 14.5km from the Old Port to Lac St-Louis. Its banks are a terrific park for cycling and walking.

Its high-energy flagship store stocks all the latest styles.

CHEAP THRILLS   Music Store
(Map p230; http://cheapthrills.ca; 2044 Rue Metcalfe) It's easy to lose track of time as you browse through this big selection of used books and music (CDs and some vinyl), both with a mainstream and off-beat bent and sold at bargain prices.

ℹ️ Information

Tourist Information

Montréal and Québec province maintain a central phone service for tourist information (📞514-873-2015, 877-266-5687).

Centre Infotouriste (Map p230; www.bonjour quebec.com; 1255 Rue Peel; 🕐9am-6pm Mar–mid-Jun, 8:30am-7pm mid-Jun–Aug, 9am-6pm Sep-Oct, 9am-5pm Nov-Feb) Information about Montréal and all of Québec. Free hotel, tour and car reservations, plus currency exchange.

Montréal Tourist Office (Map p230; www .tourism-montreal.org; 174 Rue Notre Dame Est; 🕐9am-5pm Jan-May & early Sep-Oct, to 7pm Jun–early Sep)

ℹ️ Getting There & Away

Air Both domestic and international airlines land at Pierre Elliott Trudeau International Airport (YUL; 📞514-394-7377, 800-465-1213; www .admtl.com), formerly known as Dorval Airport, about 20km west of downtown.

Bus The main bus station is Station Centrale de l'Autobus (505 Blvd de Maisonneuve Est).

Train Montréal's Gare Centrale (Central Train Station; 895 Rue de la Gauchetière Ouest) is the local hub for VIA Rail. There are regular services to Toronto (with wi-fi) and a delightful overnight service to Halifax. Amtrak services go to New York City.

ℹ️ Getting Around

To/From the Airport

STM (www.stm.info), the public transportation system, runs two bus lines from Montréal Trudeau airport to downtown. Rte 747 (one-way $7 in exact change, 35 minutes) is the express service. The service runs every 10 to 12 minutes from 8:30am to 8pm, every half-hour from 5:30am to 8:30am and from 8pm to 1am, and hourly other times.

A taxi to/from Trudeau airport costs $38.

Public Transportation

Montréal has a modern and convenient bus and metro system run by STM (www.stm.info). The metro is the city's subway system and runs quickly and quietly on rubber tires. It operates until at least 12:30am. Some buses provide service all night.

Tickets cost $2.75 but are cheaper by the half-dozen ($13.25). There are also 'Tourist Cards' for $7/14 for one/three days and weekly cards for $20.50 (valid Monday to Sunday). Note that bus drivers won't give change.

THE LAURENTIANS

The Laurentians, or Les Laurentides in French, are perhaps the best-kept secret of Montréal day-trippers. Just an hour's

---

'Out' & About in Montréal

Montréal is one of Canada's gayest cities with the rainbow flag flying especially proudly in The Village along Rue St-Catherine between Rue St-Hubert and Rue Dorion. Dozens of high-energy bars, cafes, restaurants, saunas and clubs flank this strip, turning it pretty much into a 24/7 fun zone. The authoritative guide to the gay and lesbian scene is **Fugues** (www.fugues.com), a free monthly mag found throughout The Village.

Bars and clubs worth checking out:

• **Sky Pub & Club** (Map p234; 1474 Rue Ste-Catherine Est) Huge place with rooftop terrace complete with Jacuzzi and pool.

• **Aigle Noir** (Map p234; 1315 Rue Ste-Catherine Est) For the leather-and-fetish crowd.

• **Le Drugstore** (Map p234; 1360 Rue Ste-Catherine Est) Fun seekers of every persuasion will be satisfied on at least one of the six multithemed floors.

GUYLAIN DOYLE

Don't Miss **Marché Jean Talon**

The gem of Little Italy in Montréal, this kaleidoscopic market **(7075 Ave Casgrain; ☉7am-6pm Mon-Wed, to 8pm Thu & Fri, to 5pm Sat & Sun; Ⓜ Jean Talon)** is perfect for assembling a gourmet picnic or partaking in a little afternoon grazing. A great stop is Marché des Saveurs, devoted entirely to Québec specialties such as wine and cider, fresh cheeses, smoked meats and preserves. The market sprawls south of Rue Jean-Talon between Blvd St-Laurent and Rue St-Denis.

drive west of the city, you'll find yourself amid gentle rolling mountains, crystal blue lakes and meandering rivers peppered with towns and villages too cute for words. A visit to this natural paradise is like putting your feet up after a long day.

Mont-Tremblant is the main skiing center. For two less-visited villages in the area, see the boxed text, p244.

ℹ️ Information

Association Touristique des Laurentides
(Laurentian Tourist Association; ☎ 450-436-8532, 800-561-6673, reservation service 450-436-3507; www.laurentides.com; ☉9am-5pm)
Regional tourist office; can answer questions on the phone, make room bookings and

mail out information. Operates a free room reservation service.

ℹ️ Getting There & Around

Drivers coming from Montréal should follow either Hwy 15 or the slower Rte 117.

Nearly all towns in the Laurentians can be accessed via Hwy 15, the Autoroute des Laurentides. The old Rte 117, running parallel to it, is slow but considerably more scenic.

Buses from Montréal serve the Laurentians area.

Ville de Mont-Tremblant

The Mont-Tremblant area is the crown jewel of the Laurentians, lorded over by the 960m-high eponymous mountain, dotted with pristine lakes and traversed by rivers. It's a hugely popular four-season playground, drawing ski bums from late October to mid-April, and hikers, bikers, golfers, water sports fans and other outdoor enthusiasts the rest of the year.

The area of Ville de Mont-Tremblant is divided into three sections: **Station Tremblant**, the ski hill and pedestrianized tourist resort at the foot of the mountain; **Mont-Tremblant Village**, a sweet and tiny cluster of homes and businesses about 4km southwest of here; and **St-Jovite**, the main town and commercial center off Rte 117, about 12km south of the mountain.

A shuttle bus ($2.25, 6am to 8pm) connects all three.

Sights & Activities

Station Tremblant (www.tremblant.com; adult lift ticket full/half-day $62/48) is among the top-ranked international ski resorts in eastern North America according to *Ski* magazine and legions of loyal fans. The mountain has a vertical drop of 645m and is laced with 95 trails and two snow parks served by 14 lifts, including an express gondola. Ski rentals start at $32 per day.

A summer attraction is the **downhill luge track** (1/3/5 rides $12.50/23/36) that snakes down the mountain for 1.4km; daredevils can reach speeds up to 50km/h. The nearby **Activity Center** (891-681-4848; www.tremblantactivities .com) can arrange for a variety of outdoor pursuits, from fishing to canoeing to horseback riding.

The southern mountain base spills over into a **pedestrian tourist village** with big hotels, shops, restaurants and an amusement-park atmosphere.

Sleeping

AUBERGE LE LUPIN   B&B **$$**
(819-425-5474, 877-425-5474; www.lelupin .com; 127 Rue Pinoteau, Mont-Tremblant Village; r $90-123; @) This 1940s log house offers snug digs just 1km away from the ski station, with private beach access to sparkling Lac Tremblant. Tasty breakfasts are whipped up by host Pierre in his homey rustic kitchen.

COUNTRY INN & SUITES BY CARLSON
                                          Hotel **$$**
(819-681-5555, 800-596-2375; 160 Chemin Curé des Lauriers, Station Tremblant; ste from $149; ✳ @ ☒) With its perfect position in the heart of the pedestrian village, the large and functional rooms of this contemporary ski lodge are comfortable and convenient. All suites have full kitchens. Children under 17 stay free.

Eating

PLUS MINUS CAFÉ
                                       Fusion **$$$**
(www.plusminuscafe.com; Station Tremblant; mains $29-40;

Basilique Notre-Dame (p226), Montréal
GUYLAIN DOYLE

⏰6am-10pm; 🍴) The healthy avant-garde menu here extends from colorful salads to elaborately designed mains incorporating high-quality lean red meats, reserve-raised wild poultry, fresh saltwater fish and funky flavor combinations such as locally grown cannabis with miso, star anise and chlorophyll.

ℹ️ Information

Mont Tremblant Tourism (📞 800-322-2932; www.tourismemonttremblant.com; 48 Chemin de Brébeuf, St-Jovite)

QUÉBEC CITY

POP 167,000

Québec, North America's only walled city north of Mexico City, is the kind of place that often crops up in trivia questions. Over the centuries, the lanes and squares of the Old Town – a World Heritage site – have housed the continent's first parish church, first museum, first stone church, first Anglican cathedral, first girls' school, first business district and the first French-speaking university.

The city's Haute Ville (Upper Town) sits atop the cliffs of Cap Diamant (Cape Diamond), while the Basse Ville (Lower Town) sits below. Each has their old and new sections. The Citadelle, a fort and landmark, stands on the highest point of Cap Diamant.

Once past Le Château Frontenac, arguably the most photographed hotel in the world, visitors find themselves torn between the various neighborhoods'

If You Like...
Mountain Villages

If you like Ville de Mont-Tremblant (p241), stoke your mountain high in these other Laurentian communities:

1 ST-SAUVEUR

(www.mssi.ca) St-Sauveur-des-Monts (or St-Sauveur, for short) is the busiest village in the Laurentians and is often deluged with day-trippers thanks to its proximity to Montréal (60km). A pretty church anchors Rue Principale, the attractive main street, flanked by restaurants, cafes and boutiques. In winter, Mont Saint-Sauveur and four other ski hills provide excellent runs for all levels of expertise. In summer, water-park action takes over.

2 VAL-DAVID

(www.valdavid.com) Val-David is a pint-sized village with an almost lyrical quality and a gorgeous setting along the Rivière du Nord and at the foot of the mountains. Its charms have made it a magnet for artists whose studios and galleries line the main street, Rue de L'Église. Outfitters also rent bicycles, kayaks and canoes, and offer cycle-canoe packages on the Rivière du Nord.

diverse charms. In Old Upper Town, the historical hub, many excellent museums and restaurants hide among the tacky fleur-de-lis T-shirt stores.

Old Lower Town, at the base of the steep cliffs, is a labyrinth, where it's a pleasure to get lost among street performers and cozy inns before emerging on the north shore of the St Lawrence River.

Sights

Old Upper Town
FORTIFICATIONS OF QUÉBEC
Landmark

The largely restored old wall is a national historic site. You can walk the 4.6km circuit on top of it all around the Old Upper Town, with much of the city's history within easy view. At the old powder magazine beside Porte St Louis, the **interpretive center** (Map p246; 100 Rue St-Louis; adult/child $4/2; ⏰10am-6pm May-Aug, to 5pm Sep–mid-Oct) examines the city's defenses through displays, models and a short film.

The center's enthusiastic guides run 90-minute **walking tours** (adult/child $10/5) from here and the Kiosk Frontenac (p253).

LA CITADELLE
Landmark

(Fort; Map p246; www.lacitadelle.qc.ca; Côte de la Citadelle; adult/child $10/5.50; ⏰10am-4pm Apr, 9am-5pm May, Jun & Sep, 9am-6pm Jul-early Sep, 10am-3pm Oct) The dominating Citadelle is North America's largest fort, covering 2.3 sq km. Begun by the French in 1750 and completed by the British in 1850, it served as part of the defense system against an American invasion that never came.

Today the Citadelle is the base of Canada's Royal 22s (known in bastardized French as the Van Doos, from the French for 22, *vingt-deux*). Founded in WWI, the regiment earned three Victoria Crosses in that conflict and WWII. Admission to the site is by one-hour guided tour, which takes in the regimental museum, numerous historical sites and a cannon called Rachel. Tours depart regularly, apart from between late October and early April, when there's only one tour a day at 1:30pm.

A separate tour of the **Governor General's Residence** (Map p246; tours free; ⏰10am-4pm Sun May & Jun, 11am-4pm late Jun–early Sep, 10am-4pm Sat & Sun Sep & Oct) is also available.

The **changing of the guard** ceremony takes place at 10am each day during the summer months. The **beating of the retreat**, which features soldiers banging on their drums at shift's end, happens at 7pm on Friday, Saturday and Sunday during July and August. It's a small bit of Canadiana right in the heart of Québec.

Latin Quarter

BASILICA NOTRE-DAME-DE-QUÉBEC
Church

(Map p246; 16 Rue de Buade; admission free;
☺8:30am-6pm) This cathedral towers
above the site of a chapel erected by
Samuel de Champlain in 1633. It became
one of the continent's first cathedrals in
1674, following the appointment of the
first bishop of Québec, Monseigneur de
Laval, whose tomb is inside. Ever bigger
replacements were constructed over the
centuries, with the last being completed
in 1925. The grandiose interior recreates
the spirit of the 17th century.

Old Lower Town

From Upper Town, you can reach this
must-see area in several ways. Walk
down Côte de la Canoterie from Rue des
Ramparts to the Old Port, or edge down
the charming and steep Rue Côte de la
Montagne. About halfway down on the
right, a shortcut, the Break-Neck Stairs
(Escalier Casse-Cou) leads down to Rue
du Petit-Champlain. You can also take
the **funicular** from Terrasse Dufferin ($2
each way).

Teeming **Rue du Petit-Champlain** is
said to be, along with Rue Sous le-Cap,
the narrowest street in North America,
and is the center of the continent's
oldest business district. Look out for the
murals decorating the 17th- and 18th-
century buildings, which, along with
numerous plaques, statues and street
performers, give this quarter its distinct,
history-meets-holiday feel.

Place Royale, Old Lower Town's
central, principal square, has had an
eventful 400-plus years. When Samuel
de Champlain founded Québec City, he

Québec City

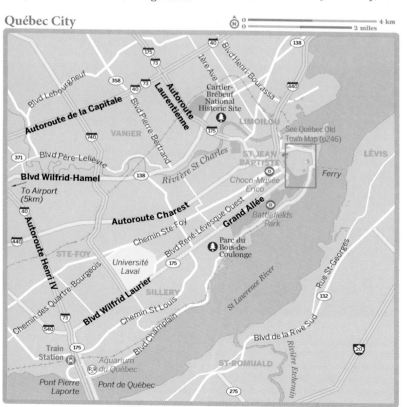

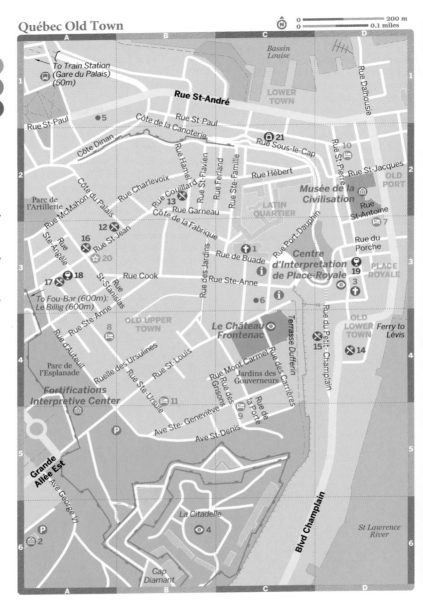

0 200 m
0 0.1 miles

settled this bit of shoreline first. In 1690 cannons placed here held off the attacks of the English naval commander Phips and his men. Today the name 'Place Royale' generally refers to the district.

Built around the old harbor, north of Place Royale and west of the Musée de la Civilisation, the **Vieux Port** (Old Port) is being redeveloped as a multipurpose waterfront area.

Québec Old Town

MUSÉE DE LA CIVILISATION   Museum
(Museum of Civilization; Map p246; www
.mcq.org; 85 Rue Dalhousie; adult/child $12/4,
free Tue Nov-May & 10am-noon Sat Jan & Feb;
⏱10am-6.30pm late Jun–Aug, to 5pm Tue-Sun
Sep–late Jun) The Museum of Civilisation
offers a dozen exhibitions in its airy
halls, including permanent shows on
the culture of Québec's 11 Aboriginal
groups, and tells the province's story
from the French settlers to today's
distinct society. Quirky displays, videos and interactive features bring the
weighty subjects to life. The striking
building incorporates some pre-existing
structures; for instance, it shares an
early-18th-century wall with Auberge
Saint Antoine.

ÉGLISE NOTRE-DAME-DES-VICTOIRES
  Church
(Our Lady of Victories Church; Map p246; 32 Rue
Sous le Fort; admission free; ⏱9:30am-5pm
May–mid-Oct, 10am-4pm mid-Oct–May) Our
Lady of Victories Church is the oldest
stone church in North America, built
in 1688 and devastated by cannon fire
in 1759. It stands on the spot where
de Champlain set up his 'Habitation,'

a small stockade. Inside are copies of
works by Rubens and Van Dyck.

**CENTRE D'INTERPRÉTATION DE
PLACE-ROYALE**   Museum
(Map p246; 27 Rue Notre-Dame; adult/child $7/2;
⏱9:30am-5pm late Jun–Aug, 10am-5pm Tue-Sun
Sep–late Jun) This interpretive center touts
the area as the cradle of French history
in North America with a series of good
participatory displays. While here, pick
up a brochure on Place Royale's 27 vaulted cellars (ancient stone basements),
five of which can be visited for free,
including the one right here, complete
with costumed barrel-maker.

Outside the Walls

BATTLEFIELDS PARK   Historic Park
(Map p245) With its hills, gardens and
monuments, this huge park looks like
any urban North American park, but
where yoga groups stretch and joggers
sweat, there was once a bloody battle-
ground that determined the course of
Canadian history. The part closest to the
cliff is known as the **Plains of Abraham** –
it was here in 1759 that the British
finally defeated the French. The British

general, Wolfe, died on the battlefield; Montcalm of France died the following morning, while his officers fled the city for Montréal.

Within the park are diverse sites. The reception center at the **Discovery Pavilion** (Map p246; 835 Ave Wilfrid-Laurier; admission free; ☺8:30am-5:30pm late Jun–early Sep, 8:30am-5pm Mon-Fri, from 9am Sat, from 10am Sun early Sep–late Jun) is a good place to start. The staff at the center offer park bus tours and multiple-attraction packages.

ST JEAN BAPTISTE   Neighborhood
Strolling along **Rue St-Jean**, west of the Old Town, is a great way to feel the pulse of this bohemian area. The first thing that strikes you, once you've recovered from crossing busy Ave Honoré Mercier, is the area's down-to-earth ambience. Good restaurants, hip cafes and bars and interesting shops, some catering to a gay clientele, line the thoroughfare as far as Rue Racine.

CHOCO-MUSÉE ÉRICO   Museum
(Map p245; www.chocomusee.com; 634 Rue St-Jean; admission free; ☺10am-5:30pm Mon-Wed & Sat, to 9pm Thu & Fri, 11am-5:30pm Sun, extended hours warm summer evenings) This museum and store is devoted to all things chocolatey. Get a history lesson, see the kitchen, and of course sample a chunk and try to resist the shop.

 **Activities**

TERRASSE DUFFERIN   Park
Outside Le Château Frontenac along the riverfront, 425m-long Terrasse Dufferin is marvelous for a stroll, with dramatic views over the river, perched as it is 60m high on a cliff. It's peppered with quality street performers vying for attention.

CYCLO SERVICES   Cycling
(Map p246; 289 Rue St-Paul; bicycles per hr/24hr $14/35; ☺8:30am-8pm) This shop rents bikes and organizes excellent cycle tours

Left: Wharf at sunset, near Tadoussac (p256); **Below:** Jumble of colorful roofs, Old Québec (p245)

PHOTOGRAPHER: (LEFT) GUYLAIN DOYLE; (BELOW) MARK HEMMINGS

of the city and outskirts, available in English. It has good cycling maps covering the vicinity.

up to four people for 40 minutes. The drivers provide some commentary.

 Tours

LES SERVICES HISTORIQUES SIX ASSOCIES   Walking
(☎ 418-692-3033; 2hr walking tours $16)
Costumed guides lead excellent walking circuits such as the ever-popular 'Lust and Drunkenness,' which creaks open the rusty door on the history of alcohol and prostitution in the city. Other tours, done in English and French, focus on epidemics and crimes. A cheery bunch, they are. Reservations should be made by phone.

CALÈCHES   Horse-Drawn Carriage
From Place d'Armes, near the information centers (Map p246) the horses give nice rides but are expensive at $80 for

 Sleeping

Midsummer and the winter Carnaval are especially busy times, so book well in advance during these times.

Old Upper Town

MAISON HISTORIQUE JAMES THOMPSON   B&B $$
(Map p246; ☎ 418-694-9042; www.bedand breakfastquebec.com; 47 Rue Ste-Ursule; r $75-135) History buffs will get a real kick out of staying in the 18th-century former residence of James Thompson, a veteran of the Battle of the Plains of Abraham. The beautifully restored house comes complete with the original murder hole next to the front door. Rooms are spacious and brightly

MARK HEMMINGS

Don't Miss **Le Château Frontenac**

Said to be the world's most photographed hotel, **Le Château Frontenac** (Map p246; 1 Rue des Carrières) was built in 1893 by the Canadian Pacific Railway (CPR) as part of its chain of luxury hotels. During WWII, Prime Minister MacKenzie King, Winston Churchill and Franklin Roosevelt planned D-Day here. Leaving every hour on the hour, slightly underwhelming 50-minute hotel **tours** (adult/child $9.50/6; ⏱10am-6pm May–mid-Oct, noon-5pm Sat & Sun mid-Oct–Apr) evoke polite society in the late 19th century.

Facing the hotel along Rue Mont Carmel is **Jardins des Gouverneurs**, with a monument to both Wolfe and Montcalm.

infused with host Guitta's cheerful artwork; and it's easy to while away an afternoon chatting with host Greg – a wealth of knowledge on all things Québec and historical.

LA MARQUISE DE BASSANO   Inn $$
(Map p246; ☎ 418-692-0316, 877-692-0316; www.marquisedebassano.com; 15 Rue des Grisons; r $99-175; P@) Rooms sporting canopy beds, claw-foot tubs or a rooftop deck are part of the allure of this serene Victorian house, run by young, gregarious owners. The sweet scent of fresh-baked croissants for breakfast will surely have you up before the alarm clock.

HÔTEL ACADIA   Hotel $$
(Map p246; ☎ 418-694-0280, 800-463-0280; www.hotelacadia.com; 43 Rue Ste-Ursule; r $99-219; P@🛜) This longtime visitor fave is carved out of three adjacent historic houses and offers rooms in a range of sizes, features and prices, from small 'classic' quarters to luxury spreads with fireplaces. There's a peaceful garden overlooking the old Ursuline convent.

Old Lower Town
AUBERGE SAINT ANTOINE
Boutique Hotel $$$
(Map p246; ☎ 418-692-2211; www.saint-antoine .com; 8 Rue St-Antoine; r $179-989; ❄@🛜) History and modernity are ecstatically

250

married in this hotel, where understated details such as a clock projected onto a wall complement one of the city's most significant archaeological sites. A daily tour takes in the 700 artifacts on display, discovered when the underground car park was installed. In the original, 250-year-old part of the complex, the rooms and historical suites are stacked with antique furniture. The views of the château are superb.

LE GERMAIN-DOMINION
Boutique Hotel **$$**

(Map p246; ☎ 418-692-2224, 888-833-5253; www.germaindominion.com; 126 Rue St-Pierre; r $169-315; ❄@☎) This winner by local luxury chain, Groupe Germain, tucked away in a cozy spot in the heart of the Lower Town, hits high notes with fresh, modern decor (renovated in 2010), a never-ending list of amenities and flawless customer service.

 Eating

For the best bargains, get the *table d'hôte,* especially at lunch.

Old Upper Town
LE PATRIARCHE
Fusion **$$$**

(Map p246; www.lepatriarche.com; 17 Rue St-Stanislas; mains $26-50; ⌚11:30am-2pm Thu-Fri, 5:30-10pm daily) The nouvelle cuisine echoes the contemporary art hanging on the 180-year-old stone walls in this top-class restaurant. On the menu stocked almost entirely with local products, starters include foie gras and pan-fried frogs legs; mains range from New Brunswick salmon fillet to Appalachian deer and Québec lamb.

CHEZ TEMPOREL
Cafe **$$**

(Map p246; 25 Rue Couillard; meals $12.50; ⌚7am-1:30am Sun-Thu, to 2:30am Fri & Sat) For a sandwich or leisurely breakfast of a perfect café au lait and fresh croissants, you can't beat this Parisian-style hideaway. Later in the day, it's the province of solitary book readers and wistful music.

UN THÉ AU SAHARA
African **$$**

(Map p246; 7 Rue Ste-Ursule; meals $14-22; ⌚11:30am-2:30pm Thu-Fri, 5pm-late daily) Bring your own wine or hit the mint tea in this basic but popular Moroccan restaurant. All the classics are available: tabbouleh, hummus, couscous, brochettes and *tagine keffa* (veal croquettes in tomato sauce).

CHEZ ASHTON
Fast Food **$**

(Map p246; 54 Côte du Palais; meals $7; ⌚11am-2am Sun-Wed, to 4am Thu, to 4.30am Fri & Sat) This snack bar is one of the establishments that claims to have invented poutine (fries smothered in cheese curds and gravy; see the boxed text, p255). It's

Cirque du Soleil, Québec City (p238)
DENIS CORRIVEAU

popular throughout the day and night for all varieties of poutine, burgers and subs.

Old Lower Town

Rue St-Paul and Rue du Petit-Champlain are lined with restaurants and their outdoor tables.

LE LAPIN SAUTÉ French **$$**
(Map p246; www.lapinsaute.com; 52 Rue du Petit-Champlain; mains $15-23; ⊙11am-10pm Sun-Thu, 9am-11pm Fri & Sat) If you only splash out once in Québec City, do it at this cozy restaurant specializing in country cooking. Naturally, le lapin (rabbit) lasagna and sausages are available, but so are duck, salmon and chicken, and there's maple syrup crème brûlée for dessert. In good weather you can sit on the flowery patio, overlooking tiny Félix Leclerc park.

LE COCHON DINGUE French **$$**
(Map p246; www.cochondingue.com; 46 Blvd Champlain; meals $10-20; ⊙8am-11pm) Since 1979, this Gallic gem among touristy eateries has delighted diners with its attentive service and outside seating. A French feel pervades its checkered tablecloths and dishes, which range from *croque monsieur* to mussels and steak frites.

Outside the Walls

LE BILLIG Cafe **$$**
(526 Rue St-Jean; crepes $3.50-16; ⊙11am-3pm & 5-9pm Tue-Sat, 11am-3pm Sun) A Breton bistro specializing in crepes, featuring winning combinations such as duck confit and onion marmalade, and buckwheat inventions such as the Roscoff, which crams in ham, asparagus, Swiss cheese, apple and béchamel sauce.

 Drinking

Wander the Grande Allée by the Old Upper Town's walls for a row of hoppin' bars, cafes and nightlife spots.

L'ONCLE ANTOINE Pub
(Map p246; 29 Rue St-Pierre; ⊙11am-late) In the Old Port area, down in the stone cellar of one of the city's oldest surviving houses (dating from 1754), this tavern pours out several drafts *(en fût)* and Québec microbrews (the coffee-tinted stout is

Ice sculpture at Québec City's Winter Carnival (p42)

GLENN VAN DER KNIJFF

Detour:
Lévis

On the 1km ferry crossing from Québec City to the town of Lévis, the best views are undoubtedly on the Québec side of the vessel. The Citadelle, the Château Frontenac and the seminary dominate the clifftop cityscape. Once you disembark, riverside Lévis is a relaxing escape from the intensity of Québec City's Old Town.

Tourisme Lévis (☎418-838-6026; ☺May-Oct), at the ferry landing, has maps and an Old Lévis package ($9), which includes return ferry and a 30-minute guided bus shuttle to several points of interest.

Near the ferry landing, the **Terrasse de Lévis**, a lookout point inaugurated in 1939 by King George VI and (the future) Queen Elizabeth II, offers excellent vistas of Québec and beyond from the top of the hill on Rue William-Tremblay.

The **ferry** (☎877-787-7483) between Québec City and Lévis runs frequently between 6am and 2am. The one-way fare is $3/2 per adult/child; including the car driver, cars cost $6.75 and bikes $3. The 10-minute crossing provides great views of the river, Le Château Frontenac and the Québec City skyline. The terminal is at Place Royale.

particularly reviving); taste four of them for $7.

BAR STE ANGÈLE Bar
(Map p246; 26 Rue Ste-Angèle; ☺8pm-late) A low-lit, intimate hideaway, where the genial staff will help you navigate the list of cocktail pitchers and local and European bottled beers.

 Entertainment

Fou-Bar Live Music
(525 Rue St-Jean; ☺3pm-3am) Laid-back and with an eclectic mix of bands, this is one of the town's classics for live music. The jazz on Tuesdays from 9pm is a winner.

Les Yeux Bleus Live Music
(Map p246; 1117 Rue St-Jean) The city's best *boîte a chanson* (live, informal singer/songwriter club), this is the place to catch newcomers and the occasional big-name Francophone concert.

 Shopping

In the Old Lower Town, Rue St-Paul has a dozen shops piled with antiques, curiosities and old Québécois relics, and incongruous **Le Roquet** (Map p246; 141 Rue St-Paul), sells funky locally made T-shirts.

❶ Information

Tourist Information

Centre Infotouriste (Map p246; www.bonjour quebec.com; 12 Rue Ste-Anne; ☺8:30am-7:30pm Jun-Aug, 9am-5pm Sep-May) Busy provincial tourist office; also handles city inquiries. Tour operators have counters here.

Kiosk Frontenac (Map p246) An information booth on Terrasse Dufferin facing Le Château Frontenac; makes reservations for activities and is the starting point for some tours.

❶ Getting There & Away

Air

Jean Lesage airport (www.aeroportdequebec .com) is west of town off Hwy 40, near where north–south Hwy 73 intersects it.

Boat

A **ferry** (☎877-787-7483) travels between Québec City and Lévis (see above for details).

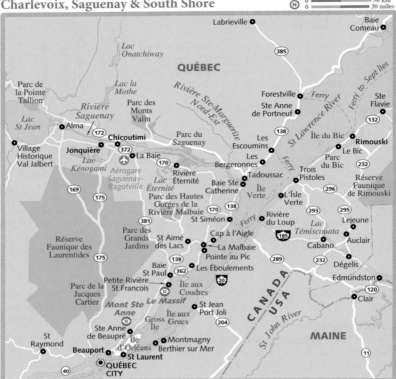

Bus

The bus station (☎418-525-3000; 320 Rue Abraham-Martin) is beside Gare du Palais.

Train

The simply gorgeous Gare du Palais (off Map p246) has a bar and cafe. Daily VIA Rail trains go to Montréal and destinations further west.

A station inconveniently across the river in the town of **Charny** serves eastern destinations. Some trains from the Gare du Palais go via Charny.

❶ Getting Around

To/From the Airport

A Taxi Co-op (☎418-525-5191) cab between town and the airport costs about $30. Some tour companies sometimes offer cheaper shuttle fares to the airport.

Bicycle

Many cycle paths run through and around the city, covered by the *Plan du Réseau Cyclable* and more-detailed *Parcours Cyclables*. Cyclo Services (p248) rents bikes (one hour/day $14/35).

Car & Motorcycle

In Québec City, driving isn't really worth the trouble. You can walk just about everywhere, the streets are narrow and crowded, and parking is limited.

Public Transportation

A ride on the city bus system (☎418-627-2511) costs $2.60, with transfer privileges, or $6.70 for a day pass. The tourist offices can supply maps.

CHARLEVOIX

Hold up a blade of Charlevoix grass and you'll see it bend in the breeze of contentment that wafts through the region's flowery farmlands. For 200 years, this pastoral strip of rolling hills has been a summer retreat for the privileged.

A driving route to consider is taking the 'River Drive' (Rte 362) one way and returning through ear-popping hills on the 'Mountain Drive' (Rte 138) inland.

Baie St Paul

The clowning, juggling troupe Cirque du Soleil may have started out in Baie St Paul, but most of the entertainment here is of a gentler nature. The small town boasts some 30 art galleries and *ateliers*, along with historic houses that have been converted into superb restaurants and *gîtes* (B&Bs).

Sights & Activities

MUSÉE D'ART CONTEMPORAIN
Art Gallery

(www.macbsp.com; 23 Rue Ambroise-Fafard; adult/child $6/free; ⊙noon-5pm Tue-Sun) Across the main drag, this architecturally attention-grabbing gallery houses contemporary art by local artists and some photographic exhibits on loan from the National Gallery of Canada.

CARREFOUR CULTUREL PAUL MÉDÉRIC
Art Gallery

(4 Rue Ambroise-Fafard; admission free; ⊙10am-5pm) This gallery is named after a local priest and writer who founded a youth movement here. It's possible to watch local artisans working in their studios.

 Sleeping

AUBERGE LA MUSE B&B $$
(☎ 418-435-6839, 800-841-6839; www.lamuse.com; 39 Rue St Jean Baptiste; r $109-209; ❄) This cheerful yellow B&B has refined the art of relaxation. The superior rooms variously feature therapeutic baths, pillow-based massage technology and terraces overlooking the flower garden. If you can, avoid No 1, the slightly noisy room next to the front door.

NATURE ET PINCEAUX B&B $$
(☎ 418-435-2366; www.natureetpinceaux.qc.ca; 33 Rue Nordet; r $125-145) Atop the mountain peeking out over the river below, the views from the spacious rooms at this charming B&B are surpassed only by the phenomenal four-course breakfasts cooked by the host, Francine. The house is east of the town, signposted off Rte 362.

Eating

LE MOUTON NOIR French $$$
(☎ 418-240-3030; 43 Rue Ste Anne; meals $30-36; ⊙11am-2pm & 5-10pm Wed-Sun) Since 1978, the rustic-looking Black Sheep has been home to fine French cuisine. Fish, including walleye, the freshwater queen, is on offer when available, as are buffalo, caribou and steak, all enlivened by a deft touch incorporating wild mushrooms and local produce. The outdoor *terrasse* (patio) overlooks the Gouffre.

Poutine, Bien Sur

Like all fast food, Québec's beloved poutine is perfect if you have a *gueule de bois* (hangover) after a night on the Boréale Blonde. In this calorie-packing culinary Frankenstein, the province's exemplary fries (fresh-cut, never frozen and served limp and greasy) are sprinkled with cheese curds and smothered in gravy. The dish was devised in the early 1980s and spread across Québec like a grease fire.

Chez Ashton in Québec City (p251) is a good place to take the poutine challenge.

LE SAINT PUB
Pub $$$

(2 Rue Racine; meals $20-30; ⊙11am-2am)
Ale lovers will foam at the mouth in
this former brewery, where the dinner
menu begins with beers and continues
with beer-based sauces, dressings and
marinades. For $6 you can sample four
regional brews including the local malt.

. . . .

ⓘ Information

Charlevoix Tourist Office (www.tourisme
-charlevoix.com; 444 Blvd Mgr de Laval;
⊙8:30am-4:30pm Apr–late Jun, 9am-7pm late
Jun–early Sep, restricted hours rest of year) On
Rte 138 just west of town.

TADOUSSAC

For many visitors, Tadoussac is the
one place in Québec province they visit
outside Montréal and Québec City. What
draws the hordes to the small spot –
where fewer than 1000 inhabitants gaze
across the St Lawrence and at those
poor souls leaving on the ferry across the
Saguenay – is the whales. Not only do
Zodiacs zip out in search of the behe-
moths, but smaller whales such as belu-
gas and minkes can be glimpsed from the
shore. Added to that are activities such
as sea kayaking, 'surfbiking,' exploring
the fjord by boat or on foot, or simply
wandering the dunes and headlands.

Activities

WHALE-WATCHING
From May to November, tourists flock to
Tadoussac for a good reason: whale-
watching. It's phenomenal, particularly
between August and October, when
blue whales are spotted. All over town,
tickets are available for boat tours, from
12-person Zodiacs to the 600-person
Grand Fleuve; check out the possibilities
carefully. **Otis Excursions** (☎418-235-
4197; 431 Rue du Bateau Passeur) is a local
company that has been running for 35
years. Its Zodiacs get closest to the
waves and offer the most exciting, if
roughest, rides. Young children aren't
permitted, however. The Zodiac oper-
ated by **Croisières AML (www.croisiere
saml.com; 177 Rue des Pionniers)** is twice the
size of the others. Adult fares are $59
for a two-hour Zodiac trip and $69 for a
three-hour boat trip. Zodiac passengers
are given waterproofs; whatever trip
you do, take lots of warm clothes.

For the adventurous, sea-
kayaking supremo **Mer et
Monde** (www.mer-et
-monde.qc.ca; 405 Rue de la
Mer, Les Bergeronnes; 3hr
from $52) offers whale-
watching expeditions and
excursions up the fjord.

HIKING
There are four 1km paths
in and around Tadous-
sac, marked on the map
given out by the tourist
office. The trails around
the peninsulas **Pointe de
l'Islet**, by the quay, and,

Lighthouse near Tadoussac
PHOTOGRAPHER: OLIVIER CIRENDINI

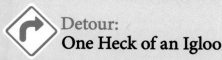

Detour:
One Heck of an Igloo

Located half an hour's drive from central Québec City, the Hôtel de Glace first opened its cool, blue doors in 2001, following similar Scandinavian establishments.

Yes, almost everything is made of ice (hot tubs and fireplaces are two understandable exceptions). This architectural feat strikes you, like an ice mallet, as soon as you step into the entrance hall: tall, sculpted columns of ice support a ceiling where a crystal chandelier hangs, and carved sculptures, tables and chairs line the endless corridors. The reception desk, the pen you sign the guest book with, the sink in your room, even your bed are also made of ice. Visitors say the bed is not as frigid as it sounds, thanks to thick sleeping bags laid on lush deer pelts.

The 3000-sq-m structure's public areas include exhibition rooms, a cinema, a chapel and the Absolut Ice Bar. The hotel melts in the spring and has to be rebuilt every winter, a job that takes five weeks, 12,000 tons of snow and 400 tons of ice.

The ice hotel offers several packages, starting at $600 per double, including a welcome vodka, dinner and breakfast. If you're not staying, simply take the tour for $15. The **Ice Hotel** (418-875-4522, 877-505-0423; www.icehotel-canada.com; **143 Rte Duchesnay, Ste Catherine de la Jacques Cartier;** Jan-Apr) is off Rte 367 to the west of Québec City, reached via Hwy 40 exit 295.

at the other end of the beach, **Pointe Rouge** are the best for spying whales.

Parc du Saguenay's interpretation center, **Maison des Dunes** (750 Chemin du Moulin à Baude; adult/child $3.50/1.50; 10am-5pm Sat & Sun late May–mid-Jun, 10am-5pm mid-Jun–early Oct), is about 5km out of town in another prime whale-watching location.

 Festivals & Events

Tadoussac's busy summer season begins with a vengeance at the **Festival de la Chanson** (Song Festival; 418-235-2002; www.chansontadoussac.com; mid-Jun), a celebration of Francophone music, mostly Québécois, and a serious party. Stages spring up all over town and accommodations fill up.

 Sleeping

AUBERGE LA STE PAIX   B&B $$
(418-235-4803; www.aubergelasaintepaix .com; 102 Rue Saguenay; r $98-133) Guests at this out-of-the-way, seven-room B&B

spot whales while savoring gourmet breakfasts ranging from French toast to Mexican omelets, cooked by the entertaining Montréaler Denis.

HÔTEL TADOUSSAC   Hotel $$
(418-235-4421; www.hoteltadoussac.com; 165 Rue du Bord de l'Eau; r from $155;) This 149-room, red-and-white landmark has extensive gardens, a pool overlooking the port, and vintage photos of steamers and the hotel looking considerably smaller in 1870. Somewhat tired and dated bedrooms have plush carpets, ceiling fans and river views.

MAISON CLAUPHI
          Motel/B&B $$
(418-235-4303; www.clauphi.com; 188 Rue des Pionniers; B&B r in studio/motel $95/119; May-Oct) The accommodations range from motel and B&B rooms to studios and suites in this building built in 1932 by the owner's parents. Bikes and waterborne 'surfbikes' can be rented.

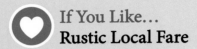

If You Like…
Rustic Local Fare

If you like Le Mouton Noir (p255), try these Charlevoix restaurants that use ingredients from the surrounding farmland:

1 LES SAVEURS OUBLIÉES
(Forgotten Flavors; ☎418-635-9888; 350 Rang St Godefroy; mains from $27; ⏰11am-9pm Wed-Mon Jun-Oct) This BYO specializes in Éboulmontaise lamb from the attached farm and organic vegetables. Stroll around the barn and ogle the shop, which sells jams, jellies, oils, vinegar, sausages and (bien sur) lamb, mostly produced on the farm. The restaurant, which serves lamb in about 10 succulent ways, is open from 5:30pm. Reservations are essential. It's in Les Éboulements, 18km northeast of Baie St Paul on Rte 362.

2 VICE VERSA
(☎418-665-6869; 216 Rue St Étienne, La Malbaie; meals $65; ⏰6-9:30pm Tue-Sun Jun-Sep, 6-9:30pm Thu-Sat Oct-May) Decided two weeks in advance, the menu is underpinned by local produce (Éboulmontaise lamb, calf's sweetbreads with Grand-Fonds oyster mushrooms, St Urbain duck, rock Cornish stew with Charlevoix beer), but the tangy, peppery sauces keep you guessing exactly which ingredient it is that tastes so good. It's in La Malbaie, about 50km northeast of Baie St Paul via Rte 362.

Eating

CHEZ MATHILDE Fusion $$$
(227 Rue des Pionniers; lunch & dinner meals from $25; ⏰11am-9:30pm Jun-Oct) The stellar chef at this cute little house utilizes plenty of local produce in his creative, though limited, menu. The innovative dishes, cooked to perfection, are served up alongside a view of the port from an airy patio.

RESTAURANT LE BATEAU
Québecois $$
(246 Rue des Forgerons; lunch/dinner meals $11/18; ⏰11am-9:30pm May-Oct) A great view comes with the buffet of traditional Québec workers' fare at this friendly restaurant. Fill up on Lac St Jean meat pie, followed by your choice of blueberry, sugar or vinegar pie.

CAFÉ BOHÈME Cafe $$
(239 Rue des Pionniers; meals $14-20; ⏰8am-10pm May-Oct) The village's hangout of choice is a prime place for a breakfast of fruit and yogurt or a panini, or just to sip fair trade coffee with the local intellectuals.

ℹ Information

Tourist information office (☎ 418-235-4744, 866-235-4744; www.tadoussac.com; 197 Rue des Pionniers; ⏰8am-9pm Jul-Sep, 9am-6pm Apr-Jun & Oct) In the middle of town with a very patient staff.

ℹ Getting There & Away

Tadoussac is right off Rte 138. The 10-minute ferry from Baie Ste Catherine in Charlevoix is free and runs around the clock. The terminal is at the end of Rue du Bateau Passeur.

ÎLES DE LA MADELEINE

Everything about the Magdalen Islands, a stringy archipelago that resembles a Mandelbrot Set on maps, is head turning. Located 105km north of Prince Edward Island, its six largest islands are connected by the 200km-long, classically named Rte 199, which curves between lumpy, verdant blotches of land on sand spits that seem about to be reclaimed by the omnipresent ocean. Between the islands' 350km of beach are iron-rich, red cliffs, molded by wind and sea into anthropomorphic forms and caves just crying out to be explored by kayak.

Despite their exposed position, the isles are a comforting place, where the horizon is normally interrupted, along with the thought that you're in the open sea, by another wing of the archipelago.

The islands are teeming with artists, often encountered looking

Rugged promontory on the Îles de la Madeleine (p258)

JIM WARK

for inspiration in a *pot-en-pot* (a local specialty, with mixed fish, seafood and sauce baked in a pie crust) or a Pas Perdus (one of three beers brewed on Cap aux Meules). A great way to meet the islanders is at *boîtes à chansons* (small drinking spots that feature music).

The islands fall in the Atlantic Time Zone, one hour ahead of mainland Québec.

ℹ️ Getting There & Around

The airport is on the northwest corner of Île du Havre aux Maisons. Air Canada Jazz offers daily flights from Montréal, Québec City and Gaspé.

The cheapest and most common arrival method is by ferry from Souris, Prince Edward Island, to Île du Cap aux Meules. **CTMA Ferries** (📞418-986-3278, 888-986-3278; www.ctma .ca) makes the five-hour cruise from April through January. The fare is $45.75/23 per adult/child aged five to 12. Bikes cost $11, cars $85.50.

Between June and October, CTMA also operates a two-day cruise from Montréal via Québec City, Tadoussac and Chandler. It's a great way of seeing the St Lawrence River, and you can take your car and returning by road.

There is no public transportation. **Le Pédalier** (📞418-986-2965; 500 Chemin Principale), in Cap aux Meules, rents bicycles. Hertz and local companies have airport car-rental outlets; book as far ahead as possible.

Île du Cap aux Meules

With more than half the archipelago's population and its only Tim Hortons, the islands' commercial center is disappointingly developed compared with its neighbors. Nonetheless, it's still 100% Madelinot and, with its amenities, accommodations and lively nightlife, it makes an ideal base for exploring the islands. You can normally catch wistful Acadian songs being strummed on summer evenings.

The **main tourist office** (📞418-986-2245, 877-624-4437; www.tourismeilesdela madeleine.com; 128 Chemin Principale; 🕐7am-9pm late Jun–Aug, 9am-8pm Sep, 9am-5pm & when ferries arrive Oct-Nov, 9am-5pm Mon-Fri Dec–late Jun), near the ferry terminal, is a helpful source of information about all the islands.

🔘 Sights & Activities

On the west side of the island, you can see the red cliffs in their glory. Their patterns of erosion can be glimpsed from the clifftop path between La Belle Anse

259

and Fatima. Southwest, the lighthouse at **Cap du Phare** (Cap Hérissé) is a popular place to watch sunsets, and a cluster of bright boutiques and cafes overlooks a shipwreck at **Anse de l'Étang du Nord**. In the middle of the island, signposted on Chemin de l'Église near the junction with Rte 199, **Butte du Vent** offers views along the sandbanks running north and south.

AEROSPORT CARREFOUR D'AVENTURES
Kayaking

(📞 418-986-6677; www.aerosport.ca; 1390 Chemin Lavernière) Young, enthusiastic thrill-seekers run this company that offers kayak expeditions and cave visits. When the wind is right, you'll have an unforgettable experience if you opt for the power kite buggy ride.

À L'ABRI DE LA TEMPÉTE
Brewery

(📞 418-986-5005; 286 Chemin Coulombe; tours $6; ⊙tours 11am-7pm Jun-Sep) Finish the day at this microbrewery on the beach.

 Tours

VERT ET MER
Kayaking

(📞 418-986-3555; www.vertetmer.com; 169 Chemin Principale) This eco-outfit offers excursions including sea kayaking and yurt lodging on Île Brion.

MA POIRIER
Bus Tour

(📞 418-986-4467; 375 Chemin Petipas; tours from $99) Runs seven-hour guided bus tours of the main sights throughout the islands.

 Sleeping & Eating

PAS PERDUS
Pub, Inn $$

(Not Lost; 📞 418-986-5151; 169 & 185 Chemin Principale; mains $12-20; s/d/tr with bathroom $40/50/65; ⊙11am-8pm) Munching on a shark burger on the *terrasse* at Pas Perdus, watching the traffic on Rte 199 cruise by, or in the red interior among curvy mirrors, is a sure way to feel the islands' bohemian pulse. Everyone drops by to surf the internet or sip a Pas Perdus from the nearby microbrewery. You can actually get a decent night's sleep in the bright bedrooms above the

restaurant now the musical entertainment has shifted next door (185 Chemin Principale). This venue hosts live acts most summer nights and, on Monday, films about the islands (7pm) and a free jam session (10pm). Pas Perdus is on the east side of the island, just west of the tourist office.

LA FACTRIE
Seafood $$

(521 Chemin du Gros Cap; mains $15-30; ⊙11am-10pm Mon-Sat, 4-10pm Sun May-Sep) Top-notch seafood is served in a cafeteria above a lobster processing plant; only in Îles de la Madeleine! Try lobster in salad, boiled, thermidore, sandwich or crepe form.

CAFÉ LA CÔTE
Cafe $$

(499 Chemin Boisville Ouest; mains $9-20; ⊙8am-10pm Jun-Sep) Near the fishermen statue in L'Etang du Nord, this beach-hutlike place is a perfect spot for breakfast or a quick lunch of seafood or pasta. The adjoining *boîte à chansons* puts on outdoor Acadian music shows on summer evenings.

Île du Havre Aubert

Heading south from Cap aux Meules to the archipelago's largest island, Rte 199 glides between dunes backed by the blue Atlantic and Baie du Havre aux Basques, popular with kite surfers.

The liveliest area of **Havre Aubert** town is La Grave, where the rustic charm of a fishing community remains in the old houses, small craft shops and restaurants. Beyond, walk along the **Sandy Hook** to feel like you're at the end of the world (apart from during the sand castle contest in August).

Économusée **Artisans du Sable** (907 Rte 199; ⊙10am-5:30pm) sells chessboards, candlesticks and other souvenirs...all made of sand. Also see the **Musée de la Mer** (1023 Rte 199; adult/child $5/2; ⊙10am-6pm late Jun-early Sep, reduced hrs rest of year).

Café de la Grave (969 Rte 199; meals $9-15; ⊙11:30am-midnight late Apr–mid-Oct) is more than a local institution, it's one of the islands' vital organs. *Pot-en-pot, croque monsieur,* soups and cakes meet

Some colorful wooden buildings, Île du Havre Aubert (p260)

EGMONT STRIGL/PHOTOLIBRARY

an appreciative crowd in the former general store.

Île du Havre aux Maisons

The home of the airport is one of the most populated islands but certainly doesn't feel it. Particularly to the east of Rte 199, it's probably the most scenic area, best viewed from Chemin des Buttes, which winds between green hills and picture-perfect cottages.

A short climb from the car park on Chemin des Échoueries near Cap Alright, the cross-topped **Butte Ronde** has wonderful views of the lumpy coastline.

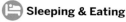 Sleeping & Eating

DOMAINE DU VIEUX COUVENT
Hotel **$$**
(418-969-2233; www.domaineduvieuxcouvent .com; 292 Rte 199; r incl breakfast $125-275;

late Feb–mid-Dec;) Smack-dab in the middle of the archipelago, the Domaine du Vieux Couvent boasts the swankiest digs in the Îles de la Madeleine. Every room overlooks the ocean through a wall of windows. The very popular **restaurant** (meals from $27; 6-9pm May-Oct, to 10pm Jul & Aug) is a must-visit for adventurous foodies, who can sample local dishes made with seafood, veal, boar, wild fruits and cheeses that are produce from the islands.

LA BUTTE RONDE
B&B **$$**
(418-969-2047; www.labutteronde.com; 70 Chemin des Buttes; r incl breakfast $100-145) With ticking clocks, classical music, beautiful rooms decorated with photos of Tuaregs, and a sea-facing conservatory, this grand home has a calming, library-like air.

Nova Scotia & Maritime Canada

At first glance, Nova Scotia appears as sweet as a storybook.
Its lupin-studded fields, gingerbread-like houses, picture-perfect lighthouses and lightly lapping waves on sandy shores make you want to wrap it all up and give it to a kid as a Christmas gift. Then another reality creeps up on you: this is also the raw Canada, of fisherfolk braving icy seas, of coal miners, of moose, of horseflies and of hockey.

Here and throughout the Maritimes, it's easy to discover empty coastal beach trails and vistas doused with briny breezes. Celtic and Acadian communities dot the landscape, and their foot-stompin', crazy-fiddlin' music vibrates through local pubs.

New Brunswick shows off its best side from its capital Fredericton down to the Fundy shore. And little Prince Edward Island, personified by Anne Shirley, LM Montgomery's spunky red-headed star of the Green Gables series, is as sweet and pretty as it is portrayed in the books.

The rustic harbor of Peggy's Cove (p282)
PHOTOGRAPHER: ANDREW BAIN

The Hopewell Rocks (p290) gaze out to sea
CHERYL FORBES

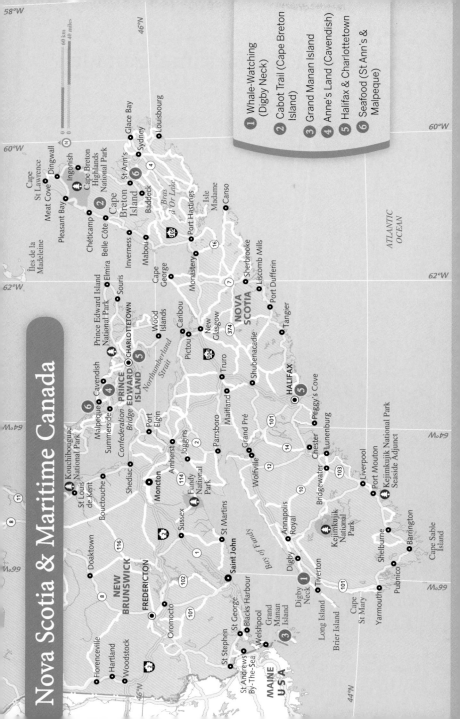

Nova Scotia & Maritime Canada

1 Whale-Watching (Digby Neck)
2 Cabot Trail (Cape Breton Island)
3 Grand Manan Island
4 Anne's Land (Cavendish)
5 Halifax & Charlottetown
6 Seafood (St Ann's & Malpeque)

ATLANTIC OCEAN

NOVA SCOTIA

NEW BRUNSWICK

PRINCE EDWARD ISLAND

MAINE USA

Cape Lawrence
St Lawrence
Meat Cove
Dingwall
Ingonish
Cape Breton Highlands National Park
Pleasant Bay
Chéticamp
Belle Côte
Inverness
Mabou
Elmira
Souris
Îles de la Madeleine

Glace Bay
Sydney
Louisbourg
St Ann's
Cape Breton Island
Baddeck
Bras d'Or Lake
Isle Madame
Port Hastings
Canso

Prince Edward Island National Park
Cavendish
Malpeque
Summerside
CHARLOTTETOWN
Confederation Bridge
Wood Islands
Cape George
Monastery
Sherbrooke
Liscomb Mills
Port Dufferin
Tangier

Caribou
Pictou
New Glasgow
Truro
Shubenacadie
HALIFAX
Peggy's Cove
Chester
Lunenburg

Kouchibouguac National Park
St Louis de Kent
Bouctouche
Shediac
Port Elgin
Amherst
Joggins
Parrsboro
Maitland
Grand Pré
Wolfville
Bridgewater
Liverpool
Port Mouton
Kejimkujik National Park Seaside Adjunct

Doaktown
Moncton
Sussex
St Martins
Fundy National Park
Annapolis Royal
Kejimkujik National Park
Shelburne
Barrington
Cape Sable Island

Florenceville
Hartland
Woodstock
FREDERICTON
Oromocto
Saint John
Digby
Tiverton
Digby Neck
Long Island
Brier Island
Cape St Mary
Yarmouth
Pubnico

St Stephen
St George
Blacks Harbour
Welshpool
Grand Manan Island
St Andrews By-The-Sea

60 km
40 miles

Nova Scotia & Maritime Canada's Highlights

① Whale-Watching

Fin, right, humpback, pilot: whales big and small lurk offshore throughout Maritime Canada, and the opportunity to see them is the region's most precious gift to visitors. The thrill of spotting a whale's spout, followed by its giant tail flukes arching and descending, can't be beat.

Need to Know

BEST TIME Mid-July to mid-September. **DON'T FORGET** Warm clothing (regardless of how hot a day it seems), sunblock, binoculars and motion-sickness pills.

Whale-Watching Don't Miss List

BY TOM GOODWIN, BIOLOGIST, GUIDE
AND OWNER OF OCEAN EXPEDITIONS IN TIVERTON,
NOVA SCOTIA

1 DIGBY NECK

Digby Neck and its islands (p280) are the best place to see big whales in the Maritimes. Fin, humpback, minke are the most common types that swim close to shore. The Fundy tides create the perfect conditions for their food source, such as herring and krill, which is what draws them. Further out in the bay we often see the North Atlantic right whale. We have sporadic blue whale sightings, too – they're the biggest of the species. To see one is like winning the lottery.

2 GRAND MANAN ISLAND

Grand Manan (p288) in New Brunswick is another top place for whale-watching, and one of the few other locations where you can see the rare North Atlantic right whale.

3 CAPE BRETON HIGHLANDS

The Cape Breton Highlands (p283) is the best area to view whales from the shore, though they're likely to be pilot whales, a smaller kind.

4 THE BACK-UP PLAN

People need a backup plan in case of bad weather. For instance, at Digby Neck, there is lots of fog in the summer and wind in the fall. Though conditions are poor here, and we don't go out, the weather might be totally fine 30 to 60 minutes up the road at, say, Annapolis Royal, where there are old forts and historic sites. Schedule an extra day, and take advantage of the region's other attractions.

5 SEAFOOD AFTER THE TOUR

You have to get fresh seafood – especially scallops – when you're in Digby. The town is famous for them. Try the Royal Fundy Seafood Market (p280), which is right by the wharf and where you'll see fleets hauling in their catch.

267

Cabot Trail, Cape Breton Island

Driving the 300km Cabot Trail (p282) is a singular, brake-smoking journey. The road winds and climbs over coastal mountains, with gawp-evoking sea views at every turn, whales visible just offshore, moose nibbling roadside and plenty of paths to stop and hike. Be sure to tote your dancing shoes – Celtic and Acadian communities pepper the region, and their high-energy fiddles blow the roof off local pubs.

Anne's Land, Cavendish

You know how spunky Anne Shirley, Lucy Maud Montgomery's immortal heroine of *Anne of Green Gables*, wins over everyone in her path? So it is with Cavendish (p295), the wildly popular little town that inspired the book. It'll charm even the biggest skeptic – eventually. Past the water parks and wax museums lie pink-sand beaches, a green patchwork of rolling fields and tidy seaside villages every bit as pastoral as in the storybook. Avonlea Village, Cavendish

Grand Manan Island

Grand Manan (p288) is a fine place to absorb clifftop lighthouses, clapboard fishing hamlets and other requisite Maritime scenery. But the island's unique geography ups the ante. Located in the Bay of Fundy, it's slapped by the world's most extreme tides. And those tides stir up serious food for whales. Fin, humpback, scarce North Atlantic right whales and mega-huge blue whales swim in to feast, making a whale-watch here extraordinary. Swallowtail Lighthouse

Halifax & Charlottetown

With heritage buildings, arty shops and cosmopolitan eateries sloping down to the waterfront, Halifax (p274) and Charlottetown (p291) let you soak up the Maritime culture at its finest. By day they're historic-site-studded capitals, offering everything from a spooky citadel to *Titanic* exhibits to Canada's birthplace for exploration. By night they morph into music centers, where rock and traditional Celtic bands plug in for crowds. Halifax

Seafood Suppers

Lobster is the Maritimes' main dish – boiled in the pot and served with a little butter – and the best place to get down and dirty with the crustacean is a community-hall supper club in a blink-of-the-eye town such as St Ann's (p296). Giant, butter-soft scallops from Digby (p280) and briny oysters from Malpeque (p296) also stoke foodies' fire, especially when procured in rustic, wharfside cafes.

Nova Scotia & Maritime Canada's Best..

Dining

● **Fid** (p276) Regional specialties made from ingredients sourced at the Halifax farmers market

● **Chanterelle Country Inn** (p284) They don't forage for their own mushrooms at St Ann's Loop for nothing

● **St Ann's Parish Lobster Supper** (p296) Top place to don a bib and get crackin'

● **Lot 30** (p293) Creative takes on local seafood, with masterful wine pairings in Charlottetown

Lighthouses

● **Peggy's Cove** (p282) Picture-perfect, red-and-white tower sends cameras clicking

● **Swallowtail** (p288) Looms atop a moss-covered cliff with seals swimming below

● **Cape Enrage** (p290) Presides over the highest, meanest tides in the world (hence the name)

● **East Quoddy Head** (p290) Lookout for whales on Campobello Island's north end

Live Music

● **Red Shoe Pub** (p283) World-renowned Celtic fiddlers scorch the strings in Mabou

● **Baddeck Gathering Ceilidhs** (p285) Nightly fiddling and dancing at the local parish hall

● **Benevolent Irish Society** (p293) Another rowdy place to catch a ceilidh, in Charlottetown

● **Lower Deck** (p278) Bands rock Halifax's most sociable pub nightly

Need to Know

Wildlife-Watching

- **Digby Neck** (p280) Endangered North Atlantic right whales, humpbacks and perhaps blue whales if you're lucky

- **Grand Manan Island** (p288) Add puffins to the humpback and right whale mix

- **Pleasant Bay** (p283) Whales, seals and a bonus Tibetan monastery

- **Cape Breton Highlands National Park** (p283) More moose than you can shake a shrub at

ADVANCE PLANNING

- **One month before** For summer, book accommodation as soon as possible. Same with rental cars.

- **Two weeks before** Book cycling and whale-watch excursions; make ferry reservations.

- **One week before** Get binoculars, motion sickness pills ready.

RESOURCES

- **Tourism Nova Scotia** (www.novascotia.com) Links to attractions, tour operators and accommodations.

- **Destination Halifax** (www.halifaxinfo.com) Halifax's tourism site.

- **Studio Map** (www.studiorally.ca) Guide to Nova Scotia's art and craft studios, plus a shortlist of eateries and B&Bs.

- **Tourism New Brunswick** (www.tourismnewbrunswick.ca) Info on scenic drives and other trip planning resources.

- **PEI Tourism** (www.peiplay.com) The low-down on local foods, Confederation Trail cycling, beaches and St Ann's sights.

- **Bay Ferries** (www.bayferries.com) Reservations for ferry between St John, New Brunswick, and Digby, Nova Scotia.

- **Northumberland Ferries** (www.peiferry.com) Reservations between Wood Islands, PEI, and Caribou, Nova Scotia.

- **Wines of Nova Scotia** (www.winesofnovascotia.ca) Information on vineyards and festivals across the province.

GETTING AROUND

- **Fly** Halifax International Airport is the hub for travel across the region; services to/from Charlottetown, PEI, and Fredericton, New Brunswick.

- **Car** The longest drive most people will do is the four-hour haul from Halifax to Cape Breton Island. Same driving time from Halifax to Charlottetown. The toll Confederation Bridge links PEI to New Brunswick.

- **Ferry** Common mode between St John, New Brunswick, and Digby, Nova Scotia; and between Wood Islands, PEI, and Caribou, Nova Scotia.

- **Train** Once daily VIA Rail train from Halifax to Montréal (21 hours).

Left: Swallowtail Lighthouse (p288);
Above: Whales off Pleasant Bay (p283)

Nova Scotia & Maritime Canada Itineraries

With three days, hopscotch through Nova Scotia's pretty wine country; the intrepid can whale-watch at Digby Neck, where behemoths congregate like nowhere else. With five days, take a bite of all the Maritime provinces.

HALIFAX TO HALIFAX
Whales & Wine
3 DAYS

Spend the first day in **(1) Halifax**. Wander the waterfront and its historic properties, making sure to tour **(2) Alexander Keith's Brewery** and the **(3) Halifax Historic Farmers' Market**. When night falls, fork into one of downtown's hip restaurants, then see what's on for live music at the local pubs.

On day two motor west to **(4) Tiverton** on Digby Neck, a 275km drive. Yes, it's a long haul, but **(5) Ocean Explorations Whale Cruises** is worth it. Buckle into a tangerine-colored flotation suit and hold on tight as you get up close and personal with humpbacks and rare North Atlantic right whales. Eat like a whale when you return to **(6) Digby**, famous worldwide for the buttery scallops plucked from its waters.

Depart Digby on day three, backtracking to **(7) Wolfville**, a university town ringed by wineries. Pull over for sparkling pours at **(8) L'Acadie Vineyards**, or sweet ice wines at **(9) Gaspereau Vineyards**, one of the region's star grape crushers. You can spend the night here in the star-filled valley – there are several inns, and some of the wineries host guests – or return to Halifax, an hour down the road.

5 DAYS

HALIFAX TO HALIFAX
Heart of the Maritimes

This 650km loop loops through Nova Scotia, New Brunswick *and* PEI.

Eat and drink in **(1) Halifax** for a day, then make a break northwest to New Brunswick. Give the province a quick kiss hello and goodbye, then barrel over the 12.9km Confederation Bridge that links New Brunswick to PEI. Voila – you're in Anne's Land (Anne being the fictional red-headed orphan of Green Gables fame), and **(2) Cavendish** is the wildly developed town that pays homage to her.

Continue the red theme by exploring the sandstone bluffs at **(3) Prince Edward Island National Park**, where there's bird-watching, beach walking and swimming. There's also lobster eating: spurting shellfish all over your shirt at a 'lobster supper' initiates you into the local lifestyle, and the church basement in nearby **(4) St Ann's** hosts an excellent venue to get juicy. It's easy to while away a few days in this area around Cavendish.

Spend a day in PEI's compact, colonial capital **(5) Charlottetown** before taking the ferry from **(6) Wood Islands** to **(7) Caribou** back in Nova Scotia. It takes about two hours to return to Halifax.

Inn in historic Charlottetown (p291)
PHOTOGRAPHER: MICHAEL GEBICKI

273

Discover Nova Scotia & Maritime Canada

HALIFAX
POP 360,000

Halifax is the kind of town that people flock to, not so much for the opportunities, but for the quality of life it has to offer. Sea breezes off the harbor keep the air clean, and parks and trees nestle between heritage buildings, cosmopolitan eateries and arty shops. Several universities ensure that the population is kept young and the bars and nightclubs full. Stroll the historic waterfront, catch some live music and enjoy the best of what the Maritimes have to offer.

 Sights

Downtown Halifax
HISTORIC PROPERTIES
Notable Buildings

The Historic Properties is a group of restored buildings on Upper Water St, built between 1800 and 1905. Originally designed as huge warehouses for easy storage of goods and cargo, they now house boutiques, restaurants and bars and are connected by the waterfront boardwalks. Artisans, merchants and buskers do business around the buildings in the summer.

ALEXANDER KEITH'S NOVA SCOTIA BREWERY
Brewery

(☎ 902-455-1474; www.keiths.ca; Brewery Market, 1496 Lower Water St; adult/child $16/8; ⏲ 11am-8pm Mon-Thu, 11am-9pm Fri & Sat, noon-4pm Sun)A tour of this brewery takes you to 19th-century Halifax via costumed thespians, quality brew and dark corridors. Finish your hour-long tour with a party in the basement pub with beer

The waterfront at Halifax
PHOTOGRAPHER: ANDREW BAIN

on tap and ale-inspired yarns. Note that you'll need your ID. (Kids are kept happy with lemonade.)

MARITIME MUSEUM OF THE ATLANTIC
Museum

(☎ 902-424-7490; www.museum.gov .ns.ca/mma; 1675 Lower Water St; adult/child $8.50/4.50; ⏱ 9:30am-5:30pm Wed-Mon, to 8pm Tue) Part of this fun waterfront museum was a chandlery, where all the gear needed to outfit a vessel was sold. You can smell the charred ropes, cured to protect them from saltwater. There's a wildly popular display on the *Titanic* and another on the Halifax Explosion. The 3-D film about the *Titanic* costs $5. Outside at the dock you can explore the CSS *Acadia*, a retired hydrographic vessel from England.

The last WWII corvette **HMCS Sackville** (adult/child $3/2; ⏱ 10am-5pm) is docked nearby and staffed by the Canadian Navy.

CITADEL HILL NATIONAL HISTORIC SITE
Historical Site

(☎ 902-426-5080; off Sackville St; adult/ child $11.70/5.80; ⏱ 9am-6pm) Canada's most visited national historic site, the huge and arguably spooky Citadel is a star-shaped fort atop Halifax's central hill. Construction began in 1749 with the founding of Halifax; this version of the Citadel is the fourth, built from 1818 to 1861. Guided tours explain the fort's shape and history.

 Tours

TALL SHIP SILVA
Harbor Tours

(☎ 902-429-9463; www.tallshipsilva.com; Queen's Wharf at Prince St; ⏱ noon, 2pm, 4pm, 6pm & 10:30pm daily May-Oct) Lend a hand or sit back and relax while taking a one-hour ($12 per person), 1½-hour (adult/ child $20/14) or evening party two-hour ($20 per person) cruise on Halifax' square masted tall ship.

TATTLE TOURS
Walking Tours

(☎ 902-494-0525; www.tattletours.ca; per person $10; ⏱ 7:30pm Wed-Sun) Lively two-hour

tours depart from the Old Town Clock and are filled with local gossip, pirate tales and ghost stories. Walking tours are also available on demand – ask at any Visitor Information Centre (VIC).

 Sleeping

WAVERLEY INN
Inn $$

(☎ 902-423-9346, 800-565-9346; www.waver leyinn.com; 1266 Barrington St; d incl breakfast $130-240; P @) Every room here is furnished uniquely and nearly theatrically with antiques and dramatic linens. Both Oscar Wilde and PT Barnum once stayed here and probably would again today if they were still living. The downtown location can't be beat.

PEBBLE BED & BREAKFAST
B&B $$

(☎ 902-423-3369, 888-303-5056; www .thepebble.ca; 1839 Armview Tce; r $110-225; P) Bathroom aficionados will find heaven at this luxurious B&B. The tub and shower are in a giant room that leads to a terrace overlooking a leafy garden. The bedrooms are equally generous with plush, high beds and a modern-meets-antique decor. Irish owner Elizabeth O'Carroll grew up with a pub-owning family and brings lively, joyous energy from the Emerald Isle to her home in a posh, waterside residential area.

HALLIBURTON
Inn $$$

(☎ 902-420-0658; www.thehalliburton.com; 5184 Morris St; r $145-350; P ⊜ @) Pure, soothing class without all that Victorian hullabaloo can be found at this exceedingly comfortable and well-serviced historic hotel right in downtown.

LORD NELSON HOTEL
Hotel $$$

(☎ 902-423-5130, 800-565-2020; www.lord nelsonhotel.com; 1515 South Park St; d $140-360; P @) When rock stars (such as the Rolling Stones) come to Halifax, they stay here. It's an elegant yet not stuffy 1920s building right across from Halifax Public Gardens. Rates drop dramatically in the off-season.

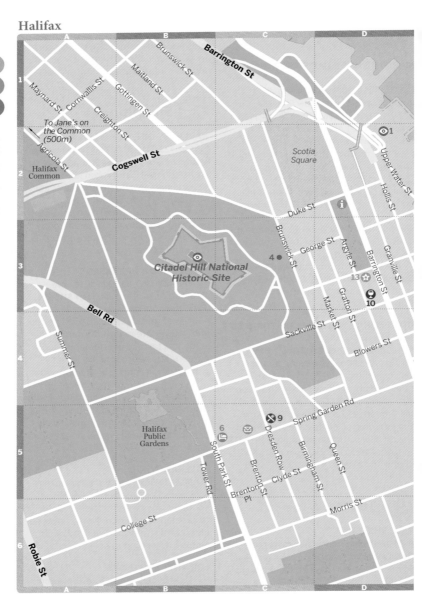

Eating

FID Fusion **$$**
(902-422-9162; www.fidcuisine.ca; 1569
Dresden Row; mains lunch $14-16, dinner

$22-27; lunch Wed-Fri, dinner Tue-Sun;)
Slow-food proponent Dennis Johnston
buys all his ingredients from the local
farmers' market, then uses them to
concoct dishes such as monkfish with
shell peas, asparagus, maple-glazed

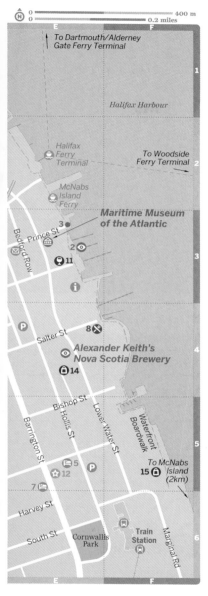

Halifax

◎ Top Sights

JANE'S ON THE COMMON Canadian $$
(☎ 902-431-5683; 2394 Robie St; mains lunch $11-13, dinner $16-19; ⊙lunch Tue-Fri, dinner Tue-Sun, brunch Sat & Sun) The shiny black diner-style tables fill up early at this increasingly popular eatery. Try a delectable starter such as the arugula, apple and ricotta tart or seared scallops in a curried apricot vinaigrette, then move on to to-die-for mains such as a smoked pork chop stuffed with spinach, sage and cheddar. Divine!

BISH Canadian $$$
(☎ 902-425-7993; 1475 Lower Water St; mains $30-36; ⊙dinner Mon-Sat) If a sizzling

pork belly with sweet potato and a beautiful pad thai. Needless to say, it's a great place to sample regional foods; the menu changes weekly and carries vegetarian options.

AUSTIN MANNETTE

Don't Miss **Halifax Historic Farmers' Market**

North America's oldest **farmers' market** (📞 902-492-4043; 1496 Lower Water St; 🕐 8am-1pm Sat Jan–mid-May, 7am-1pm Sat mid-May–Dec), in the 1820s Keith's Brewery Building, is the ultimate shopping experience. Head here to people-watch and buy organic produce, locally crafted jewelry, clothes and more. In fact, the market has become so popular it's going to be expanded in 2011 to the newly built **Seaport Market**, a second location near Pier 21 – it will be a daily event with more vendors and cafes as well as more parking.

platter of shellfish including king crab, scallops and lobster doesn't up the ante of Maritime cuisine, not much will. There's no better place to celebrate or get very, very romantic than waterside Bishop's Harbour.

DA MAURIZIO   Italian $$$
(📞 902-423-0859; 1496 Lower Water St; mains $28-34; 🕐 dinner Mon-Sat) Many locals cite this as their favorite Halifax restaurant. The ambience is as fine as the cuisine; exposed brick and clean lines bring out all the flavors of this heritage brewery building. Reservations strongly recommended.

EPICURIOUS MORCELS   Fusion $$
(📞 902-455-0955; Hydrostone Market, 5529 Young St; mains around $12; 🕐 11:30am-8pm Tue-

Thu, 10:30am-8pm Fri & Sat, 10:30am-2:30pm Sun) The specialties here are smoked salmon, *gravlax* (dill-cured salmon) and unusual but extremely tasty homemade soups. The rest of the internationally inspired menu is also fantastic.

 **Drinking**

LOWER DECK   Pub
(📞 902-422-1501; 1869 Lower Water St) A first stop for a real Nova Scotian knee-slapping good time. Think pints in frothy glasses, everyone singing, and live music all spilling out over the sidewalks on summer nights. When someone yells 'sociable!' it's time to raise your glass.

ECONOMY SHOE SHOP Pub

(☎ 902-423-8845; 1663 Argyle St) This has been the 'it' place to drink and people-watch in Halifax for almost a decade. On weekend nights actors and journalists figure heavily in the crush. It's a pleasant place for afternoon drinks and the kitchen dishes out tapas until last call at 1:45am.

 Entertainment

Check out the *Coast* to see what's on – a free weekly publication available around town, it's the essential guide for music, theater, film and events.

CARELTON Live Music

(☎ 902-422-6335; 1685 Argyle St) Catch acoustic sets then enjoy the reasonable meals including a late-night menu.

BEARLY'S HOUSE OF BLUES & RIBS
Live Music

(☎ 902-423-2526; 1269 Barrington St; cover $3) The best blues musicians in Atlantic Canada play here at incredibly low cover charges. Wednesday karaoke nights draw a crowd and some fine singers.

ℹ Information

Tourism Nova Scotia (☎ 902-425-5781, 800-565-0000; www.novascotia.com) Operates VICs in Halifax.

ℹ Getting There & Away

Air There are multiple daily flights to Toronto, Calgary and Vancouver.
Train A daily VIA Rail (www.viarail.ca) train goes from Halifax to Montréal (21 hours) via Charny (Québec City).

ℹ Getting Around

To/From the Airport

Halifax International Airport is 40km northeast of town on Hwy 102. Airbus (☎ 902-873-2091; one-way/return $19/27) runs between 5am and 11pm and picks up at major hotels. If you arrive in the middle of the night, as many flights do, your only choice is a taxi, which costs $54 to downtown Halifax.

Public Transportation

Metro Transit (☎ 902-490-6600; one-way fare $2.25) runs the city bus system. 'Fred' is a free

Maritime Museum of the Atlantic (p275), Halifax

ANDREW BAIN

city bus that loops around downtown every 30 minutes in the summer.

ANNAPOLIS VALLEY & FRENCH SHORE

Digby

Digby has been a tourist mecca for more than a century and it's a good base from which to explore Digby Neck and some lesser-known hiking trails in the area. If you're here in passing, the best things to do are to stroll the waterfront, watch the scallop draggers come and go, and eat as much of their catch as you can get your hands on.

Sleeping & Eating

BAYSIDE INN B&B　　　　　B&B $$
(902-245-2247, 888-754-0555; www.bay sideinn.ca; 115 Montague Row; r $60-100; @)
In continuous operation since the late 1800s, the historic 11-room Bayside is Digby's oldest inn. Centrally located in town, it has views over the scallop fleet and Fundy tides. It was remodeled in 2010.

ROYAL FUNDY SEAFOOD MARKET
　　　　　　　　　　　　　Cafe $$
(902-245-5411; 144 Prince William St; mains $6-14; 11am-8pm) Get your seafood from the source at this little fishmonger-cum-cafe. Local seafood is made into all the usual fried suspects as well as soups.

ⓘ Getting There & Away

Bay Ferries (888-249-7245; www.bay ferries.com; adult/under 5 yrs/6-13 yrs/senior $40/5/25/30, car/motorcycle/bicycle $80/50/10) has a three-hour trip from Digby to St John, New Brunswick.

Digby Neck

Craning out to take a peek into the Bay of Fundy, Digby Neck is a giraffe's length strip of land that's a haven for whale- and seabird-watchers. At the far western end of the appendage are Long and

Brier Islands, connected by ferry with the rest of the peninsula.

Plankton stirred up by the strong Fundy tides attracts finback, minke and humpback whales and this is the best place in the world to see the endangered North Atlantic right whale.

Long Island

Most people head straight to Brier Island, but Long Island has better deals on whale-watching as well as a livelier community. At the northeastern edge of Long Island, **Tiverton** is an active fishing community.

One of the best whale-watching tours in the province is found just near the Tiverton ferry dock. **Ocean Explorations Whale Cruises** (902-839-2417, 877-654-2341; www.oceanexplorations.ca; half-day tours adult/child $59/40; Jun-Oct), led by biologist Tom Goodwin, has the adventurous approach of getting you low to whale-level in a Zodiac. Shimmy into an orange coastguard-approved flotation suit and hold on tight!

At the southwestern end of Long Island, **Freeport** is central for exploring both Brier and Long Islands.

Getting There & Away

Two ferries connect Long and Brier Islands to the rest of Digby Neck. The Petit Passage ferry leaves East Ferry (on Digby Neck) 25 minutes after the hour and Tiverton on the hour; ferries are timed so that if you drive directly from Tiverton to Freeport (18km) there is no wait for the Grand Passage ferry to Westport (on Brier Island). Both ferries operate hourly, 24 hours a day, year-round. Round-trip passage is $5 for a car and all passengers. Pedestrians ride free.

Wolfville

Wolfville is a college town with several wineries nearby so as you'd expect there are plenty of drinking holes, good eating establishments and culture.

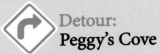

Detour:
Peggy's Cove

Peggy's Cove is one of the most visited fishing towns in Canada but for a good reason: the rolling granite cove highlighted by a perfect red-and-white lighthouse exudes a dreamy seaside calm even through the parading tour buses. Most visitors hop off their air-con bus, snap a few pictures then get right back on the bus. If you stick around you'll find it surprisingly easy to chat with the friendly locals (there are only 45 of them) and settle into a fishing-village pace. At 43km west of Halifax on Hwy 333 it makes a mellow day trip from the city.

It's best to visit before 10am in summer as tour buses arrive in the middle of the day and create one of the province's worst traffic jams. There's free parking with washrooms and a **tourist information office** (☎902-823-2253; 109 Peggy's Cove Rd; ☉9am-7pm Jul & Aug, to 5pm mid-May–Jun, Sep & Oct) as you enter the village. Free 45-minute walking tours are led from the tourist office daily from mid-June through August.

Sights

L'ACADIE VINEYARDS
Winery

(☎902-542-8463; www.lacadievineyards.ca; 310 Slayter Rd; ☉10am-5pm May-Oct) Overlooking Gaspereau Valley just south of Wolfville, this geothermal winery grows certified organic grapes to make unique traditional-method sparkling and dried-grape wines. You can also stay in one of three country-style two-bedroom, kitchen-equipped cottages ($150 per night), which of course include a free bottle of wine.

GASPEREAU VINEYARDS
Winery

(☎902-542-1455; www.gaspereauwine.com; 2239 White Rock Rd; ☉10am-5pm mid-May–Oct, tours noon, 2pm & 4pm daily mid-May–Oct) In Gaspereau, 3km south of Wolfville, this is one of the province's best known wineries with award-winning icewine.

CAPE BRETON ISLAND

Floating over the rest of Nova Scotia like an island halo, Cape Breton is a heavenly, forested realm of bald eagles, migrating whales, palpable history and foot-tapping music. Starting up the Ceilidh Trail along the western coastline, Celtic music vibrates through the pubs and community centers, eventually reaching the Cabot Trail where more eclectic Acadian-style tunes ring out around **Chéticamp**.

The 300km **Cabot Trail** continues around Cape Breton Highlands National Park. It winds and climbs around and over coastal mountains, with heart-stopping ocean views at every turn; there are moose on the roads and hiking trails to entice you from your vehicle.

Mabou

Although it looks unlikely at first glance, micro Mabou is the not-so-underground hot spot of Cape Breton's Celtic music scene. Among lush hills and quiet inlets you can hike away your days and dance away your nights.

Sights & Activities

GLENORA INN & DISTILLERY
Inn & Distillery

(☎902-258-2662, 800-839-0491; www.glenora distillery.com; Hwy 19; guided tours incl tasting $7; ☉tours on the hour 9am-5pm mid-Jun–mid-Oct) Glenora Inn & Distillery is the only distillery making single malt whiskey in Canada. After a tour and a taste of the rocket fuel, stop for a meal at the gourmet pub (there are daily lunchtime and dinner ceilidhs) or even for the night;

cave-like rooms ($125 to $150 per night) are perfect for sleeping it off if you've been drinking the local beverage but the chalets ($175 to $240) are a better choice if you want brighter surroundings. It's 9km north of Mabou.

RED SHOE PUB
Pub $$

(902-945-2996; www.redshoepub.com; 11533 Hwy 19; mains $9-22; 11:30am-midnight Wed, 11:30am-2am Thu-Sat, noon-midnight Sun) Straddling the spine of the Ceilidh Trail, this pub is the beating heart of Mabou. Gather round a local fiddle player (often from the Rankin family) while enjoying a pint and a superb meal – the desserts, including the gingerbread with rum-butterscotch sauce and fruit compote, are divine.

Cape Breton Highlands National Park

There are two park entrances: one at Chéticamp and one at Ingonish. Buy an **entry permit** (adult/child/up to 7 people in a vehicle $7.80/3.90/19.60) at either park entrance. A one-day pass is good until noon the next day. Wheelchair-accessible trails are indicated on the free park map available at either entrance. The park is a great place for spotting moose.

CO-OP ARTISANALE RESTAURANT
Restaurant $$

(902-224-2170; 15067 Main St, Chéticamp; mains $8-16; 9am-9pm) This restaurant specializes in Acadian dishes such as a stewed chicken dinner ($13) and *pâté à la viande* (meat pie) for $8. Delicious potato pancakes ($8) with apple sauce, molasses or sour cream are the only vegetarian option.

Pleasant Bay

A perfect base for exploring the park, Pleasant Bay is a carved-out bit of civilization hemmed on all sides by wilderness.

🔘 Sights & Activities

GAMPO ABBEY
Buddhist Monastery

(902-224-2752; www.gampoabbey.org; tours 1:30-3:30pm Mon-Fri mid-Jun–mid-Sep) This abbey, 8km north of Pleasant Bay past the village of Red River, is a monastery for followers of Tibetan Buddhism. Ane Pema Chödrön is the founding director of the abbey and a noted Buddhist author, but you aren't likely to see her here as she is often on the road. You can visit the grounds any time during the day but you get a more authentic experience with a tour – a friendly monk escorts you.

CAPTAIN MARK'S WHALE & SEAL CRUISE
Whale-Watching

(902-224-1316, 888-754-5112; www.whaleandsealcruise.com; adult $25-39, child $12-19; mid-May–Sep) Two to five daily tours (depending on the season) can be taken in the lower-priced 'Cruiser' motor boat

Cape Breton Island (p282)

PHOTOGRAPHER: MICHAEL GEBICKI

or closer to the action in a Zodiac. Captain Mark promises not only guaranteed whales but also time to see seabirds and seals as well as Gampo Abbey. There's a discount of 25% if you reserve a spot on the earliest (9:30am) or latest (5pm) tour. Tours leave from the wharf next to the Whale Interpretive Centre.

 Sleeping

SCOTTISH HILLSIDE B&B B&B **$$**
(☎ 877-223-8111, 902-224-21156; scottishhill sidebnb@hotmail.com; 23562 Cabot Trail; r $85-135; ☎) Run by a friendly young family, this new Victorian-style home sits right on the Cabot Trail and is a comfortable and convenient base for hiking and whale-watching. Ornately decorated rooms are big and the buffet-style breakfasts feature everything from local fruit to authentic oatcakes.

CABOT TRAIL HOSTEL Hostel **$**
(☎ 902-224-1976; www.cabottrail.com/hostel; 23349 Cabot Trail; dm/r $27/59; @ ☎) Bright and basic, this very friendly 18-bed hostel has a common kitchen and barbecue area. The office for Cabot Trail Whale Watching is here.

St Ann's Loop
Settle into the artsy calm of winding roads, serene lakes, eagles soaring overhead and a never-ending collection of artists' workshops that dot the trail like Easter eggs.

CHANTERELLE COUNTRY INN & COTTAGES Inn **$$$**
(☎ 902-929-2263, 866-277-0577; www .chanterelleinn.com; 48678 Cabot Trail, North River; r $145-225; ◷ May-Nov; @ ☎ ⚐) Unparalleled as an environmentally friendly place to stay, the house and cabins are on 60 hectares overlooking rolling pastures and bucolic bliss. Meals (breakfast and dinner) are served on the screened-in porch. If you're not staying here, you can reserve for dinner at the highly reputed restaurant (mains $20 to $28, prix-fixe four courses veg/non-veg $38/45; open 6pm to 8pm May to November).

Baddeck
An old resort town in a pastoral setting, Baddeck is the most popular place to stay for those who intend to do the Cabot Trail as a one-day scenic drive.

 Sights & Activities

ALEXANDER GRAHAM BELL NATIONAL HISTORIC SITE Museum
(☎ 902-295-2069; www.parkscanada.gc.ca; 559 Chebucto St; adult/child $7.80/3.90; ◷ 9am-6pm) The inventor of the telephone is buried near his summer home, Beinn Bhreaghm, which is visible across the bay from Baddeck. The excellent museum of the Alexander Graham Bell National Historic Site, at the eastern edge of town, covers all aspects of his inventions and innovations. See medical and electrical devices, telegraphs, telephones, kites and seaplanes and then learn about how they all work.

 Sleeping & Eating

BROADWATER INN & COTTAGES
Inn **$$**
(☎ 902-295-1101, 877-818-3474; www.broad water.baddeck.com; Bay Rd; r $90-140, ste $199, cottages $95-200; ☎) In a tranquil spot 1.5km east of Baddeck, this c 1830 home once belonged to JAD McCurdy, who worked with Alexander Graham Bell on early aircraft designs. The rooms in the inn are full of character, have bay views and are decorated with subtle prints and lots of flair. Modern self-contained cottages are set in the woods and are great for families. Only the B&B rooms include breakfast. It's gay friendly.

HIGHWHEELER CAFE & DELI Cafe **$**
(486 Chebucto St; sandwiches $8; ◷ 6am-8pm) This place bakes great bread and goodies (some gluten-free), makes big tasty sandwiches (including vegetarian), quesadillas, soups and more. Finish off on the sunny deck licking an ice-cream cone. Box lunches for hikers are also available.

STEPHEN SAKS

Don't Miss **Louisbourg National Historic Site**

Budget a full day to explore this extraordinary **historic site** (📞902-733-2280; 259 Park Service Rd; adult/child $17.60/8.80; ⏱9am-5:30pm) that faithfully re-creates Fortress Louisbourg as it was in 1744 right down to the people – costumed thespians take their characters and run with them. Built to protect French interests in the region, it was also a base for cod fishing and an administrative capital.

Free guided tours around the site are offered throughout the day. Be prepared for lots of walking, and bring a sweater and raincoat even if it's sunny when you start out.

Though the scale of the reconstruction is massive, three-quarters of Louisbourg is still in ruins. The 2.5km **Ruins Walk** guides you through the untouched terrain and out to the Atlantic coast.

Three restaurants serve food typical of the time. **Hotel de la Marine** and the adjacent **L'Épée Royale** (grilled cod with soup $14, 3-course meal $20) are where sea captains and prosperous merchants would dine on fine china with silver cutlery. Servers in period costume also dish out grub at **Grandchamps House** (meals $9-15), a favorite of sailors and soldiers. Wash down beans and sausage with hot buttered rum ($4).

Entertainment

BADDECK GATHERING CEILIDHS
Live Music
(📞902-295-2794; www.baddeckgathering
.com; St Michael's Parish Hall, 8 Old Margaree
Rd; adult/child $10/5; ⏱7:30pm Jul & Aug) The
parish hall hosts nightly fiddling and
dancing. It's just opposite the VIC right
in the middle of town.

Louisbourg

Louisbourg, 37km southeast of Sydney, is famous for its historic fortress (see the boxed text above). The town itself has plenty of soul, with its working fishing docks, old-timers and a friendly vibe.

Starting from the lighthouse at the end of Havenside Rd, a rugged 6km **trail** follows the coast over bogs, barrens and pre-Cambrian polished granite. Bring your camera to capture the views back toward the fortress at the national historic site.

Sleeping & Eating

CRANBERRY COVE INN Inn **$$**
(☎ 902-733-2171, 800-929-0222; www.cranberrycoveinn.com; 12 Wolfe St; r $105-160; ✆May-Nov; ☎) From the dark pink facade to the period-perfect interior of mauves, dusty blues and antique lace, you'll be transported back in time through rose-colored glasses at this stunning B&B. Each room is unique and several have Jacuzzis and fireplaces.

BEGGAR'S BANQUET Restaurant **$$$**
(☎ 888-374-8439; Point of View Suites, 15 Commercial St Extension; meals $35; ✆6-8pm late Jul-Sep) Finally here's a chance for you to get into period costume and gorge on a feast of local seafood in a replicated 18th-century tavern. There's a choice of four delicious and copious mains including crab and lobster.

NEW BRUNSWICK
Fredericton
POP 50,500

This sleepy provincial capital does quaint very well. On warm weekends, 'The Green,' as it's known, looks like something out of a watercolor painting – families strolling, kids kicking soccer balls, couples picnicking.

Sights

BEAVERBROOK ART GALLERY Museum
(www.beaverbrookartgallery.org; 703 Queen St; adult/senior/student/family $8/6/3/18, pay as you wish Thu after 5:30pm; ✆9am-5:30pm, to 9pm Thu, noon-5pm Sun Sep-Jun, closed Mon in winter) The exceptional collection includes works by international heavyweights and is well worth an hour or so. Among others, you will see Constable, Dali, Gainsborough and Turner, Canadian artists Tom Thompson, Emily Carr and Cornelius Kreighoff, as well as changing contemporary exhibits of Atlantic art.

Hopewell Rocks (p290) at low tide

OFFICERS' SQUARE Historical Site
(www.downtownfredericton.ca; btwn Carleton & Regent Sts; ⏱ceremonies 11am & 4pm mid-July–3rd week Aug, additional performances 7pm Tue & Thu) Once the military parade ground, the Garrison District's Officers' Square now hosts a full-uniform changing-of-the-guard ceremony in summertime. Also in summer the Calithumpians Outdoor Summer Theatre performs daily at 12:15pm on weekdays and 2:30pm on weekends. The free historical skits are laced with humor.

 Tours

Heritage Walking Tours (free; ⏱10am, 2:30pm & 5pm daily Jul-Oct) Enthusiastic, historic-costume-wearing young people lead free hour-long tours of the river, the government district or the Historic Garrison District, departing from City Hall.

 Sleeping

CARRIAGE HOUSE INN B&B $$
(☎ 506-452-9924, 800-267-6068; www.carriagehouse-inn.net; 230 University Ave; r with breakfast $99-129; ᴾ♨❄🛜) Located in a shady Victorian neighborhood near the Green, this beautifully restored 1875 Queen Anne was built for a lumber baron and former Fredericton mayor. The grand common room has polished hardwood floors, antiques, comfy sofas, fireplaces and a grand piano. Upstairs, the guest rooms have high ceilings, four-posters, period wallpapers and vintage artwork.

BRENNAN'S B&B B&B $$
(☎ 506-455-7346; www.bbcanada.com/3892.html; 146 Waterloo St; r incl breakfast $95-135; ᴾ♨❄@) Built for a wealthy merchant family in 1885, this turreted white riverfront mansion is now a handsome four-room B&B. The better rooms have hardwood floors and water views.

 Eating

WW BOYCE FARMERS' MARKET Farmers Market $
(www.boycefarmersmarket.com; 665 George St; ⏱6am-1pm Sat) This Fredericton institution is great for picking up fresh fruit, vegetables, meat, cheese, handicrafts, dessert and flowers. Many of the 150 or so stalls recall the city's European heritage, with everything from German-style sausage to French duck pâtés to British marmalade. There is also a restaurant where Frederictonians queue to chat and people-watch.

RACINE'S Fusion $$$
(www.racinesrestaurant.ca; 536 Queen St; mains $17-33; ⏱dinner) Faux leather tablecloths and touches of neon green lend an urban mod look to this trendy downtown bistro. The internationally influenced menu is heavy on seafood and grilled meats – Malpec oysters on the half-shell, curried crab cakes, Szechuan-spiced duck, filet mignon with herb butter – all artfully displayed on white plates like abstract paintings.

 Drinking

GARRISON DISTRICT ALE HOUSE Pub
(www.thegarrison.ca; 426 Queen St; ⏱Mon-Sat) Dim lighting and a leather-and-wood decor make this popular Queen St pub feel like an old-school British hunting club. Preppy crowds munch burgers and sip a wide variety of craft brews.

LUNAR ROGUE PUB Pub
(www.lunarrogue.com; 625 King St; ⏱daily) This jolly locals' joint has a good beer selection and a fine assortment of single malts. The patio is wildly popular in warm weather.

 Information

Visitors Center (☎ 506-460-2129, 888-888-4768; www.tourismfredericton.ca; City Hall, 397 Queen St; ⏱8am-4:15pm Mon-Fri Oct-May, longer hours in summer) Free city parking passes provided here.

ℹ️ Getting There & Away

Air Fredericton International Airport (www .yfcmobile.ca) is on Hwy 102, 14km southeast of town.

Car & Motorcycle Cars with out-of-province license plates are eligible for a free three-day parking pass for downtown Fredericton May to October, available at the Fredericton Tourism Office at 11 Carleton St.

ℹ️ Getting Around

A taxi to the airport costs $16. Bicycle rentals are available at Radical Edge (📞506-459-3478; www.radicaledge.ca; 386 Queen St; per hr/day $7.50/25).

Grand Manan Island

Grand Manan is a peaceful, unspoiled place. There are no fast-food restaurants, no trendy coffeehouses or nightclubs, no traffic lights and no traffic. Just lots of fresh air and a ruggedly beautiful coastline of high cliffs and sandy coves interspersed with spruce forest and fields of long grass. Along the eastern shore and joined by a meandering coastal road sit a string of pretty and prosperous fishing villages. Some people make a day trip to the island, but lingering for a while is recommended.

The ferry disembarks at the village of **North Head** at the north end of the island. The main road, Rte 776, runs 28.5km down the length of the island along the eastern shore. If you wish to, you can drive from end to end in about 45 minutes.

◎ Sights

SWALLOWTAIL LIGHTHOUSE
Lighthouse

Whitewashed Swallowtail Lighthouse (1860) is the island's signature vista, cleaving to a rocky promontory about 1km north of the ferry wharf. Access is via steep stairs and a slightly swaying suspension bridge. Since the light was automated in 1986, the site has been left to the elements. Nevertheless, the grassy bluff is a stupendous setting for a picnic. It has a wraparound view of the horizon and seals raiding the heart-shaped fishing weirs (an ancient type of fishing trap made from wood posts) below.

SEAL COVE
Historical Site

Seal Cove is the island's prettiest village. Much of its charm comes from the fishing boats, wharves and herring smoking sheds clustered around the tidal creek mouth. For a century, smoked herring was king on Grand Manan. A thousand men and women worked splitting, stringing and drying fish in 300 smokehouses up and down the island.

Fishing shacks, Cape Manan Island
PHOTOGRAPHER: DONALD VERGER/PHOTOLIBRARY

Detour:
Scenic Drive: Fredericton to Fundy Shore

Start on the north side of the river in Fredericton, and follow Rte 105 south through Maugerville to Jemseg. At Exit 339, pick up Rte 715 South, which will take you to the **Gagetown ferry landing** (admission free; ☺24hr year-round). This is the first of a system of eight free cable ferries that crisscross the majestic St John River en route to the city of St John. You will never have to wait more than a few minutes for the crossing, which generally takes five to 10 minutes.

From Gagetown, head south on Rte 102, known locally as 'the Old River Road.' The hilly 42km piece of road between Gagetown and the ferry landing at **Evandale** (admission free; ☺24hr year-round) is especially picturesque, with glorious panoramic views of fields full of wildflowers, white farm houses and clots of green and gold islands set in the intensely blue water of the river.

A hundred years ago, tiny Evandale was a bustling little place, where a dance band would entertain riverboat passengers stopping off for the night at the **Evandale Resort** (☏506-468-2222; ferry landing; r $139-199), now restored to its Victorian grandeur with six rooms and a fine-dining restaurant. On the other side of the water, Rte 124 takes you the short distance to the **Belleisle ferry** (admission free; ☺24hr year-round). The ferry deposits you on the rural Kingston Peninsula, where you can cross the peninsula to catch the **Gondola Point Ferry** (admission free; ☺24hr year-round) and head directly into St John.

The last smokehouse shut down in 1996. Although herrings are still big business around here, they're now processed at a modern cannery. Today, the sheds house an informal **Sardine Museum** (admission by donation; ☺open most days).

ROLAND'S SEA VEGETABLES   Market
(www.rolandsdulse.com; 174 Hill Rd; ☺9am-6pm daily) Grand Manan is one of the few remaining producers of dulse, a type of seaweed that is used as a snack food or seasoning in Atlantic Canada and around the world. Dark Harbour, on the west side of the island, is said to produce the world's best. Dulse gatherers wade among the rocks at low tide to pick the seaweed, then lay it out on beds of rocks to dry just as they've been doing for hundreds of years. Buy some at this little roadside market, which sells various types of edible local seaweeds from nori to sea lettuce to Irish moss. Sandy, Roland's son, recommends sprinkling powdered dulse on fried eggs or baked fish.

 Activities

SEA WATCH TOURS   Puffin-Watching
(☏ 506-662-8552, 877-662-8552; www.sea watchtours.com; Seal Cove fisherman's wharf; adult/child $85/45; Mon-Sat late Jun–mid-Aug) Make the pilgrimage out to isolated Machias Seal Island to see the Atlantic puffins waddle and play on their home turf. Access to the puffins is limited to 15 visitors a day, so reserve a place well in advance. Getting onto the island can be tricky, as the waves are high and the rocks slippery. So be sure to wear sturdy shoes.

WHALES-N-SAILS ADVENTURES
Whale-Watching
(☏ 506-662-1999, 888-994-4044; www.whales -n-sails.com; North Head fisherman's wharf; adult/child $65/45; ☺late Jun-late Sep) A marine biologist narrates these exhilarating whale-watching tours aboard the sailboat *Elsie Menota*. You'll often see puffins, razorbills, murre and other seabirds.

If You Like...
Coastal Scenery

If Grand Manan Island (p288) floats your boat, check out these other highlights along the Fundy coast:

1 ST ANDREWS BY-THE-SEA
(www.townofstandrews.ca) A genteel summer resort town of inns, spas and pubs, St Andrews is where folks come to dine on lobster and windowshop with an ice cream cone. High tea or afternoon gin at the castle-like Algonquin Hotel is de rigueur. Blessed with a fine climate and picturesque beauty, it also has a colorful history being founded by Loyalists in 1783.

2 CAMPOBELLO ISLAND
(www.campobelloislandtourism.com) Campobello feels as much a part of the USA as of Canada, and indeed it is connected to Lubec, Maine by a bridge. The island's southern half is parkland. Look for whales offshore from East Quoddy Head Lighthouse.

3 FUNDY NATIONAL PARK
(www.pc.gc.ca/fundy; daily permit adult/child/family $7.80/3.90/19.60) One of the country's most popular parks, its highlights include the world's highest tides, irregularly eroded sandstone cliffs and 120km of walking trails.

4 CAPE ENRAGE
(www.capenrage.org; off Rte 905; adult/child $4/2.50; ⏱9am-5pm late May–mid-Oct, to 8pm Jul & Aug) The 150-year-old clifftop lighthouse provides dramatic views. There's an onsite climbing and rapelling school (beginners welcome) and excellent meals in the lightkeeper's house.

5 HOPEWELL ROCKS
(www.thehopewellrocks.ca; off Hwy 114; adult/child/family $8.50/6.25/23, shuttle extra $2; ⏱9am-5pm mid-May–mid-Oct, later hours in summer; 👶) Some look like arches, others like massive stone mushrooms. Crowds come from all over the world to marvel at the rocks' Dr Seussian vibe. Be prepared for crowds.

HIKING TRAILS   Hiking
About 70km of hiking trails crisscross and circle the island. For an easy hike, try the shoreline path from Long Pond to Red Point (a 1.6km/one hour round-trip that's suitable for children).

🛏 Sleeping

INN AT WHALE COVE   Inn $$
(☎506-662-3181; www.whalecovecottages.ca; Whistle Rd, North Head; s/d $120/130; ⏱May-Oct) 'Serving rusticators since 1910,' including writer Willa Cather, who wrote several of her novels here in the 1920s and '30s. The main lodge (built in 1816) and half a dozen vine-covered and shingled cottages retain the charm of that earlier era. They are fitted with polished pine floors and stone fireplaces, antiques, chintz curtains and well-stocked book-shelves. Some have kitchens.

SHORECREST LODGE   Inn $
(☎506-662-3216; www.shorecrestlodge.com; 100 Rte 776, Seal Cove; r $65-89; ⏱May-Oct; 🛜👶) Near the ferry landing, this big comfy farmhouse has 10 sunny rooms with quilts and antique furniture.

Eating

Reservations are essential for dinner due to limited table space island-wide, particularly off season when many places close. That said, there are some fine dining options on the island.

INN AT WHALE COVE
                        New Canadian $$$
(☎506-662-3181; www.whalecovecottages.ca; Whistle Rd, North Head; mains $22-28; ⏱dinner late Jun–mid-Oct, weekends May-Jun) This place serves absolutely wonder-ful food in a relaxed country setting on the cove. The menu changes daily, but includes mouth-watering upscale meals such as Provençal-style rack of lamb, scallop ravioli and a to-die-for hazelnut crème caramel for dessert.

NORTH HEAD BAKERY
Bakery $

(www.northheadbakery.ca; 199 Rte 776, North Head; items $1-5; ⏱6:30am-5:30pm Tue-Sat May-Oct) Scrumptious Danish pastries, fruit pies and artisanal breads made with organic flour make this cheerful red-and-white bakery the first stop for many folks just off the ferry.

ℹ Information

For further information on the area try the tourist information office (www.grandmanannb.com; 130 Rte 776, North Head; ⏱8am-4pm Mon-Fri, 9am-noon Sat).

ℹ Getting There & Away

The only way to get on and off the island from Blacks Harbour on the mainland to North Head on Grand Manan is by the **government ferry** (☎506-662-3724; www.coastaltransport.ca; ticket office at North Head ferry terminal). Service (adult/child $10.90/5.40, automobiles $32.55, bicycles $3.70, seven departures daily in summer) is on a first-come, first-served basis at Blacks Harbour; plan on arriving at least 45 minutes before departure. The crossing takes 1½ hours. Watch for harbor porpoises and whales en route.

PRINCE EDWARD ISLAND
Charlottetown
POP 38,114

It's been said that Charlottetown is too small to be grand and too big to be quaint. In fact, PEI's capital is just about the perfect size with a collection of stylish eateries and a lively cultural scene.

◉ Sights

PROVINCE HOUSE NATIONAL HISTORIC SITE
Historic Site

(☎902-566-7626; 165 Richmond St; admission $3.40; ⏱8:30am-5pm) It was here in 1864, within the Confederation Chamber, that 23 representatives of Britain's North American colonies first discussed the creation of Canada (p312). Along with being the 'birthplace of Canada,' the site is home to Canada's second-oldest active legislature.

Several rooms have been restored, and in July and August you may find yourself face to face with Canada's first

One of the many historical properties in Charlottetown

STEPHEN SAKS

Detour:
Distilleries

In the last few years two distinctly different distilleries have opened on PEI, echoing the province's fame for bootlegging during prohibition.

Prince Edward Distillery (☎902-687-2586; www.princeedwarddistillery.com; Rte 16, Hermanville; ☉11am-6pm) specializes in potato vodka that even in its first year of production turned international heads that have called it among the finest of its class. Stop in for tours (with/without tasting $10/2) of the immaculate distillery and to taste the different vodkas (potato, grain and blueberry) as well as the newer products such as bourbon, rum and a very interesting and aromatic gin.

Myriad View Distillery (☎902-687-1281; www.straightshine.com; 1336 Rte 2, Rollo Bay; ☉11am-6pm Mon-Sat, 1-5pm Sun) produces Canada's first and only legal moonshine. The hardcore Straight Lightning Shine is 75% alcohol and so potent it feels like liquid heat before it evaporates on your tongue. Take our advice and start with a micro-sip! A gulp could knock the wind out of you. The 50% alcohol Straight Shine lets you enjoy the flavor a bit more. Tours and tastings are free and the owner is happy to answer any questions.

The distilleries are 75km east of Charlottetown. It's about a 10-minute drive on Hwy 307 between the two places.

prime minister: actors in period garb wander the halls and regularly coalesce to perform reenactments of the famous conference.

Tours

Self-guided walking tour booklets are available for just a Loonie ($1) at the tourist office.

CONFEDERATION PLAYERS
Walking Tours

(☎902-368-1864; 6 Prince St; adult/child $10/5) There is no better way to tour Charlottetown. Playing the fathers and ladies of Confederation, actors garbed in 19th-century dress educate and entertain through the town's historic streets. Tours leave from Founders' Hall, and there are three variations on the theme: historic Great George St, Island Settlers and the haunts of local ghosts.

PEAKE'S WHARF BOAT CRUISES
Boat cruises

(☎902-566-4458; 1 Great George St; 70min cruise $20; ☉2:30pm, 6:30pm & 8pm Jun-Aug) Observe sea life, hear interesting stories and witness a wonderfully different perspective of Charlottetown from the waters of its harbor. An excellent seal-watching trip ($28) departs at 2:30pm, returning at 5pm.

Sleeping

FAIRHOLM INN
B&B $$$

(☎902-892-5022, 888-573-5022; www.fairholm .pe.ca; 230 Prince St; ste incl breakfast $129-289) This historic inn was built in 1838 and is a superb example of the picturesque movement in British architecture. Take tea while enjoying the morning sun in the beautiful conservatory, wander the gardens or hole up with a book in the library. Luxurious English fabrics, beautiful PEI artwork and grand antiques fill each suite.

GREAT GEORGE
Inn $$$

(☎ 902-892-0606, 800-361-1118; www.innson greatgeorge.com; 58 Great George St; d incl breakfast $175-219, ste $269-899; P ✳ @ 🛜) A colorful collage of celebrated buildings along Charlottetown's most famous street has rooms ranging from plush and historic to bold and contemporary – but all are simply stunning. It's both gay- and family-friendly. A babysitting service is available, as is a fitness room.

CHARLOTTE'S ROSE INN
Inn $$

(☎ 902-892-3699, 888-237-3699; www.char lottesrose.ca; 11 Grafton St; r incl breakfast $155-205, apt $180; P ⇨ ✳ @ 🛜) Miss Marple must be around here somewhere. This decadent Victorian place has true English flair with bodacious rose-printed wallpaper, lace canopies, big fluffy beds and grand bathrooms. There's a fire in the parlor for guests to enjoy along with complimentary tea and cakes.

Eating

LOT 30
Restaurant $$$

(☎ 902-629-3030; 151 Kent St; lunch mains $22-55; ⏰from 5pm Tue-Sun) Anyone who's anyone goes to Lot 30 but show up unknown and in jeans and you'll be treated just as well. Tables are in view of each other so you can see the ecstatic expressions of food bliss on the merry diners' faces; dishes from beurre blanc to curry are spiced to perfection. For a treat, try the excellent-value five-course tasting menu ($55) – small servings of a starter, three mains and a dessert sampler.

WATER PRINCE CORNER SHOP
Restaurant $$

(☎ 902-368-3212; 141 Water St; meals $10-17; ⏰9:30am-8pm) When locals want

seafood they head to this inconspicuous, sea-blue eatery near the wharf. It is deservedly famous for its scallop burgers but it's also the best place in town for fresh lobster. You'll probably have to line up for a seat or order takeout lobster, which gets you a significant discount.

SIRINELLA
Restaurant $$

(☎ 902-628-2271; 83 Water St; lunch mains $8-17, dinner $15-28; ⏰lunch & dinner Mon-Fri, dinner Sat) Cross the threshold of this diner-looking restaurant and you are transported to seaside Italy. It's nothing fancy, just little round, white-clothed tables, some Mediterranean oil paintings and incredibly authentic Italian fare.

⭐ Entertainment

BENEVOLENT IRISH SOCIETY
Hall

(☎ 902-963-3156; 582 North River Rd; admission $10; ⏰8pm Fri mid-May–Oct) On the north side of town, this is a great place to catch a ceilidh. Come early, as seating is limited.

Cycling the Confederation Trail (p330)

PHOTOGRAPHER: ANDREW BAIN

ANDREW BAIN

Don't Miss **House of Green Gables**

Cavendish is the home town of Lucy Maud Montgomery (1874–1942), author of *Anne of Green Gables*. Here she is simply known as Lucy Maud or LM. Owned by her grandfather's cousins, the now-famous **House of Green Gables and its Victorian surrounds** (☏902-672-7874; Rte 6; adult/under 17yr/family $5.75/3/14.50; ◷9am-8pm) inspired the setting for her fictional tale. In 1937 the house became part of the national park and it's now administered as a national heritage site.

The site celebrates Lucy Maud and Anne with exhibits and audio-visual displays. The trails leading from the house through the green, gentle creek-crossed woods are worthwhile. The 'Haunted Wood' and 'Lover's Lane' have maintained their idealistic childhood ambience.

ⓘ Information

Visit Charlottetown (www.visitcharlottetown.com) Website with upcoming festival information and visitor information.

Visitors Centre (☏ 902-368-4444, 888-734-7529; www.peiplay.com; @)

ⓘ Getting There & Away

Air

Charlottetown Airport is 8km north of the city center at Brackley Point and Sherwood Rds. A taxi to/from town costs $12, plus $4 for each additional person.

Car & Motorcycle

During the summer rental cars are in short supply, so book ahead.

ⓘ Getting Around

Bicycle

Cycling is a great way to get around this quaint town. **MacQueen's Bicycles** (☏902-368-2453; www.macqueens.com; 430 Queen St; per day/week $25/125) rents a variety of quality bikes.

Car & Motorcycle

The municipal parking lots near the tourist office and Peak's Wharf charge $6 per day.

Prince Edward Island National Park

Heaving dunes and red sandstone bluffs provide startling backdrops for some of the island's finest stretches of sand; welcome to **Prince Edward Island National Park** (☎ 902-672-6350; www.pc.gc.ca/pei; day pass adult/child $7.80/3.90).

Beaches lined with marram grasses and wild rose span almost the entire length of the park's 42km coastline. In most Canadians' minds, the park is almost synonymous with the beaches. **Dalvay Beach** sits to the east, and has some short hiking trails through the woods. The landscape flattens and the sand sprawls outward at **Stanhope Beach**. Here, a boardwalk leads from the campground to the shore.

Backed by dunes, and slightly west, is the expansive and popular **Brackley Beach**. On the western side of the park, the sheer size of **Cavendish Beach** makes it the granddaddy of them all. During summer this beach sees copious numbers of visitors beneath its hefty dunes. If crowds aren't your thing, there are always the pristine sections of sand to the east. Lifeguards are on duty at Cavendish, Brackley and Stanhope Beaches in midsummer. A new bike lane now runs all the way along this coast.

Cavendish

Anyone familiar with *Anne of Green Gables* might have lofty ideas of finding Cavendish as a quaint village bedecked in flowers and country charm; guess again. While the Anne and Lucy Maud Montgomery sites are right out of the imagination-inspiring book pages, Cavendish itself is a mishmash of manufactured attractions with no particular town center. The junction of Rte 6 and Hwy 13 is the tourist center and the area's commercial hub.

Sights

AVONLEA VILLAGE   Theme Park
(☎ 902-963-3050; www.avonlea.ca; Rte 6; adult/child/family $19/15/65; ☻9am-5pm) Delve deeper into Anne fantasy at this theme park where costumed actors portray characters from the book and perform dramatic moments and scenes

One of the many beaches on Prince Edward Island (p291)

ANDREW BAIN

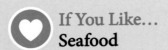

If You Like...
Seafood

If you like the Water Prince Corner Shop (p293), head to these seafood hot spots, all within an hour of Charlottetown and a half-hour of Cavendish:

1 NEW GLASGOW LOBSTER SUPPER
(📞902-964-2870; Rte 258, New Glasgow; lobster dinners $26-35; ⏱4-8:30pm) You can make a right mess with the lobster here, while also gorging on an endless supply of great chowder, mussels, salads, breads and homemade desserts.

2 ST ANN'S PARISH
(📞902-621-0635; Rte 224, St Ann's; supper $26-34; ⏱4:30-8:30pm) Crack into a crustacean in this quintessential PEI church basement, complete with chowder, steamed blue mussels and melted butter. Many islanders rank St Ann's as their favorite lobster supper.

3 MALPEQUE OYSTER BARN
(Malpeque Wharf; ½ dozen oysters $14; ⏱11am-9pm Mon-Sat, noon-9pm Sun) The hamlet of Malpeque is where the namesake oysters come from, famed for their moist, briny taste that's perfect with a beer. This ambient cafe sits atop a fisherman's barn overlooking the bay.

from Green Gable chapters. Beyond the theatrical exploits, the park offers you cow-milking demonstrations, a ride in horse-drawn wagon and other period farm activities. Check the website for the day's schedule.

SITE OF LUCY MAUD MONTGOMERY'S CAVENDISH HOME　　　Historic Site
(📞902-963-2231; Rte 6; adult/child $4/2; ⏱9am-6pm) This is considered hallowed ground to Anne fans worldwide. Raised by her grandparents, Lucy Maud lived in this house from 1876 to 1911 and it is here that she wrote *Anne of Green Gables*. The land is now owned and tended to by Lucy Maud's grandson who also runs a small on-site museum and bookshop.

 **Sleeping & Eating**

KINDRED SPIRITS COUNTRY INN & COTTAGES　　　Inn $$
(📞902-963-2434, 800-461-1755; www.kindredspirits.ca; Rte 6; d $55-285, ste $125-285; P❄🛜♨) Huge and immaculate, this complex has something for everyone from a storybook-quality inn-style B&B to deluxe suites. Rooms are every Anne fan's dream with dotty floral prints, glossy wood floors and fluffy, dreamlike beds.

PARKVIEW FARM TOURIST HOME & COTTAGES　　　B&B $$
(📞902-963-2027, 800-237-9890; www.peionline.com/al/parkview; 8214 Rte 6; r with shared bathroom incl light breakfast $60-65, 2-bedroom cottage $160-225; 🛜) This fine choice is set on a working dairy farm, 2km east of Cavendish. Ocean views, bathrooms and the prerequisite flowered wallpaper and frills abound in this comfortable and roomy place.

THE PEARL　　　Restaurant $$
(📞902-963-2111; 7792 Cavendish Rd; mains $22-32, brunch $8-12; ⏱from 4:30pm daily, 10am-2pm Sun) This shingled house surrounded by flowers just outside Cavendish is an absolutely lovely place to eat. There are plenty of unusual and seasonally changing options and locally inspired mains such as butter-poached scallops.

CARR'S OYSTERS　　　Restaurant $$
(📞902-886-3355; Stanley Bridge Wharf, Rte 6; mains $14-32; ⏱10am-7pm) Dine on oysters straight from Malpeque Bay or lobster, mussels and seafood you've never even heard of like quahogs from this place's saltwater tanks. There are also plenty of fish on offer from salmon to trout. The setting over the bay is sociable and bright and there's also on on-site market selling fresh and smoked sea critters.

ⓘ Information
Cavendish Visitor Centre (📞902-963-7830; cnr Rte 6 & Hwy 13; ⏱9am-9pm)

The Best of the Rest

The Yukon (p298)
Rugged northern region with a frontier flavor and spectacular scenery

Manitoba (p300)
Prairie heartland with polar-bear watching and a bustling main city

Newfoundland & Labrador (p302)
Rustic east coast communities teeming with stories and characters

Top: Polar bears near Churchill (p301); **Bottom:** Fall in the Yukon (p298)

PHOTOGRAPHER: (TOP):LEE FOSTER; (BOTTOM) MARK NEWMAN

The Yukon

HIGHLIGHTS

1 **Klondike National Historic Sites (p299)** Collection of fascinating Dawson City heritage buildings.

2 **MacBride Museum (p298)** Illuminating the region's gold rush past.

3 **Bombay Peggy's (p299)** A sleepover with a difference in a former brothel.

Making the most of winter, Dawson City
PHOTOGRAPHER: ANDREW BAIN

Whitehorse

The regional capital of this vast and thinly populated wilderness is usually the first port of call. The territory's two great highways, the Alaska and the Klondike, cross here; it's a hub for transport. You'll also find all manner of outfitters and services for outfitters here. Fuel up at city eateries and peruse historic sites before hitting the road or perhaps taking a gorgeous train trip (see www.wpyr .com). Check out the website www .visitwhitehorse.com.

Sights & Activities

MACBRIDE MUSEUM Museum
(www.macbridemuseum.com; cnr 1st Ave & Wood St; adult/child $8/4.50; ☉9am-6pm mid-May–Sep, noon-4pm Tue-Sat Oct–mid-May) Covering the gold rush, First Nations and more with period photos and taxidermy.

YUKON HISTORICAL & MUSEUMS ASSOCIATION Tours
(☎ 867-667-4704; 3126 3rd Ave; admission $4; ☉9am-3pm Mon-Sat Jun-Aug) Downtown walking tours; four times daily.

Sleeping & Eating

HIGH COUNTRY INN Hotel $$
(☎ 867-667-4471; www.highcountryinn.ca; 4051 4th Ave; r $90-220; ❋@☎) Towering four stories over Whitehorse, some of the 84 large rooms have whirlpool baths.

KLONDIKE RIB & SALMON BAKE Canadian $$
(2116 2nd Ave; mains $12-25; ☉4-9pm) It looks touristy and is touristy but the food is excellent. Consider the fresh halibut.

ℹ Getting There & Away

Whitehorse airport (www.gov.yk.ca/yxy/) is five minutes drive west of downtown.

Klondike Highway

Allow up to seven hours for the Whitehorse to Dawson City drive via this sparse, rugged-landscape route, unmatched across Canada. Pit stops include **Carmacks**, a historic gold-rush

Northern Lights in NWT

Head to **Yellowknife** in the Northwest Territories for one of Canada's most memorable sights. Commonly called the Northern Lights, the mysterious aurora borealis stripes the night sky with a kaleidoscope of breathtaking colors you'll likely remember for the rest of your life. Best viewing is from December to March and local operators include **Aurora Village** (☎ 867-669-0006; www .auroravillage.com: 5203 54th St, Yellowknife). Its viewing vehicles have heated seats ($120) but it also offers dog-sledding ($90) and snowshoeing ($95) alternatives.

Yellowknife can be reached by air from Edmonton and Whitehorse.

village now home to the **Tage Cho Hudan Interpretive Centre** (☎ 867-863-5830; admission by donation; ⊙9am-4pm May-Sep) covering aboriginal life past and present. The village is also popular as a kayaking destination for trips from Whitehorse.

Next up is **Stewart Crossing**. If you've brought your canoe, it's a popular spot to hit the river. From here, it's 181km to Dawson City.

Dawson City

It's easy to fall for the historic buildings, the beauty and rich cultural life of delightful Dawson, which was the center of the Klondike Gold Rush. Immerse yourself in its funky vibe for a day or three. For information see www.dawsoncity.ca.

Sights & Activities

KLONDIKE NATIONAL HISTORIC SITES

Historic Park

Relive the gold rush at the numerous preserved sites administered by **Parks Canada** (www.pc.gc.ca/dawson), including **Robert Service Cabin** and **SS Keno**. It also runs city **walking tours** (adult $7; ⊙daily) that illuminate local history.

JACK LONDON INTERPRETIVE CENTRE

Museum

(Firth St; admission $5; ⊙11am-6pm) In 1898 Jack London lived in the Yukon, the setting for his most popular stories, including *Call of the Wild* and *White Fang*. At the writer's cabin there are daily interpretive talks.

Sleeping & Eating

BOMBAY PEGGY'S Inn $

(☎ 867-993-6969; www.bombaypeggys.com; cnr 2nd Ave & Princess St; r $90-200; ⊙Mar-Dec; ✲ ⊚) A renovated brothel, Peggy's allure is its period furnishings and spunky attitude.

KLONDIKE KATE'S Fusion $$

(☎ 867-993-6527; cnr King St & 3rd Ave; mains $8-25; ⊙8am-9pm) Fine sandwiches, fresh Yukon fish and great breakfasts.

❶ Getting There & Away

Dawson City airport is 19km east of town off the Klondike Hwy. There are flights to Whitehorse; otherwise public transportation between the two towns is unreliable.

Note that there are no car rentals available in Dawson City.

Manitoba

HIGHLIGHTS

1 **Winnipeg Art Gallery (p300)**
Breathtaking Inuit art collection.

2 **Fort Prince of Wales (p301)**
Hulking old stone fort from the 1700s.

3 **Lazy Bear Lodge (p301)** Evocative log-built sleepover with polar-bear tour excursions.

On the trail of polar bears, Churchill
PHOTOGRAPHER: LEE FOSTER

Winnipeg

Rising above the prairies, this historic metropolis surprises with its rich cultural scene and many attractions. Winnipeg's main sights are mostly concentrated around the walkable downtown area. For information see www.destination winnipeg.ca.

Sights & Activities

WINNIPEG ART GALLERY   Art Gallery
(www.wag.ca; 300 Memorial Blvd; adult/child $8/4; ⊙11am-5pm Tue, Wed & Fri-Sun, to 9pm Thu) A ship-shaped gallery showcasing contemporary Manitoban and Canadian artists, including the world's largest Inuit collection.

FORKS NATIONAL HISTORIC SITE
                              Historic Park
(www.parkscanada.ca/forks) A beautiful riverside setting for interpretive exhibits outlining the area's history. Footpaths line the riverbank.

**HISTORIC EXCHANGE DISTRICT
WALKING TOURS**   Tours
(☎ 204-942-6716; www.exchangedistrict.org; adult/child $7/free; ⊙call for times) Themed and history tours departing from Old Market Sq.

Sleeping & Eating

RIVER GATE INN   B&B **$$**
(☎ 204-474-2761; www.rivergateinn.com; 186 West Gate, r $80-140; P✿🛜🌀) A 1919 mansion sleepover offering sumptuous accommodation plus free snacks.

NORWOOD HOTEL   Hotel **$$**
(☎ 204-233-4475, 888-888-1878; www .norwood-hotel.com; 112 Marion St; r $80-120; P✿@🛜) A friendly, five-story modern hotel with a newish, soothing decor.

CHEZ SOPHIE   French, Italian **$$**
(www.chezsophie.net; 248 Av de la Cathédrale; meals $9-15; ⊙11am-9pm Tue-Sat) A chatty spot with a well-priced French menu of salads, crepes and quiche. Pizzas and pasta add an Italian flair.

Getting There & Away

Winnipeg International Airport (www.waa.ca) is 10km west of downtown.

VIA Rail (www.viarail.ca) runs trains west to Edmonton, Jasper and Vancouver, north to Churchill, and east to Toronto.

Churchill

Luring visitors to frigid Hudson Bay with its polar bears and beluga whales, there's also a huge historic site here. The town has a hearty seductive spirit that makes the rest of the world seem – thankfully – even further away than it really is. For information, check out: www.churchill.ca.

Sights & Tours

It took 40 years to build and its cannons have never fired, but the 18th-century star-shaped **Fort Prince of Wales** (204-675-8863; www.parkscanada.ca; Jul & Aug) still stands prominently on the banks of the Churchill River.

Parks Canada also administers **Sloop's Cove**, once a winter harbor for old European ships, and **Cape Merry** where the crumbling walls overlook a spectacular waterfront – look for beluga whales offshore.

If you're more interested in polar bears – September to early November is the season – consider these operators:

Great White Bear Tours (204-675-2781; www.greatwhitebeartours.com; 266 Kelsey Blvd)

Lazy Bear Lodge (204-675-2869; www.lazybearlodge.com)

Sleeping & Eating

LAZY BEAR LODGE Inn $$
(204-675-2869, 866-687-2327; www.lazybearlodge.com; 313 Kelsey Blvd; r from $110, bear season from $200; Jun-Nov;) This log lodge offers tours and a good eatery.

GYPSY'S BAKERY Canadian $$
(Kelsey Blvd; mains $7-25; 7am-9pm) Suffused with luscious baked goods and a long cafeteria-style menu.

Getting There & Away

Access is by plane or train only. Churchill Airport is 11km east of town. **VIA Rail** (www.viarail.com) trains trundle in from Winnipeg.

THE BEST OF THE REST MANITOBA

Newfoundland & Labrador

HIGHLIGHTS

1. **Signal Hill National Historic Site (p302)** Landmark waterfront site with amazing views.

2. **Duke of Duckworth (p303)** Friendly party pub in the heart of St Johns.

3. **Labrador Straits (p303)** Pretty coastal drive through colorful small communities.

St John's clings to the hillside
PHOTOGRAPHER: STEPHEN SAKS

St John's

Huddled on the steep harbor slopes, St John's jelly-bean-colored row houses and welcoming vibe make it one of Canada's friendliest cities. It's the home of many artists and musicians. At night sample the eateries, funky shops and music-filled pubs. Apart from the town the area is mostly wee fishing villages freckling the crenulated coastline. Check out www.stjohns.ca.

Sights & Activities

Hike up to **Signal Hill National Historic Site** (www.pc.gc.ca/signalhill; Signal Hill Rd; grounds admission free; ☺grounds 24hr) for the glorious views and check out the **interpretive center** (adult/child $3.90/1.90; ☺10am-6pm, reduced mid-Oct–mid-May) for interactive history displays.

Peruse the remnants of the 18th-century British battery at **Queen's Battery & Barracks** further up the hill. The tiny castle at the summit is **Cabot Tower** (admission free; ☺9am-9pm Jun–early Sep, to 5pm rest of yr, closed mid-Jan–Mar). An awesome way to return to downtown is along the **North Head Trail** (1.7km), which connects Cabot Tower with the harborfront Battery neighborhood. Because much of the trail runs along the bluff's sheer edge, this walk isn't something to attempt in icy, foggy or dark conditions.

If you fancy spotting whales or icebergs, tour with **Iceberg Quest** (www.icebergquest.com; Pier 7; 2hr tour adult/child $55/25).

Sleeping & Eating

BALMORAL HOUSE   B&B $$
(☎709-754-5721; www.balmoralhouse.com; 38 Queen's Rd; d $99-179; ☺❄@) An antiquey B&B with self-serve breakfast.

BACALAO   Seafood $$$
(www.bacalaocuisine.ca; 65 Lemarchant Rd; mains $28-35; ☺noon-2:30pm Tue-Fri, from 11am Sat & Sun, 6-10pm Tue-Sun) Go for salt cod du jour or caribou in partridgeberry sauce.

DUKE OF DUCKWORTH   Pub
(www.thedukenl.ca; McMurdo's Lane, 325 Duckworth St; 🔊) English-style pub where the locals know how to have a good time.

. . . .

❶ Getting There & Around

St John's Airport (www.stjohnsairport.com) is 6km north of the city. The Metrobus (www.metrobus.com) system covers most of the city (fare $2.25).

Labrador Straits

Covering Labrador's southern coast, your first stop here will actually be in Québec province: the ferry terminal and airport are in Blanc Sablon. Sail the 28km across the Strait of Belle Isle and behold a windswept landscape of black rocks. Clouds rip across aqua-and-gray skies, and the water that slaps the shore is so cold it's purplish.

From Blanc Sablon, take the pretty coastal drive northeast on Rte 510 to the town of **L'Anse au Clair**. Recharge your batteries with a B&B stay at **Beachside Hospitality Home** (☎ 709-931-2338; normanletto@yahoo.ca; 9 Lodge Rd; r with shared bathroom $48-58).

Continuing northeast on Rte 510, pass Forteau and come to **L'Anse Amour**, which includes **L'Anse Amour Burial Mound** (L'Anse Amour Rd), a stone pile placed by the Maritime Archaic Aboriginals: it's North America's oldest burial monument. Further on is **Point Amour Lighthouse Provincial Historic Site** (www.seethesites.ca; L'Anse Amour Rd; admission $3; ⏱10am-5:30pm mid-May–late Sep).

Continue past Pinware and you'll arrive at **Red Bay**, 80km from your starting point. Visit **Red Bay National Historic Site** (www.pc.gc.ca/redbay; Rte 510; adult/child/family $7.80/3.90/19.60; ⏱9am-6pm early Jun–mid-Oct), which chronicles the seabed discovery of three 16th-century galleons.

Finally, check into **Basinview B&B** (☎ 709-920-2022; blancheearle@hotmail.com; 145 Main St; r $50-80), a cozy home on the waterfront in Red Bay.

Canada
In Focus

People take to the ice (p232) with the arrival of winter, Montréal
PHOTOGRAPHER: BRIAN CRUICKSHANK

Canada Today

The start of fall beside Georgian Bay (p206)

66

extracting and developing [resources] comes with an ecological price

99

belief systems
(% of population)

43 Roman Catholic

28 Other

23 Protestant

4 Christian

2 Muslim

if Canada were 100 people

28 would be of British Isles origin
23 would be of French origin
15 would be of European origin
34 would be of Other origin

population per sq km

↑ ≈ 4 people

Canada · USA · France

Loonie Boons

The Canadian economy kicked butt from 1993 through 2007. That's the year the loonie reached parity with the US dollar for the first time in three decades, with oil and natural gas as the driving force. But like many countries around the world, the global economic crisis brought things to a halt. The economy dropped into a recession, and Ottawa posted its first fiscal deficit in 2009 after 12 years of surplus.

And then: Canadian banks bounced back, thanks to their tradition of conservative lending. Even with a pesky deficit, Canada is doing a-OK compared to its global brethren. The International Monetary Fund predicts it'll be the only one of the seven major industrialized democracies to return to surplus by 2015.

The High Price of Oil

Voltaire may have written off Canada as 'a few acres of snow' back in the mid-18th century, but those 'few acres' have yielded vast

Table Talk

The nation's much-cherished but ailing universal healthcare system sparks serious debate. Although no one will admit it, a two-tiered system is in place, and those with deep pockets can access additional, often quicker care in private facilities. Newfoundland premier and millionaire Danny Williams, for instance, went to Florida in 2010 for heart surgery that was available in Canada, which sent newspaper headlines screaming.

Still, a free, portable healthcare system that's available to everyone is quite a feat. To many citizens, it's at the very root of what makes Canada great. So are progressive views on same-sex marriage, immigration and marijuana use.

DON JOHNSTON/PHOTOLIBRARY

amounts of oil, timber and other natural resources, that in turn have propelled Canada to a very enviable standard of living.

The only issue: extracting and developing the resources comes with an ecological price, and Canadians debate what to do about it. Oil, in particular, is a conundrum. Northern Alberta's Athabasca Tar Sands are the world's second-biggest oil reserves, and they've done a heckuva job boosting the economy. They also produce 5% of Canada's greenhouse gas emissions, according to Environment Canada. Environmentalists say the sands are massive polluters. The pro-industry camp says improvements are being made and, when compared to other oil producers such as Saudi Arabia and Venezuela, the oil sands measure up, especially when human-rights issues and decreased transportation distances are factored in (most of Canada's oil goes to the USA).

Politics

In 2006 the Conservative Party took over from the Liberals for the first time in 12 years. Stephen Harper became the new prime minister, but he led Canada's smallest minority government since Confederation. In 2008 he called for early elections hoping to boost the Conservatives' grip. They did, but only 22% of Canadians went to the polls, the lowest voter turnout in history.

Amid controversy, Harper suspended Parliament twice in 2009. The first time, he did it to avoid a no-confidence vote by opposition parties. The second time he did it to deal with the economy, he said. Opponents say he did it to muzzle allegations of Afghan detainee torture. (Reports had surfaced that the Canadian government and troops turned a blind eye to torture going on at the hand of Afghan troops.) That the shutdown occurred right before the Winter Olympics in Vancouver added fuel to the fire.

History

Replica of a Viking boathouse, Newfoundland

CINDY HOPKINS/

The human story of Canada begins around 15,000 years ago when Aboriginal locals began carving thriving communities from the abundant wilderness. Everything changed, though, when the Europeans rolled in from the late 15th-century onwards, staking claims that triggered rumbling conflicts and eventually shaped a vast new nation. Much of this colorful heritage is accessible to visitors, with 956 national historic sites covering everything from forts to battlefields to famous homes.

Early Locals & Viking Visitors

The first Canadians most likely came from Asia, chasing down elk and bison across the one-time land link between Siberia and Alaska and eventually settling throughout the Americas. The north proved particularly popular for its abundance of tasty fish and seal dinners and these early Aboriginal

Circa 15,000 BC

Humans arrive via a lan bridge from Siberia, following herds of caribou and bison.

communities eventually spread to four main regions in what would become Canada: the Pacific, the Plains, southern Ontario/St Lawrence River and the northeast woodlands.

About 2500 BC, a second major wave of migration from Siberia brought the ancestors of the Inuit to Canada. These early Inuit were members of the Dorset Culture, named after Cape Dorset on Baffin Island, where its remains were first unearthed. Around AD 1000, a separate Inuit cultural group – the whale-hunting Thule of northern Alaska – began making its way east through the Canadian Arctic. As these people spread, they overtook the Dorset Culture. The Thule are the direct ancestors of Canada's modern-day Inuit.

These original communities lived and thrived for thousands of years before anyone else turned up and stayed. Around AD 1000, Viking explorer Leif Eriksson and his hairy posse poked ashore on the east coast, sticking around long enough to establish winter settlements and a few hardy outposts. Life was tough for these interlopers and the hostile reception from the locals eventually sent them back where they came from. Without a glowing recommendation from these first European visitors, it was several centuries before anyone else bothered to make the epic journey across the Atlantic.

Return of the Europeans

After Christopher Columbus made heading west from Europe across the ocean fashionable again with his 1492 expedition in search of Asia, avaricious European monarchs began queuing up to sponsor expeditions. In 1497 Giovanni Caboto – better known as John Cabot – sailed under a British flag as far west as Newfoundland and Cape Breton. His great discovery turned out to be a surfeit of cod stocks, triggering a hungry rush of boats from Europe, including Spanish whaling vessels.

King François I of France looked over the fence at his neighbors, stroked his beard, and ordered Jacques Cartier to appear before him. By this time, the hunt was on not only for the fabled Northwest Passage route but also for gold, given the shiny discoveries made by Spanish conquistadors among the Aztec and Inca civilizations.

But upon arrival in Labrador, Cartier found only 'stones and horrible rugged rocks.' He kept exploring, though, and soon went ashore on Québec's Gaspé Peninsula to claim the land for France. The local Iroquois thought he was a good neighbor at first, until he kidnapped two of the chief's sons and took them to Europe. Rather surprisingly, Cartier returned them a year later when sailing up the St Lawrence River.

AD 1000
Viking Leif Eriksson lands his crew on the east coast, setting up winter encampments.

1497
Sailing from Britain, John Cabot lands in Newfoundland, sparking a hungry rush for local cod.

1534
Jacques Cartier sails into what is now Québec, claiming the land for France.

The Best Historic Sites

Fur: the New Gold

While these early explorers were always looking for gold to please their royal sponsors back home, it eventually become clear that the riches of the new land were not quite so sparkly. With fur the latest fashion of the French court – almost extinct in the Old World, beaver-trimmed chapeaux were a highly sought after accessory there – the New World's lustrous and abundant pelts were suddenly in huge demand across Europe.

In 1588 the French crown granted the first trading monopoly in Canada, only to have other merchants promptly challenge the claim. And so the race for control of the fur trade was officially on. The economic value of this enterprise and, by extension, its role in shaping Canadian history, cannot be underestimated. It was the main reason behind the country's European settlement, at the root of the struggle for dominance between the French and the British, and the source of strife and division between various Aboriginal groups.

To support their claims, French pioneers established a tentative foothold on Île Ste-Croix (a tiny islet in the river on the present US border with Maine) in 1604. They soon moved to Port Royal (today's Annapolis Royal) in Nova Scotia. Exposed and difficult to defend, neither site was ideal for controlling the inland fur trade. As the would-be colonists moved up the St Lawrence River, they came upon a spot their leader, Samuel de Champlain, considered prime real estate – where today's Québec City now stands. It was 1608 and 'New France' had landed.

Brits Take Over

While the French paraded around in their exclusive Canadian fur headgear for decades, the jealous – and presumably hatless – Brits eventually mounted a challenge in 1670 when King Charles II formed the Hudson's Bay Company. He granted it a trade monopoly over a vast northern area that would today encompass about 40% of Canada.

As both countries reaffirmed and expanded their claims, skirmishes broke out between groups of colonizers, mirroring the wars that were engulfing Europe in the first half of the 18th century. Things came to a head with the Treaty of Utrecht,

1608
Samuel de Champlain establishes the first permanent settlement of 'New France.'

1670
King Charles II creates Hudson's Bay Company to shore up fur trade for the Brits.

RENAULT PHILIPPE

which forced the French to recognize British claims in the region.

But the enmity and military skirmishes between the two continued for several decades, culminating in a 1759 battle on Québec's Plains of Abrahams that is remembered today as one of Canada's most important military events. Besieging the city in a surprise and bloody attack that left both commanding generals dead, the Brits eventually won the day and the French were forced to hand over control of Canada in the resulting 1763 Treaty of Paris.

Managing their newly acquired territory was a tricky challenge for the Brits, who had to contend with aboriginal uprisings as well as resentment from French Canadians. Next, the restless American colonies started rumbling from the south. To keep the French Canadians on side, the Québec Act of 1774 confirmed the French Canadians' right to their religion, allowed them to assume political office and restored the use of French civil law. It worked: during the American Revolution (1775–83), most French Canadians refused to take up arms in support of the American cause.

After the revolution, the English-speaking population exploded when some 50,000 settlers from the newly independent USA migrated north. Called United Empire Loyalists due to their presumed allegiance to Britain, the majority ended up living in Nova Scotia and New Brunswick, while a smaller group settled along the northern shore of Lake Ontario and in the Ottawa River Valley (forming the nucleus of what became Ontario). About 8000 settlers moved to Québec, creating the first sizeable Anglophone community in the French-speaking bastion.

What's in a Name?

Explorer Jacques Cartier is said to have picked up the name 'Kanata' from two Huron-Iroquois youths. It means 'settlement' in the Huron-Iroquois language and the lads were showing him the way to the village of Stadacona – later known as Québec City – rather than referring to an entire country. But the name stuck and Cartier used it in his journals to define the large 'new' region he had hit upon. As the known area grew, the name stayed the same: maps from 1547 designated everything north of the St Lawrence River as 'Canada.'

Canada Splits...then Unites

Accommodating the interests of Loyalist settlers, the British government passed the Constitutional Act of 1791, which divided the colony into Upper Canada (today's southern Ontario) and Lower Canada (now southern Québec). Lower Canada retained French civil laws, but both provinces were governed by the British criminal code.

1759
Famous Plains of Abraham battle for Québec City. France loses to Britain.
Plains of Abraham tower (left)

1763
Treaty of Paris boots France out of Canada, cementing British rule over the region.

1775
American Revolution rebels try enticing Québec to join the revolt against the British; they refuse.

The Best Historic Neighborhoods

These divisions didn't help matters, with rising tensions and arguments caused by the clear dominance of the British over the French in administrative matters across the two regions. Two French rebellions kicked off in the 1830s and although each was swiftly quelled, it was an indication that the ill-conceived division was unsustainable. The Brits then tried a different approach.

The Union Act of 1840 sought to crush French nationalism by legislating that British laws, language and institutions were superior across both regions, now joined together as the Province of Canada. If anything, the union's clear underlying objective of destroying French identity made Francophones cling together even more tenaciously – the wounds can still be seen in Canada today.

With the rise of the USA after the American Civil War (1861–65), fragile Canada, whose border with the USA was established on the 49th parallel in 1818, sought to further solidify its status and prevent annexation. In 1864 Charlottetown, Prince Edward Island (PEI), became the birthing room for modern Canada when the 'Fathers of Confederation' – a group of representatives from Nova Scotia, New Brunswick, PEI, Ontario and Québec – got together and hammered out the framework for a new nation. The British North America Act was passed in 1867, creating a modern, self-governing nation originally known as the Dominion of Canada. The day the act became official, July 1, is now celebrated across the country as Canada's national holiday.

Creating Confederation

Under Canada's first prime minister, John A Macdonald, land and colonies were slowly added to the confederation. The government acquired a vast northern swathe, now called the Northwest Territories (NWT), in 1869 for the paltry sum of £300,000 – about $11.5 million in today's money – from the Hudson's Bay Company. The land was sparsely populated, mostly by Plains First Nations and several thousand Métis (may-*tee*), a racial blend of Cree, Ojibwe or Saulteaux and French-Canadian or Scottish fur traders, who spoke French as their main language. Their biggest settlement was the Red River Colony around Fort Garry (today's Winnipeg).

The Canadian government immediately clashed with the Métis people over land-use rights, causing the latter to form a provisional government led by the

1793

Explorer Alexander Mackenzie makes the first transcontinental journey across the land.

1858

Prospectors discover gold along BC's Fraser River, spurring thousands of get-rich-quick dreamers to head north.

1864

The Fathers of Confederation meet in Charlottetown, molding a new country called Canada.

charismatic Louis Riel. He sent the Ottawa-appointed governor packing and, in November 1869, seized control of Upper Fort Garry, thereby forcing Ottawa to the negotiating table. However, with his delegation already en route, Riel impulsively and for no good reason executed a Canadian prisoner he was holding at the fort.

Although the murder caused widespread uproar in Canada, the government was so keen to bring the west into the fold it agreed to most of Riel's demands, including special language and religious protections for the Métis. As a result, the then-pint-sized province of Manitoba was carved out of the NWT and entered the dominion in July 1870. Macdonald sent troops after Riel but he narrowly managed to escape to the USA. He was formally exiled for five years in 1875.

Rail Link to the West

Despite the progress toward confederation, the West Coast remained a distant and forbidding frontier. British Columbia (BC), created in 1866 by merging the colonies of New Caledonia and Vancouver Island, finally joined in 1871 in exchange for the Canadian government assuming all its debt and promising to link it with the east within 10 years via a vast transcontinental railroad.

Historic trestle bridge, now part of the Trans Canada Trail, Vancouver Island
PHOTOGRAPHER: JEFFREY BOSDET

1885
In Craigellachie, BC, workers drive in the spike that completes the Canadian Pacific Railway.

1896
Klondike Gold Rush kicks off in the Yukon; 40,000 hopefuls roll into Dawson City.

1913
Immigration crests, with more than 400,000 embracing the maple leaf, mostly Americans and Eastern Europeans.

The Maple Leaf Symbol

It's on the penny, on Air Canada planes, on Toronto hockey jerseys – you can't escape the maple leaf, considered a national symbol for almost two centuries. In 1836 *Le Canadien*, a newspaper published in Lower Canada, called it a suitable emblem for the nation. Ontario and Québec both were using it on their coat of arms by 1868. The Canadian Armed Forces used it during the world wars. Finally, after much wrangling over the design (one leaf? three leaves? 13 points?), the current 11-point leaf was granted national symbol status and went on the flag in 1965.

The Canadian Pacific Railway's construction is one of the most impressive and decisive chapters in Canada's history. Though essential in uniting the nation, it was a costly proposition, made even more challenging by the rough and rugged terrain the tracks had to traverse. To entice investors, the government offered major benefits, including massive land grants in western Canada. Workers drove the final spike into the track at Craigellachie, BC, on November 7, 1885.

Canada rang in the 20th century on a high note. Industrialization was in full swing, prospectors had discovered gold in the Yukon, and Canadian resources – from wheat to lumber – were increasingly in demand. In addition, the new railroad opened the floodgates to immigration. Between 1885 and 1914 about 4.5 million people arrived in Canada. This included large groups of Americans and Eastern Europeans, especially Ukrainians, who went to work cultivating the prairies.

By the time the guns of WWI fell silent in 1918, most Canadians were fed up with sending their sons and husbands to fight in distant wars for Britain. Under the government of William Lyon Mackenzie King, Canada made it clear that Britain could no longer automatically draw upon the Canadian military and even sent its own ambassador to Washington. This forcefulness led to the Statute of Westminster, passed by the British Parliament in 1931. It formalized the independence of Canada and other Commonwealth nations, although Britain retained the right to pass amendments to those countries' constitutions – a right only removed with the 1982 Canada Act. The British monarch remains Canada's head of state, although this is predominantly a ceremonial role and does not diminish the country's sovereignty.

Twentieth-Century Canada

The period after WWII brought another wave of economic expansion and immigration, especially from Europe. And, in 1949, Newfoundland finally elected to join Canada after a bruising campaign by local politician Joey Smallwood.

1933
Three out of 10 people are unemployed, as Canada struggles through the Great Depression.

1961
Saskatchewan introduces the first universal healthcare plan, an idea that soon spreads across Canada.

ROSS BA

The only province truly left behind during the 1950s boom years was Québec. For a quarter century, it remained in the grip of ultraconservative Maurice Duplessis and his Union Nationale party, with support from the Catholic Church and various business interests. Only after Duplessis' death did the province finally start getting up to speed during the 'Quiet Revolution' of the 1960s. Advances included expanding the public sector, investing in public education and nationalizing the provincial hydroelectric companies. Still, progress wasn't swift enough for radical nationalists who claimed independence was the only way to ensure Francophone rights. Québec has spent the ensuing years flirting with separatism, culminating in a cliffhanger 1994 referendum when a majority of less than 1% voted that the province should remain a part of Canada.

In 1960 Canada's Aboriginal peoples were finally granted Canadian citizenship. And, in 1985, Canada became the first country in the world to pass a national multicultural act and establish a federal department of multiculturalism. Today 40% of Canadians claim their origins are in places other than Britain or France.

For information on the events shaping present-day Canada, see p306.

The Best
History
Museums

1 Maritime Museum of the Atlantic, Halifax (p275)

2 Canadian War Museum, Ottawa (p199)

3 Musée d'Archéologie et d'Histoire Pointe-à-Callière, Montréal (p228)

4 Royal BC Museum, Victoria (p88)

5 Glenbow Museum, Calgary (p150)

1963
Trans-Canada Hwy completed, spanning 7821km from St John's, Newfoundland, to Victoria, BC. Trans-Canada Hwy (left)

1982
Queen Elizabeth II signs the Canada Act, giving Canada complete sovereignty.

1998
Government apologizes to Aboriginal peoples for 'attitudes of racial and cultural superiority...'

Family Travel

Lodge in the wilderness, Sunshine Coast (p84)

There are so many experiences in Canada guaranteed to leave your kids wide-eyed with wonder: the challenge is choosing what to focus on. Consider their interests when you decide between the wow factor of watching a whale slide by, zip-lining along a mountain canyon, catching an NHL hockey game or beachcombing among shiny purple starfish. And you can expect a warm welcome: Canada is one of the world's most kid-friendly countries.

When to Go

Canada is a year-round destination but if you're planning to bring your children to highlights such as Montréal, Québec or Toronto in winter make sure they have plenty of thick clothing: temperatures can dip to -20°C in these cities and if you're not prepared, your kids will be miserable.

Beyond that, Canada's weather welcomes children of all ages. The school vacation summer season is popular with families, since there's always plenty of outdoor action to be had and there are hundreds of festivals and community events across the country, many with a dedicated family focus – favorites include the Vancouver International Children's Festival (www.childrens festival.ca; May or Jun). It offers storytelling, performances and activities in the tents at Vanier Park in mid-May.

Of course, summer season is the peak for most hotel accommodation prices, so consider spring or fall: if you can wrest them from the clutches of school you can save a packet.

The second most popular time for family travel is winter – especially December to February – when parents bring older children and teenagers to ski resorts across the country. Your usually sullen teens might even smile and thank you profusely if you give them the best snowboarding experience of their lives. And if you come in time for Christmas, you'll also enjoy some seasonal treats – such as Santa Claus parades and festive light displays – that will make your visit unforgettable.

For more tips and tricks on hitting Canada with your kids, see Lonely Planet's *Travel with Children*.

Where to Go

It's a big place and you're spoilt for choice, so if you really want to show your kids a good time put some thought into which regions they (and you) might enjoy most. Hit Vancouver for beaches and snow sports on the same day; look out for elk, moose or wolves in the Rocky Mountains; dive into the rich history and cobbled streets of old Québec; or take a splashtastic boat tour at spectacular Niagara Falls.

Most kids will enjoy a visit to a museum or two on their trip and many in Canada are dedicated to children: there are space and science centers (as well as aquariums) across the country. Even 'stuffy' galleries or history museums have made great strides in recent years to cater to children: check ahead on their websites for kid-friendly events and programming.

Many of these attractions offer free entry to under-fives as well as reduced rates for older children and school students. Also, make sure you ask about family tickets, a special group rate that's offered at many attractions in Canada.

For information on travel with children in Canada's major cities, see p73 (Vancouver), p182 (Toronto), p202 (Ottawa) and p237 (Montréal).

What to Do

If your kids are an active bunch, consider hiring bikes for them on their visit: you'll find many city parks have great trails – Vancouver's Stanley Park may be the best. Mountain biking teens may be more into the challenges of some parts of the Trans Canada Trail (TCT) or downhill bike parks such as the summer facility in Whistler. Horseback riding is a very Canadian alternative – especially if you combine it with a visit to cowboy country around the Rocky Mountains region.

If a quick thrill is more their style, consider a white-water rafting excursion or you could try a slightly more sedate kayaking tour. Stay on the water for a marine

The Best
Children's Attractions

1 Vancouver Aquarium, Vancouver (p65)

2 Canadian Museum of Nature, Ottawa (p198)

3 Centre des Sciences de Montréal (p228)

4 Choco-Musée Érico, Québec City (p248)

5 Avonlea Village, Cavendish, Prince Edward Island (p295)

6 Royal Ontario Museum, Toronto (p173)

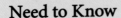

Need to Know

- **Changing facilities** Found in most stores, malls and cinemas
- **Cots** Available at most mid- to high-end accommodation
- **Health** See the general health section (p346)
- **Highchairs** Generally available, especially in midrange restaurants
- **Kids' menus** Offered at many midrange restaurants
- **Nappies (diapers)** Widely available
- **Strollers** Cities and towns are generally stroller friendly
- **Transport** Fully accessible to children; under-fives usually travel free

wildlife-viewing trip – the east or west coasts are ideal for whale-watching – or consider paying for them to learn surfing in Tofino on Vancouver Island.

They can also hit the slopes with skiing or snowboarding lessons at one of Canada's excellent, family-friendly winter resorts. And if that's a little too challenging for some, they'll also love tramping through the snow between the icicle-covered 'Christmas trees' on a seasonal snowshoeing expedition.

Sleeping & Eating

Hotels and motels typically have rooms with two double beds. Most can also bring in rollaways or cots, usually for a small charge. Larger hotels may offer adjoining rooms with lockable doors separating them, so you can keep an eye on the kids and also gain some privacy.

Some properties offer 'kids stay free' promotions and some – usually resorts or larger hotels – have special kids clubs with scheduled activities. B&Bs are often pickier, so make sure you clarify who you're bringing with you when you book: some B&Bs are adult-only, while others will roll out the red carpet for your precious offspring.

If you're concerned about the costs of eating out with a large group at every meal (or just aware of that ultrapicky young eater you have traveling with you), consider a hotel room with a kitchen or even a self-catering apartment: either will enable you to keep dining costs down and please everyone's palate at the same time. Tourism bureaus across the country will be able to help you find this type of accommodation easily, especially in larger cities.

Which brings us to eating. Children are welcome at the vast majority of restaurants across Canada, the exceptions being some high-end eateries where a level of adult sophistication will likely have other diners frowning into their soup if the room is suddenly hit with a tantrum. Many restaurants – especially in the midrange – have dedicated children's menus. If they don't, ask for a half-order and you'll find that most eateries will happily oblige.

What to Pack

Aside from the aforementioned winter clothing, layers are the key to successfully packing for your kids here: it can get spontaneously cool in Canada during the summer months. And relentlessly rainy days (we're talking about you British Columbia) can make everyone miserable, so make sure they have some good rain gear if traveling outside the peak summer period. Don't worry too much about packing, though: Canada is well-stocked with shops and department stores and children's clothing is generally well-priced (unless you have a Gucci-loving baby).

Sunscreen, of course, is a must and bug spray is a good idea if you're going to be in the great outdoors for any length of time. And if you're planning any long drives – and Canada is the home of the long drive – bring every activity you can think of to keep the kids occupied, unless you want your energetic backseat drivers to drive you nuts.

Culture

Montréal sways to the rhythm of fine music (p238)

GUYLAIN DO

Looking specifically at artistic output, overseas visitors might be forgiven for thinking that culture in Canada simply means Celine Dion, William Shatner, Margaret Atwood and a few totem poles. But while Canadians rarely shout about it, the country's creative and artistic scenes are rich and vibrant across the nation, offering a deep well of creativity for visiting culture vultures to sink their beaks into.

Literature

Canada's earliest inhabitants built their cultures on storytelling, passing important tales from generation to generation. Later authors created a written body of Canadian literature – the phrase 'Canlit' is still used here – that defined the struggles of creating a new life in a vast, sometimes barren wilderness. These often deeply affecting novels are the ideal accompaniment for an epic train ride across the prairies. Recommended authors for the long haul include Margaret Laurence and Robertson Davies, while many will also enjoy Lucy Maud Montgomery's *Anne of Green Gables*.

But if you want to hit an adult blockbuster during your travels, there are two main authors to focus on. If you read Mordecai Richler's *The*

Apprenticeship of Duddy Kravitz while hanging around in Montréal's Plateau district, you'll almost feel the story on the streets around you (his later epic, *Barney's Version*, was recently made into a movie). And a trip to Canada that doesn't include a Margaret Atwood novel is like visiting a bar without having a drink. Consider top titles such as *Oryx and Crake*, *The Blind Assassin* or *The Handmaid's Tale* or dive into *Surfacing*, an enigmatic story where the Canadian wilderness is a character in itself.

It's unlikely you'll have much time to read while on the road, so you might want to fill your suitcase with a few choice volumes to take home. Canadian authors to look out for in the local bookstore include, Carol Shields, Alice Munro, Douglas Coupland, William Gibson and Michael Ondaatje. And if you time your visit well, you can join the local bookworms at literary events including the Vancouver Readers & Writers Festival (www.writersfest.bc.ca), Toronto's International Festival of Authors (www.readings.org) and the annual five-city Word on the Street (www.thewordonthestreet.ca).

Visual Arts

Canada's artistic bent was founded thousands of years ago when early Aboriginal inhabitants began adorning their homes with visual representations of the natural world. Later, European painters continued to use nature as their muse, often adding images of the mysterious Aboriginal locals to their canvases.

But the most famous artistic school in Canadian cultural history is the Group of Seven, a clutch of painters who banded loosely together in the early 1920s, creating bold stylized representations of the striking Canadian landscape that still seem fresh and vibrant today. Members of the group – which included famed luminaries such as Tom Thomson, Lawren Harris and Arthur Lismer, and which later expanded beyond the original seven – would often disappear into the wilderness for months on end, which is where Thomson met his demise, drowning in a lake in 1917, just as he was at the height of his creative powers.

While Group of Seven paintings still attract huge prices at auction and exhibitions of their work typically lure large crowds, Canada also has an energetic contemporary art scene. Internationally renowned latter-day stars – look out for their works at galleries across the country – include photoconceptualist Jeff Wall, painter and sculptor Betty Goodwin and painter and avant-garde filmmaker Michael Snow. And don't forget to check out the celebrated public art scenes on the streets of Vancouver, Toronto and Montréal.

Music

Ask visitors to name a few Canadian musicians and they'll stutter to a halt after Celine Dion, Bryan Adams and perhaps Leonard Cohen. But ask the locals to do the same and they'll hit you with a roster of performers you've probably never heard of as well as a few that you always assumed were US born. For the

Aboriginal Artists

There was little outside recognition of the art produced by Aboriginal communities until the 20th century. But over the last 50 years or so, there's been a strong and growing appreciation of this unique creative force, led initially by the paintings, sculptures and carvings or revered Haida artist Bill Reid (1920–98) who's work appears on the back of the $20 bill. Also look out for colorful paintings by Norval Morriseau; mixed-media works by Saskatchewan-born Edward Poitras; and challenging younger artists, such as Marianne Nicholson and Brian Jungen.

The Best Art Galleries

1 National Gallery of Canada, Ottawa (p197)

2 Art Gallery of Ontario, Toronto (p172)

3 Musée des Beaux-Arts, Montréal (p228)

4 Vancouver Art Gallery, Vancouver (p64)

5 Art Gallery of Alberta, Edmonton (p144)

record, this is the homeland of classic legends such as Neil Young and Joni Mitchell as well as latter-day superstars such as Michael Buble, Sarah McLachlan, Diana Krall, who lives in British Columbia (BC) with her hubby, and someone called Elvis Costello.

Working their list into a lather, it won't be long before most Canadians also mention the Tragically Hip, Barenaked Ladies, Blue Rodeo, Guess Who, Rush, Feist, New Pornographers, Oscar Peterson, Great Big Sea, Gordon Lightfoot or Bruce Cockburn: seminal Canadian musicians past and present that define the country's musical soundscape yet often have very little profile outside the country: the Hip, for example, can easily pack stadiums in Canada while they'd struggle to fill a midsized venue in most other countries.

To tap into the scene on your visit, drop into a local independent record store and ask for some recommendations. They'll likely point you to the area's best live-music venues and offer you some tips on who to look out for. And if you're a true die-hard traveling muso, consider timing your visit for a music festival. The Montréal International Jazz Festival (www.montrealjazzfest.com) is one of the biggest in the world (see p216 for more details), while Vancouver offers summer events including the Vancouver Folk Music Festival (www.thefestival.bc.ca) and the classical, jazz and world music-focused MusicFest Vancouver (www.musicfestvancouver.ca).

Film

There are two distinct sides to Canada's burgeoning movie industry. As a production hot spot, it's often used as a visual stand-in for US cities, which means you usually don't know you're watching a Canadian-made flick when you sit down to *X-Men*, *I Robot* or *Catwoman* (OK, you probably won't want to sit down to that one). But aside from being a busy back lot for Hollywood – the nickname Hollywood North is frequently used here – there's a healthy independent Canadian movie-making scene with a flavor all its own.

Celebrated films made here over the years and which are about as far from Hollywood blockbusters as you can imagine include *Away from Her* (2006, directed by Sarah Polley), *The Sweet Hereafter* (1997, directed by Atom Egoyan), *The Barbarian Invasions* (2003, directed Denys Arcand), *Thirty Two Short Films About Glenn Gould* (1993, directed by Francois Girard) and *The Red Violin* (1998), co-written by Don McKellar, who has often seemed like a one-man movie industry unto himself.

You can dip into both sides of the Canadian film industry coin at the country's two main movie festivals. The Toronto International Film Festival (www.tiff.net) is a glitzy affair where Hollywood megastars drop by to promote their new offerings. In contrast, the Vancouver International Film Festival (www.viff.org) showcases arthouse and independent flicks from Canada and around the world.

Food, Wine & Microbrews

Vancouver offers some fine dining (p75)

LAWRENCE WORCESTER

While Canadians used to eat only to lag themselves for a harsh winter, big cities such as Montréal, Toronto and Vancouver now offer world-leading dining scenes. At the same time, regions across the country have rediscovered distinctive local ingredients produced on their doorsteps. The approach has also spread to drink: celebrated wines are produced in the Okanagan, Niagara and beyond, while microbrewed beer has added local flavor to pub nights.

Local Flavors

From East Coast lobster to prairie pierogis and West Coast spot prawns, distinctive dishes define Canada's regions. These provincial soul foods reflect local ingredients and the diverse – often immigrant – influences of their cooks.

Starting from the east, the main dish of the Maritimes is lobster – boiled in the pot and served with a little butter – and the best place to get stuck into it is a community hall 'kitchen party' with the chatty locals. Try some hearty seafood chowder while waiting for your meal to arrive, but don't eat too much; you'll need room for the mountainous fruit pie coming your way afterwards.

Visitors to Nova Scotia should save their appetites for butter-soft Digby scallops and rustic Lunenberg sausage, while the favored food of nearby Newfoundland and Labrador combines rib-sticking cod cheeks and sweet snow crab.

Along with broiled Atlantic salmon, French-influenced New Brunswick serves-up *poutine râpée*, potatoes stuffed with pork and boiled for a few hours. It's been filling the bellies of locals here for decades and is recommended if you haven't eaten for a week or two.

Over in the even more French-influenced province of Québec, fine food is a way of life. Cosmopolitan Montréal has long claimed to be the nation's fine-dining capital, but there's an appreciation of food here at all levels that includes hearty pea soups, exquisite cheeses and tasty pâtés sold at bustling markets. In addition, there's poutine – irresistible dark golden fries topped with gravy and cheese curds – and huge, bulging smoked meat sandwiches that will fill you for a week.

Ontario – especially Toronto – is a microcosm of Canada's melting pot of cuisines. Like Québec, maple syrup is a super-sweet flavoring of choice here, found in desserts such as beavertails (sugary pastries with rich toppings) and on fluffy breakfast pancakes the size of Frisbees.

Canada's Aboriginal people have many fascinating culinary traditions. Reliant on meat and seafood – try a juicy halibut stew on British Columbia's (BC) Haida Gwaii – there's also a tradition of bannock (pan-fried bread) that was imported by the Scots and appropriated by Canada's first locals.

In contrast, the central provinces of Manitoba, Saskatchewan and Alberta have their own culinary ways. The latter is the nation's beef capital – you'll find top-notch Alberta steak on menus here and across the country. Pierogis (dumplings), introduced by Ukrainian immigrants, are a staple across the border in Manitoba, while Saskatchewan serves up striking Saskatoon berry pies to all who pass through.

In the far west, British Columbians have traditionally fed themselves from the sea and the fertile farmlands of the interior. Okanagan Valley peaches, cherries and blueberries are the staple of many summer diets. But it's the seafood that attracts the lion's share of culinary fans. Tuck into succulent wild salmon, juicy Fanny Bay oysters and velvet-soft regional scallops and you may (rightfully) think you've found foodie nirvana.

Top Dining Districts

Ask anyone in Toronto, Montréal or Vancouver to name Canada's leading foodie city and they'll likely inform you that you've just found it. But while each of the big three

Extreme Cuisine

Unique foods for traveling taste-trippers include Prince Edward Island's (PEI) Solomon Gundy, a marinated herring and chopped-meat combo, and geoduck (pronounced 'gooey duck'), a giant saltwater clam that's a popular British Columbian (BC) Chinese dish. In Alberta, search out some 'prairie oysters' for your fellow travelers, then sit back and watch them tuck into a plate of bull's testicles. If you make it to Nunavut, frozen raw char served like a Popsicle with soy dipping sauce is a favorite. Backcountry foraging is also big in Canada: BC is a popular mushroom picking spot, while New Brunswick is ideal for fiddleheads (edible fern fronds).

claims to be at the head of the top table, their strengths are so diverse that they're more accurately defined as complimentary courses in one great meal – in fact, if you jog between them, you might work off a little of that belt-challenging excess.

First dish on the table is Montréal, which was Canada's dine-out capital long before the upstarts threw off their donut-based shackles. Renowned for introducing North America's finest French-influenced cuisine, it hasn't given up its crown lightly. Chefs here are often treated like rock stars as they challenge Old World conventions with daring, even artistic approaches. You should also expect a great restaurant experience: Montréalers have a bacchanalian love for eating out, from cozy old town heritage restaurants to the lively patios of Rue Prince Arthur and the sophisticated eateries of the Plateau.

If Montréal is an ideal starter, that makes Toronto the main course – although that's a reflection of its more recent elevation rather than its preeminence. Fusion is the default approach in Canada's largest city, with contemporary immigration adding modern influences from Asia to a foundation of British, Greek and Italian cuisines. With 7000 restaurants to choose from, though, it can be a tough choice figuring out where to unleash your appetite. Your best approach is to hit the neighborhoods: the Financial District and Old York areas are studded with classy, high-end joints where swank is a typical side-dish.

And while that appears to make Vancouver the dessert, it could be argued that this glass-towered metropolis is the best of the bunch. Some of the country's most innovative chefs have set up shop here, inspired by a distinctive local larder of unique ingredients and Canada's most cosmopolitan – especially Asian – population. Fusion is the starting point in fine-dining districts such as Yaletown and Kitsilano. But there's also a high level of authentic ethnic dining across the city: the best sushi bars and Japanese *izakayas* outside Tokyo jostle for attention with superb Vietnamese and Korean eateries. And if you want to discover what Pacific

Testing out microbrews in Vancouver's Yaletown (p77)
PHOTOGRAPHER: CHRISTOPHER HERWIG

Northwest or West Coast cuisine means, this is the place to tuck in and conduct some lip-smacking field research.

The Best Restaurants

1 C Restaurant, Vancouver (p75)

2 The Swan, Toronto (p181)

3 ZenKitchen, Ottawa (p202)

4 L'Express, Montréal (p237)

5 Le Lapin Sauté, Québec City (p252)

6 Camille's, Victoria (p93)

Price Icons

In this guide eating choices are flagged with price indicators, based on the cost of an average main course from the dinner menu.

Eating Price Indicators	
$	up to $12
$$	from $12 to $25
$$$	more than $25

Wine Regions

While international visitors are often surprised to learn that wine is produced here, their suspicions are tempered after a drink or two. Canada's wines have gained ever-greater kudos in recent years and while smaller-scale production and the industry dominance of other wine regions means they'll never be a global market leader, there are some tasty treats waiting for thirsty grape lovers.

And since the best way to sample any wine is to head straight to the source – where you can taste the region in the glass – consider doing some homework and locating the nearest vineyards on your visit. Don't miss the top table wineries in Ontario's Niagara region or BC's Okanagan Valley – the country's leading producers – but a visit to the smaller, often rustic wineries of Québec and the charming boutique operations of Nova Scotia and Vancouver Island can be just as rewarding.

Wherever your tipple-craving takes you, drink widely and deeply and prepare to be surprised. And make sure you have plenty of room in your suitcase – packing materials are always available, but you'll probably drink everything before you make it to the airport anyway.

For background and further information, check the website of Wines of Canada (www.winesofcanada.com) and visit the blog Canadian Wine Guy (www.canadian wineguy.com).

Here for the Beer?

Canadians don't only drink wine, of course – beer is at least as important as a national beverage here. And while you'll soon come across the mass-produced fizz of brewing behemoths Labatt and Molson, a little digging uncovers a thriving regional microbrewing scene dripping with fantastic ales, bitters and lagers.

Midsized breweries such as Moosehead in New Brunswick, Alexander Keith's in Nova Scotia, Sleemans in Ontario, Big Rock in Alberta and Okanagan Springs in BC produce some easy-to-find, highly quaffable tipples. It's worth noting that several of these have been taken over by the two big boys in recent years, although they haven't been stupid enough to change much about these successful operations.

It's at the local level where you'll find the real treats. Canada is suffused with a foamy head of small-batch brewers and visiting beer geeks should search these out by asking for the local brew wherever they find themselves. Highlights include Québec's Boréale, Alberta's Wild Rose Brewery and Nova Scotia's Propeller Brewing. In Ontario, keep your tongue alert for beers from Wellington Brewery, Kawartha Lake Brewing Company and Steam Whistler Brewing. And in BC, it's all about Phillips Brewing, Tree Brewing and Central City Brewing, among many others. Cheers!

Food Festivals

Canada is dripping with palate-pleasing food and wine events, which makes it especially important to check the dates of your trip: they're among the best ways to hang out and get to know the locals. And if you're on the West Coast, don't miss the ever-popular Vancouver Playhouse International Wine Festival (www.playhousewinefest.com).

On the BC Farm Trail

Ask Vancouverites where the food on their tables comes from and most will point vacantly at a nearby supermarket, but others will tell you about the Fraser Valley (p103). This lush interior region starts about 30km from the city and is studded with busy farms. Now, farmers and the people they feed are getting to know each another on a series of Circle Farm Tours. These self-guided driving treks take you around several food-producing communities, highlighting recommended pit stops – farms, markets, wineries and dining suggestions – along the way. Downloaded free tour maps at www.circlefarmtour.ca.

Recommended events – large and small – include PEI's International Shellfish Festival (www.peishellfish.com), New Brunswick's Shediac Lobster Festival (www.shediaclobsterfestival.ca) and Nova Scotia's Fall Wine Festival (www.nsfalwinefestival.ca).

Alternatively, Québec-bound visitors should hit the Eastern Townships' Magog-Orford area for the Fête des Vendanges (www.fetedesvendanges.com), which focuses on regional food and wine. Traveling chocoholics might prefer the province's Fête du Chocolat de Bromont (www.feteduchocolat.ca) instead.

Across the border in Ontario, Niagara stages more than one annual event to celebrate its winey wealth, including January's Icewine Festival, June's New Vintage Festival and September's giant, nine-day Niagara Wine Festival. For information on these events, visit www.niagarawinefestival.com. Toronto's Salut Wine & Food Festival (www.salutwinefestival.com) is also a popular annual draw in this region.

And if you're still hungry and thirsty by the time you make it out to the West Coast, it's hard to miss one of the Okanagan Valley's four main wine festivals – one for each season. They include the 10-day Fall Wine Festival, staged in October, and the highly enjoyable Winter Festival of Wine in January, which focuses on icewine. For more information on these events, visit www.thewinefestivals.com.

If you fancy sampling all those local BC microbrewed beers instead, drop into Vancouver Craft Beer Week (www.vancouvercraftbeerweek.com) in May. Food-wise, head across the water to Vancouver Island for the Cowichan Wine & Culinary Festival (www.wines.cowichan.net). Both are great ways to meet the locals and tuck into some tasty regional treats.

Outdoors

Canada is blessed with a number of superb ski slopes

PAUL KENNE

While the great Canadian outdoors looks undeniably pretty on postcards, the wild wilderness here is not just about good looks. Locals have been jumping in head first – sometimes literally – for decades, interacting on land and on water by means of activities ranging from hiking to kayaking and from biking to climbing. For visitors, there are countless operators across the country that can help you gear up and get out there.

Skiing & Snowboarding

While it might have taken the 2010 Winter Olympic and Paralympic Winter Games in Vancouver to show just how special Canada's snow sports facilities are, it was certainly no secret to the locals. From Québec to Ontario and from Alberta to British Columbia (BC), this is the country where it seems like almost everyone was born to ski. Visitors will find world-renowned resorts here, but it's also worth asking the locals where exactly they like to hit the slopes: for every big-time swanky resort, there are several smaller spots where the terrain and the welcome can be even better.

Québec boasts some big slopes – Le Massif, near Québec City, has a vertical drop of 770m – located handily close to the cities. Most of these nonalpine hills, such as Mont-Tremblant, are a day's drive from Toronto and less than an hour from Québec City and Montréal. Ski areas in Québec's Eastern Townships, offer renowned gladed runs – runs that weave through a thinned forest.

Head west and you'll hit the big mountains and vast alpine terrains. Glide down gargantuan slopes at Whistler-Blackcomb, which has North America's highest vertical drop *and* most impressive terrain variation. You'll also slide through stunning postcard landscapes in the Canadian Rockies, especially at Sunshine in Banff National Park.

In BC's Okanagan Valley, resorts such as Apex and Big White boast good snow year after year (no droughts here). Snowpack ranges from 2m to 6m-plus, depending on how close the resort is to the Pacific Ocean.

For cross-country skiing, Alberta offers some popular trails that were part of that other Canadian Winter Olympics, Calgary in 1988. For further information and resources covering the national scene, check the website of the Canadian Ski Council (www.skicanada.org).

The Best
Day Hikes

1 Sunshine Meadows, Banff (p119)

2 Lake Louise, Banff (p133)

3 Stanley Park, Vancouver (p65)

4 Bruce Trail, Ontario (p209)

5 Nokomis Trail in Lake Superior Provincial Park, Ontario (p209)

Hiking

You don't have to be a hiker to go hiking in Canada. While there are plenty of multi-day jaunts for those who like tramping through the wilderness equipped only with a small Swiss Army Knife, there are also innumerable opportunities for those whose idea of a hike is a gentle stroll around a lake with a pub visit at the end. Canada, luckily, is more than blessed with both approaches.

The country's hiking capital is Banff National Park, crisscrossed with stunning vistas accessible to both hard and soft eco adventurers. In the park's Sunshine Meadows area, for example, you can wind through landscapes teeming with alpine flora – as bald eagles circle overhead – and enjoy mountain panoramas arguably unmatched in Canada. Also in the Rockies region, areas near Jasper offer breathtaking glacier views.

In BC's provincial parks system (www.bcparks.ca) you'll have a choice of more than 100 parks, each with distinct landscapes to hike through, including ancient volcanoes. And since you're in BC, head over to Grouse Mountain and hit the Grouse Grind, a steep forest hike that's known as 'mother nature's Stairmaster.' You'll understand why by the time you get to the top (*if* you get to the top).

Out east, awe-inspiring trails stripe the landscape. In southern Ontario, the Bruce Trail (www.brucetrail.org) tracks from Niagara Falls to Tobermory. It's the oldest and longest continuous footpath in Canada and spans more than 800km. Though portions are near cities such as Hamilton and Toronto, it's surprisingly serene. In contrast, Newfoundland's trails make for fantastic shoreline hiking and often provide whale views.

And don't forget the cities. Canada's major metropolises offer some great urban hikes, an ideal way to get to know the communities you're visiting. Slip into your runners for a stroll (or a jog) with the locals in Montréal's Parc du Mont Royal or Vancouver's gemlike Stanley Park, where the idyllic seawall winds alongside

towering trees and lapping ocean. It's the kind of breathtaking, vista-packed stroll that gives hiking a good name.

Mountain Biking

Mountain biking is a big deal in Canada. While cycling enthusiasts in other countries might be into trundling around town or along a gentle riverside trail, in Canada you're more likely to find them hurtling down a mountainside covered in mud and punishing their bike as if they were riding a bucking bronco. Given the landscape, of course, it was just a matter of time before the wheels hit the off-road here.

If you need to ease yourself in, start gently with BC's Kettle Valley Rail Trail (www .kettlevalleyrailway.ca), near Kelowna. This dramatic segment of converted railbed barrels across picturesque wooden trestle bridges and through canyon tunnels.

Looking for more of an adrenalin rush? In North Vancouver (see www.nsmba .ca), you can ride on much narrower and steeper 'trestles.' Birthplace of 'freeride' mountain biking (which combines downhill and dirt jumping), this area offers elevated bridges, log rides and skinny planks that loft over the wet undergrowth. It's a similar story up at Whistler where the melted ski slopes are transformed into a summertime bike park that draws thousands every year – especially during the July Crankworx Mountain Bike Festival (www.crankworx.com/whistler).

For road touring, Canada's east coast, with more small towns and less emptiness, is a fantastic place to pedal, either as a single-day or a multiday trip. In Québec province, try any part of the 4000km Route Verte (www.routeverrte.com), the longest network of bicycle paths in the Americas. Or alternatively follow PEI's bucolic red roads (www.tourismpei.com/pei-cycling), which includes the 279km Confederation Trail that extends from near the island's northern tip to near its eastern tip. The trail passes by some idyllic villages where riders can stop for a bite to eat or to rest for the night.

Climber emerges at the Canadian Rockies
PHOTOGRAPHER: PHILIP & KAREN SMITH

And if you're in one of Canada's big cities and you feel like stretching your legs, consider renting a bike for a half-day trundle: Vancouver and Victoria in BC have particularly good city-spanning bike trails.

Climbing

All those inviting crags you've spotted on your trip are an indication that Canada is a major climbing capital, ideal for short scales or multiday crampon-picking jaunts.

BC's Squamish region, located between Vancouver and Whistler, is a climbing centre, with dozens of accessible (and not so accessible) peaks. Tap into the scene via Squamish Rock Guides (www.squamishrockguides .com). If mountaineering is more your thing, the Rockies are not surprisingly the recommended first stop. The area near Banff is an ideal first stop for rock climbers, no matter what your skill level. Yamnuska (www.yamnuska.com) is one company that offers ice and other climbs in this region.

If your trip takes you out east instead, Ontario's favorite climbing destinations dot the Bruce Peninsula.

If you prefer the European approach, the Matterhorn of Canada is BC's Mt Assiniboine, located between the Kootenay and Banff national parks. There are other fine peaks in Canada's west.

And if you need a guide, check in with the excellent Alpine Club of Canada (www .alpineclubofcanada.ca).

The One that Didn't Get Away

Built on its Aboriginal and pioneer past, Canada has a strong tradition of fishing and you can expect to come across plenty of opportunities to hook walleye, pike, rainbow or lake trout on your travels. Among the best fishing holes to head for are Lunenburg (west of Halifax) in Nova Scotia and the Miramichi River in New Brunswick. And while salmon are the usual draw on the Pacific coastline, hopping aboard a local vessel for some sea fishing off Haida Gwaii can deliver the kind of giant catches you'll be bragging about for years to come.

Windsurfing Wonders

It would seem that Québec's Îles de la Madeleine – a small chain in the Gulf of St Lawrence, accessible by ferry from Québec or Prince Edward Island – were made for wind sports. It's the kind of place so blessed that if the wind is blowing the wrong way, you can drive a few minutes down to another beach where it's just perfect. Sheltered lagoons offer safe learning locations for testing kiteboards or seeking shelter during heavy days.

Kayaking & Boating

If you're on a tight schedule and don't have time for some of Canada's multiday sea kayaking odysseys – think remote Canadian Arctic or the West Coast wilderness of Vancouver Island – there are plenty of other, more accessible ways to get your paddling fix here. Big cities such as BC's Vancouver and Victoria offer tours and lessons near town, while the province's Sunshine Coast and Salt Spring Island offer crenulated coastlines combined with tranquil sea inlets.

Playboats – tiny plastic kayaks with flat hulls like surfboards – are designed to surf on a river's stationary and recirculating waves. The world's

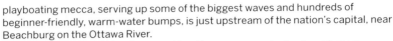

playboating mecca, serving up some of the biggest waves and hundreds of beginner-friendly, warm-water bumps, is just upstream of the nation's capital, near Beachburg on the Ottawa River.

Playboating's gnarly brother, creekboating, uses rounder boats with more flotation to help paddlers career down steep, narrow, waterfall-riddled rivers. Make sure you have a solid Eskimo roll for righting yourself when you flip. Go with a team of safety-conscious boaters in hot spots across BC and in Québec.

Surfing

If you're aiming to become a temporary beach bum on your Canada trip, head to the wild west coast of BC's Vancouver Island and hang out on the beaches around Tofino. Surfing schools and gear rental operations stud this region and you'll have an awesome time riding the swells or just watching everyone else as you stretch out on the sand. Backed by verdant rain forest, it's an idyllic spot to spend your time.

June to September is the height of the season here but serious surfer dudes also like to drop by in winter to face down the lashing waves. Check Surfing Vancouver Island (www.surfingvancouverisland.com) for a taste of what to expect.

Some 5500km away, the east coast of Nova Scotia can also dish out some serious surf. The US south coast's hurricane season (August to November) brings Canadians steep fast breaks, snappy right and left point breaks, and offshore reef and shoal breaks in areas just outside Halifax, as well as the entire south shore region. There are also a couple of surf schools in the province. Scotia Surfer (www .scotiasurfer.com) has the lowdown.

Sports

A frozen pond is all Canadians need for a game of hockey

TODD LAWSON

While Canadians have a solid repu-
tation for being mild-mannered,
that all changes when it comes to
watching sports. Meek and peace-
loving most of the time, locals will
paint their faces, down a few too
many Molsons and chant, scream
and sing at the top of their lungs
at hockey games that somehow
seem to define their existence. For
visitors, watching sports with
these passionate locals is an eye-
opening cultural experience.

Hockey

While Canada is a multifaith country, there's one religion that rises above all others. Hockey – don't even bother calling it *ice* hockey here – rouses rabid emotions in die-hard fans and can trigger group hugging and uncontrollable sobbing at the drop of a puck, especially when the local team has just lost (like they have always done lately) in the annual Stanley Cup play-offs.

Canada has six teams in the elite, US-dominated National Hockey League (NHL): the Vancouver Canucks, Calgary Flames, Edmonton Oilers, Ottawa Senators, Montréal Canadiens and Toronto Maple Leafs (don't make the mistake of calling them 'the Leaves').

But although it's the country's national sport and Wayne Gretzky – its most famous former player – is Canadian, no team north of the border has won that illusive cup since

1993. It's a touchy subject here, which might explain why riots have ensued in some cities when another annual run at the trophy comes to naught.

While tickets for games in some areas can be hard to come by – Vancouver Canucks games routinely sell out, for example, and booking as far ahead as possible for the September to June season is essential – you don't have to hit a stadium to catch a game. For a glimpse at what it feels like to be unreservedly in love with a Canadian hockey side, head to any local pub on game night and you'll be swept up in the emotion. And the beer will be better than the overpriced plastic cups of generic fizz on offer at the games themselves.

After the game, make sure you ask your new beer buddies about the 2010 Winter Olympics in Vancouver. Their faces will light up as they regale you with the story of the US versus Canada men's hockey gold medal battle, a movie-style epic in which the local boys scored a nail-biting 3-2 overtime win. On the night, the entire country rose as one to hug each other and cheer.

For an introduction to Canada's hockey scene, visit CBC television's website at www.cbc.ca/sports/hockey.

Football

We're not talking about soccer and we're not even talking about American Football here. With eight major teams across the country, the Canadian Football League (CFL) is second only to hockey in the hearts and minds of many north-of-the-border sports nuts. And while it's similar to American Football – think hefty padding, an egg-shaped ball and the kind of crunching tackles that would stop a grizzly bear – the Canadian version involves teams of 12 players and is fought out on a larger pitch.

Like hockey, the main annual aim of the Hamilton Tiger-Cats, Montréal Alouettes, Toronto Argonauts, Winnipeg Blue Bombers, Saskatchewan Roughriders, Calgary Stampeders, Edmonton Eskimos and BC Lions is to win that elusive trophy, this one called the Grey Cup. Play-off games trigger raucous street celebrations in host cities, with fans from visiting teams parading around in team shirts hollering their undying love for their side.

Established in 1958, the fortunes of the CFL have ebbed and flowed over the decades but recent years have seen solid popularity and the improvement of stadium facilities as well as the awarding of a franchise: the as-yet unnamed Ottawa team will be the third CFL team the city has had and they are expected to debut soon.

For visitors, tickets for Grey Cup games can be hard to get hold of but regular matches during the June to November season are much more accessible: expect a family atmosphere and a partylike vibe with cheerleaders and noisy crowd interaction. For more information on the league, check out its official website at www.cfl.ca.

How about an Alternative?

Vancouver's hottest new alternative sports league, Terminal City Rollergirls (www.terminalcityroller girls.com) pits all-female amateur flat-track roller derby teams against each other as they whistle around the track at breakneck speeds. The battles are between teams with names such as Riot Girls and Bad Reputations. But you don't have to be in Vancouver to catch the action: roller derby leagues are growing across Canada and you can check out the options where you are at www.derbygirls.ca.

Soccer

Canada's most popular participation sport, soccer – you won't get very far calling it football here – has traditionally mirrored the US experience by never quite reaching the heights of the continent's more established professional sports. But you can't keep a good pastime down, and while they struggled with early attempts at building support here (by importing fading stars from Europe and South America), recent leagues are on a much more solid footing.

The three biggest Canadian professional teams are Toronto FC, Montréal Impact and the Vancouver Whitecaps. Toronto entered the sport's US-based top level Major League Soccer (MLS) in 2007 and Vancouver will be joining them in 2011. The Montréal side plays in the second rung of the US pro league but has been awarded an expansion franchise to join the MLS in 2012. The third level of what's often called the soccer pyramid is the Canadian Soccer League. It's dominated by teams from Ontario, including the Brampton Lions and the North York Astros.

Soccer is growing in popularity as a spectator sport in Canada, but tickets for top level games are still relatively easy to buy – book ahead via club websites, though, if you have a particular date in mind.

Baseball

Following the 2004 relocation of the Montréal Expos to Washington (they're now called the Washington Nationals), Canada's only Major League Baseball (MLB) team is the Toronto Blue Jays, a member of the American League's Eastern Division. Founded in 1977 and playing in the city's cavernous downtown SkyDome – now known as the Rogers Centre – they are the only non-US team to win the World Series (in 1993). Follow the team and check out ticket options for the April to early November season at www.toronto.bluejays.mlb.com.

There is also one professional minor league side in Canada: the Vancouver Canadians, affiliated with the Oakland Athletics and playing in the Northwest League. Their recently refurbished outdoor stadium with mountain views is one of the best diamonds in Canada, so hit the bleachers and feel the nostalgic ambiance of old-school summertime baseball.

Additional lower level teams across the country – including the Edmonton Capitals and Winnipeg Goldeyes – offer a similar family-friendly feel, while college teams are also popular if you want to catch the atmosphere of a game without paying Blue Jay prices.

The Best Professional Sports Teams

1 Toronto Maple Leafs (hockey; p183)

2 Vancouver Canucks (hockey; p79)

3 Toronto Blue Jays (baseball; p183)

4 Edmonton Oilers (hockey; p147)

5 Vancouver Whitecaps (soccer; p79)

6 Calgary Stampeders (football)

Wildlife

A polar bear does a bit of sunbaking, Labrador Straits (p303)

GAB/IMAGEBROCK

On land, in the water and in the air, Canada is teeming with the kind of camera-worthy critters that make visitors wonder if they haven't stepped into a safari park by mistake. And when we say 'critters,' we're not talking small fry: this is the home of grizzlies, wolves, moose and bald eagles, as well as a perfect viewing spot for huge whales. Pack your camera.

Grizzly Bears & Black Bears

The main wildlife viewing target for many Canada-bound visitors, grizzly bears – *ursus arctos horribilis* to all you Latin scholars out there – are most commonly found in the Rocky Mountain regions of British Columbia (BC) and Alberta. Standing up to 3m tall, you'll know them by their distinctive shoulder hump. Solitary animals with no natural enemies (except us), they enjoy crunching on elk, moose or caribou but they're usually content to fill their bellies with berries and – if they're available – juicy fresh salmon. Keep in mind that you should never approach any bear. And in remote areas, be sure to travel in groups.

Just to confuse you, grizzlies are almost black, while their smaller relation, the black bear, is sometimes brown. More commonly spotted in the wild than grizzlies, Canada is home to around half a million black bears and they're spread out across the country, except for Prince Edward Island (PEI), southern Alberta and southern Saskatchewan. In regions such as northern BC as well as Banff and Jasper National Parks, seeing black bears feasting on berries as you drive past on the highway is surprisingly common.

In 1994, coastal BC's Khutzeymateen Grizzly Bear Sanctuary (www.greatcanadianparks.com/bcolumbia/khutzey/index.htm) near the northern town of Prince Rupert) was officially designated for protected status. Over 50 grizzlies currently live on this 45,000-hectare refuge. A few ecotour operators have permits for viewing these animals if you want to check them out face-to-face.

Polar Bears

Weighing less than a kilogram at birth, the fiercest member of the bear clan is not quite so cute when it grows up to be a hulking 600kg. But these mesmerizing animals still pack a huge visual punch for visitors. If your visit to Canada won't be complete until you've seen one, there's really only one place to go: Churchill, Manitoba, on the shores of Hudson Bay (late September to early November is the viewing season). About 900 of the planet's roughly 20,000 white-furred beasts prowl the tundra here.

Operators will tour you around the Polar Bear Capital of the World in elevated tundra buggies. Just don't step out: these carnivorous, ever-watchful predators are not cuddly cartoon critters and will view you as an easy take-out dinner. Unlike grizzlies and black bears, polar bears actively prey on people, whether or not they have cameras.

While Churchill is a polar bear–watching magnet, it's not Canada's only potential viewing spot. The animals occasionally show up in Newfoundland and Labrador, coming ashore from drifting pack ice. And while northern Nunavut is home to nearly half of the world's polar bear population, its bear-rich spots such as Ukkusiksalik National Park are notoriously difficult and expensive to visit.

Moose

Canada's iconic shrub-nibbler, the moose is a massive member of the deer family that owes its popularity to a distinctively odd appearance: skinny legs supporting a humungous body and a cartoonish head that looks permanently inquisitive and clueless at the same time. And then there are the antlers: males grow a spectacular rack every summer, only to discard them come November.

Adding to their *Rocky & Bullwinkle* appeal, a moose can move at more than 50km per hour and easily out-swim two men paddling a canoe – all on a vegetarian diet comprised mostly of leaves and twigs.

You'll spot moose foraging for these yummy treats near lakes, muskegs and streams, as well as in the forests of the western mountain ranges in the Rockies and the Yukon. Newfoundland is perhaps the moosiest place of all. In 1904 the

The Best Wildlife-Watching

1 Jasper National Park (p140), Alberta

2 Algonquin Provincial Park (p201), Ontario

3 Icefields Parkway (p139), Alberta

4 Churchill (p301), Manitoba

5 Cape Breton Island (p282), Nova Scotia

province imported and released four beasts into the wild. They enjoyed the good life of shrub-eating and hot sex, ultimately spawning the 120,000 inhabitants that now roam the woods.

Generally not aggressive, moose will often stand stock still for photographs. They can be unpredictable, though, so don't startle them. During mating season (September), the giant males can become belligerent, so keep your distance: great photos are not worth an antler charge from 500kg of angry moose.

Elk, Deer & Caribou

Moose are not the only animals that can exhibit a Mr Hyde personality change during rutting season. Usually placid, male elk have been known to charge vehicles in Jasper National Park, believing their reflection in the shiny paintwork to be a rival for their harem of eligible females. It's rare, though, and Jasper is generally one of the best places in Canada to see this large deer species wandering around attracting cameras on the edge of town.

White-tailed deer can be found anywhere from Nova Scotia's Cape Breton to the Northwest Territories' Great Slave Lake. Its bigger relative, the caribou, is unusual in that both males and females sport enormous antlers. Barren-ground caribou feed on lichen and spend most of the year on the tundra from Baffin Island to Alaska. Woodland caribou roam further south, with some of the mightiest herds trekking across northern Québec and Labrador. These beasts, which have a reputation for not being especially smart, also show up in the mountain parks of BC, Alberta and Newfoundland, which is where many visitors catch a glimpse of them.

Wolves

It's fitting that wolves follows elk, deer and caribou in this chapter since that's what they spend much of their time doing in the wild. Perhaps the most intriguing and mysterious of all Canada's wild animals, they hunt cleverly and tenaciously in packs and have no qualms about taking on prey much bigger than themselves – although human attacks are extremely rare.

Clearly wary of human contact, they're also not the easiest animals to spot. If you do catch sight of one – perhaps in the Rockies – it will likely be from a distance.

Fairly common in sparsely populated areas throughout the country, you may also hear wolves howling at the moon if you're out in the bush. In Ontario's Algonquin Provincial Park, you can actually take part in a public 'howl.' Wolves will readily respond to human imitations of their calls, so the park's staff conducts communal sessions on various summer evenings to give visitors a 'wail' of an experience.

Salmon Runs Wild

After years of declining returns, the 2010 wild Pacific sockeye salmon run on BC's Fraser River surprised scientists and local fishing operators by being the largest for almost 100 years. More than 34 million gasping salmon reportedly pushed themselves up the river to lay their eggs and die, a spectacle that turned regional rivers red with millions of crimson sockeye. The previous year had seen less than two million fish return to the area in what was regarded as a catastrophic low.

Whales

More than 22 species of whale and porpoise lurk offshore in Atlantic Canada, including camera-hogging superstars

such as the humpback whale, which averages 15m and 36 tons; the North Atlantic right whale, the world's most endangered leviathan, with an estimated population of just 350; and the mighty blue whale, the largest animal on earth at 25m and around 100 tons. Then there's the little guy, the minke, which grows to 10m and often approaches boats, delighting with acrobatics as it shows off. Whale-watching tours are not surprisingly very popular throughout this region.

You can also spot humpbacks and gray whales off the West Coast. But it's the orca – or killer whale – that dominates viewing here. Their aerodynamic bodies, signature black-and-white color and incredible speed (up to 40km/h) make them the Ferraris of the aquatic world and their diet includes seals, belugas and other whales (hence the 'killer whale' tag). The waters around Vancouver Island, particularly in the Johnstone Strait, teem with orcas every summer. Whale-watching tours depart from points throughout this region: Tofino and Victoria are particularly hot spots for operators.

Belugas glide in Arctic waters to the north. These ghostly white whales are one of the smallest members of the whale family, typically measuring no more than 4m and weighing about one ton. They are chatty fellows who squeak, groan and peep while traveling in close-knit family pods. If you tire of the polar bears in Churchill, Manitoba, you can also view belugas here via a boat or kayak tour. The more adventurous can also don a wetsuit and go snorkeling with them.

Birdlife

Canada's wide skies are home to 462 bird species, with BC and Ontario boasting the greatest diversity. The most famous feathered resident is the common loon, Canada's national bird – if you don't spot one in the wild, you'll see it on the back of the $1 coin. Rivaling it in the ubiquity stakes are Canada geese, hardy fowls that can fly up to 1000km per day and seem to have successfully colonized parks

Spotting a moose is a highlight of any naturalist's visit
PHOTOGRAPHER: DENIS CORRIVEAU

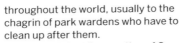

throughout the world, usually to the chagrin of park wardens who have to clean up after them.

The most visually arresting of Canada birds are its eagles, especially the bald variety. The bald eagle wingspan can reach up to 2m and, like wolves, they provide a spine tingling experience for anyone lucky enough to see one in the wild. Good viewing sites include Brackendale, between Vancouver and Whistler in BC, where up to 4000 eagles nest in winter. Also train your camera on Bras d'Or Lake in Cape Breton, Nova Scotia and on Vancouver Island's southern and western shorelines.

Seabirds flock to Atlantic Canada to breed. You'll be able to feast your eyes upon razorbills, kittiwakes, arctic terns, common murres and yes, puffins. Everyone loves these cute little guys, a sort of waddling penguin-meets-parrot with black-and-white feathers and an orange beak. They nest around Newfoundland, in particular.

On the Brink

According to the Committee on the Status of Endangered Wildlife, there are 602 endangered species in Canada. These include the eastern cougar and the tiny Vancouver Island marmot. Also on the list is the whooping crane, North America's tallest bird. Happily, the crane's situation is improving: down to just 21 individuals in 1941, the population dropped a further 10% after a bad winter in 2009. But in 2010, a near-record number of chicks hatched in northern Canada and the flock – which winters in Texas – is now estimated to be at around 300.

The seabird colonies can be up to one million strong, their shrieks deafening and their smell, well, not so fresh. Still, it's an amazing sight to behold. The preeminent places to get feathered are New Brunswick's Grand Manan Island and Newfoundland's Witless Bay and Cape St Mary's (both on the Avalon Peninsula near St John's). The best time is May through August, before the birds fly away for the winter.

Survival
Guide

Icy highway through the Yukon (p298)
PHOTOGRAPHER: ANDREW BAIN

A-Z

Directory

●●●

Accommodations

In Canada, you'll be choosing from a wide range of B&Bs, chain motels, hotels and hostels. Provincial tourist offices publish comprehensive directories of accommodations, and some take bookings online.

If camping, be aware that most government-run sites are available on a first-come first-served basis. Several national parks participate in **Parks Canada's camping reservation program** (☎ 877-737-3783; www.pc camping.ca; reservation fees $10.80).

SEASONS

○ Peak season is summer, from late May to early September, when prices are highest.

○ It's best to book ahead during summer, as well as during ski season at winter resorts, and during holidays and major events, as rooms can be scarce.

PRICE ICONS

○ The price indicators in this book are: $ (budget),

$$ (midrange) and $$$ (top end) and apply to the cost of a double room.

○ Prices listed in this book are for peak-season travel and, unless stated otherwise, do not include taxes (which can be up to 17%). If breakfast is included and/or a bathroom is shared, that information is included in our listing.

ACCOMMODATION PRICE INDICATORS	
$	up to $80
$$	from $80 to $180
$$$	more than $180

○ The budget category comprises campgrounds, hostels and simple hotels and B&Bs where you'll likely share a bathroom. Rates rarely exceed $80 for a double.

○ Midrange accommodation options, such as most B&Bs, inns (*auberges* in French), motels and some hotels, generally offer the best value for money. Expect to pay between $80 and $180 for a comfortable, decent-sized double with a private bathroom and TV.

○ Top-end accommodations (more than $180 per double) offer an international standard of amenities, including fitness and business centers and other upmarket facilities.

AMENITIES

○ Most properties offer in-room wi-fi. It's typically free in budget and midrange lodgings, while top-end hotels often charge a fee.

○ Many smaller properties, especially B&Bs, ban smoking. Marriott and Westin brand hotels are 100% smoke free. All other properties have rooms set aside for nonsmokers. In this book, we have used the nonsmoking icon (🚭) to mean that *all* rooms within a property are nonsmoking.

○ Air-conditioning is not a standard amenity at most budget and midrange places. If you want it, be sure to ask about it when you book.

DISCOUNTS

○ In winter, prices can plummet by as much as 50%.

○ Membership in the American Automobile Association (AAA) or an associated automobile association, American Association of Retired Persons (AARP) or other organizations also yields modest savings (usually 10%).

○ Check the hotel websites listed throughout this book for special online rates. The usual suspects also offer discounted room prices throughout Canada:

Book Your Stay Online

For more accommodations reviews by Lonely Planet authors, check out hotels.lonelyplanet .com/Canada. You'll find independent reviews, as well as recommendations on the best places to stay. Best of all, you can book online..

Expedia (www.expedia.com)

Hotwire (www.hotwire.com)

Priceline (www.priceline.com)

Travelocity (www.travelocity
.com)

Tripadvisor (www.tripadvisor
.com)

B&BS

Bed & Breakfast Online
(www.bbcanada.com) is the
main booking agency for
properties nationwide.

In Canada, B&Bs (*gîtes*
in French) are essentially
converted private homes
whose owners live on site.
People who like privacy may
find B&Bs too intimate, as
walls are rarely soundproof
and it's usual practice to
mingle with your hosts and
other guests.

Standards vary widely,
sometimes even within a single
B&B. The cheapest rooms tend
to be small with few amenities
and a shared bathroom. Nicer
ones have added features such
as a balcony, a fireplace and an
en suite bathroom. Breakfast
is always included in the rates
(though it might be continental
instead of a full cooked affair).

Not all B&Bs accept
children. Minimum stays
(usually two nights) are
common, and many B&Bs are
only open seasonally.

HOTELS & MOTELS

Most hotels are part of
international chains (see list,
p346), and the newer ones
are designed for either the
luxury market or business-
people. Rooms have cable
TV and wi-fi; many also have

Practicalities

o **Newspapers & Magazines** The most widely
available newspaper is the Toronto-based *Globe
and Mail*. Other principal dailies are the *Montréal
Gazette*, *Ottawa Citizen*, *Toronto Star* and *Vancouver
Sun*. *Maclean's* (www.macleans.ca) is Canada's
weekly news magazine.

o **TV & Radio** The Canadian Broadcasting
Corporation (CBC) is the dominant nationwide
network for both radio and TV. The Canadian
Television Network (CTN) is the major
competition.

o **Weights & Measures** Canada officially uses the
metric system, but imperial measurements are used
for many day-to-day purposes. To convert between
the two systems, see the chart on the inside front
cover.

o **Smoking** Smoking is banned in all restaurants,
bars and other public venues nationwide.

swimming pools and fitness
and business centers.

Rooms with two double or
queen-sized beds sleep up to
four people, although there is
usually a small surcharge for
the third and fourth person.
Many places advertise that
'kids stay free' but sometimes
you have to pay extra for a crib
or a rollaway (portable bed).

In Canada, as in the
USA (both lands of the
automobile), motels are
ubiquitous. They dot the
highways and cluster in
groups on the outskirts of
towns and cities. Although
most motel rooms won't win
any style awards, they're
usually clean and comfortable
and offer good value for
travelers. Many regional
motels remain your typical
'mom and pop' operations,
but plenty of North American
chains have also opened up

around the region (see p346
for contact information).

Activities

Snowboarding, hiking, sea
kayaking, mountain biking –
there's so much to do we've
devoted a whole chapter to
Canada's outdoor activities
(see p328). Other resources:

Alpine Club of Canada
(www.alpineclubofcanada.ca)
Climbing and mountaineering.

Canada Trails (www.canada
trails.ca) Hiking, biking, cross-
country skiing.

Canadian Ski Council
(www.skicanada.org) Skiing
and snowboarding.

Paddling Canada (www
.paddlingcanada.com) Kayaking
and canoeing.

Climate

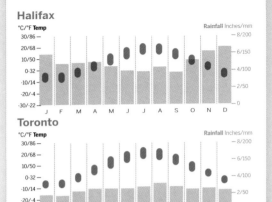

Halifax

Toronto

Vancouver

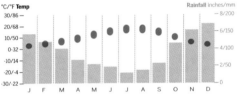

Parks Canada (www.pc.gc
.ca) National park action.

Business Hours

The following list provides
'normal' opening hours for
businesses. Reviews throughout this book show specific
hours only if they vary from
these standards. Note, too,
that hours often vary by
season. Our listings depict
the peak season operating
times.

Banks 10am-5pm Mon-Fri;
some banks open 9am-noon
Sat

General office hours 9am-
5pm Mon-Fri

Museums 10am-5pm daily,
sometimes they are closed
on Mon

Restaurants breakfast
8-11am, lunch 11:30am-
2:30pm Mon-Fri, dinner
5-9:30pm daily; some open
for brunch 8am-1pm Sat &
Sun

Bars 5pm-2am daily

Clubs 9pm-2am Wed-Sat

Shops 10am-6pm Mon-Sat,
noon-5pm Sun, some open to
8 or 9pm Thu and/or Fri

Supermarkets 9am-8pm,
some open 24hr

Customs Regulations

The **Canada Border Serv-
ices Agency** (CBSA; www
.cbsa.gc.ca) has the customs
lowdown. A few regulations
to note:

Alcohol You can bring in 1.5L
of wine, 1.14L of liquor or 24
355mL beers duty free.

Gifts You can bring in gifts
totaling up to $60.

Money You can bring in/
take out up to $10,000; larger
amounts must be reported to
customs.

Personal effects Camping
gear, sports equipment,
cameras and laptop
computers can be brought
in without much trouble.
Declaring these to customs
as you cross the border might
save you some hassle when
you leave, especially if you'll
be crossing the US-Canadian
border multiple times.

Pets You must carry a signed
and dated certificate from a
veterinarian to prove your dog
or cat has had a rabies shot in
the past 36 months.

Prescription drugs You
can bring in/take out a 90-
day supply for personal use
(though if you're bringing it to
the USA, know it's technically
illegal, but overlooked for
individuals).

Tobacco You can bring in
200 cigarettes, 50 cigars,

200g of tobacco and 200 tobacco sticks duty free.

● ● ●
Discount Cards

Discounts are commonly offered for seniors, children, families and people with disabilities, though no special cards are issued (you get the savings on site when you pay). AAA and other automobile association members also receive various travel-related discounts.

International Student Identity Card (ISIC; www .isiccard.com) Provides students with discounts on travel insurance and admission to museums and other sights. There are also cards for those who are aged under 26 but not students, and for full-time teachers.

Parks Canada Discovery Pass (www.pc.gc.ca/voyage -travel/carte-pass/index_e .asp; adult/child 6-16yr/family $68/33/136) Provides access to 27 national parks and 77 historic sites for a year. Can pay for itself in as few as seven visits over daily entry fees; also provides quicker entry into sites.

Many cities have discount cards for local attractions; see destinations for details. These include:

Montréal Museum Pass

Ottawa Culture Passport

UBC Attractions Passport (Vancouver)

Winnipass (Winnipeg)

● ● ●
Electricity

120V/60Hz

120V/60Hz

● ● ●
Food

In this guide eating choices are flagged with price indicators, based on the cost of an average main course from the dinner menu. For details on Canadian food, wine and microbrews, see p323.

EATING PRICE INDICATORS	
$	up to $12
$$	from $12 to $25
$$$	more than $25

● ● ●
Gay & Lesbian Travelers

Canada is tolerant when it comes to gays and lesbians, though this outlook is more common in the big cities than in rural areas. Same-sex marriage is legal throughout the country (Canada is one of only 10 nations worldwide that permits this).

Montréal, Toronto and Vancouver are by far Canada's gayest cities, each with a humming nightlife scene, publications and lots of associations and support groups. All have sizeable Pride celebrations, too, which attract big crowds. For more details, see the boxed texts, p240, p178 and p77.

Attitudes remain more conservative in the northern regions. Throughout Nunavut, and to a lesser extent in the Aboriginal communities of the Northwest Territories, there are some retrogressive attitudes toward homosexuality. The Yukon, in contrast, is more like British Columbia, with a live-and-let-live West Coast attitude.

The following are good resources for gay travel; they include Canadian information, though not all are exclusive to the region.

ℹ The Chain Gang

BUDGET

Days Inn (📞 800-329-7466; www.daysinn.com)

Econo Lodge (📞 877-424-6423; www.econolodge.com)

Super 8 (📞 800-800-8000; www.super8.com)

MIDRANGE

Best Western (📞 800-780-7234; www.bestwestern.com)

Clarion Hotel (📞 877-424-6423; www.clarionhotel.com)

Comfort Inn (📞 877-424-6423; www.comfortinn.com)

Fairfield Inn (📞 800-228-2800; www.fairfieldinn.com)

Hampton Inn (📞 800-426-7866; www.hamptoninn.com)

Holiday Inn (📞 888-465-4329; www.holidayinn.com)

Howard Johnson (📞 800-446-4656; www.hojo.com)

Quality Inn & Suites (📞 877-424-6423; www.qualityinn.com)

Travelodge/Thriftlodge (📞 800-578-7878; www.travelodge.com)

TOP END

Delta (📞 877-814-7706; www.deltahotels.com)

Fairmont (📞 800-257-7544; www.fairmont.com)

Hilton (📞 800-445-8667; www.hilton.com)

Hyatt (📞 888-591-1234; www.hyatt.com)

Marriott (📞 888-236-2427; www.marriott.com)

Radisson (📞 888-201-1718; www.radisson.com)

Ramada (📞 800-272-6232; www.ramada.com)

Sheraton (📞 800-325-3535; www.sheraton.com)

Westin (📞 800-937-8461; www.westin.com)

Damron (www.damron.com) Publishes several travel guides, including *Men's Travel Guide*, *Women's Traveller* and *Damron Accommodations*; gay-friendly tour operators are listed on the website, too.

Gay Canada (www.gaycanada.com) Search by province or city for queer-friendly businesses and resources.

Gay Travel News (www.gaytravelnews.com) Website listing gay-friendly destinations and hotels.

Out Traveler (www.outtraveler.com) Gay travel magazine.

Purple Roofs (www.purpleroofs.com) Website listing queer accommodations, travel agencies and tours worldwide.

Queer Canada (www.queercanada.ca) A general resource.

Xtra (www.xtra.ca) Source for gay and lesbian news nationwide.

Health

BEFORE YOU GO

INSURANCE

Canada offers some of the finest healthcare in the world. The problem is that, unless you are a Canadian citizen, it can be prohibitively expensive. It's essential to purchase travel-health insurance if your regular policy doesn't cover you when you're abroad. Check out www.lonelyplanet

.com/travel_services for insurance information.

Bring medications you may need clearly labeled in their original containers. A signed, dated letter from your physician that describes your medical conditions and medications, including generic names, is also a good idea.

AVAILABILITY & COST OF HEALTH CARE

Medical services are widely available. For emergencies, the best bet is to find the nearest hospital and go to its emergency room. If the problem isn't urgent, call a nearby hospital and ask for a referral to a local physician, which is usually cheaper than a trip to the emergency room (where costs can be $500 or so before any treatment).

Pharmacies are abundant, but prescriptions can be expensive without insurance. However, US citizens may find Canadian prescription drugs to be cheaper than drugs at home. You're allowed to take out a 90-day supply for personal use (though know it's technically illegal to bring them into the USA, but overlooked for individuals).

RECOMMENDED VACCINATIONS

No special vaccines are required or recommended for travel to Canada. All travelers should be up to date on routine immunizations, listed below.

MEDICAL CHECKLIST

o acetaminophen (eg Tylenol) or aspirin

o anti-inflammatory drugs (eg ibuprofen)

o antihistamines (for hay fever and allergic reactions)

o antibacterial ointment (eg Neosporin) for cuts and abrasions

o steroid cream or cortisone (for poison ivy and other allergic rashes)

o bandages, gauze, gauze rolls

o adhesive or paper tape

o safety pins, tweezers

o thermometer

o DEET-containing insect repellent for the skin

o permethrin-containing insect spray for clothing, tents and bed nets

o sunblock

o motion-sickness medication

WEBSITES

For Canada

Public Health Agency of Canada (www.publichealth .gc.ca)
General resources:

MD Travel Health (www .mdtravelhealth.com)

World Health Organization (www.who.int)

Other Travel Health Websites

Australia (www.smart traveller.gov.au)

UK (www.nhs.gov/ healthcareabroad)

USA (www.cdc.gov/travel/)

INFECTIOUS DISEASES

Most are acquired by mosquito or tick bites, or environmental exposure. The **Public Health Agency of Canada** (www.publichealth. gc.ca) has details on all listed below.

Giardiasis Intestinal infection. Avoid drinking

Recommended Vaccinations

VACCINE	RECOMMENDED FOR	DOSAGE	SIDE EFFECTS
tetanus-diphtheria	all travelers who haven't had booster within 10 years	one dose lasts 10 years	soreness at injection site
measles	travelers born after 1956 who've had only one measles vaccination	one dose	fever, rash, joint pains, allergic reactions
chickenpox	travelers who've never had chickenpox	two doses one month apart	fever, mild case of chickenpox
influenza	all travelers during flu season (November through March)	one dose	soreness at the injection site, fever

directly from lakes, ponds, streams and rivers.

Lyme Disease Occurs mostly in southern Canada. Transmitted by deer ticks in late spring and summer. Perform a tick check after you've been outdoors.

Severe Acute Respiratory Syndrome (SARS) At the time of writing, SARS is not a problem in Canada.

West Nile Virus Mosquito-transmitted in late summer and early fall. Prevent by keeping covered (wear long sleeves, long pants, hats, and shoes rather than sandals) and apply a good insect repellent, preferably one containing DEET, to exposed skin and clothing.

ENVIRONMENTAL HAZARDS

Cold exposure This can be a significant problem, especially in the northern regions. Keep all body surfaces covered, including the head and neck. Watch out for the 'Umbles' – stumbles, mumbles, fumbles and grumbles – which are signs of impending hypothermia.

Heat exhaustion Dehydration is the main contributor. Symptoms include feeling weak, headache, nausea and sweaty skin. Lay the victim flat with their legs raised, apply cool, wet cloths to the skin, and rehydrate.

Insurance

See p346 for health insurance and p359 for car insurance.

TRAVEL INSURANCE

Make sure you have adequate travel insurance, whatever the length of your trip. At a minimum, you need coverage for medical emergencies and treatment, including hospital stays and an emergency flight home. Medical treatment for non-Canadians is very expensive.

Also consider insurance for luggage theft or loss. If you already have a home-owners or renters policy, check what it will cover and only get supplemental insurance to protect against the rest. If you have prepaid a large portion of your vacation, trip cancellation insurance is worthwhile.

Worldwide travel insurance is available at www.lonely planet.com/travel_services. You can buy, extend and claim online at anytime – even if you're already on the road. Also check the following providers.

Insure.com (www.insure.com)

Travel Guard (www.travel guard.com)

Travelex (www.travelex.com)

Internet Access

It's easy to find internet access. Libraries, schools and community agencies in practically every town provide free high-speed internet terminals for public use, travelers included. The only down-sides are that usage time is limited (usually 30 minutes), facilities have erratic hours and you may not be able to upload photos (it depends on

the facility). The government's **Community Access Program** (C@P) provides the services.

Internet cafes are limited to the main tourist areas, and access generally costs $3 to $4 per hour.

Wi-fi is widely available. Most lodgings have it (in-room, with good speed), as do many urban coffee shops and bars. We've identified sleeping, eating and drinking listings that have wi-fi with a 🛜. We've denoted lodgings that offer internet terminals for guest use with a @.

Check the regional Information sections throughout the book for suggested facilities where you can go online.

Legal Matters

POLICE

If you're arrested or charged with an offense, you have the right to keep your mouth shut and to hire any lawyer you wish (contact your embassy for a referral, if necessary). If you cannot afford one, ask to be represented by public counsel. There is a presumption of innocence.

DRUGS & ALCOHOL

The blood-alcohol limit is 0.08% and driving cars, motorcycles, boats and snowmobiles while drunk is a criminal offense. If you are caught, you may face stiff fines, license suspension and other nasty consequences.

Consuming alcohol anywhere other than at a residence or licensed premises is also a no-no,

Legal Age

○ Driving a car: 16

○ Smoking tobacco: 18 (19 in British Columbia, Ontario and the Atlantic provinces)

○ Voting in an election: 18

○ Drinking alcoholic beverages: 19 (18 in Alberta, Manitoba and Québec)

which puts parks, beaches and the rest of the great outdoors off limits, at least officially.

Avoid illegal drugs, as penalties may entail heavy fines, possible jail time and a criminal record. The only exception is the use of marijuana for medical purposes, which became legal in 2001. Meanwhile, the decriminalization of pot possession for personal use remains a subject of ongoing public and government debate.

OTHER MATTERS

Abortion is legal.

Travelers should note that they can be prosecuted under the law of their home country regarding age of consent, even when abroad.

●●●

Money

All prices quoted in this book are in Canadian dollars ($), unless stated otherwise.

Canadian coins come in 1¢ (penny), 5¢ (nickel), 10¢ (dime), 25¢ (quarter), $1 (loonie) and $2 (toonie or twoonie) denominations. The gold-colored loonie features the loon, a common Canadian water bird, while the two-toned toonie is decorated with a polar bear.

Paper currency comes in $5 (blue), $10 (purple), $20 (green) and $50 (red) denominations. The $100 (brown) and larger bills are less common, and are tough to change.

The Canadian dollar has seen fluctuations over the last decade, though since 2007 it has tracked quite closely to the US dollar.

For changing money in the larger cities, currency exchange offices may offer better conditions than banks.

See p49 for exchange rates and costs.

ATMS

Many grocery and convenience stores, airports, and bus, train and ferry stations have ATMs. Most are linked to international networks, the most common being Cirrus, Plus, Star and Maestro.

Most ATMs also spit out cash if you use a major credit card. This method tends to be more expensive because, in addition to a service fee, you'll be charged interest immediately (in other words, there's no interest-free period as with purchases). For exact fees, check with your own bank or credit card company.

Visitors heading to Canada's more remote regions (such as in Newfoundland) won't find an abundance of ATMs, so it is wise to cash up beforehand.

Scotiabank, common throughout Canada, is part of the Global ATM Alliance. If your home bank is a member, fees may be less if you withdraw from Scotiabank ATMs.

CASH

Most Canadians don't carry large amounts of cash for everyday use, relying instead on credit and debit cards. Still, carrying some cash, say $100 or less, comes in handy when making small purchases. In some cases, cash is necessary to pay for rural B&Bs and shuttle vans; inquire in advance to avoid surprises. Shops and businesses rarely accept personal checks.

CREDIT CARDS

Major credit cards such as MasterCard, Visa and American Express are widely accepted in Canada, except in remote, rural communities where cash is king. You'll find it difficult or impossible to rent a car, book a room or order tickets over the phone without having a piece of plastic. Note that some credit-card companies charge a 'transaction fee' (around 3% of whatever you purchased); check with your provider to avoid surprises.

For lost or stolen cards, these numbers operate 24 hours:

American Express (☏ 866-296-5198; www.american express.com)

MasterCard (☏ 800-307-7309; www.mastercard.com)

Visa (☏ 800-847-2911; www .visa.com)

TAXES & REFUNDS

Canada's federal goods and services tax (GST), which is

variously known as the 'gouge and screw' or 'grab and steal' tax, adds 5% to just about every transaction. Most provinces also charge a provincial sales tax (PST) on top of it. Several provinces have combined the GST and PST into a harmonized sales tax (HST). Whatever the methodology, expect to pay 10% to 15% in all.

Unless otherwise stated, taxes are not included in prices given in this book.

TAX RATES (GST + PST)	
Alberta	5%
British Columbia*	12%
Manitoba	12%
New Brunswick*	13%
Newfoundland*	13%
Nova Scotia*	15%
Ontario*	13%
PEI	15%
Québec	13.5%
Saskatchewan	10%
* has a combined HST	

You might be eligible for a rebate on some of these taxes. If you've booked your accommodations in conjunction with a rental car, plane ticket or other service (ie if it all appears on the same bill from a 'tour operator'), you should be eligible to get 50% of the tax refunded from your accommodations. Fill out the GST/HST Refund Application for Tour Packages form available from the **Canada Revenue Agency** (☎ 902-432-5608, 800-668-4748; www.cra-arc.gc.ca/E/pbg/gf/gst115).

TIPPING

Tipping in Canada is a standard practice.

- Restaurant waitstaff
  15% to 20% (though use your judgement if service has been unacceptable)

- Bar staff
  $1 per drink

- Hotel bellhop
  $1 to $2 per bag

- Hotel room cleaners
  $2 per day

- Taxis
  10% to 15%

TRAVELER'S CHECKS

Traveler's checks are becoming more and more obsolete in the age of ATMs. Traveler's checks issued in Canadian dollars are generally treated like cash by businesses. Traveler's checks in most other currencies must be exchanged for Canadian dollars at a bank or foreign-currency office. The most common issuers:

American Express (www.americanexpress.com)

MasterCard (www.mastercard.com)

Visa (www.visa.com)

Post

Canada's national postal service, **Canada Post/Postes Canada** (www.canadapost.ca), is neither quick nor cheap, but it is reliable. Stamps are available at post offices, drugstores, convenience stores and hotels.

Postcards or standard letters cost 57¢ within Canada, $1 to the USA and $1.70 to all other countries.

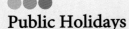

Public Holidays

Canada observes 10 national public holidays and more at the provincial level. Banks, schools and government offices close on these days. See p352 for info on unique Canadian celebrations.

NATIONAL HOLIDAYS

New Year's Day January 1

Good Friday March or April

Easter Monday March or April

Victoria Day Monday before May 25

Canada Day July 1; called Memorial Day in Newfoundland

Labour Day First Monday of September

Thanksgiving Second Monday of October

Remembrance Day November 11

Christmas Day December 25

Boxing Day December 26

PROVINCIAL HOLIDAYS

Some provinces also observe their local holidays, with Newfoundland leading the pack.

Family Day Third Monday of February in Alberta, Ontario, Saskatchewan and Manitoba; known as Louis Riel Day in Manitoba

St Patrick's Day Monday nearest March 17

Postal Abbreviations

PROVINCES & TERRITORIES	ABBREVIATIONS
Alberta	AB
British Columbia	BC
Manitoba	MB
New Brunswick	NB
Newfoundland & Labrador	NL
Northwest Territories	NT
Nova Scotia	NS
Nunavut	NU
Ontario	ON
Prince Edward Island	PE
Québec	QC
Saskatchewan	SK
Yukon Territory	YT

St George's Day Monday nearest April 23

National Day Monday nearest June 24 in Newfoundland; June 24 in Québec (aka St-Jean-Baptiste Day)

Orangemen's Day Monday nearest July 12 in Newfoundland

Civic Holiday First Monday of August everywhere *except* Newfoundland, PEI, Québec and Yukon Territory

Discovery Day Third Monday of August in Yukon Territory

SCHOOL HOLIDAYS

Kids break for summer holidays in late June and don't return to school until early September. University students get even more time off, usually from May to early or mid-September. Most people take their big annual vacation during these months.

Telephone

Canada's phone system is almost identical to the USA's.

DOMESTIC & INTERNATIONAL DIALING

Canadian phone numbers consist of a three-digit area code followed by a seven-digit local number. In many parts of Canada, you must dial all 10 digits preceded by 1, even if you're calling across the street. In other parts of the country, when you're calling within the same area code, you can dial the seven-digit number only, but this is slowly changing. The pay phone or phone book where you are should make it clear which system is used.

For direct international calls, dial 011 + country code + area code + local phone number. The country code for Canada is 1 (the

same as for the USA, although international rates still apply for all calls made between the two countries).

Toll-free numbers begin with 800, 877 or 866 and must be preceded by 1. Some of these numbers are good throughout Canada and the USA, others only work within Canada, and some work in just one province.

EMERGENCY NUMBERS

Dial 911. Note it is *not* the emergency number in the Northwest Territories or Nunavut.

CELL PHONES

Local SIM cards can be used in European and Australian phones. Other phones must be set to roaming

If you have a European, Australian or other type of unlocked GSM phone, buy a SIM card from local providers such as **Telus** (www.telus .com), **Rogers** (www.rogers .com) or **Bell** (www.bell.ca).

US residents can often upgrade their domestic cell phone plan to extend to Canada. **Verizon** (www .verizonwireless.com) provides good results.

Reception is poor in rural areas no matter who your service provider is.

PUBLIC PHONES

Coin-operated public pay phones are fairly plentiful. Local calls cost 25¢ (sometimes 35¢); many phones also accept prepaid phonecards and credit cards. Dialing the operator (0) or directory assistance (411 for local calls, 1 + area code + 555-1212 for long-distance calls) is free of charge from public phones;

Uniquely Canadian Celebrations

◦ **National Flag Day** (February 15) Commemorates the first time the maple-leaf flag was raised above Parliament Hill in Ottawa, at the stroke of noon on February 15, 1965.

◦ **Victoria Day** (late May) This day was established in 1845 to observe the birthday of Queen Victoria and now celebrates the birthday of the British sovereign who's still Canada's titular head of state. Victoria Day marks the official beginning of the summer season (which ends with Labour Day on the first Monday of September). Some communities hold fireworks.

◦ **National Aboriginal Day** (June 31) Created in 1996, it celebrates the contributions of Aboriginal peoples to Canada. Coinciding with the summer solstice, festivities are organized locally and may include traditional dancing, singing and drumming; storytelling; arts and crafts shows; canoe races; and lots more.

◦ **Canada Day** (July 1) Known as Dominion Day until 1982, Canada Day was created in 1869 to commemorate the creation of Canada two years earlier. All over the country, people celebrate with barbecues, parades, concerts and fireworks.

◦ **Thanksgiving Day** (mid-October) First celebrated in 1578 in what is now Newfoundland by explorer Martin Frobisher to give thanks for surviving his Atlantic crossing, Thanksgiving became an official Canadian holiday in 1872 to celebrate the recovery of the Prince of Wales from a long illness. These days, it's essentially a harvest festival involving a special family dinner of roast turkey and pumpkin, very much as it is practiced in the USA.

it may incur a charge from private phones.

PHONECARDS

Prepaid phonecards usually offer the best per-minute rates for long-distance and international calling. They come in denominations of $5, $10 or $20 and are widely sold in drugstores, supermarkets and convenience stores. Beware of cards with hidden charges such as 'activation fees' or a per-call connection fee. A surcharge ranging from 30¢ to 85¢ for calls made from public pay phones is common.

Time

Canada spans six of the world's 24 time zones. The Eastern zone in Newfoundland is unusual in that it's only 30 minutes different from the adjacent zone. This means that the time difference from coast to coast is 4½ hours.

Canada observes daylight saving time, which comes into effect on the second Sunday in March, when clocks are put forward one hour, and ends on the first Sunday in November. Saskatchewan and small pockets of Québec, Ontario and British Columbia are the only areas that do not switch to daylight saving time.

In Québec province especially, times for shop hours, train schedules, film screenings etc are usually indicated by the 24-hour clock.

Tourist Information

The **Canadian Tourism Commission** (www.canada.travel) is loaded with information, packages and links.

All provincial tourist offices maintain comprehensive websites packed with information helpful in planning your trip. Staff also field telephone inquiries and, on request, will mail out free maps and directories about accommodations, attractions and events. Some offices can also help with making hotel, tour or other reservations.

For detailed information about a specific area, contact the local tourist office, aka visitors center. Just about every city and town has at least a seasonal branch with helpful staff, racks of free pamphlets and books and maps for sale. Visitor center addresses are listed in the Information sections for individual destinations throughout this book.

PROVINCIAL TOURIST OFFICES

Newfoundland & Labrador Tourism (☏ 800-563-6353; www.newfoundlandlabrador .com)

Northwest Territories Tourism (☏ 800-661-0788; www.spectacularnwt.com)

Nunavut Tourism (☏ 866-686-2888; www.nunavuttourism .com)

Ontario Tourism (☏ 800-668-2746; www.ontariotravel .net)

Prince Edward Island Tourism (☏ 800-463-4734; www.peiplay.com)

Tourism British Columbia (☏ 800-435-5622; www .hellobc.com)

Tourism New Brunswick (☏ 800-561-0123; www .tourismnewbrunswick.ca)

Tourism Nova Scotia (☏ 800-565-0000; www .novascotia.com)

Tourism Saskatchewan (☏ 877-237-2273; www .sasktourism.com)

Tourisme Québec (☏ 877-266-5687; www.bonjourquebec .com)

Travel Alberta (☏ 800-252-3782; www.travelalberta.com)

Travel Manitoba (☏ 800-665-0040; www.travelmanitoba .com)

Yukon Department of Tourism (☏ 800-661-0494; www.travelyukon.com)

Travelers with Disabilities

Canada is making progress when it comes to easing the everyday challenges facing people with disabilities, especially the mobility impaired. Many public buildings, including museums, tourist offices, train stations, shopping malls and cinemas, have access ramps and/or lifts. Most public restrooms feature extra-wide stalls equipped with hand rails. Many pedestrian crossings have sloping curbs.

Newer and recently remodeled hotels, especially chain hotels, have rooms with extra-wide doors and spacious bathrooms.

Interpretive centers at national and provincial parks are usually accessible, and many parks have trails that can be navigated in wheelchairs.

Car-rental agencies offer hand-controlled vehicles and vans with wheelchair lifts at no additional charge, but you must reserve them well in advance. See p359 for a list of rental agencies.

For accessible air, bus, rail and ferry transportation check **Access to Travel** (www.accesstotravel.gc.ca), the federal government's website. In general, most transportation agencies can accommodate people with disabilities if you make your needs known when booking.

Other organizations specializing in the needs of travelers with disabilities:

Access-Able Travel Source (www.access-able.com) Lists accessible lodging, transport, attractions and equipment rental by province.

Canadian National Institute for the Blind (www.cnib.ca)

Canadian Paraplegic Association (www.canparaplegic.org) Has information about facilities for mobility-impaired travelers in Canada.

Mobility International (www.miusa.org) Advises travelers with disabilities on mobility issues and runs an educational exchange program.

Society for Accessible Travel & Hospitality (www .sath.org) Travelers with

Time Difference Between Cities

Vancouver	3pm
Montréal	6pm
New York City	6pm
Newfoundland	7:30pm
London	11pm

disabilities share tips and blogs.

Visas

For information about passport requirements, see p355.

Citizens of dozens of countries – including the USA, most Western European nations, Australia, New Zealand, Japan and South Korea – do not need visas to enter Canada for stays of up to 180 days. US permanent residents are also exempt. **Citizenship & Immigration Canada** (CIC; www.cic.gc.ca) has the details.

Nationals of other countries – including China, India and South Africa – must apply to the Canadian visa office in their home country for a temporary resident visa (TRV). A separate visa is required if you plan to study or work in Canada.

Single-entry TRVs ($75) are usually valid for a maximum stay of six months from the date of your arrival in Canada. Multiple-entry TRVs ($150) allow you to enter Canada from all other countries multiple times while the visa is valid (usually two or three years), provided no single stay exceeds six months.

VISITING THE USA

Admission requirements are subject to rapid change. The **US State Department** (www.travel.state.gov) has the latest information, or check with a US consulate in your home country.

Under the US visa-waiver program, visas are not required for citizens of 36 countries – including most EU members, Australia and New Zealand – for visits of up to 90 days (no extensions allowed), as long as you can present a machine-readable passport and are approved under the **Electronic System for Travel Authorization** (ESTA; www.cbp.gov/esta). Note you must register at least 72 hours before arrival, and there's a $14 fee for processing and authorization.

Canadians do not need visas, though they do need a passport or document approved by the **Western Hemisphere Travel Initiative** (www.getyouhome .gov). Citizens of all other countries need to apply for a US visa in their home country before arriving in Canada.

All foreign visitors (except Canadians) must pay a US$6 'processing fee' when entering at land borders. Note that you don't need a Canadian multiple-entry TRV for repeated entries into Canada from the USA, unless you have visited a third country.

Women Travelers

Canada is generally a safe place for women to travel, even alone and even in the cities. Simply use the same common sense as you would at home.

In bars and nightclubs, solo women are likely to attract a lot of attention, but if you don't want company, most men will respect a firm 'no thank you.' If you feel threatened, protesting loudly will often make the offender slink away – or will at least spur other people to come to your defense. Note that carrying mace or pepper spray is illegal in Canada.

Physical attack is unlikely, but if you are assaulted, call the police immediately (☎911 except in the Northwest Territories and Nunavut) or contact a rape crisis center. A complete list of these is available from the **Canadian Association of Sexual Assault Centres** (☎604-876-2622; www.casac.ca).

Hotlines in some of the major cities:

Calgary (☎403-237-5888)

Halifax (☎902-425-0122)

Montréal (☎514-934-4504)

Toronto (☎416-597-8808)

Vancouver (☎604-255-6344)

Resources for women travelers include the following:

Her Own Way (www.voyage .gc.ca/publications/woman -guide_voyager-feminin -eng.asp) Published by the Canadian government for Canadian travelers, but it contains a great deal of general advice.

Journeywoman (www .journeywoman.com)

Transport

Getting There & Away

Flights, tours and rail tickets can be booked online at www.lonelyplanet.com/travel_services.

ENTERING THE COUNTRY

Entering Canada is pretty straightforward. First, you will have to show your passport (and your visa if you need one; see p354). The border officer will ask you a few questions about the purpose and length of your visit. After that, you'll go through customs. See **Going to Canada** (www.goingtocanada.gc.ca) for details.

US citizens at land and sea borders have other options besides using a passport, such as an enhanced driver's license or passport card. See the **Western Hemisphere Travel Initiative** (www.getyouhome.gov) for approved identification documents.

Note that questioning may be more intense at land border crossings and your car may be searched.

For updates (particularly regarding land-border crossing rules), check the websites for the **US State Department** (www.travel.state.gov) and **Citizenship & Immigration Canada** (www.cic.gc.ca).

 AIR

AIRPORTS

Toronto is far and away the busiest airport, followed by Vancouver. The international gateways you're most likely to arrive at include the following:

Calgary (YYC; www.calgaryairport.com)

Edmonton (YEG; www.flyeia.com)

Halifax (YHZ; www.hiaa.ca)

Montréal (Trudeau; YUL; www.admtl.com)

Ottawa (YOW; www.ottawa-airport.ca)

St John's (YYT; www.stjohnsairport.com)

Toronto (Pearson; YYZ; www.gtaa.com)

Vancouver (YVR; www.yvr.ca)

Winnipeg (YWG; www.waa.ca)

 LAND

BORDER CROSSINGS

There are 22 official border crossings along the Canada–US border, from British Columbia to New Brunswick.

The website of the **Canadian Border Services Agency** (www.cbsa-asfc.gc.ca/general/times/menu-e.html) shows current wait times at each. You can also access it via the government's wireless portal (www.wap.gc.ca) or on Twitter (@CBSA_BWT).

In general, waits rarely exceed 30 minutes, except during the peak summer season, and on Friday and Sunday afternoons, especially on holiday weekends, when you might get stuck at the border for several hours. Some entry points are especially busy:

○ Windsor, Ontario, to Detroit, Michigan

○ Fort Erie, Ontario, to Buffalo, New York State

○ Niagara Falls, Ontario, to Niagara Falls, New York State

○ Québec to Rouse's Point/Champlain, New York State

○ Surrey, British Columbia, to Blaine, Washington State

Other border points tend to be quieter, sometimes so quiet that the officers have nothing to do except tear apart your luggage. When approaching the border, turn off any music, take off your sunglasses and be exceptionally polite. Most officers do not welcome casual conversation, jokes or clever remarks.

When returning to the USA, check the website for the **US Department for Homeland Security** (http://apps.cbp.gov/bwt) for border wait times.

All foreign visitors (except Canadians) must pay a $6 'processing fee' when entering the USA by land; payment by credit card is not accepted.

For information on documents needed to enter Canada, see p355.

BUS ROUTE	DURATION	FREQUENCY	FARE (US$)
Boston–Montréal	from 7hr	up to 8 daily	105
Detroit–Toronto	from 5½hr	up to 5 daily	73
New York–Montréal	10hr	up to 2 daily	84
Seattle–Vancouver	4hr	up to 5 daily	38

BUS

Greyhound (www.greyhound .com) and its Canadian equivalent, **Greyhound Canada** (www.greyhound.ca), operate the largest bus network in North America. There are direct connections between main cities in the USA and Canada, but you usually have to transfer to a different bus at the border (it takes a good hour for all passengers to clear customs/immigration). Most international buses have free wi-fi. See the table for sample fares and durations.

Other notable international bus companies (with free wi-fi) include the following:

Megabus (www.megabus .com) Runs between Toronto and New York City, and Toronto and Philadelphia; usually cheaper than Greyhound. Tickets can only be purchased online.

Quick Coach (www.quick coach.com) Runs between Seattle and Vancouver; typically a bit quicker than Greyhound.

CAR & MOTORCYCLE

The highway system of the USA connects directly with the Canadian highway system at numerous points along the border. These Canadian highways then meet up with the east–west Trans-Canada Hwy further north. Between the Yukon and Alaska, the main routes are the Alaska, Klondike and Haines Hwys.

If you're driving into Canada, you'll need the vehicle's registration papers, proof of liability insurance and your home driver's license. Cars rented in the USA can usually be driven into Canada and back, but make sure your rental agreement says so in case you are questioned by border officials. If you're driving a car registered in someone else's name, bring a letter from the owner authorizing use of the vehicle in Canada. For details about driving within Canada, see p359.

TRAIN

Amtrak (www.amtrak.com) and **VIA Rail Canada** (www .viarail.ca) run three routes between the USA and Canada (see table, p357), two in the east and one in the west. Customs inspections happen at the border, not upon boarding.

 SEA

FERRY

Various ferry services on the coasts connect the US and Canada.

Bar Harbor, Maine–Yarmouth, NS Service halted in 2010 but due to start again in 2011; check Bay Ferries (www.nfl-bay.com).

Seattle–Victoria, BC Victoria Clipper (www.clipper vacations.com); see p96.

Getting Around

 AIR

AIRLINES IN CANADA

Air Canada operates the largest domestic-flight network serving some 150 destinations together with its regional subsidiary, Air Canada Jazz.

Low-cost, low-frills carriers are chasing Air Canada's wings. The biggest is Calgary-based WestJet. In response, Air Canada entered the discount game by introducing inexpensive 'Tango' fares, which sometimes undercut even the discount carriers, on its regular flights.

The Canadian aviation arena also includes many independent regional and local airlines, which tend to focus on small, often-remote regions, mostly in the north. Depending on the destination, fares in such noncompetitive markets can be high.

Air Canada (888-247-2262; www.aircanada.com) Nationwide flights.

Air Canada Jazz (888-247-2262; www.aircanada.com) Regional flights throughout western and eastern Canada.

Air North (📞 in Canada 867-668-2228, in USA 800-661-0407; www.flyairnorth.com) Flies from the Yukon to British Columbia, Alberta, Northwest Territories and Alaska.

Calm Air (📞 204-778-6471, 800-839-2256; www.calmair.com) Flights throughout Manitoba, including Churchill.

Harbour Air (📞 800-665-0212; www.harbour-air.com) Seaplane service from the city of Vancouver to Vancouver Island, Gulf Islands and the Sunshine Coast.

Hawkair (📞 866-429-5247; www.hawkair.ca) Serves northern British Columbia from Vancouver and Victoria.

Kivalliq Air (📞 204-888-5619, 877-855-1500; www.kivalliqair.com) Flies from Winnipeg to Churchill and Nunavut.

Pacific Coastal Airlines (📞 800-663-2872; www.pacific-coastal.com) Vancouver-based airline with service to many British Columbia locales.

Porter Airlines (📞 888-619-8622; www.flyporter.com) Flies turboprop planes from Montréal, Halifax and Ottawa to Toronto's quicker, more convenient City Centre Airport downtown.

Provincial Airlines (📞 800-563-2800; www.provincialairlines.com) St John's–based airline with service throughout Newfoundland and to Labrador.

Seair Seaplanes (📞 604-273-8900, 800-447-3247; www.seairseaplanes.com) Flies from Vancouver to Nanaimo and the Southern Gulf Islands in British Columbia.

West Coast Air (📞 800-347-2222; www.westcoastair.com) Seaplane service from Vancouver city to Vancouver Island and the Sunshine Coast.

WestJet (📞 800-538-5696, 888-937-8538; www.westjet.com) Calgary-based low-cost carrier serving destinations throughout Canada.

AIR PASSES

Star Alliance (www.staralliance.com) members Air Canada, Continental Airlines, United Airlines and US Airways have teamed up to offer the North American Airpass, which is available to anyone not residing in the USA, Canada, Mexico, Bermuda or the Caribbean. It's sold only in conjunction with an international flight operated by any Star Alliance–member airline. You can buy as few as three coupons (US$399) or as many as 10 (US$1099).

🚲 BICYCLE

Much of Canada is great for cycling. Long-distance trips can be done entirely on quiet back roads, and many cities (including Edmonton, Montréal, Ottawa, Toronto and Vancouver) have designated bike routes.

Cyclists must follow the same rules of the road as vehicles, but don't expect drivers to always respect your right of way.

Helmets are mandatory for all cyclists in British Columbia, New Brunswick, Prince Edward Island and Nova Scotia, as well as for anyone under 18 in Alberta and Ontario.

The **Better World Club** (📞 866-238-1137; www.betterworldclub.com) provides emergency roadside assistance. Membership costs $40 per year, plus a $12 enrollment fee, and entitles you to two free pick-ups, and transport to the nearest repair shop, or home, within a 50km radius of where you're picked up.

For information on Canada's sweetest mountain biking and cycling trails, see p330.

TRANSPORTATION

By air: most airlines will carry bikes as checked luggage without charge on international flights, as long as they're in a box. On domestic flights they usually charge

TRAIN ROUTE	DURATION	FREQUENCY	FARE (US$)
New York–Toronto (*Maple Leaf*)	14hr	1 daily	125
New York–Montréal (*Adirondack*)	11hr	1 daily	62
Seattle–Vancouver (*Cascades*)	4hr	2 daily	44

between $30 and $65. Always check details before you buy the ticket.

By bus: you must ship your bike as freight on Greyhound Canada. In addition to a bike box ($10), you'll be charged according to the weight of the bike, plus an oversize charge ($30) and GST. Bikes only travel on the same bus as the passenger if there's enough space. To ensure that yours arrives at the same time as (or before) you do, ship it a day early.

By train: VIA Rail will transport your bicycle for $20, but only on trains offering checked-baggage service (which includes all long-distance and many regional trains).

RENTAL

Outfitters renting bicycles exist in most tourist towns; some are listed throughout this book.

Rentals cost around $15 per day for touring bikes and $25 per day for mountain bikes. The price usually includes a helmet and lock. Most companies require a security deposit of $20 to $200.

 BOAT

Ferry services are extensive, especially throughout the Atlantic provinces and in British Columbia. For schedule information, see the Getting There & Away and Getting Around sections of the destination chapters.

Walk-ons and cyclists should be able to get aboard at any time, but call ahead for vehicle reservations or if you require a cabin berth. This is especially important during summer peak season and holidays. Main operators include the following:

Bay Ferries (☎ 888-249-7245; www.bayferries.com) Year-round service between St John, New Brunswick, and Digby, Nova Scotia.

BC Ferries (☎ 250-386-3431, 888-223-3779; www.bcferries.com) Huge passenger-ferry systems with 25 routes and 46 ports of call, including Vancouver Island, the Gulf Islands, the Sechelt Peninsula along the Sunshine Coast and the islands of Haida Gwaii, all in British Columbia.

Coastal Transport (☎ 506-662-3724; www.coastal .transport.ca) Ferry from Blacks Harbour to Grand Manan in the Fundy Isles, New Brunswick.

CTMA Ferries (☎ 418-986-3278, 888-986-3278; www .ctma.ca) Daily ferries to Québec's Îles de la Madeleine from Souris, Prince Edward Island.

Labrador Marine (☎ 709-535-0810, 866-535-2567; www .labradormarine.com) Connects Newfoundland to Labrador.

Marine Atlantic (☎ 800-341-7981; www.marine-atlantic .ca) Connects Port aux Basques and Argentia in Newfoundland with North Sydney, Nova Scotia.

Northumberland Ferries (☎ 902-566-3838, 888-249-7245; www.peiferry.com) Connects Wood Islands, Prince Edward Island, and Caribou, Nova Scotia.

 BUS

Greyhound Canada (☎ 800-661-8747; www.grey hound.ca) is the king, plowing along an extensive network in central and western Canada. In eastern Canada, it is part of an alliance of regional carriers, including Orléans Express in Québec and Acadian Lines in the Maritime provinces. You can usually transfer from one carrier to another on a single ticket.

Buses are generally clean, comfortable and reliable. Amenities may include onboard toilets, air-con (bring a sweater), reclining seats and onboard movies. Smoking is not permitted. On long journeys, buses make meal stops every few hours, usually at highway service stations.

Acadian Lines (☎ 800-567-5151; www.acadianbus .com) Service throughout New Brunswick, Nova Scotia and Prince Edward Island.

Coach Canada (☎ 800-461-7661; www.coachcanada.com) Scheduled service within Ontario and from Toronto to Montréal.

Intercar (☎ 888-861-4592; www.intercar.qc.ca) Connects Québec City, Montréal and Tadoussac, among other towns in Québec.

Malaspina Coach Lines (☎ 604-886-7742, 877-227-8287; www.malaspinacoach .com) Service between Vancouver and the Sunshine Coast in British Columbia.

Orléans Express (☎ 888-999-3977; www.orleansexpress

.com) Service to eastern Québec.

....

Pacific Coach Lines
(📞 250-385-4411, 800-661-1725; www.pacificcoach.com) Service between Vancouver Island and mainland British Columbia.

🚗 CAR & MOTORCYCLE

AUTOMOBILE ASSOCIATIONS

Auto-club membership is a handy thing to have in Canada. The **Canadian Automobile Association** (CAA; 📞 800-268-3750; www.caa.ca) offers services, including 24-hour emergency roadside assistance, to members of international affiliates such as AAA in the USA, AA in the UK and ADAC in Germany. The club also offers trip-planning advice, free maps, travel-agency services and a range of discounts on hotels, car rentals etc.

The **Better World Club** (📞 866-238-1137; www.betterworldclub.com), which donates 1% of its revenue to environmental cleanups, has emerged as an alternative. It offers service throughout the USA and Canada, and also has a roadside-assistance program for bicycles.

BRING YOUR OWN VEHICLE

There's minimal hassle driving into Canada from the USA as long as you have your vehicle's registration papers, proof of liability insurance and your home driver's license.

DRIVER'S LICENSE

In most provinces visitors can legally drive for up to three months with their home driver's license. In some, such as British Columbia, this is extended to six months.

If you're spending considerable time in Canada, think about getting an International Driving Permit (IDP), which is valid for one year. Your automobile association at home can issue one for a small fee. Always carry your home license together with the IDP.

FUEL

Gas is sold in liters. At the time of writing, the average for midgrade fuel was $1.08 per liter (about C$4.10 per US gallon). Prices are higher in remote areas, with Yellowknife usually setting the national record; drivers in Calgary typically pay the least for gas.

Fuel prices in Canada are usually higher than in the USA, so fill up south of the border.

INSURANCE

Canadian law requires liability insurance for all vehicles, to cover you for damage caused to property and people.

The minimum requirement is $200,000 in all provinces except Québec, where it is $50,000.

US citizens traveling to Canada in their own car should ask their insurance company for a Nonresident Interprovince Motor Vehicle Liability Insurance Card (commonly known as a 'yellow card'), which is accepted as evidence of financial responsibility anywhere in Canada. Although not mandatory, it may come in handy in an accident.

Car-rental agencies offer liability insurance. Collision Damage Waivers (CDW) reduce or eliminate the amount you'll have to reimburse the rental company if there's damage to the car itself. Some credit cards cover CDW for a certain rental period, if you use the card to pay for the rental, and decline the policy offered by the rental company. Always check with your card issuer to see what coverage it offers in Canada.

Personal accident insurance (PAI) covers you and any passengers for medical costs incurred as a result of an accident. If your travel insurance or your health-insurance policy at home does this as well (and most do, but check), then this is one expense you can do without.

RENTAL
Car

To rent a car in Canada you generally need to:

○ be at least 25 years old

○ hold a valid driver's license (an international one may be required if you're not from an English- or French-speaking country; see Driver's License, earlier)

○ have a major credit card

Some companies will rent to drivers between the ages of 21 and 24 for an additional charge.

You should be able to get an economy-sized vehicle for about $35 to $65 per day. Child safety seats are compulsory (reserve them when you book) and cost about $8 per day.

Major international car-rental companies usually have branches at airports, train stations and in city centers.

Avis (📞 800-437-0358; www.avis.com)

Budget (📞 800-268-8900; www.budget.com)

Dollar (📞 800-800-4000; www.dollar.com)

Enterprise(📞 800-736-8222; www.enterprise.com)

Hertz (📞 800-263-0600; www.hertz.com)

National (📞 800-227-7368; www.nationalcar.com)

Thrifty (📞 800-847-4389; www.thrifty.com)

Practicar (📞 800-327-0116; www.practicar.ca), formerly known as Rent a Wreck, often has lower rates. It's also affiliated with Backpackers Hotels Canada and Hostelling International.

In Canada, on-the-spot rentals often are more expensive than pre-booked packages (ie rental cars booked with your flight).

Motorcycle

Several companies offer motorcycle rentals and tours. A Harley Heritage Softail Classic costs about $210 per day, including liability insurance and 200km mileage. Some companies have minimum rental periods, which can be as much as seven days. Riding a hog is especially popular in British Columbia.

Coastline Motorcycle Tours & Rentals (📞 250-335-1837, 866-338-0344; www.coastlinemc.com) Operates out of Victoria and Vancouver in British Columbia.

McScoots Motorcycle & Scooter Rentals (📞 250-763-4668; www.mcscoots.com) Big selection of Harleys, also operates motorcycle tours, based in Kelowna, British Columbia.

Open Road Adventure (📞 250-494-5409; www.canadamotorcyclerentals.com) Rentals and tours out of Summerland, near Kelowna, British Columbia.

Recreational Vehicles

The RV market is biggest in the west, with specialized agencies in Calgary, Edmonton, Whitehorse and Vancouver. For summer travel, book as early as possible. The base cost is roughly $160 to $265 per day in high season for midsized vehicles, although insurance, fees and taxes add a hefty chunk. Diesel-fueled RVs have considerably lower running costs.

Some recommended companies:

Canadream Campers (📞 403-291-1000, 800-461-7368; www.canadream.com) Based in Calgary with rentals (including one-ways) in eight cities, including Vancouver, Whitehorse, Toronto and Halifax.

Go West Campers (📞 800-661-8813; www.go-west.com) Rents out of Calgary and Coquitlam, British Columbia (near Vancouver).

ROAD CONDITIONS & HAZARDS

Road conditions are generally good, but keep in mind:

● Fierce winters can leave potholes the size of landmine craters. Be prepared to swerve. Winter travel in general can be hazardous due to heavy snow and ice, which may cause roads and bridges to close periodically. **Transport Canada** (📞 800-387-4999; www.tc.gc.ca/road) provides links to road conditions and construction zones for each province.

● If you're driving in winter or in remote areas, make sure your vehicle is equipped with four-seasonal radial or snow tires, and emergency supplies in case you're stranded.

● Distances between services can be long in sparsely populated areas such as the Yukon, Newfoundland or northern Québec, so keep your gas topped up whenever possible.

● Moose, deer and elk are common on rural roadways, especially at night. There's no contest between a 534kg bull moose and a Subaru, so keep your eyes peeled.

ROAD RULES

● Canadians drive on the right-hand side of the road.

● Seat belt use is compulsory. Children under 18kg must be strapped in child-booster seats, except infants, who must be in a rear-facing safety seat.

● Motorcyclists must wear helmets and drive with their headlights on.

- Distances and speed limits are posted in kilometers. The speed limit is generally:
  - 40km/h to 50km/h in cities
  - 90km/h to 110km/h outside town
- Slow down to 60km/h when passing emergency vehicles (such as police cars and ambulances) stopped on the roadside with their lights flashing.
- Turning right at red lights after coming to a full stop is permitted in all provinces (except where road signs prohibit it, and on the island of Montréal, where it's always a no-no). There's a national propensity for running red lights, however, so don't take your 'right of way' at intersections for granted.
- Driving while using a hand-held cell phone is illegal in British Columbia, Newfoundland, Nova Scotia, Ontario, PEI, Québec and Saskatchewan.
- Radar detectors are not allowed in most of Canada (Alberta, British Columbia and Saskatchewan are the exceptions). If you're caught driving with a radar detector, even one that isn't being operated, you could receive a fine of $1000 and your device may be confiscated.
- The blood-alcohol limit for drivers is 0.08%. Driving while drunk is a criminal offense.

LOCAL TRANSPORTATION

For fares and other details, see Getting Around under city and town listings throughout this book.

BICYCLE

Cycling is a popular means of getting around during the warmer months, and many cities have hundreds of kilometers of dedicated bike paths. Bicycles typically can be taken on public transportation (although some cities have restrictions during peak travel times). All the major cities rent bikes.

BUS

Buses are the most ubiquitous form of public transportation, and practically all towns have their own systems. Most are commuter oriented, and offer only limited or no services in the evenings and on weekends.

TRAIN

Both Toronto and Montréal have subway systems. Vancouver's version is mostly an above-ground monorail. Calgary, Edmonton and Ottawa have efficient light rail systems. Route maps are posted in all stations.

TAXI

Most of the main cities have taxis. They are usually metered, with a flag-fall fee of roughly $2.70 and a per-kilometer charge around $1.75. Drivers expect a tip of between 10% and 15%. Taxis can be flagged down or ordered by phone.

TOURS

Tour companies are another way to get around this great big country. We've listed some in the Tours sections for destinations throughout this book. Reliable companies operating in multiple provinces across Canada include the following:

Arctic Odysseys (✆ 206-325-1977, 800-574-3021; www.arcticodysseys.com) Experience Arctic Canada close up on tours chasing the northern lights in the Northwest Territories, heli-skiing on Baffin Island or polar-bear spotting on Hudson Bay.

Backroads (✆ 510-527-1555, 800-462-2848; www.backroads.com) Guided cycling, walking and/or paddling tours in the Rockies, Nova Scotia and Québec.

Moose Travel Network (✆ in eastern Canada 416-504-7514, 888-816-6673, in western Canada 604-777-9905, 888-244-6673; www.moosenetwork.com) Operates backpacker-type tours in small buses throughout British Columbia, Alberta, Québec, Ontario, Nova Scotia and PEI. The two- to 19-day trips hit Whistler, Banff, Jasper, Calgary, Toronto, Montréal and Halifax, among others, and you can jump on or off anywhere along the route. In winter, various skiing and snowboarding packages are available.

Nahanni River Adventures (✆ 867-668-3180, 800-297-6927; www.nahanni.com) Operates rafting and kayaking expeditions in the Yukon, British Columbia and Alaska, including trips on the Firth, Alsek and Babine Rivers, as well as down the Tatshenshini-Alsek watershed in north BC.

Road Scholar (✆ 800-454-5768; www.roadscholar.org) This is the new name for the programs run by Elderhostel. The nonprofit organization offers study tours in nearly all provinces for active people aged over 55, including train trips, cruises, and bus and walking tours.

Routes to Learning

(☎ 613-530-2222, 866-745-1690; www.routestolearning .ca) From bird-watching in the Rockies to trekking around Québec City to walking in the footsteps of Vikings on Newfoundland, this nonprofit group has dozens of educational tours throughout Canada.

Salty Bear Adventure Tours

(☎ 902-202-3636, 888-425-2327; www.saltybear .ca) Backpacker-oriented van tours through the Maritimes with jump-on/jump-off flexibility. There's a three-day circuit around Cape Breton, Nova Scotia, and a five-day route that goes into PEI.

Trek America

(☎ in USA 800-221-0596, ☎ in UK 0870-444-8735; www.trekamerica .com) Active camping, hiking and canoeing tours in small groups, geared primarily for people aged between 18 and 38, although some are open to all ages.

🚈 TRAIN

VIA Rail (☎ 888-842-7245; www.viarail.ca) operates most of Canada's intercity and transcontinental passenger trains, chugging over 14,000km of track. In some remote parts of the country, such as Churchill, Manitoba, trains provide the only overland access.

Rail service is most efficient in the corridor between Québec City and Windsor, Ontario – particularly between Montréal and Toronto, the two major hubs. The rail network does not extend to Newfoundland, Prince Edward Island or the Northern Territories.

Free wi-fi is available on trains in the corridor. Via Rail was set to expand the service to additional trains in fall 2010.

Smoking is prohibited on all trains.

CLASSES

There are four main classes:

o Economy class buys you a fairly basic, if indeed quite comfortable, reclining seat with a headrest. Blankets and pillows are provided for overnight travel.

o Business class operates in the southern Ontario/Québec corridor. Seats are more spacious and have outlets for plugging in laptops. You also get a meal and priority boarding.

o Sleeper class is available on shorter overnight routes. You can choose from compartments with upper or lower pullout berths, and private single, double or triple roomettes, all with a bathroom.

o Touring class is available on long-distance routes and includes sleeper class accommodations plus meals, access to the sightseeing car and sometimes even a tour guide.

COSTS

Taking the train is more expensive than the bus, but most people find it a more comfortable way to travel. June to mid-October is peak season, when prices are about 40% higher. Buying tickets in advance (even just five days before) can yield significant savings.

LONG-DISTANCE ROUTES

VIA Rail has several classic trains:

Canadian A 1950s stainless-steel beauty between Toronto and Vancouver, zipping through the northern Ontario lake country, the western plains via Winnipeg and

TRAIN ROUTE	DURATION	FREQUENCY	FARE (US$)
Toronto–Vancouver (Canadian)	87hr	3 per week	890
Winnipeg–Churchill (Hudson Bay)	43hr	2 per week	309
Victoria–Courtenay (Malahat)	4½hr	1 daily	59
Halifax–Montréal (Ocean)	22hr	1 daily (except none Tue)	258
Prince Rupert–Jasper (Skeena)	33hr	3 per week	206

Edmonton, and Jasper in the Rockies over three days.

Hudson Bay From the prairie (slowly) to the subarctic: Winnipeg to polar-bear hangout Churchill.

Malahat Carves through Vancouver Island's magnificent countryside; get off and back on as many times as you'd like.

Ocean Chugs from Montréal along the St Lawrence River through New Brunswick and Nova Scotia to Halifax.

Skeena An all-daylight route from Jasper, Alberta, to coastal Prince Rupert, British Columbia; there's an overnight stop in Prince George (you make your own hotel reservations).

Privately run regional train companies offer additional rail-touring opportunities:

Rocky Mountaineer Railtours (www.rocky mountaineer.com) Gape at Canadian Rockies scenery on swanky trains between Vancouver, Whistler, Banff, Kamloops and Calgary.

Royal Canadian Pacific (www.royalcanadianpacific .com) A cruise-ship-like luxury line between and around the Rockies via Calgary.

White Pass & Yukon Route (www.wpyr.com) Gorgeous route paralleling the original White Pass trail from Whitehorse, Yukon, to Fraser, British Columbia.

RESERVATIONS

Seat reservations are highly recommended, especially in summer, on weekends and around holidays. During peak season (June to mid-October), some of the most popular sleeping arrangements sell out

months in advance, especially on long-distance trains such as the *Canadian*. The *Hudson Bay* often books solid during polar-bear season (late September to early November).

TRAIN PASSES

VIA Rail offers a couple of passes that provide good savings:

○ The Canrailpass-System is good for seven trips on any train during a 21-day period. All seats are in economy class; upgrades are not permitted. You must book each leg at least three days in advance (you can do this online). It costs $941/588 in high/low season.

○ The Canrailpass-Corridor is good for seven trips during a 10-day period on trains in the Québec City–Windsor corridor (which includes Montréal, Toronto and Niagara). It costs $337 year-round.

A-Z

Language

The sounds used in spoken French can almost all be found in English. There are a couple of exceptions: nasal vowels (represented in our pronunciation guides by 'o' or 'u' followed by an almost inaudible nasal consonant sound 'm', 'n' or 'ng'), the 'funny' *u* sound ('ew' in our guides) and the deep-in-the-throat *r*. Bearing these few points in mind and reading our pronunciation guides below as if they were English, you'll be understood just fine.

To enhance your trip with a phrasebook, visit **lonelyplanet.com**. Lonely Planet iPhone phrasebooks are available through the Apple App store.

BASICS

Hello./Goodbye.
Bonjour./Au revoir.   bon·zhoor/o·rer·vwa
How are you?
Comment allez-vous?   ko·mon ta·lay·voo
I'm fine, thanks.
Bien, merci.   byun mair·see
Excuse me./Sorry.
Excusez-moi./Pardon.   ek·skew·zay·mwa/par·don
Yes./No.
Oui./Non.   wee/non
Please.
S'il vous plaît.   seel voo play
Thank you.
Merci.   mair·see
That's fine./You're welcome.
De rien.   der ree·en
Do you speak English?
Parlez-vous anglais?   par·lay·voo ong·glay
I don't understand.
Je ne comprends pas.   zher ner kom·pron pa
How much is this?
C'est combien?   say kom·byun

ACCOMMODATION

I'd like to book a room.
Je voudrais réserver   zher voo·dray ray·zair·vay
une chambre.   ewn shom·brer
How much is it per night?
Quel est le prix par nuit?   kel ay ler pree par nwee

EATING & DRINKING

I'd like ..., please.
Je voudrais ...,   zher voo·dray ...
s'il vous plaît.   seel voo play
That was delicious!
C'était délicieux!   say·tay day·lee·syer
Bring the bill/check, please.
Apportez-moi l'addition,   a·por·tay·mwa la·dee·syon
s'il vous plaît.   seel voo play

I'm allergic (to peanuts).
Je suis allergique   zher swee a·lair·zheek
(aux cacahuètes).   (o ka·ka·wet)
I don't eat ...
Je ne mange pas de ...   zher ner monzh pa de ...

fish	*poisson*	pwa·son
(red) meat	*viande (rouge)*	vyond (roozh)
poultry	*volaille*	vo·lai

EMERGENCIES

I'm ill.
Je suis malade.   zher swee ma·lad
Help!
Au secours!   o skoor
Call a doctor!
Appelez un médecin!   a·play un mayd·sun
Call the police!
Appelez la police!   a·play la po·lees

DIRECTIONS

I'm looking for (a/the) ...
Je cherche ...   zher shairsh ...
  bank
  une banque   ewn bongk
  ... embassy
  l'ambassade de ...   lam·ba·sahd der ...
  market
  le marché   ler mar·shay
  museum
  le musée   ler mew·zay
  restaurant
  un restaurant   un res·to·ron
  toilet
  les toilettes   lay twa·let
  tourist office
  l'office de tourisme   lo·fees der too·rees·mer

Behind the Scenes

Author Thanks

KARLA ZIMMERMAN

Thanks to stalwart colleague John Lee, unflappable in the deadline madness and a plain awesome writer. Thanks to LPers Heather, Jennye and Sasha for patience and book-style wisdom. You all top my Best List. Thanks most to Eric Markowitz, partner-for-life supremo, who kept the home fires burning while I disappeared down the rabbit hole to write.

JOHN LEE

Hearty thanks to coordinating author Karla for her great support during this project, and thanks also to Jennye and Heather at LP for answering all my late-breaking questions. Since this was my fourth LP book project of a busy year, I'd also like to thank all my friends and family for keeping me relatively sane throughout this assignment, especially during the beard-growing, pajama-wearing write-up phase. And thanks, of course, to the local hairdresser for making me look relatively normal again at the end of it all.

Acknowledgments

Climate map data adapted from Peel MC, Finlayson BL & McMahon TA (2007) 'Updated World Map of the Köppen-Geiger Climate Classification', *Hydrology and Earth System Sciences,* 11, 163344.

Vancouver Translink Map © Translink Shirley Pal, Subsidiary Marketing 2011

Cover photographs
Front: Icefields Parkway, Philip & Karen Smith/LPI
Back: Niagara Falls, Eoin Clarke/LPI
Many of the images in this guide are available for licensing from Lonely Planet Images: www.lonelyplanetimages.com.

This Book

This 1st edition of *Discover Canada* was researched and written by Karla Zimmerman and John Lee. Some content was written by Catherine Bodry, Celeste Brash, Emily Matchar, Brandon Presser, Sarah Richards, Brendan Sainsbury and Ryan Ver Berkmoes. The guidebook was commissioned in Lonely Planet's Oakland office, and produced by the following:

Commissioning Editors Jennye Garibaldi, Heather Dickson

Coordinating Editor Evan Jones

Coordinating Cartographer Corey Hutchison

Coordinating Layout Designer Kerrianne Southway

Managing Editors Sasha Baskett, Brigitte Ellemor

Managing Cartographers David Connolly, Hunor Csutoros, Alison Lyall

Managing Layout Designers Jane Hart, Celia Wood

Assisting Editors Anna Metcalfe, Susie Ashworth

Assisting Cartographers Jennifer Johnston, Xavier Di Toro

Cover Research Aude Vauconsant

Cover Mazzy Prinsep

Internal Image Research Jane Hart

Language Content Branislava Vladisavljevic

Thanks to Shahara Ahmed, Judith Bamber, Melanie Dankel, Janine Eberle, Bruce Evans, Ryan Evans, Chris Girdler, Laura Jane, Indra Kilfoyle, Yvonne Kirk, Nic Lehman, Katie Lynch, John Mazzocchi, Wayne Murphy, Piers Pickard, Malisa Plesa, Raphael Richards, Averil Robertson, Lachlan Ross, Mik Ruff, Rebecca Skinner, Laura Stansfeld, Juan Winata

NOTES

NOTES

Index

How to Use
This Book

These symbols will help you find the listings you want:

⊙	Sights	😊	Festivals & Events	☆	Entertainment
✦	Activities	🛏	Sleeping	🛍	Shopping
⊖	Courses	✕	Eating	ⓘ	Information/Transport
⊕	Tours	🍷	Drinking		

These symbols give you the vital information for each listing:

☏	Telephone Numbers	🖥	Wi-Fi Access	🚌	Bus
⊙	Opening Hours	≋	Swimming Pool	🚢	Ferry
P	Parking	🍃	Vegetarian Selection	Ⓜ	Metro
⊖	Nonsmoking	📖	English-Language Menu	Ⓢ	Subway
✳	Air-Conditioning	👪	Family-Friendly	⊖	London Tube
@	Internet Access	🐾	Pet-Friendly	🚋	Tram
				🚆	Train

Reviews are organised by author preference.

Look out for these icons:

FREE No payment required

🍃 A green or sustainable option

Our authors have nominated these places as demonstrating a strong commitment to sustainability – for example by supporting local communities and producers, operating in an environmentally friendly way, or supporting conservation projects.

Map Legend

Sights
- ⊙ Beach
- ⊛ Buddhist
- ⊙ Castle
- ⊙ Christian
- ⊙ Hindu
- ⊙ Islamic
- ⊙ Jewish
- ⓞ Monument
- ⊜ Museum/Gallery
- ⊙ Ruin
- ⊙ Winery/Vineyard
- ⊙ Zoo
- ⊙ Other Sight

Activities, Courses & Tours
- ⊜ Diving/Snorkelling
- ⊛ Canoeing/Kayaking
- ⊕ Skiing
- ⊕ Surfing
- ⊜ Swimming/Pool
- ⊙ Walking
- ⊙ Windsurfing
- • Other Activity/Course/Tour

Sleeping
- 🛏 Sleeping
- ⊙ Camping

Eating
- ✕ Eating

Drinking
- ⊖ Drinking
- ⊖ Cafe

Entertainment
- ⊙ Entertainment

Shopping
- ⊕ Shopping

Information
- ⊜ Post Office
- ⓘ Tourist Information

Transport
- ⊙ Airport
- ⊗ Border Crossing
- ⊜ Bus
- ⊷⊕⊶ Cable Car/Funicular
- -⊙- Cycling
- -⊖- Ferry
- Ⓜ Metro
- ⊷⊕⊶ Monorail
- P Parking
- ⊖ S-Bahn
- ⊙ Taxi
- ⊷⊕⊶ Train/Railway
- ⊷⊕⊶ Tram
- ⊖ Tube Station
- ⓤ U-Bahn
- • Other Transport

Routes
- Tollway
- Freeway
- Primary
- Secondary
- Tertiary
- Lane
- Unsealed Road
- Plaza/Mall
- Steps
-)=(Tunnel
- Pedestrian Overpass
- Walking Tour
- Walking Tour Detour
- Path

Boundaries
- — — International
- ---- State/Province
- — — Disputed
- - - - Regional/Suburb
- Marine Park
- Cliff
- Wall

Population
- ⊙ Capital (National)
- ◉ Capital (State/Province)
- ⊙ City/Large Town
- ⊙ Town/Village

Geographic
- ⊙ Hut/Shelter
- 🔒 Lighthouse
- ⊜ Lookout
- ▲ Mountain/Volcano
- ⊙ Oasis
- ⊙ Park
-)(Pass
- ⊙ Picnic Area
- ⊙ Waterfall

Hydrography
- River/Creek
- Intermittent River
- Swamp/Mangrove
- Reef
- Canal
- Water
- Dry/Salt/Intermittent Lake
- Glacier

Areas
- Beach/Desert
- Cemetery (Christian)
- Cemetery (Other)
- Park/Forest
- Sportsground
- Sight (Building)
- Top Sight (Building)

in love with the crisp air and is an unabashed Anne fan. After this trip she moved from the tropics to a similar latitude in Oregon to start more temperate adventures involving salmon and blackberries.

EMILY MATCHAR

Nova Scotia & Maritime Canada Though American by birth, Emily has long suffered acute Canada-envy (and not just for the healthcare, either!). She's had some of her best adventures in the True North, from paddling with seals off the coast of British Columbia to eating poutine at 3am in Montréal to hanging out with canoe-makers in rural New Brunswick. These days, she makes her home quite a bit further south, in Chapel Hill, North Carolina, where she writes for a variety of magazines, newspapers and websites. She's contributed to half a dozen Lonely Planet guides, including *USA*, *Mexico* and *Trips: The Carolinas, Georgia and the South*.

BRANDON PRESSER

Toronto, Niagara Falls & Ontario For this, his second time co-authoring the Canada guide, Brandon had the distinct honor of tracing his father's old trucking route through the moose-clad recesses of northern Ontario. Brandon is himself no stranger to the area – he was born in Ottawa and spent much of his childhood in the region. After living in Paris, Tokyo and Boston, Brandon strapped on a backpack and joined the glamorous ranks of eternal nomadism. As a fulltime freelance travel writer he's contributed to over 20 Lonely Planet titles from Iceland to Thailand and many '-lands' in between.

SARAH RICHARDS

Montréal & Québec Loyal to the mountains and forest of her native BC, Sarah vowed never to love another Canadian province. But when she started her undergraduate degree at McGill University, a torrid love affair with the enticing vibe of Québec threatened to break her ties with home forever. After graduation, she roamed Asia and Europe for six years, before finding her way back into the arms of Montréal. She blames the soft scents of freshly baked croissants in the wind and the sinful delights of the city's vibrant nightlife for her betrayal.

BRENDAN SAINSBURY

Banff & the Canadian Rockies An expat Brit from Hampshire, England, Brendan is a former fitness instructor, volunteer teacher, wannabe musician and travel guide who now writes about travel full-time. In 2003 he met a Canadian girl from Saskatoon in Spain. After romancing in Cuba and getting married in Mexico, they now live (with their son, Kieran) in White Rock, BC. Brendan is a long time lover of Alberta's national parks and is the co-author of Lonely Planet's current *Banff, Jasper & Glacier National Parks* guide.

RYAN VER BERKMOES

Vancouver & British Columbia, Manitoba, Yukon Territory Ryan's been bouncing around BC and the Yukon for more than two decades. This time he added Manitoba and Saskatchewan. But what he really added was more critter-spotting than he'd ever imagined possible. But it's fitting given Ryan's background with moose. At his first newspaper job he was tasked with placing random moose jokes in the classifieds to pique reader interest (eg What's a moose's favorite philosopher? Cam-moose). For better jokes than that, surf over to ryanverberkmoes.com.

Our Story

A beat-up old car, a few dollars in the pocket and a sense of adventure. In 1972 that's all Tony and Maureen Wheeler needed for the trip of a lifetime – across Europe and Asia overland to Australia. It took several months, and at the end – broke but inspired – they sat at their kitchen table writing and stapling together their first travel guide, *Across Asia on the Cheap*. Within a week they'd sold 1500 copies. Lonely Planet was born.

Today, Lonely Planet has offices in Melbourne, London and Oakland, with more than 600 staff and writers. We share Tony's belief that 'a great guidebook should do three things: inform, educate and amuse'.

Our Writers

KARLA ZIMMERMAN

Coordinating author; Plan Your Trip chapters; Toronto, Niagara Falls & Ontario; Montréal & Québec; Nova Scotia & Maritime Canada; Newfoundland & Labrador; Survival Guide During her years covering Canada coast to coast for Lonely Planet, Karla has paddled by icebergs, hiked in polar bear territory, inhaled an embarrassing number of Tim Horton's Maple Cream donuts and braked for moose more times than she can count. When she's not north of the border, Karla lives in Chicago, where she writes travel features for newspapers, books, magazines and websites. She has authored or co-authored several Lonely Planet guidebooks to the USA, Canada, Caribbean and Europe.

JOHN LEE

Vancouver & British Columbia, Banff & the Canadian Rockies, The Best of the Rest, In Focus chapters Born in St Albans in southeast England, John moved to Canada's West Coast to study at the University of Victoria in the 1990s, relocating to Vancouver and launching a full-time independent travel writing career in 1999. Since then, he's been covering the region (and beyond) for major newspapers and magazines around the world. Becoming a Lonely Planet author in 2005, he has contributed to 19 titles, including writing the most recent edition of the *Vancouver City Guide* and penning a daily blog for the LP website from the 2010 Olympic Winter Games. To read his latest stories and see what he's up to next, visit www.johnleewriter.com.

CATHERINE BODRY

Toronto, Niagara Falls & Ontario Catherine grew up just below the Canadian border, in Washington State, and has made countless trips to visit her northern neighbors. During her youth she camped on Vancouver Island, and when she got a little older she snuck across the border for the coveted 19-year-old drinking age. Since then, she's driven the Alaska Hwy five times, explored the western coast by ferry, and filled her belly repeatedly across Ontario's farmland. Writing for Lonely Planet feeds (and often fuels) her wanderlust: you'll find her in Lonely Planet's Alaska, Pacific Northwest Trips and Thailand. Check out www.catherinebodry.com for more of her work.

CELESTE BRASH

Nova Scotia & Maritime Canada 'This is where people from Tahiti go on vacation?' – this question is often asked of Celeste during her voyages through the Maritimes. Lighthouses and lupine are a far cry from palm trees and hibiscus of her island home of 15 years, but Celeste became certain long ago that Atlantic lobster is the best food on Earth, fell

 More Writers ....

Published by Lonely Planet Publications Pty Ltd
ABN 36 005 607 983
1st edition – May 2011
ISBN 978 1 74220 284 6
© Lonely Planet 2011 Photographs © as indicated 2011
10 9 8 7 6 5 4 3 2 1
Printed in China